LIBRARY OF NEW TESTAMENT STUDIES

666

Formerly Journal for the Study of the New Testament Supplement Series

Editor
Chris Keith

Editorial Board
Dale C. Allison, Lynn H. Cohick, R. Alan Culpepper, Craig A. Evans,
Jennifer Eyl, Robert Fowler, Simon J. Gathercole, Juan Hernández Jr.,
John S. Kloppenborg, Michael Labahn, Matthew V. Novenson, Love L. Sechrest,
Robert Wall, Catrin H. Williams, Brittany E. Wilson

A CASE FRAME GRAMMAR AND LEXICON
FOR THE BOOK OF REVELATION

Paul L. Danove

LONDON • NEW YORK • OXFORD • NEW DELHI • SYDNEY

T&T CLARK
Bloomsbury Publishing Plc
50 Bedford Square, London, WC1B 3DP, UK
1385 Broadway, New York, NY 10018, USA
29 Earlsfort Terrace, Dublin 2, Ireland

BLOOMSBURY, T&T CLARK and the T&T Clark logo
are trademarks of Bloomsbury Publishing Plc

First published in Great Britain 2022
Paperback edition published 2024

Copyright © Paul L. Danove, 2022

Paul L. Danove has asserted his right under the Copyright, Designs and Patents Act, 1988, to be identified as Author of this work.

For legal purposes the Acknowledgments on p. xiii constitute an extension of this copyright page.

All rights reserved. No part of this publication may be reproduced or transmitted in any form or by any means, electronic or mechanical, including photocopying, recording, or any information storage or retrieval system, without prior permission in writing from the publishers.

Bloomsbury Publishing Plc does not have any control over, or responsibility for, any third-party websites referred to or in this book. All internet addresses given in this book were correct at the time of going to press. The author and publisher regret any inconvenience caused if addresses have changed or sites have ceased to exist, but can accept no responsibility for any such changes.

A catalogue record for this book is available from the British Library.

Library of Congress Cataloging-in-Publication Data

Names: Danove, Paul L., author.
Title: A case frame grammar and lexicon for the Book of Revelation / by Paul L. Danove.
Description: London ; New York : T&T Clark, 2022. | Series: Library of New Testament studies, 2513-8790 ; 666 | Includes bibliographical references and index. | Summary: "Paul Danove provides a step-by-step introduction to Case Frame analysis of the Book of Revelation, helping readers to comprehend syntactic, semantic, and lexical requirements and guiding the interpretation and translation of each predicator"-- Provided by publisher.
Identifiers: LCCN 2021060452 (print) | LCCN 2021060453 (ebook) | ISBN 9780567705983 (hardback) | ISBN 9780567706027 (paperback) | ISBN 9780567705990 (pdf) | ISBN 9780567706010 (epub)
Subjects: LCSH: Greek language, Biblical--Case grammar. | Greek language, Biblical--Lexicology. | Bible. Revelation--Language, style.
Classification: LCC PA813 .D36 2022 (print) | LCC PA813 (ebook) | DDC 228/.048--dc23/eng/20220127
LC record available at https://lccn.loc.gov/2021060452
LC ebook record available at https://lccn.loc.gov/2021060453

ISBN:	HB:	978-0-5677-0598-3
	PB:	978-0-5677-0602-7
	ePDF:	978-0-5677-0599-0
	ePUB:	978-0-5677-0601-0

Series: Library of New Testament Studies, volume 666
ISSN 2513-8790

Typeset by: Trans.form.ed SAS

To find out more about our authors and books visit www.bloomsbury.com and sign up for our newsletters.

For my students

CONTENTS

Preface   xi
Acknowledgments   xiii
Abbreviations   xv

Part I
THE METHOD OF ANALYSIS AND DESCRIPTION

1
CASE FRAME ANALYSIS AND DESCRIPTION   3
  1. Presuppositions and Concepts of Case Frame Analysis   3
  2. Syntactic Analysis and Description   5
  3. Semantic Analysis and Description   12
  4. Lexical Analysis and Description   20
  5. Required Complement Omission   26
  6. Applications of the Case Frame Method   29

2
EVENTS, EVENT FEATURES, AND NON-EVENTS   30
  1. Events and Non-Events   30
  2. The Twenty-Three Events Grammaticalized in the Text of Revelation   31
  3. Base and Alternate Configurations of Event Entities: Event Features   35
  4. Event Feature: Entity Incorporation   36
  5. Event Feature: Entity Reinterpretation   39
  6. Event Feature: Entity Bifurcation   41
  7. The Three Non-Events Grammaticalized in the Text of Revelation   42
  8. Event and Non-Event Configurations   45
  9. Applications of Events, Event Features, and Non-Events   46

3
USAGES AND USAGE FEATURES   47
  1. Usages and Their Conceptualization   47
  2. Usage Features for the Events of Transference and Delegation   48
  3. Usage Features for the Event of Motion: Part 1   55
  4. Usage Features for the Event of Motion: Part 2   60
  5. Usage Feature for the Event of Location   65

6. Usage Features for the Event of Communication	66
7. Usage Features for the Event of Experience	70
8. Usage Features for Events Containing a Patient Entity	74
9. Applications of Usages and Usage Features	78

4
THE FURTHER SPECIFICATION OF VALENCE DESCRIPTIONS — 79
1. Semantic Feature: ±Animate — 79
2. Semantic Feature: ±Response — 83
3. Licensing Alignment: Λέγω Melding — 85
4. Redundant Complements — 87
5. Indeclinable Greek Noun Phrases — 88
6. Polysemous Occurrences — 89
7. Applications of the Further Specifications — 91

Part II
USAGES AND PREDICATORS

5
USAGES OF EVENTS WITH A THEME (Θ), EXPERIENCER (E), OR OCCURRENCE (O) — 95
1. Usages of Transference (Tra.) — 96
2. Usages of Motion (Mot.) — 104
3. Usages of Location (Loc.) — 110
4. Usages of Communication (Cmm.) — 112
5. Usages of Experience (Exp.) — 117
6. Usages of Capacity (Cap.) — 123
7. Events with Only One Usage — 125

6
PREDICATOR USAGES OF OTHER EVENTS AND OF THREE NON-EVENTS — 129
1. Usages of Benefaction (Ben.) — 130
2. Usages of Communion (Com.) — 137
3. Usages of Effect (Eff.) — 138
4. Usages of Instrumentality (Ins.) — 141
5. Usages of Materiality (Mat.) — 145
6. Usages of Modification (Mod.) — 148
7. Usages of Partition (Par.) — 150
8. Usages of Separation (Sep.) — 152
9. Events with Only One Usage — 153
10. Usages of the Non-Event Qualification (Qual.) — 156
11. Usages of the Non-Event Coordination (Coor.) — 158
12. Usage of the Non-Event Specification (Spec.) — 159
13. Applications of the Ninety-Two Usages — 160

7
Distinctive Grammatical Characteristics of the Text of Revelation — 161
1. Novel Predicator Usages — 161
2. Novel Realizations of Required Complements — 169
3. Disharmonious Coordination by Conjunction Predicators — 174
4. The Omission of Εἰμί (Be) — 176
5. The Omission of Other Predicators — 178
6. Distant Predicator Retrieval — 179
7. Contribution of the Study of the Distinctive Grammatical Characteristics — 180
8. Conclusion to the Case Frame Study — 180

Part III
Lexicon Entries

8
From Valence Descriptions to Lexicon Entries — 185
1. Valence Descriptions for the Verb Predicator Ποιέω — 185
2. Generalized Valence Descriptions for the Verb Predicator Ποιέω — 191
3. Lexicon Entries for the Verb Predicator Ποιέω — 194
4. Lexicon Entries for Polysemous Predicator Occurrences — 196
5. Further Specifications of Lexicon Entries with General Application — 199
6. Further Specifications of Lexicon Entries with Particular Application — 202
7. Application of the Protocols for Generating Lexicon Entries — 207

9
The Case Frame Lexicon for Predicators in the Text of Revelation — 208

Appendix — 272
A. Thematic Role Definitions (Abbreviations in Valence Descriptions— Event Configurations/Usage Labels) — 272
B. Event and Non-Event Designations, Abbreviations, and Configurations — 273
C. Usage Labels by Event or Non-Event (92 Usages) — 273

Bibliography — 277
Index of Authors — 281

PREFACE

The following study develops and adapts the method of Case Frame analysis of predicators, that is, words and phrases that require and/or permit the completion of their meaning by other words and phrases (Part I), applies this method to identify, describe, and illustrate the ninety-two distinct usages of predicators observed in the Greek text of the book of Revelation (Part II), and formulates lexicon entries that specify a thorough grammatical description of each predicator occurrence in the text (Part III). The study has three goals. The first is to provide a step-by-step introduction to Case Frame analysis that incorporates various adaptations and extensions to address the needs of the study of the Greek of the New Testament. The second is to produce a comprehensive Case Frame grammar and description of each predicator's licensing properties, that is, the syntactic, semantic, and lexical requirements that each predicator imposes on its complements. The third is to generate a Case Frame lexicon that guides the interpretation and translation of each predicator occurrence in its grammatical contexts. The following discussion specifies the order and content of the presentation and identifies three significant contributions of the study.

The discussion of the development and adaptation of the method of Case Frame analysis (Part I) proceeds in four stages. The initial discussion introduces the guidelines for analyzing and describing the syntactic, semantic, and lexical requirements that predicators impose on their complements and establishes the conventions for noting these requirements in a framework called a Valence Description (Chapter 1). The adaptation of the method begins by identifying and describing the events and non-events that predicators grammaticalize in the text of Revelation and establishing the procedure for noting the event or non-event being grammaticalized in the Valence Description for each predicator occurrence (Chapter 2). The adaptation continues by identifying usage features that constrain the conceptualizations of specific events, illustrating the manner in which different sets of usage features characterize different predicator usages, and establishing the procedure for noting usage features in Valence Descriptions (Chapter 3). The adaptation concludes by developing further notations that clarify the interpretation of specific lexical realizations of complements and conventions for noting the possible interpretations of polysemous occurrences in Valence Descriptions (Chapter 4).

The discussion of predicator usages (Part II) resolves each occurrence of each predicator in the text of Revelation into one or more of the ninety-two observed usages. The presentation identifies the predicators with the usage, specifies the event being grammaticalized and the features of the event's conceptualization, provides illustrative examples of the interpretation and translation of each category of predicator with the usage, and generates the Valence Description for each illustrative example (Chapters 5 and 6). This information then permits the identification of predicator usages and lexical realizations of complements that differ from those found elsewhere in the New Testament and the recognition of a series of distinctive grammatical characteristics of the text of Revelation (Chapter 7).

The discussion concludes with the generation of lexicon entries (Part III). This requires an initial exposition on the conventions for re-presenting in a single lexicon entry all syntactic, semantic, lexical, and further grammatical information in the Valence Descriptions of all occurrences of a predicator with a given usage (Chapter 8). These conventions then accommodate the formulation of lexicon entries for all predicators in the text of Revelation (Chapter 9).

The Appendix reprises the definitions of the thematic roles used in the semantic analysis of the complements of predicators, lists the event and non-event designations, abbreviations, and configurations, and identifies each of the ninety-two usages by its label and the sectional heading in which it receives description and illustration.

The following study makes three significant contributions to the Case Frame analysis of predicators of the New Testament. First, the presentation on the method of analysis (Part I) provides a careful, step-by-step introduction to the method and its major adaptations for the study of the Greek of the New Testament. Second, the descriptions and illustrations of the ninety-two predicator usages in the text of Revelation (Part II) provide a comprehensive introduction to the most frequently observed predicator usages in the New Testament and, in the process, establish that the licensing properties of all predicators in the text of Revelation fall within the range of grammaticality in comparison to other texts in the Septuagint and New Testament. Third, the lexicon entries (Part III) appear in a format that combines all syntactic, semantic, lexical, and further descriptive grammatical information in a manner that guides the interpretation and translation of predicators in their various contexts.

ACKNOWLEDGMENTS

I wish to acknowledge the contributions of Mr. Andre Price (Villanova University) who proofed the text of the Lexicon (Chapter 9), of Dr. Ann Elizabeth Mayer (Associate Professor Emeritus of Legal Studies, The Wharton School, University of Pennsylvania) who proofed the English text of the manuscript, and of Ms. Anna Barnett (Brown University) who proofed the final version of the entire text.

ABBREVIATIONS

BDF	Friedrich Blass, Albert Debrunner and Robert W. Funk, *A Greek Grammar of the New Testament and Other Early Christian Literature* (Cambridge: Cambridge University Press, 1961)
BLS	*Berkeley Linguistics Society*
CAL	Constructional Approaches to Language
CogLing	*Cognitive Linguistics*
CSLI	Center for the Study of Language and Information
FN	*Filología Neotestamentaria*
JSNTSup	*Journal for the Study of the New Testament*, Supplement Series
JLing	*Journal of Linguistics*
L&P	*Linguistics and Philosophy*
LBS	Linguistic Biblical Studies
LInq	*Linguistic Inquiry*
LNTS	Library of New Testament Studies
MIT	Massachusetts Institute of Technology
SNTG	Studies in New Testament Greek
SPIB	Scripta Pontificii Instituti Biblici
WPiFG	*Working Papers in Functional Grammar*

Part I

THE METHOD OF ANALYSIS AND DESCRIPTION

1

CASE FRAME ANALYSIS AND DESCRIPTION

This chapter introduces the method of Case Frame analysis and describes its application in the study of the 870 words and phrases in the text of the book of Revelation that require or permit the completion of their meaning by other words and phrases. The following discussions clarify the presuppositions and concepts of the method, develop its procedures for describing the syntactic, semantic, and lexical requirements that words and phrases impose on their complements, and propose conventions for representing the conditions under which Greek grammar permits the omission of required complements. The concluding discussion specifies the manner in which the method receives application in the following study. All illustrative examples of words and phrases in this chapter are from the text of Revelation.

1. Presuppositions and Concepts of Case Frame Analysis

Case Frame analysis describes the licensing properties of "predicators," that is, words and phrases that license the presence of other elements in a phrase. Predicators are both simple (words) and complex (phrases). Simple predicators include all verbs, participles, adjectives, prepositions, interjections, and conjunctions, as well as those nouns, pronouns, and adverbs that either require or permit the completion of their meaning by other phrasal elements.[1] This list distinguishes participles from their associated verbs because participles exhibit the licensing properties of both verbs and adjectives. Complex predicators are phrases formed by linking either simple non-verb predicators or non-predicators and the verb εἰμί (be).[2] For example, the simple/complex predicator "tall"/"tall + be" licenses the phrase/clause, "tall men"/"the men are tall."

Case Frame analysis resolves elements licensed by predicators into "arguments" that are required to complete the meaning of a predicator and "adjuncts" that provide a specification of meaning beyond that required for the grammatical use

---

[1] The "licensing" of elements is part of the more comprehensive principle of "government"; cf. Charles J. Fillmore and Paul Kay, *Construction Grammar* (Stanford: CSLI, 1999), 4:9–12.
[2] Further discussion of complex predicators appears in Paul L. Danove, *Linguistics and Exegesis in the Gospel of Mark: Applications of a Case Frame Analysis and Lexicon* (JSNTSup 218; SNTG 10; Sheffield: Sheffield Academic Press, 2001), 55–58.

of a predicator.³ The number of arguments that a predicator requires is equal to the number of entities that must be referenced to relate the predicator's concept or meaning. For example, the verb predicator δίδωμι (give) most frequently requires completion by three arguments that specify a giver, what is given, and a recipient of what is given.⁴ Among the words that consistently function as predicators, verbs and participles require completion by one, two, or three arguments, prepositions and conjunctions by two arguments, adjectives by one or two arguments, and interjections by one argument. Among the words that do not consistently function as predicators, specific nouns require completion by two or three arguments and specific adverbs and pronouns by one argument. The following sentences clarify the use of the terms "predicator," "argument," and "adjunct":⁵

και ἔδωκα αὐτῇ χρόνον ἵνα μετανοήσῃ (2:21)
And I gave her time so that she might repent.

και δώσω αὐτῷ τὸν ἀστέρα τὸν πρωϊνόν (2:28)
And I will give him the morning star.

In both examples, the conjunction καί (and) requires completion by two arguments that are realized as complements constituted by the words of the following phrase and the words of the preceding phrase, and the words of the following phrases are licensed by the verb predicator δίδωμι (give). In the former example, δίδωμι licenses three arguments that are required to complete its meaning: "time" (what is given) and "her" (recipient), with "I" (giver) introduced by the verbal ending. The remaining element of the phrase, "so that she might repent," realizes an adjunct that offers a non-required specification of the purpose of the giving. In the latter example, δίδωμι licenses three arguments that are realized by "morning star" (what is given) and "him" (recipient), with "I" (giver) again introduced by the verbal ending. The latter example also admits to further resolution: the adjective predicator πρωϊνός (morning) requires completion by "star," and, although ἀστήρ (star) requires completion by no arguments, it is a noun predicator insofar as it admits to completion by adjuncts, as apparent in "the stars of heaven" (οἱ ἀστέρες τοῦ οὐρανοῦ, 6:13).

In general, arguments and adjuncts are realized lexically as a predicator's syntactic complements. In Greek and English, arguments and complements frequently stand in a one-to-one relationship, although Greek grammar permits the omission of the complement of verb, participle, and adjective predicators whose referent may be retrieved from the linkage of the predicator's ending and contextual information.

---

[3] The concepts of "argument" and "adjunct" have their origins in the field of logic; cf. Randy Allen Harris, *The Linguistics Wars* (New York: Oxford University Press, 1993), 115–17; James D. McCawley, *Grammar and Meaning* (New York: Academic Press, 1976), 136–39; and Frederick J. Newmeyer, *Linguistic Theory in America* (New York: Academic Press, 1980), 148–50.
[4] The determination of the number of arguments required by predicators is based on the internal logic of the predicator and is confirmed by its characteristic NT use.
[5] All NT citations are taken from Barbara Aland *et al.* (eds), *The Greek New Testament* (Stuttgart: Biblia-Druck, 4th rev. edn, 1993). The translations are my own.

1. Case Frame Analysis and Description

Since predicators require completion of their meaning by arguments but only permit completion of their meaning by adjuncts, a complement that lexically realizes an argument is deemed a "required complement," and a complement that lexically realizes an adjunct is deemed a "non-required complement."

Case Frame analysis utilizes a framework called a Valence Description to describe syntactic, semantic, and lexical information about the arguments and adjuncts licensed by a predicator.[6] The generation of a Valence Description proceeds in two stages. The first stage identifies the number of arguments that a predicator requires and the number of adjuncts that it permits. As the previous examples indicate, the number of arguments varies from predicator to predicator: three for δίδωμι, two for καί, one for πρωϊνός, and zero for ἀστήρ. These are designated three-place, two-place, one-place, and zero-place predicators respectively.[7] Some predicators, most frequently verbs and participles, require different numbers of arguments associated with different meanings.[8] The second stage of generating Valence Descriptions specifies the syntactic function, semantic function, and lexical realization of each argument and adjunct. This permits a preliminary distinction of predicator "usages" that are constituted by all occurrences of a predicator that require completion by arguments with the same syntactic and semantic functions. As a result, distinct usages of a predicator are described by distinct Valence Descriptions.

The Valence Description of a predicator places the Greek predicator on top followed by its location in the text in parentheses, ( ). All predicators except participles are listed in their dictionary forms, and participles are listed in their masculine singular nominative form in the observed tense and voice. The remainder of the Valence Description resembles a matrix with varying numbers of columns and three rows of information that appear beneath the predicator and citation. The number of columns equals the number of arguments and adjuncts licensed by the predicator. The columns specify for each argument and adjunct its syntactic function (first row), semantic function (second row), and lexical realization (third row).

2. Syntactic Analysis and Description

The top row of the Valence Description provides a generalized statement of the syntactic functions of the predicator's arguments and adjuncts. There are five possible syntactic functions: "0," "1," "2," "3," and "C." Greek grammar, like English grammar, restricts predicators to license at most three arguments, which are assigned syntactic functions "1," "2," and "3." These are referenced as the first, second, and third arguments. Since zero-place predicators do not license arguments, "0" appears as the

---

[6] Fillmore and Kay, *Construction Grammar*, 4:11–12, 29–34. An introduction to valency appears in Mirjam Fried and Jan-Ola Östman, "Construction Grammar: A Thumbnail Sketch," in *Construction Grammar in a Cross-Language Perspective* (ed. Mirjam Fried and Jan-Ola Östman; Amsterdam/Philadelphia: Benjamins, 2004), 40–43.
[7] Lucien Tesnière, *Éléments de Syntaxe Structurale* (Paris: C. Klincksieck, 1959), 106–110.
[8] An investigation of variable valence verbs appears in Beth Levin, *English Verb Classes and Alternations: A Preliminary Investigation* (Chicago: University of Chicago Press, 1993).

first noted syntactic function. All adjuncts are assigned the syntactic function "C." The following discussion develops the protocols for assigning syntactic functions to the arguments of zero-, one-, two-, and three-place predicators.

a. Zero-Place Predicators

The syntactic function "0" appears in first position for all zero-place predicators. In the text of Revelation, the only zero-place predicators are nouns, as illustrated in the following examples of ἄνεμος (wind) and ἀρνίον (lamb). The translations set off the non-required complements that realize the predicators' adjuncts in brackets, [ ], and label the syntactic function of the adjuncts, "C," in parentheses, ( ).

ἀνέμους τῆς γῆς (7:1a)
Winds (ἄνεμος) [of the earth (C)].

τὸ ἀρνίον τὸ ἀνὰ μέσον τοῦ θρόνου (7:17)
The lamb (ἀρνίον) [in the middle of the throne (C)].

The Valence Descriptions for these examples place the abbreviation for the syntactic function (syn.) at the left and separate the "0" syntactic function of the lacking argument from the syntactic function of the adjuncts "C" by a vertical line, |.

	ἄνεμος (7:1a)		ἀρνίον (7:17)	
syn.	0	| C	0	| C

b. One-Place Predicators

The syntactic function of the sole argument of all one-place predicators is "1." The one-place predicators in the text of Revelation include some verbs (verb) and their associated participles (part.), most adjectives (adj.), all interjections (int.), and complex predicators (cp-) that combine εἰμί (be) with one-place participles (cp-p.) and adjectives (cp-adj) or with zero-place nouns and pronouns (cp-n), that is, nouns and pronouns that do not require completion by arguments. One-place complex predicators also arise when εἰμί (be) combines with non-predicator nouns and pronouns (cp-n) or non-predicator adverbs (cp-a). For all one-place complex predicators formed by combining εἰμί and a one-place predicator, the sole argument of "be" and the sole argument of the one-place predicator coalesce into the complex predicator's single argument, and, for one-place complex predicators formed by combining εἰμί and a zero-place predicator or a non-predicator, the sole argument of "be" becomes the single argument of the complex predicator.

One-place predicators receive illustration in the following examples of the verb κλαίω (cry), the participle ζῶν (living), the adjective ἀληθινός (true), the interjection ἰδού (look!), and the complex predicators ζῶν + εἰμί (be living), ἀληθινός + εἰμί (be true), διάβολος + εἰμί (be a devil), and ὧδε + εἰμί (be here). These examples appear in groups of two or three followed immediately by the Valence Descriptions for their licensing predicators. The translations set off the complements that realize the predicators' arguments and adjuncts in brackets, [ ], and label the syntactic function of the arguments, "1," and adjuncts, "C," in parentheses, ( ). For ease of reference, the examples link complex predicators with their associated simple predicators. The Valence Descriptions separate the syntactic functions (syn.) of the arguments and any adjuncts by a vertical line, |.

    verb   ἔκλαιον πολύ, ὅτι οὐδεὶς ἄξιος εὑρέθη ἀνοῖξαι τὸ βιβλίον οὔτε βλέπειν αὐτό (5:4)
             [I (1)] was crying (κλαίω) [a lot (C)] [because no one was found worthy to open the scroll or see it (C)].

    part.   θεοῦ ζῶντος (7:2)
             Living (ζῶν) [God (1)].

    cp-p   ζῶν εἰμι εἰς τοὺς αἰῶνας τῶν αἰώνων (1:18b)
             [I (1)] am living (ζῶν + εἰμί) [into the ages of the ages (C)].

	κλαίω (5:4)			ζῶν (7:2)	ζῶν + εἰμί (1:18b)		
syn.	1	|	C C	1	1	|	C

    adj.   ὁ δεσπότης ὁ...ἀληθινός (6:10)
             True (ἀληθινός)...[master (1)].

    cp-adj οὗτοι οἱ λόγοι ἀληθινοὶ τοῦ θεοῦ εἰσιν (19:9)
             [These words of God (1)] are true (ἀληθινός + εἰμί).

    int.   ἰδοὺ ἕστηκα ἐπὶ τὴν θύραν καὶ κρούω (3:20)
             Look! (ἰδού) [I stand at the door and knock (1)].

	ἀληθινός (6:10)	ἀληθινός + εἰμί (19:9)	ἰδού (3:20)
syn.	1	1	1

    cp-n   ὅς ἐστιν Διάβολος (20:2)
             [Who (1)] is the Devil (διάβολος + εἰμί).

    cp-a   ὧδε ἡ σοφία ἐστίν (13:8)
             Here is (ὧδε + εἰμί) [wisdom (1)].

	διάβολος + εἰμί (20:2)	ὧδε + εἰμί (13:8)
syn.	1	1

c. Two-Place Predicators

The syntactic functions of the arguments of two-place predicators vary according to the category of predicator. For verbs (verb), the argument referencing the verbal subject when the verb is not passivized has syntactic function "1" and the remaining argument has syntactic function "2." For participles (part.) and adjectives (adj.), the argument referencing the modified entity has syntactic function "1" and the remaining argument has syntactic function "2." For prepositions (prep.), the argument referencing the entity set in relation to the object of the preposition has syntactic function "1" and the argument referencing the object of the preposition has syntactic function "2." For conjunctions (conj.), the argument referencing the former conjoined entity or entities of a series has syntactic function "1" and the argument referencing the following entity has syntactic function "2."[9] For nouns (noun), the argument referencing the entity that makes, experiences, possesses, constitutes, or is reciprocally related to the entity designated by the noun has syntactic function "1," and the argument referencing the entity that is made, experienced, possessed, constituted, or in reciprocal relationship has syntactic function "2." Reciprocally related nouns typically designate human biological, legal, religious, or ownership relationships and are defined in terms of those relationships: e.g., "father" is defined in terms of one or more biological or legal "children" and "slave" is defined in terms of an "owner" or "master."[10] For the majority of two-place noun predicators in the text of Revelation, the referent of the second argument is identical to the referent of the noun predicator itself, and with such nouns, the second argument never is realized as a complement.[11] Valence Descriptions note this second, never-realized argument by placing its syntactic function in braces, { }.

Complex predicators (cp-) formed by joining "be" and simple two-place participles (cp-p), adjectives (cp-adj), and prepositions (cp-pr) consistently are two-place and the single argument of "be" coalesces with the first argument of their associated simple two-place predicator. As a consequence the arguments of the resulting two-place complex predicators have the same syntactic functions as those of the associated simple two-place predicators. Complex predicators formed by joining "be" and two-place nouns (cp-n) also consistently are two-place, but the single argument of "be" coalesces not with the first but with the second (never-realized) argument of the two-place noun. As a result, the never-realized second argument of the simple two-place noun predicator becomes the consistently realized first argument of the

---

[9] In sequences of conjoined entities, conjunctions coordinate all in the sequence before the conjunction to the following entity: [[[[wretched and pitiable] and poor] and blind] and naked] (3:1).
[10] Further discussion of reciprocally related nouns appears in Paul L. Danove, *Theology of the Gospel of Mark: A Semantic, Narrative, and Rhetorical Study of the Characterization of God* (London/New York: T&T Clark, 2019), 14, 179–84.
[11] The two-place noun predicators that never realize their second arguments appear to set their first arguments directly in relation to themselves as, for example, in the phrases, "God's house" or "pot of gold," which appear to relate "God" directly to "house" and "gold" directly to "pot." The setting of entities directly in relation to themselves, however, is not a function of predicators which, instead, directly relate only their arguments to each other. In light of this fact, the Case Frame study attributes to such nouns the capacity to license an argument that is co-referential to themselves but never to realize this argument because its referent can be derived directly from the predicator. This phenomenon receives further consideration in §§3.7a, 3.8a, 3.8b, 3.8c, 3.8d, and 3.8e.

associated complex predicator, and the first argument of the simple noun predicator becomes the second argument of the associated complex noun predicator.

Two-place predicators receive illustration in the following examples of the verb ἀποκτείνω (kill), the participle ἔχων (having), the adjective ὅμοιος (like), the preposition ἐν (in), the conjunction καί (and), the noun ἄγγελος (angel), and the complex predicators, ὅμοιος + εἰμί (be like), ἔχων + [εἰμί] (be having), ἐν + εἰμί (be in), and ἄγγελος + εἰμί (be an angel). The brackets, [ ], around εἰμί indicate that this verb is permissibly omitted by Greek grammar in occurrences of the complex predicators.

The translations set off the complements that realize the predicators' arguments and adjuncts in brackets, [ ], label their syntactic functions, "1," "2," or "C" in parentheses, ( ), and introduce the never-realized complement of the noun predicator ἄγγελος (angel) in braces, { }. The Valence Descriptions separate the syntactic functions (syn.) of the arguments and any adjuncts by a vertical line, |. For examples in which the εἰμί (be) component of a complex predicator is permissibly omitted by Greek grammar, the εἰμί appears in brackets, [ ]. In 1:1, the syntactic function of the never-realized argument of the noun predicator ἄγγελος (angel) appears in braces, { }, and receives analysis in the typical fashion. For ease of reference, examples of complex predicators appear immediately after their associated simple predicators.

verb   τὰ τέκνα αὐτῆς ἀποκτενῶ ἐν θανάτῳ (2:23)
         [I (1)] will kill (ἀποκτείνω) [her children (2)] [by death (C)].

part.   τοὺς καθημένους ἐπ' αὐτῶν, ἔχοντας θώρακας πυρίνους καὶ ὑακινθίνους καὶ θειώδεις (9:17)
         [The ones sitting on them (1)] having (ἔχων) [red and blue and yellow breastplates (2)].

cp-p   τὸ τεῖχος τῆς πόλεως ἔχων θεμελίους δώδεκα (21:14)
         [The wall of the city (1)] was having (ἔχων + [εἰμί]) [twelve foundations (2)].

	ἀποκτείνω (2:23)		ἔχων (9:17)	ἔχων + [εἰμί] (21:14)
syn.	1 2 | C	1 2	1 2

adj.   θάλασσα ὑαλίνη ὁμοία κρυστάλλῳ (4:6)
         [A glass sea (1)] like (ὅμοιος) [crystal (2)].

cp-adj   τὸ θηρίον ὃ εἶδον ἦν ὅμοιον παρδάλει (13:2a)
         [The beast which I saw (1)] was like (ὅμοιος + εἰμί) [a leopard (2)].

prep.   ταῖς ἑπτὰ ἐκκλησίαις ταῖς ἐν τῇ Ἀσίᾳ (1:4)
         [The seven churches (1)] in (ἐν) [Asia (2)].

cp-pr   ὅ ἐστιν ἐν τῷ παραδείσῳ τοῦ θεοῦ (2:7)
         [Which (1)] is in (ἐν + εἰμί) [the garden of God (2)].

	ὅμοιος (4:6)		ὅμοιος + εἰμί (13:2a)		ἐν (1:4)		ἐν + εἰμί (2:7)	
syn.	1	2	1	2	1	2	1	2

noun τοῦ ἀγγέλου αὐτοῦ (1:1)
The angel (ἄγγελος) [of him (1)] {angel (2)}.

cp-n οἱ ἑπτὰ ἀστέρες ἄγγελοι τῶν ἑπτὰ ἐκκλησιῶν εἰσιν (1:20)
[The seven stars (1)] are angels (ἄγγελος + εἰμί) [of the seven churches (2)].

conj. ἡμέρας καὶ νυκτός (7:15b)
[Day (1)] and (καί) [night (2)].

	ἄγγελος (1:1)		ἄγγελος + εἰμί (1:20)		καί (7:15b)	
syn.	1	{2}	1	2	1	2

d. Three-Place Predicators

The syntactic functions of the arguments of three-place predicators vary according to the category of predicator. For verbs (verb), the argument referencing the verbal subject when the verb is not passivized has syntactic function "1." If the verb admits to passivization, the argument referencing the verbal subject when passivized has syntactic function "2," and the remaining argument has syntactic function "3." If the verbs do not admit to passivization, the assignment of the second and third syntactic functions is arbitrary. For participles (part.), the argument referencing the modified entity has syntactic function "1." For active and middle participles, the syntactic functions of their remaining arguments parallel those of their associated verbs. For passive participles, however, the first argument of their associated verbs has syntactic function "2" and the remaining argument has syntactic function "3." For nouns (noun), the argument attributed with making, possessing, or constituting the entity designated by the noun has syntactic function "1"; the argument designating what is made, possessed, or constituted has syntactic function "2," and the remaining argument has syntactic function "3." For some three-place nouns, the referent of the second argument is identical to the noun predicator and never realized as a complement.

The arguments of three-place complex participle predicators (cp-p) have the same syntactic functions as their associated participles. The only observed three-place complex noun predicator (cp-n) follows the pattern of two-place complex noun predicators: the never-realized second argument of the associated noun has syntactic function "1," the first argument of the associated noun has syntactic function "2," and the remaining argument has syntactic function "3."

Three-place predicators receive illustration in the following examples of the verb λέγω (say), the active participle λέγων (saying), the passive participle περιβεβλημένος (wrapped), the noun προσευχή (prayer), and the complex predicators, λέγων + εἰμί (be saying), περιβεβλημένος + εἰμί (be wrapped), and προσευχή + εἰμί (be a prayer).

The translations set off the complements that realize the predicators' arguments in brackets, [ ], and the (never-realized) second complement of προσευχή in braces, { }, label the syntactic functions of the arguments "1," "2," or "3" in parentheses, ( ), and, for illustrative purposes, introduce the definite referents of arguments that are not realized as complements. Valence Descriptions note the permissible omission of the εἰμί (be) component of a complex predicator by placing it in brackets, [ ]. Valence Descriptions also place in brackets, [ ], the syntactic functions of unrealized arguments with definite referents and in parentheses, ( ), the syntactic function of the never-realized argument of προσευχή. The passive participle and its associated complex predicator also do not realize their second arguments as complements, and these unrealized arguments have no retrievable referents. In these examples, the translations introduce "someone" for the referent of these unrealized arguments, and Valence Descriptions note the lack of definite referents for these arguments by placing their syntactic functions in parentheses, ( ). In the second example (19:17), the referent of the first argument, "angel," must be retrieved from the previous clause. In the third example (4:1), the third argument is not realized as a complement and the translation introduces its definite contextual referent, "me," and, in the sixth and seventh examples (8:3 and 5:8), the third argument is not realized as a complement and the translation introduces its definite referent, "God." Examples of complex predicators appear immediately after their associated simple predicators.

Note that the lack of syntactic case concord between ἄγγελον (accusative) and λέγων (nominative) in 19:17, of gender concord between φωνὴ (feminine) and λέγων (masculine) in 4:1, and of syntactic case, gender, and/or number concord elsewhere in the text of Revelation is not attributable to the licensing properties of predicators and so falls outside the purview of the Case Frame analysis.

verb   εἶπέν μοι· γέγοναν (21:6)
       [He (1)] said (λέγω) [to me (3)] ["They have happened" (2)].

part. ἕνα ἄγγελον...λέγων πᾶσιν τοῖς ὀρνέοις τοῖς πετομένοις ἐν μεσουρανήματι· Δεῦτε συνάχθητε εἰς τὸ δεῖπνον τὸ μέγα τοῦ θεοῦ (19:17)
       [An angel (1)]...saying (λέγων) [to all the birds flying in mid-heaven (3)] ["Come gather for the great feast of God" (2)].

cp-p   ἡ φωνὴ ἡ πρώτη ἣν ἤκουσα ὡς σάλπιγγος λαλούσης μετ' ἐμοῦ λέγων· ἀνάβα ὧδε... (4:1)
       [The first voice which I heard as of a trumpet speaking with me (1)] was saying (λέγων + [εἰμί]) [to me (3)] ["Come up here..." (2)].

	λέγω (21:6)			λέγων (19:17)			λέγων + [εἰμί] (4:1)		
syn.	1	2	3	1	2	3	1	2	[3]

part. γυνὴ περιβεβλημένη τὸν ἥλιον (12:1)
[A woman (1)] wrapped (περιβεβλημένος) [by someone (2)] [with the sun (3)].

cp-p ἡ γυνὴ ἣν περιβεβλημένη πορφυροῦν καὶ κόκκινον (17:4)
[The woman (1)] was wrapped (περιβεβλημένος + εἰμί) [by someone (2)] [with purple and scarlet (3)].

	περιβεβλημένος (12:1)			περιβεβλημένος + εἰμί (17:4)	
syn.	1	(2)	3	1	(2)	3

noun ταῖς προσευχαῖς τῶν ἁγίων πάντων (8:3)
The prayers (προσευχή) [of all the holy ones (1)] {prayers (2)} [to God (3)].

cp-n αἵ εἰσιν αἱ προσευχαὶ τῶν ἁγίων (5:8)
[Which (1)] are the prayers (προσευχή + εἰμί) [of the holy ones (2)] [to God (3)].

	προσευχή (8:3)			προσευχή + εἰμί (5:8)	
syn.	1	{2}	[3]	1	2	[3]

3. Semantic Analysis and Description

The second row of the Valence Description provides a generalized description of the semantic functions of the predicator's arguments and adjuncts. The Case Frame analysis employs thematic roles to describe the relationships imposed on arguments and adjuncts by predicators.[12] The following discussion introduces, defines, and provides examples of the twenty-seven thematic roles necessary to describe the arguments and adjuncts of all predicators in the text of Revelation.[13] The discussion provides the name of each thematic role, its three-letter abbreviation in parentheses,

---

[12] Thematic roles are similar to the semantic cases originally proposed in Charles J. Fillmore, "The Case for Case," in *Universals in Linguistic Theory* (ed. Emmon Bach and Robert T. Harms; New York: Holt, Reinhart and Winston, 1968), 24–25. The relationship between frame-specific roles and thematic roles receives development in David R. Dowty, "Thematic Proto-Roles and Argument Selection," *Language* 67 (1991): 574–619; John I. Saeed, *Semantics* (Oxford: Blackwell, 1997), 150–52; and Farrell Ackerman and John Moore, "Valence and the Semantics of Causativization," *BLS* 20 (1994): 2–4.

[13] These and following definitions of thematic roles are developed from those proposed in Danove, *Linguistics and Exegesis*, 31–45, and Saeed, *Semantics*, 139–71. The development of a finite set of thematic roles with universally accepted definitions has proved unsuccessful for a series of reasons that receive examination in H. L. Somers, *Valency and Case in Computational Linguistics* (Edinburgh: Edinburgh University Press, 1987), 109–44. As a consequence, most contemporary Case Frame analyses employ thematic roles defined in relation to specific frames, such as the domain specific roles of the FrameNet project <https://framenet.icsi.berkeley.edu/fndrupal/home>. Although the predicators in the text of Revelation reference a number of different frames, the proposed definitions are sufficiently general to describe all of the complements of its predicators.

1. Case Frame Analysis and Description

( ), the definition of the thematic role, one or more illustrative examples of its use, and the Valence Descriptions of the illustrative examples. The translations set off the complements that realize the predicators' arguments and adjuncts in brackets, [ ], and label the syntactic function of the arguments and the three-letter abbreviations of the thematic roles separated by a slash, /, in parentheses, ( ). The Valence Descriptions separate the syntactic (syn.) and semantic (sem.) functions of the arguments and any adjuncts by a vertical line, |. Valence Descriptions also note the permissible omission of the εἰμί (be) component of a complex predicator by placing εἰμί in brackets, [ ]. An alphabetical list of all thematic roles, their three-letter abbreviations, and definitions appears in the Appendix. The concluding discussion offers a clarification concerning specific noun predicators.

The first four thematic roles pertain to communication and its interpretation, although the first defined thematic role, Agent, has extensive use with other categories of predicators.

Agent (Agt): The animate entity that actively instigates an action and/or is the ultimate cause of a change in another entity.[14]

Content (Con): What is experienced in a sensory, cognitive, or emotional event or activity.

Experiencer (Exp): The animate entity that undergoes a sensory, cognitive, or emotional event or activity.

Topic (Top): That which a sensory, cognitive, or emotional event or activity concerns.

These thematic roles receive illustration in the following examples of λέγω (say), ἀκούων (hearing), μετανοέω (repent), and μαρτυρέω (testify). In the fourth example (22:16), the infinitive retrieves its subject from the second required complement of πέμπω (send).

εἷς ἐκ τῶν πρεσβυτέρων λέγει μοι· μὴ κλαῖε (5:5)
[One of the elders (1/Agt)] says (λέγω) [to me (3/Exp)] ["Do not cry!" (2/Con)].

οἱ ἀκούοντες τοὺς λόγους τῆς προφητείας (1:3)
[The ones (1/Exp)] hearing (ἀκούων) [the words of the prophecy (2/Con)].

μὴ μετανοήσωσιν ἐκ τῶν ἔργων αὐτῆς (2:22)
[They (1/Exp)] do not repent (μετανοέω) [of/concerning her works (2/Top)].

---

[14] The second half of the definition of Agent is formulated to include such natural forces as the wind; cf. D. A. Cruse, "Some Thoughts on Agentivity," *JLing* 9 (1973): 16.

τὸν ἄγγελόν μου μαρτυρῆσαι ὑμῖν ταῦτα ἐπὶ ταῖς ἐκκλησίαις (22:16)
To [my angel (1/Agt)] testify (μαρτυρέω) [to you (3/Exp)] [these things (2/Con)] [concerning the churches (C/Top)].

	λέγω (5:5)			ἀκούων (1:3)		
	1	2	3	1	2	
	Agt	Con	Exp	Exp	Con	

	μετανοέω (2:22)		μαρτυρέω (22:16)			
syn.	1	2	1	2	3	| C
sem.	Exp	Top	Agt	Con	Exp	| Top

The next four thematic roles pertain to transference, motion, and state.

Goal (Goa): The literal or figurative entity towards which something moves.

Locative (Loc): The literal or figurative place in which an entity is situated or an event occurs.

Source (Sou): The literal or figurative entity from which something moves.

Theme (Thm): The entity moving from one place to another or located in a place.

These thematic roles receive illustration in the following examples of βάλλω (throw), ἐν + εἰμί (be in), λαμβάνω (take), and ἐξέρχομαι (come out).

ἔβαλεν αὐτοὺς εἰς τὴν γῆν (12:4)
[It (1/Agt)] cast (βάλλω) [them (2/Thm)] [to the earth (3/Goa)].

ὅ ἐστιν ἐν τῷ παραδείσῳ τοῦ θεοῦ (2:7)
[Which (1/Thm)] is in (ἐν + εἰμί) [the garden of God (2/Loc)].

ἔλαβον τὸ βιβλαρίδιον ἐκ τῆς χειρὸς τοῦ ἀγγέλου (10:10)
[I (1/Agt)] took (λαμβάνω) [the little book (2/Thm)] [from the hand of the angel (3/Sou)].

ἐκ τοῦ καπνοῦ ἐξῆλθον ἀκρίδες εἰς τὴν γῆν (9:3)
[Locusts (1/Thm)] came out (ἐξέρχομαι) [from the smoke (C/Sou) [onto the land (2/Goa)].

1. Case Frame Analysis and Description

	βάλλω (12:4)			ἐν + εἰμί (2:7)	
syn.	1	2	3	1	2
sem.	Agt	Thm	Goa	Thm	Loc

	λαμβάνω (10:10)			ἐξέρχομαι (9:3)			
syn.	1	2	3	1	2	|	C
sem.	Agt	Thm	Sou	Thm	Goa	|	Sou

The next two thematic roles are restricted to arguments and may be placed in relation to each other.

Occurrence (Occ): The complete circumstantial scene of an action or event.

Unspecified (Uns): The entity awaiting specification of its semantic function.

These thematic roles receive illustration in the following examples of ἰδού (look!), ἀποστέλλω (send), and δύναμαι (be able). Although δύναμαι does not impose a specific semantic function on its first argument, it does impose the requirement that its first argument retrieve a definite semantic function from the subject complement of the governing verb predicator of its second (Occurrence) argument. As a consequence, the first argument may retrieve a number of different semantic functions: e.g., one may be able to hear (1/Exp) or testify (1/Agt) or go (1/Thm).

Ἰδοὺ ἔρχεται μετὰ τῶν νεφελῶν (1:7)
Look! (ἰδού) [he is coming with the clouds (1/Occ)].

ὁ κύριος ὁ θεὸς τῶν πνευμάτων τῶν προφητῶν ἀπέστειλεν τὸν ἄγγελον αὐτοῦ δεῖξαι τοῖς δούλοις αὐτοῦ ἃ δεῖ γενέσθαι ἐν τάχει (22:6)
[The Lord the God of the spirits of the prophets (1/Agt)] sent (ἀποστέλλω) [his angel (2/Thm)] [to show his slaves the things which are necessary to happen quickly (3/Occ)].

οὐ δύνῃ βαστάσαι κακούς (2:2)
[You (1/Uns)] are not able (δύναμαι) [to tolerate evil people (2/Occ)].

	ἰδού (1:7)	ἀποστέλλω (22:6)			δύναμαι (2:2)	
syn.	1	1	2	3	1	2
sem.	Occ	Agt	Thm	Occ	Uns	Occ

The next four thematic roles are Patient, which is restricted to arguments, and three further thematic roles that most frequently or consistently are imposed on arguments when they are set in relation to an argument with the Patient thematic role.

Benefactive (Ben): The ultimate entity for which an action is performed or for which, literally or figuratively, something happens or exists.

Instrument (Ins): The means by which an action is performed or something happens.

Patient (Pat): The entity undergoing an action or the object of predication.

Resultative (Rst): The final state of an entity.

These thematic roles receive illustration in the following examples of ἄγγελος + εἰμί (be an angel), περιεζωσμένος (wrapped), ἀποκτείνω (kill), and ποιέω (make). In the second example (1:13), the second argument of the passive participle has no retrievable referent; the translation introduces "someone" for its indefinite referent; and the associated Valence Description recognizes this by placing its syntactic function in parentheses, ( ).

οἱ ἑπτὰ ἀστέρες ἄγγελοι τῶν ἑπτὰ ἐκκλησιῶν εἰσιν (1:20)
[The seven stars (1/Pat)] are angels (ἄγγελος + εἰμί) [of the seven churches (2/Ben)].

υἱὸν ἀνθρώπου...περιεζωσμένον πρὸς τοῖς μαστοῖς ζώνην χρυσᾶν (1:13)
[A son of man (1/Pat)]...wrapped (περιεζωσμένος) [by someone (2/Agt)] [at his breasts (C/Loc)] [with/by a golden belt (3/Ins)].

τὰ τέκνα αὐτῆς ἀποκτενῶ ἐν θανάτῳ (2:23)
[I (1/Agt)] will kill (ἀποκτείνω) [her children (2/Pat)] [by death (C/Ins)].

ἐποίησας αὐτοὺς τῷ θεῷ ἡμῶν βασιλείαν καὶ ἱερεῖς (5:10)
[You (1/Agt)] made (ποιέω) [them (2/Pat)] [a kingdom and priests (3/Rst)] [for our God (C/Ben)].

	ἄγγελος + εἰμί (1:20)			περιεζωσμένος (1:13)			
syn.	1	2	1	(2)	3	|	C
sem.	Pat	Ben	Pat	Agt	Ins	|	Loc

	ἀποκτείνω (2:23)				ποιέω (5:10)			
syn.	1	2	|	C	1	2	3	|	C
sem.	Agt	Pat	|	Ins	Agt	Pat	Rst	|	Ben

When imposed on arguments, the next five thematic roles consistently are set in relation to an argument with the Patient thematic role.

Cause (Cau): the circumstantial motivation for an action or event.

Comparative (Cmp): The entity or event compared to another entity or event.

1. Case Frame Analysis and Description

Material (Mat): The sensible or metaphorical substance of an entity.

Partitive (Par): The entity specified as part of a whole or as part of a series.

Temporal (Tem): The time, either durative or punctual, of an action or event.

These thematic roles receive illustration in the following examples of εἰμί (be), ὅμοιος (like), γέμων (being full), ἕκαστος (each), εἰς (into), and πίπτω (fall).

διὰ τὸ θέλημά σου ἦσαν (4:11b)
[They (1/Pat)] are/exist (εἰμί) [because of your will (C/Cau)].

κάλαμος ὅμοιος ῥάβδῳ (11:1)
[A reed (1/Pat)] like (ὅμοιος) [a staff (2/Cmp)].

φιάλας χρυσᾶς γεμούσας θυμιαμάτων (5:8)
[Golden bowls (1/Pat)] being full (γέμων) [of incense (2/Mat)].

εἷς ἕκαστος τῶν πυλώνων (21:21)
Each (ἕκαστος) [one (1/Pat)] [of the gates (2/Par)].

ὁ καπνὸς αὐτῆς...εἰς τοὺς αἰῶνας τῶν αἰώνων (19:3)
[Its smoke (1/Pat)]...into (εἰς) [the ages of the ages (2/Tem)].

ὅτε εἶδον αὐτόν, ἔπεσα πρὸς τοὺς πόδας αὐτοῦ ὡς νεκρός (1:17)
[When I saw him (C/Tem)] [I (1/Thm)] fell (πίπτω) [at his feet (2/Loc)] [like a dead [man] (C/Cmp)].

	εἰμί (4:11b)		ὅμοιος (11:1)		γέμων (5:8)		ἕκαστος (21:21)	
syn.	1	C	1	2	1	2	1	2
sem.	P	Cau	Pat	Cmp	Pat	Mat	Pat	Par

	εἰς (19:3)		πίπτω (1:17)			
syn.	1	2	1	2	C	C
sem.	Pat	Tem	Thm	Loc	Cmp	Tem

The following three thematic roles need not be imposed on arguments in relation to a Patient argument and most frequently specify adjuncts.

Comitative (Com): The entity or event associated with another entity or event.

Current (Cur): The present state of an entity.

Measure (Mea): The quantification of an action or event or price of an entity.

These thematic roles receive illustration in the following examples of ἀναβαίνω (go up), λαμβάνω (receive), and ἔχων (having). In the second example (17:12b), the Source argument is not realized as a complement; the translation introduces its definite contextual referent, "the dragon"; and the associated Valence Description places its syntactic function in brackets, [ ].

ἀνέβη ὁ καπνὸς τῶν θυμιαμάτων ταῖς προσευχαῖς τῶν ἁγίων ἐκ χειρὸς τοῦ ἀγγέλου ἐνώπιον τοῦ θεοῦ (8:4)
[The smoke of the incenses (1/Thm)] [together with the prayers of the holy ones (C/Com)] went up (ἀναβαίνω) [from the hand of the angel (C/Sou)] [before God (2/Goa)].

ἐξουσίαν ὡς βασιλεῖς μίαν ὥραν λαμβάνουσιν μετὰ τοῦ θηρίου (17:12b)
[They (1/Goa)] receive (λαμβάνω) [from the dragon (3/Sou)] [authority (2/Thm)] [as kings (C/Cur)] [with the beast (C/Com)] [for one hour (C/Tem)].

ἄλλος ἄγγελος...ἔχων καὶ αὐτὸς δρέπανον ὀξύ (14:17)
[Another angel (1/Ben)]...[himself (C/Cur)] [also (C/Mea)] having (ἔχων) [a sharp sickle (2/Pat)].

	ἀναβαίνω (8:4)				λαμβάνω (17:12b)					
syn.	1	2	C	C	1	2	[3]	C	C	C
sem.	Thm	Goa	Com	Sou	Soa	Thm	Goa	Com	Cur	Tem

	ἔχων (14:17)			
syn.	1	2	C	C
sem.	Ben	Pat	Cur	Mea

The remaining five thematic roles are imposed only on adjuncts.

Condition (Cnd): The entity or event required for another event to occur.

Manner (Man): The circumstantial qualification of an action or event.

Purpose (Pur): The goal of a complete action or event.

Result (Res): The consequence of a complete event.

Vocative (Voc): The directly addressed entity.

These thematic roles receive illustration in the following examples of ἔρχομαι (come), ἥκω (come), ἐξέρχομαι (come out), and μέλλω (be about to). The translation of the first example (2:16) introduces the contextual referent of the verb of the conditional clause (repent). In the second example (3:3a), the Goal argument is not realized as a complement; the translation introduces its definite contextual referent, "you"; and the Valence Description places its syntactic function in brackets, [ ].

Note that the translation of the third example (and all future examples) introduces the referent of the first complement of imperative verbs.

εἰ δὲ μή, ἔρχομαί σοι ταχύ (2:16)
[If [you] do not [repent] (C/Cnd)] [I (1/Thm)] am coming (ἔρχομαι) [to you (2/Goa)] [soon (C/Tem)].

ἐὰν οὖν μὴ γρηγορήσῃς, ἥξω ὡς κλέπτης (3:3a)
[Therefore (C/Res)] [if you do not stay awake (C/Cnd)] [I (1/Thm)] will come (ἥκω) [to you (2/Goa)] [like a thief (C/Cmp)].

ἐξέλθατε ὁ λαός μου ἐξ αὐτῆς ἵνα μὴ συγκοινωνήσητε ταῖς ἁμαρτίαις αὐτῆς... ὅτι ἐκολλήθησαν αὐτῆς αἱ ἁμαρτίαι ἄχρι τοῦ οὐρανοῦ... (18:4-5)
[You (1/Thm)] [my people (C/Voc)] come out (ἐξέρχομαι) [from her (2/Sou)] [so that you may not participate in her sins (C/Pur)]...[because her sins are piled as far as the sky... (C/Cau)].

οὕτως ὅτι χλιαρὸς εἶ καὶ οὔτε ζεστὸς οὔτε ψυχρός, μέλλω σε ἐμέσαι ἐκ τοῦ στόματός μου (3:16)
[In this way (C/Man)] [because you are lukewarm and neither hot nor cold (C/Cau)] [I (1/Uns)] am about (μέλλω) [to spit you out of my mouth (2/Occ)].

	ἔρχομαι (2:16)				ἥκω (3:3a)				
syn.	1	2	C	C	1	[2]	C	C	C
sem.	Thm	Goa	Cnd	Tem	Thm	Goa	Cmp	Cnd	Res

	ἐξέρχομαι (18:4-5)					μέλλω (3:16)			
syn.	1	2	C	C	C	1	2	C	C
sem.	Thm	Sou	Cau	Pur	Voc	Uns	Occ	Cau	Man

Finally, the notation "—" in the semantic function position signals the absence of a thematic role in Valence Descriptions. Although this notation has multiple uses, at present it signals only the absence of a thematic role associated with the syntactic function "0" with zero-place predicators. This notation receives illustration in the following examples of the noun predicators ἀστήρ (star) and βότρυς (bunch of grapes).

οἱ ἀστέρες τοῦ οὐρανοῦ (6:13)
The stars (ἀστήρ) [of heaven (C/Ben)].

τοὺς βότρυας τῆς ἀμπέλου τῆς γῆς (14:18)
The bunches of grapes (βότρυς) [of the vineyard of the earth (C/Ben)].

	ἀστήρ (6:13)		βότρυς (14:18)	
syn.	0	C	0	C
sem.	—		—	Ben

4. Lexical Analysis and Description

In Greek, the arguments and adjuncts licensed by predicators are realized lexically by one of five categories of phrases: the noun phrase (N), "a noun with its modifiers or a pronoun"; the adjective phrase (Adj), "an adjective with its modifiers"; the verb phrase (V), "a verb with its arguments and adjuncts"; the preposition phrase (P), "a preposition with its arguments"; and the adverb phrase (A), "an adverb with its arguments and adjuncts." By convention, a subject complement that is lexically realized only by the verbal ending is listed as a noun phrase (N), and simple participle complements are listed as adjectives except in the case of the genitive absolute which is listed as Part+gen. Lexical realizations appear in the third row of the Valence Description immediately beneath the semantic functions of their associated arguments and adjuncts.

Noun (N), prepositional (P), adverb (A), and adjective (Adj) phrases always are "maximal" because they consistently include all of their modifiers (N & Adj) or arguments (P & A). Verb phrases, however, may include their subject complement and be maximal (V+) or not include their subject complement and be non-maximal (V-).

The notations in Valence Descriptions expand on this basic framework by providing specific information about all phrases except noun phrases that lexically realize the subject complements of verbs. This exclusion reflects the fact that the syntactic case of a verbal subject is determined by its governing grammatical construction: nominative case in indicative and subjunctive clauses, genitive in the genitive absolute, and either dative or accusative in various classes of infinitive phrases. The remaining phrases receive specification in a manner appropriate to the phrase.

a. Noun and Adjective Phrase Lexical Realizations

The specification of noun and adjective phrase lexical realizations is straightforward. Non-subject noun phrases (N) are maximal (+). Most frequently predicators directly impose on the noun phrase lexical realizations (lex.) of their non-first (subject) arguments the genitive (N+gen), dative (N+dat), accusative (N+acc), or vocative (N+voc) syntactic case, as illustrated in the following examples of δείκνυμι (show), ἄγγελος (angel), and μέγας + [εἰμί] ([be] great]). In the second example (1:1), the translation introduces in braces, { }, the second argument, which is co-referential to the noun predicator and never realized as a complement, and the Valence Description places braces around its syntactic function and lists its lexical realization as {N}. In the third example (15:3), Greek grammar permissibly omits the εἰμί (be) of the complex predicator, and the Valence Description places brackets, [ ], around the εἰμί component of the complex predicator.

δείξω σοι τὴν νύμφην τὴν γυναῖκα τοῦ ἀρνίου (21:9)
[I (1/Agt)] will show (δείκνυμι) [to you (3/Exp)] [the bride, the wife of the Lamb (2/Con)].

τοῦ ἀγγέλου αὐτοῦ (1:1)

The angel (ἄγγελος) [of him (1/Ben)] {angel (2/Pat)}.

μεγάλα...τὰ ἔργα σου, κύριε ὁ θεὸς ὁ παντοκράτωρ (15:3)
Great are (μέγας + [εἰμί]) [your works (1/Pat)] [Lord God Almighty (C/Voc)].

	δείκνυμι (21:9)			ἄγγελος (1:1)		μέγας + [εἰμί] (15:3)		
syn.	1	2	3	1	{2}	1	|	C
sem.	Agt	Con	Exp	Ben	Pat	Pat	|	Voc
lex.	N	N+acc	N+dat	N+gen	{N}	N	|	N+voc

Predicators impose on all remaining noun phrase complements and on all adjective and participle phrase complements the same syntactic case as either their first or their second required complement. This typically is the situation with Resultative and Current complements. When predicators impose on noun phrase (N) and adjective phrase (Adj) complements the same syntactic case as their first required complement, the lexical realizations are listed as N+1 and Adj+1. When predicators impose on noun phrase and adjective phrase complements the same syntactic case as their second required complement, the lexical realizations are listed as N+2 and Adj+2. Measure adjuncts introduce these specifications by εἰ μή (if not, except), and Comparative adjuncts introduce these specifications by ὡς (as, like). These realizations receive illustration in the following examples of ποιέω (make), γίνομαι (become), εὑρίσκω (find), οἶδα (know), and λέγων (calling).

καινὰ ποιῶ πάντα (21:5)
[I (1/Agt)] make (ποιέω) [all things (2/Pat)] [new (3/Rst)].

ἐγένετο τὸ τρίτον τῆς θαλάσσης αἷμα (8:8)
[A third of the sea (1/Pat)] became (γίνομαι) [blood (2/Rst)].

εὗρες αὐτοὺς ψευδεῖς (2:2)
[You (1/Exp)] found (εὑρίσκω) [them (2/Con)] [false (3/Cur)].

ὃ οὐδεὶς οἶδεν εἰ μὴ ὁ λαμβάνων (2:17)
[Which (2/Con)] [no one (1/Exp)] [except the one receiving it (C/Mea)] knows (οἶδα).

ἡ λέγουσα ἑαυτὴν προφῆτιν (2:20)
[The one (1/Agt)] calling (λέγων) [herself (2/Pat)] [a prophet (3/Rst)].

	ποιέω (21:5)			γίνομαι (8:8)		εὑρίσκω (2:2)		
syn.	1	2	3	1	2	1	2	3
sem.	Agt	Pat	Rst	Pat	Pat	Exp	Con	Con
lex.	N	N+acc	Adj+2	N	N+1	N	N+acc	Adj+2

	οἶδα (2:17)			λέγων (2:20)		
syn.	1	2	C	1	2	3
sem.	Exp	Con	Mea	Agt	Pat	Rst
lex.	N	N+acc	εἰ μή N+1	N	N+acc	N+2

b. Preposition and Adverb Phrase Lexical Realizations

The specification of preposition and adverb phrase lexical realizations places the preposition or adverb after its category abbreviation (P or A) and a slash, /. When prepositions govern more than one syntactic case, the syntactic case appears after the preposition in brackets, [ ], preceded by a plus sign, +. When adverbs introduce noun or adjective phrases, the noun or adjective phrase follows the adverb. The following preposition phrase realizations appear in the text of Revelation:

P/ἀνὰ μέσον (between), P/ἀπό (from, by), P/ἀπὸ μακρόθεν (from afar), P/ἄχρι (until), P/διά [+acc] (because of), P/διά [+gen] (through), P/εἰς (to, into), P/ἐκ (out of), P/ἔμπροσθεν (before), P/ἐν (in, by [means of], with), P/ἐν μέσῳ (in the middle of), P/ἐνώπιον (before), P/ἔξωθεν (outside of), P/ἐπί [+acc] (on, onto), P/ἐπί [+dat] (on, at, about, concerning), P/ἐπί [+gen] (on, before), P/κατά [+acc] (according to, down), P/κατά [+gen] (against), P/κυκλόθεν (from around), P/κύκλῳ (around), P/μετά [+acc] (after), P/μετά [+gen] (with, against), P/ὀπίσω (behind, after), P/παρά [+dat] (with), P/παρά [+gen] (from), P/περί [+acc] (around), P/πρός [+acc] (to, at), P/πρός [+dat] (at), P/ὑπό [+gen] (by), and P/ὑποκάτω (under).

The following adverb phrase realizations appear in the text of Revelation:

A/ἀνά (up), A/ἄρτι (still), A/δεύτερον (again), A/δωρεάν (freely), A/Ἑβραϊστί (in Hebrew), A/ἐκεῖ (there), A/ἐκεῖθεν (from there), A/ἔμπροσθεν (in front), A/ἐντεῦθεν (from within), A/ἔσωθεν (from the inside), A/ἔτι (still), A/εὐθέως (immediately), A/καί (also), A/μακρόθεν (from afar), A/ὀλίγον (a lttle), A/ὁμοίως (like), A/ὄπισθεν (from behind), A/οὐκέτι (no longer), A/οὖν (thus), A/οὔπω (nowhere), A/οὕτω (in this way), A/οὕτως (in this way), A/πάλιν (again), A/πνευματικῶς (spiritually), A/πόθεν (from where), A/πολύ (much, a lot), A/πῶς (how), A/σφόδρα (very), A/ταχύ (quickly, soon), A/ὧδε (here), and A/ὡς (as, like).

These preposition and adverb realizations receive illustration in the following examples of ἀναβαίνω (go up), πίπτω (fall), and ἔχω (have).

ἀνέβησαν εἰς τὸν οὐρανὸν ἐν τῇ νεφέλῃ (11:12)
[They (1/Thm)] went up (ἀναβαίνω) [to heaven (2/Goa)] [by [means of] a cloud (C/Ins)].

ἔπεσαν ἐνώπιον τοῦ θρόνου ἐπὶ τὰ πρόσωπα αὐτῶν (7:11)
[They (1/Thm)] fell (πίπτω) [before the throne (2/Loc)] [onto their faces (C/Goa)].

οὕτως ἔχεις καὶ σὺ κρατοῦντας τὴν διδαχὴν [τῶν] Νικολαϊτῶν ὁμοίως (2:15)
[In this way (C/Man)] [likewise (C/Cmp)] [you (1/Ben)] [also (C/Mea)] have (ἔχω) [ones holding the teaching of the Nicolaitans (2/Pat)].

	ἀναβαίνω (11:12)			πίπτω (7:11)		
syn.	1	2	C	1	2	C
sem.	Thm	Goa	Ins	Thm	Loc	Goa
lex.	N	P/εἰς	P/ἐν	N	P/ἐνώπιον	P/ἐπί [+acc]

	ἔχω (2:15)				
syn.	1	2	C	C	C
sem.	Ben	Pat	Cmp	Man	Mea
lex.	N	N+acc	A/ὁμοίως	A/οὕτως	A/καί

c. Verb Phrase Lexical Realizations

The specification of verb phrase (V) complements is more complicated because these phrases may contain their own subject complement and be maximal (V+) or may not contain their own subject and be non-maximal (V-). Greek, like English, shows great variety in maximal verb phrases. The simple specification V+ characterizes complete verb phrases (independent clauses), and this notation is expanded to V+quo when complete verb phrases realize a quotation with predicators of communication and experience. All remaining categories of maximal verb phrases begin with V+ to which is appended the introductory word[s] or, in the case of the maximal infinitive phrase (infinitive with subject accusative), a small letter "i":

V+, V+quo, V+ἄχρι (until), V+ἄχρι[ς] οὗ (until), V+ἀφ' οὗ (from when), V+ἐάν (if), V+εἰ (if), V+ἕως (as far as), V+ἵνα (so that), V+ὅ (who, which), V+ὅμοιος (like), V+ὅπου (where), V+ὁσάκις ἐάν (as often as), V+ὅσος (as much as), V+ὅσος ἐάν (as much as), V+ὅταν (when), V+ὅτε (when), V+ὅτι (that, because), V+οὗ (when), V+ποῖος (what sort of), V+ὡς (when, as), V+ὡς Part+gen (as when), V+ὥσπερ (as), and V+i (that).

Maximal verb phrase lexical realizations receive illustration in the following examples of ἰδού (look!), λέγω (say), κρατέω (hold [onto]), φεύγω (flee), and γινώσκω (know)

ἰδοὺ ἔρχομαι ταχύ... (22:12)
Look! (ἰδού) ["I am coming soon..." (1/Occ)].

λέγουσιν τοῖς ὄρεσιν καὶ ταῖς πέτραις· πέσετε ἐφ' ἡμᾶς... (6:16)
[They (1/Agt)] say (λέγω) [to the mountains and to the rocks (3/Exp)] ["Fall on us...!" (2/Con)].

ὃ ἔχετε κρατήσατε ἄχρι[ς] οὗ ἂν ἥξω (2:25)
[You (1/Agt)] hold (κρατέω) [what you have (2/Pat)] [until I come (C/Tem)].

ἡ γυνὴ ἔφυγεν εἰς τὴν ἔρημον, ὅπου ἔχει ἐκεῖ τόπον ἡτοιμασμένον ἀπὸ τοῦ θεοῦ, ἵνα ἐκεῖ τρέφωσιν αὐτὴν ἡμέρας χιλίας διακοσίας ἑξήκοντα (12:6)
[The woman (1/Thm)] fled (φεύγω) [into the desert (2/Goa)] [where she had [there] a place prepared by God (C/Loc)] [so that there they might feed her for one thousand two hundred and sixty days (C/Pur)].

οὐ μὴ γνῷς ποίαν ὥραν ἥξω ἐπὶ σέ (3:3)
[You (1/Exp)] may not know (γινώσκω) [during which hour I will come to you (2/Con)].

	ἰδού (22:12)	λέγω (6:16)			κρατέω (2:25)			
syn.	1	1	2	3	1	2	|	C
sem.	Occ	Agt	Con	Exp	Agt	Pat	|	Tem
lex.	V+	N	V+quo	N+dat	N	V+ὅ	|	V+ ἄχρι[ς] οὗ

	φεύγω (12:6)					γινώσκω (3:3)	
syn.	1	2	|	C	C	1	2
sem.	Thm	Goa	|	Loc	Pur	Exp	Con
lex.	N	P/εἰς	|	V+ὅπου	V+ἵνα	N	V+ποῖος

All non-maximal verb phrases are infinitive phrases (V-i) that do not realize their own subject complement. Instead, the infinitive retrieves the referent of its first complement from the first (1), second (2), or third (3) required complement of the predicator that licenses the infinitive complement, and the specifications note this by appending "1," "2," or "3" onto the infinitive marker, "i."[15] When the non-maximal infinitive also does not realize its second complement but retrieves the second complement's referent from a different required complement of the licensing predicator, the specification notes this by appending "1," "2," or "3" to the infinitive marker (i) immediately after the numerical referent of the first complement and separated by a comma (,).

V-i1, V-i1,2, V-i1,3, V-i2, V-i2,1, V-i3, V-i3,2.

[15] Technically, the first, second, or third required complement of the licensing predicator is deemed to coinstantiate the first complement of the infinitive phrase that realizes another complement of the licensing predicator. A general introduction to coinstantiation appears in Fried and Östman, "Construction Grammar," 63–66; cf. Paul Kay and Charles J. Fillmore, "Grammatical Constructions and Linguistic Generalizations: The 'What's X doing Y?' Construction," *Language* 75, no. 1 (1999): 22–23.

The non-maximal infinitive phrase lexical realizations receive illustration in the following examples of δύναμαι (be able), ποιέω (make), ἐξουσία (authority), δίδωμι (give), and μετά + [εἰμί] ([be] with). In order to clarify the retrieval of referents from the licensing predicator, the non-maximal infinitive phrases receive separate analysis beneath their licensing predicator phrases preceded by a right arrow, →, and introduce the retrieved referents in double brackets, [[ ]]. In the third example (6:8), since the first argument is not realized but has a definite referent retrievable from the context, the Valence Description places its syntactic function in brackets, [ ] and the lexical realization is left empty pending the discussion of §1.5.

τίς δύναται πολεμῆσαι μετ' αὐτοῦ; (13:4)
[Who (1/Uns)] is able (δύναμαι) [to battle against him (2/Occ)]?
→to [[who]] battle against him.

καὶ πῦρ ποιῇ ἐκ τοῦ οὐρανοῦ καταβαίνειν εἰς τὴν γῆν ἐνώπιον τῶν ἀνθρώπων (13:13b)
[It 1/Agt] [also (C/Mea)] may make (ποιέω) [fire (2/Pat)] [come down from heaven to the earth before human beings (3/Occ)].
→[[fire]] come down to the earth before human beings.

ἐξουσία ἐπὶ τὸ τέταρτον τῆς γῆς ἀποκτεῖναι ἐν ῥομφαίᾳ καὶ ἐν λιμῷ καὶ ἐν θανάτῳ καὶ ὑπὸ τῶν θηρίων τῆς γῆς (6:8)
[[Their] (1/Ben)]] authority (ἐξουσία) [over a fourth of the earth (3/Loc)] [to kill by sword and by famine and by death and by the beasts of the earth (2/Occ)].
→to [[them]] kill [[a fourth of the earth]] by sword and by famine and by death and by the beasts of the earth.

αἷμα αὐτοῖς [δ]έδωκας πιεῖν (16:6)
[You (1/Agt)] have given (δίδωμι) [them (3/Goa)] [blood (2/Thm)] [to drink (C/Pur)].
→to [[them]] drink [[blood]].

ὁ μισθός μου μετ' ἐμοῦ ἀποδοῦναι ἑκάστῳ ὡς τὸ ἔργον ἐστὶν αὐτοῦ (22:12)
[My wage (1/Thm)] is with (μετά + [εἰμί]) [me (2/Loc)] [to pay back to each one as is his work (C/Pur)].
→to [[me]] pay back [[my wage]] to each one as is his work.

	δύναμαι (13:4)		ποιέω (13:13b)				
syn.	1	2	1	2	3	|	C
sem.	Uns	Occ	Agt	Pat	Occ	|	Mea
lex.	N	V-i1	N	N+acc	V-i2	|	A/καί

	ἐξουσία (6:8)			δίδωμι (16:6)				
syn.	[1]	2	3	1	2	3	|	C
sem.	Ben	Occ	Loc	Agt	Thm	Goa	|	Pur
lex.		V-i1,3	P/ἐπί [+acc]	N	N+acc	N+dat	|	V-i3,2

	μετά + [εἰμί] (22:12)			
syn.	1	2	|	C
sem.	Thm	Loc	|	Pur
lex.	N	N+gen	|	V-i2,1

5. Required Complement Omission

In addition to the non-realization of required first complements of verbs, participles, adjectives and complex predicators, Greek grammar permits the omission of other required complements in specific circumstances.[16] This discussion examines three categories of required complement omission associated with definite null complements, indefinite null complements, and passivization.

a. Definite Null Complements

The text of Revelation presents numerous occurrences in which predicators do not realize as required complements second and/or third arguments with definite semantic referents. When this occurs, the complement that would have realized the argument is labeled a definite null complement (DNC).[17] The definite referent of such unrealized required complements most frequently is retrievable from the context, as in the immediately preceding illustrative example of ἐξουσία (authority) in 6:8. In that verse, the statement that "authority was given to them" implies "their authority."

Less frequently, the referent of the definite null complement must be supplied directly by the interpreter, that is, the reader. This can occur only if the interpreter belongs to a group characterized by specific social, cultural, or religious presuppositions. For example, the noun predicator προσευχή (prayer) requires completion by

---

[16] An introduction to non-subject complement omission appears in Francis Cornish, "Implicit Internal Arguments, Event Structures, Predication and Anaphoric Reference," in *The Grammar-Pragmatics Interface: Essays in Honor of Jeanette K. Gindel* (ed. Nancy Hedberg and Ron Zacharski; Amsterdam/Philadelphia: Benjamins, 2007), 198–99; cf. D. García Valesco and C. Portrero Muñiz, "Understood Objects in Functional Grammar," *WPiFG* 76 (2002): 1–22; Charles J. Fillmore, "Pragmatically Controlled Zero Anaphora," *BLS* 12 (1986): 95–107; and idem, "Topics in Lexical Semantics," in *Current Issues in Linguistic Theory* (ed. Roger W. Cole; Bloomington: Indiana University Press, 1977), 96–97.

[17] Definite Null Complements receive investigation under the designations, "definite object deletion" in Anita Mittwoch, "Idioms and Unspecified N[oun] P[hrase] Deletion," *LInq* 2 (1971): 255–59, "latent object" in Peter Hugoe Matthews, *Syntax* (Cambridge: Cambridge University Press, 1981), 125–26, "contextual deletion" in D. J. Allerton, *Valency and the English Verb* (New York: Academic Press, 1982), 34, 68–70, and "definite null objects" in Knud Lambrecht and K. Lemoine, "Definite Null Objects in (Spoken) French: A Construction Grammar Account," in *Grammatical Constructions: Back to the Roots* (ed. Mirjam Fried and Hans C. Boas; CAL 4; Amsterdam/Philadelphia: Benjamins, 2005), 13–55.

three arguments that function as a Benefactive, a Content, and an Experiencer, and the Experiencer must have a definite referent when left unrealized. Although the Experiencer never receives realization or explicit clarification anywhere in the text of Revelation, the phrases containing this noun predicator remain grammatical because Revelation is a document written for a Christian audience for whom there is only one possible referent for the Experiencer, God.[18] The text of Revelation presents numerous predicators, especially passivized verb predicators, for which a Christian interpreter readily is able to supply "God" or "Jesus" for the referent of an unrealized argument with no retrievable contextual referent. Such unrealized arguments also are treated as definite null complements.

Definite null complements receive illustration in the following examples of ἀκούω (hear) and προσευχή + εἰμί (be a prayer). For ease in interpretation, the translations introduce in double brackets, [[ ]], the referents of the definite null complements. In the first example (22:8b), John states earlier in the verse that he is the one hearing "these things," and in the second example (5:8), the interpreter supplies "God" as the definite referent of the Experiencer.

ἤκουσα (22:8b)
[1 (1/Exp)] heard (ἀκούω) [[these things (2/Con)]].

αἵ εἰσιν αἱ προσευχαὶ τῶν ἁγίων (5:8)
[Which (1/Con)] are the prayers (προσευχή + εἰμί) [of the holy ones (2/Ben)] [[to God (3/Exp)]].

Valence Descriptions place the syntactic function of definite null complements in brackets, [ ], and list their lexical realizations as DNC.

	ἀκούω (22:8b)		προσευχή + εἰμί (5:8)		
syn.	1	[2]	1	2	[3]
sem.	Exp	Con	Con	Ben	Exp
lex.	N	DNC	N	N+gen	DNC

b. Indefinite Null Complements

Many predicators in Greek and English come "prepackaged" with indefinite but circumscribed interpretations for one or more of their arguments. For example, although the English verb "eat" requires completion by two arguments that function as an Agent and a Patient, the verb designates the action of consuming "food/something edible by the referent of the Agent." As a consequence, when a writer or speaker sees no need to specify the exact referent of the Patient beyond "food/something edible by the referent of the Agent," the Patient argument may remain unrealized as an

---

[18] Further discussion of such interpreter-supplied definite referents, especially in the context of predicators of communication, appears in Paul L. Danove, *New Testament Verbs of Communication: A Case Frame and Exegetical Study* (LNTS 520; London: Bloomsbury, 2015), 60–61.

indefinite null complement (INC).[19] The noted indefinite null complement accounts for the fact that "My guest arrived while I was eating" is a well-formed sentence despite the absence of a definite retrievable referent for the required Patient complement of "eat." Indefinite null complements receive illustration in the following examples of βλέπω (see), δειπνέω (eat), and κηρύσσων (proclaiming). The translations introduce in double brackets, [[ ]], the non-specific but circumscribed referents of the indefinite null complements.

βλέπῃς (3:18)
[You (1/Exp)] may see (βλέπω) [[visible things (2/Con)]].

δειπνήσω μετ' αὐτοῦ (3:20)
[I (1/Agt)] will eat (δειπνέω) [[food (2/Pat)]] [with him (C/Loc)].

ἄγγελον ἰσχυρὸν κηρύσσοντα ἐν φωνῇ μεγάλῃ· τίς ἄξιος ἀνοῖξαι τὸ βιβλίον καὶ λῦσαι τὰς σφραγῖδας αὐτοῦ; (5:2)
[A strong angel (1/Agt)] proclaiming (κηρύσσων) [with a loud voice (C/Ins)] [[to those able to hear (3/Exp)]] ["Who is worthy to open the book and undo its seals? (2/Con)]

Valence Descriptions place the syntactic function of indefinite null complements in parentheses, ( ), and note their lexical realizations as INC.

	βλέπω (3:18)		δειπνέω (3:20)		
syn.	1	(2)	1	(2)	C
sem.	Exp	Con	Agt	Pat	Loc
lex.	N	INC	N	INC	P/μετά [+gen]

	κηρύσσων (5:2)			
syn.	1	2	(3)	C
sem.	Agt	Con	Exp	Ins
lex.	N	V+quo	INC	P/ἐν

c. Passivization

The passivization constructions in both Greek and English raise verb and active participle predicators' second argument as first required complement, lower the predicators' first argument to second required complement, and permit the newly lowered complement to remain unrealized even when it has no retrievable definite referent.[20] This construction also introduces the possibility that the first argument of verb

---

[19] Indefinite null complements receive investigation in Bruce Fraser and John R. Ross, "Idioms and Unspecified N[oun] P[hrase] Deletion," *LInq* 1 (1970): 264–65, and in Ivan Sag and Jorge Hankamer, "Toward a Theory of Anaphoric Processing," *L&P* 7 (1984): 325–45.
[20] An introduction to the passivization construction appears in Fillmore and Kay, *Construction Grammar*, 8:20, 30. Within the text of Revelation, this construction is reserved to verb and participle predicators with active and middle base forms.

predicators, which must have a definite referent when the verb is not passivized, to become an indefinite null complement (INC) when passivized. Passivization has no impact on the Valence Descriptions of verb predicators because Case Frame analysis uses the passivization construction to transform passivized occurrences of verb predicators into their active or middle counterparts and analyzes them accordingly. The situation is different with the passive participle predicators because modification demands that the modified entity become the first argument of the passivized participle. As a consequence, the corresponding verb or active participle's second argument becomes the passive participle predicator's first argument and the verb and active participle's second argument becomes the passive participle predicator's first argument, as illustrated in the following examples of σφάζω (slay), which requires completion by an Agent first argument and a Patient second argument, and ἐσφαγμένος (slain), which requires completion by a Patient first argument and an Agent second argument. The translation of the second example (5:12) introduces in double brackets, [[ ]], "someone" as the indefinite but circumscribed referent of the Agent complement, and the Valence Description places parentheses, ( ), around the syntactic function of the indefinite null Agent complement and lists its lexical realization as INC.

ἀλλήλους σφάξουσιν (6:4)
[They (1/Agt)] will slay (σφάζω) [one another (2/Pat)].

τὸ ἀρνίον τὸ ἐσφαγμένον (5:12)
[The lamb (1/Pat)] slain (ἐσφαγμένος) [[by someone (2/Agt)]].

	σφάζω (6:4)		ἐσφαγμένος (5:12)	
syn.	1	2	1	(2)
sem.	Agt	Pat	Pat	Agt
lex.	N	N+acc	N	INC

6. Applications of the Case Frame Method

The concepts, definitions, and method of Case Frame analysis and description presented in this chapter are foundational to all further developments in this study. Subsequent presentations will augment the information in Valence Descriptions by introducing a series of further notations that clarify the category of the predicator (Chapter 2), general qualifications of the conceptualizations grammaticalized by predicators (Chapter 3), further specifications of lexical realizations of complements (Chapter 4), the specific conceptualization grammaticalized by each occurrence of each predicator (Chapters 5 and 6), and distinctive grammatical characteristics of the text of Revelation (Chapter 7). The resulting fully articulated Valence Descriptions for each occurrence of each predicator in the text of Revelation then will receive restatement according to protocols (Chapter 8) into lexicon entries that maintain all of the syntactic, semantic, lexical, and further specifications of their associated Valence Descriptions (Chapter 9).

2

EVENTS, EVENT FEATURES, AND NON-EVENTS

This chapter introduces the concept "event," establishes the criteria for distinguishing events from non-events, and investigates the characteristics of the twenty-three events and three non-events grammaticalized by predicators in the text of Revelation. The discussion of each event proposes a distinctive name for the event, specifies the entities native to the event, develops protocols for labeling the configuration of entities within the event, and investigates three "event features" that accommodate alternate configurations of entities within some events. The discussion of each non-event proposes a distinctive name for the non-event, specifies the entities native to the non-event, and develops protocols for labeling the configurations of entities within the non-event. The concluding discussion reprises the configurations of all observed events and non-events in the text of Revelation and specifies the use of events, event features, and non-events in the following study.

1. Events and Non-Events

In addition to the syntactic, semantic, and lexical information developed in the previous chapter, the Valence Description for each occurrence of a predicator specifies the event or non-event grammaticalized in that occurrence. An event is a cognitive schema of an action, process, or state in which four, three, or two logical entities are set in particular relation to each other.[1] The cognitive schema constitutes a bare concept of an action, process, or state that may be grammaticalized by many predicators. Non-events, in contrast, do not set two or more logical entities in specific relation to each other. As developed in this chapter, non-events also are bare concepts that may be grammaticalized by multiple predicators. Among the 870 predicators in the text of Revelation, 656 consistently grammaticalize one or more of twenty-three events, 209 consistently grammaticalize one of three non-events, and five grammaticalize events in some occurrences and non-events in other occurrences.

---

[1] Cliff Goddard, *Semantic Analysis: A Practical Introduction* (Oxford: Oxford University Press, 1998), 197–98.

2. The Twenty-Three Events Grammaticalized in the Text of Revelation

The twenty-three events resolve into categories depending on whether they set four, three, or two logical entities in specific relation to each other. Predicators grammaticalize these events by raising some or all of their logical entities as arguments. This permits the description of the event entities according to the thematic roles most closely associated with their specific relations within the bare concept of the event. Once a logical entity is associated with a specific thematic role, it receives reference as an "event entity."

For example, the bare concept of the event of transference sets its four entities in specific relation that may be expressed in binary fashion: mover to what is moved, what is moved to its initial locale, what is moved to its final locale, and initial locale to final locale. Respectively, these specific relations are most closely associated with the thematic roles Agent and Theme, Theme and Source, Theme and Goal, and Source and Goal. Predicators that grammaticalize the event of transference most frequently raise the logical entities of this event as Agent, Theme, Source, and Goal arguments. This permits description of the event of transference according to the configuration of the associated thematic roles of its four event entities in the order of their grammaticalization first by verb, active participle, complex active participle, complex adjective, and complex noun predicators or, lacking these, by passive participle, complex passive participle, and complex preposition predicators, or, lacking these, by preposition predicators. These descriptive configurations place one-letter abbreviations of the most frequently occurring thematic roles in the order of their grammaticalization. Once the first letter of a thematic role is used, however, the complete three-letter abbreviation of the thematic role appears in the descriptive configurations.

Since verb predicators grammaticalize the event of transference, the descriptive configuration places the one-letter abbreviations of the thematic roles associated with its event entities in the order of their grammaticalization by verb predicators, with the entity associated with the Agent (A) thematic role as first event entity and with the Theme (Θ) thematic role as second event entity. Since different verb predicators grammaticalize this event by raising the entity associated with either the Source (S) or the Goal (G) thematic role as third argument, the sequencing of the two remaining event entities is arbitrary and set as Source entity followed by Goal entity. This yields the event configuration AΘSG for the event of transference.

The following discussion designates the twenty-three events grammaticalized by predicators in the text of Revelation, provides italicized three-letter abbreviations for each event designation, identifies the thematic roles associated with the entities of each event, and generates descriptive configurations for each event. The discussion develops first events containing four entities, then those containing three entities, and finally those containing two entities.

a. Events Containing Four Entities

The events of delegation and transference set four entities in relation to each other. The four entities of the event of delegation are associated with the thematic roles Agent (A), Occurrence (O), Source (S), and Goal (G). This yields the configuration AOSG, which is formed by listing the first letter of the thematic roles associated with its four entities in the order of their grammaticalization. As previously discussed, the four entities of the event of transference are associated with the thematic roles Agent (A), Theme (Θ), Source (S), and Goal (G), which yields the configuration AΘSG. These two events pose special complications for grammaticalization because Greek grammar, like English grammar, constrains predicators to raise at most three event entities as arguments. The manner in which the predicators raise three of these four entities as arguments receives clarification in the discussions of usage features (§3.2a).

This and following discussions propose for each event designation a three-letter abbreviation that has the first letter capitalized and that ends in a period (.). Since some of the three-letter abbreviations are similar or identical to the three-letter thematic role abbreviations, the following study distinguishes abbreviated event designations by consistently placing them in italics. The respective abbreviated designations for the events of delegation and transference are *Del.* and *Tra.* These events receive respective illustration in the following examples of δίδωμι (give, delegate) and ὁδηγέω (guide, lead). The translation of the first example (13:7a) introduces in double brackets, [[ ]], the indefinite referent (someone) of the INC Agent.

Del. ἐδόθη αὐτῷ ποιῆσαι πόλεμον μετὰ τῶν ἁγίων καὶ νικῆσαι αὐτούς (13:7a)
[To make war against the holy ones and to conquer them (2/Occ)] was given (δίδωμι) [to them (3/Goa)] [[by someone (1/Agt)]].

Tra. ὁδηγήσει αὐτοὺς ἐπὶ ζωῆς πηγὰς ὑδάτων (7:17)
[He (1/Agt)] will guide (ὁδηγέω) [them (2/Thm)] [to springs of the waters of life (3/Goa)].

The following and all subsequent Valence Descriptions incorporate the italicized three-letter abbreviation of the event designation in chevrons, < >, after the predicator and its citation. As previously discussed (§1.5c), Case Frame analysis uses the passivization construction to transform the passivized occurrence of δίδωμι in 13:7a into its active counterpart.

	δίδωμι (13:7a) <*Del.*>			ὁδηγέω (7:17) <*Tra.*>		
syn.	1	2	3	1	2	3
sem.	Agt	Occ	Goa	Agt	Thm	Goa
lex.	N	V-i3	N+dat	N	N+acc	P/ἐπί [+acc]

The following table presents from left to right the event designation, the italicized designation abbreviation (*abb.*), the thematic roles associated with the event's four entities, and the configuration (conf.) of the event.

event	abb.	event entities	conf.
delegation	*Del.*	Agent, Occurrence, Source, Goal	AOSG
transference	*Tra.*	Agent, Theme, Source, Goal	AΘSG

b. Events Containing Three Entities

Six events place three entities in relation: authority (*Aut.*), communication (*Cmm.*), compulsion (*Cpl.*), disposition (*Dis.*), motion (*Mot.*), and separation (*Sep.*). Greek grammar permits predicators to raise three event entities as arguments, and, except for the event of motion, predicators raise all three entities of these events as arguments. The manner in which some predicators raise only two of three entities of motion as arguments receives clarification in the discussion of usage features (§3.3a). The following examples of ποιέω (make) and ἐξαλείφω (erase) illustrate respectively the grammaticalization of the three-entity events of compulsion (*Cpl.*) and of separation (*Sep.*).

Cpl.   ποιεῖ τὴν γῆν καὶ τοὺς ἐν αὐτῇ κατοικοῦντας ἵνα προσκυνήσουσιν τὸ θηρίον τὸ πρῶτον (13:12b)
[It (1/Agt)] makes (ποιέω) [the earth and the ones dwelling in it (2/Pat)] [that they worship the first beast (3/Occ)].

Sep.   οὐ μὴ ἐξαλείψω τὸ ὄνομα αὐτοῦ ἐκ τῆς βίβλου τῆς ζωῆς (3:5)
[I (1/Agt)] will not erase (ἐξαλείφω) [his name (2/Pat)] [from the book of life (3/Sou)].

	ποιέω (13:12b) <*Cpl.*>			ἐξαλείφω (3:5) <*Sep.*>		
syn.	1	2	3	1	2	3
sem.	Agt	Pat	Occ	Agt	Pat	Sou
lex.	N	N+acc	V+ἵνα	N	N+acc	P/ἐκ

The following table presents from left to right the event designation, the italicized designation abbreviation (*abb.*), the thematic roles associated with the event's three entities, and the configuration (conf.) of the event.

event	abb.	event entities	conf.
authority	*Aut.*	Benefactive, Occurrence, Locative	BOL
communication	*Cmm.*	Agent, Content, Experiencer	ACE
compulsion	*Cpl.*	Agent, Patient, Occurrence	APO
disposition	*Dis.*	Agent, Theme, Occurrence	AΘO
motion	*Mot.*	Theme, Source, Goal	ΘSG
separation	*Sep.*	Agent, Patient, Source	APS

c. Events Containing Two Entities

The remaining fifteen events place two entities in relation, and, except for events already designated in my previous writings, receive designation according to the entity not associated with the Content, Occurrence, Patient, or Theme thematic role: benefaction (*Ben.*), capacity (*Cap.*), causation (*Cau.*), communion (*Com.*), comparison (*Cmp.*), effect (*Eff.*), experience (*Exp.*), instrumentality (*Ins.*), location (*Loc.*), materiality (*Mat.*), measurement (*Mea.*), modification (*Mod.*), necessity (*Nec.*), partition (*Par.*), and temporality (*Tem.*). Predicators raise both entities of all fifteen events as arguments. The following examples of ἱερεύς + εἰμί (be a priest), σφάζω (slay), and ἀγαπάω (love) illustrate respectively the grammaticalization of the two-entity events of benefaction (*Ben.*), effect (*Eff.*), and experience (*Exp.*).

Ben.   ἔσονται ἱερεῖς τοῦ θεοῦ καὶ τοῦ Χριστοῦ (20:6)
[They (1/Pat)] will be priests (ἱερεύς + εἰμί) [of God and of Christ (2/Ben)].

Eff.   ἀλλήλους σφάξουσιν (6:4)
[They (1/Agt)] will slay (σφάζω) [one another (2/Pat)].

Exp.   ἐγὼ ἠγάπησά σε (3:9)
[I (1/Exp)] loved (ἀγαπάω) [you (2/Con)].

	ἱερεύς + εἰμί (20:6) <*Ben.*>		σφάζω (6:4) <*Eff.*>	
syn.	1	2	1	2
sem.	Pat	Ben	Agt	Pat
lex.	N	N+gen	N	N+acc

	ἀγαπάω (3:9) <*Exp.*>	
syn.	1	2
sem.	Exp	Con
lex.	N	N+acc

The following table presents from left to right the event designation, its italicized abbreviation (*abb.*), the thematic roles associated with the event entities, and the event configuration (conf.). As previously discussed, thematic roles starting with a letter already utilized in the previous configurations receive their full three-letter abbreviations.

event	abb.	event entities	conf.
benefaction	*Ben.*	Patient, Benefactive	PB
capacity	*Cap.*	Unspecified, Occurrence	UO
causation	*Cau.*	Patient, Cause	PCau
communion	*Com.*	Patient, Comitative	PCom
comparison	*Cmp.*	Patient, Comparative	PCmp

effect	*Eff.*	Agent, Patient	AP
experience	*Exp.*	Experiencer, Content	EC
instrumentality	*Ins.*	Patient, Instrument	PI
location	*Loc.*	Theme, Locative	ΘL
materiality	*Mat.*	Patient, Material	PM
measurement	*Mea.*	Patient, Measure	PMea
modification	*Mod.*	Patient, Resultative	PR
necessity	*Nec.*	Occurrence, Instrument	OI
partition	*Par.*	Patient, Partitive	PPar
temporality	*Tem.*	Patient, Temporal	PTem

3. Base and Alternate Configurations of Event Entities: Event Features

The previous discussion (§2.2) distinguished among events that set four, three, or two entities in particular relationship and specified the designation for each event, its italicized designation abbreviation, and its event configuration derived from the thematic roles associated with the entities of each event. Analysis of the predicators in the text of Revelation, however, reveals that some of its predicators grammaticalize different configurations of entities for eight of these twenty-three events. The defining characteristic of these different configurations is that they in no way change the relation between (for seven two-entity events) or among (for one three-entity event) the entities of the events as previously described. This permits the distinction between the configuration previously established for entities as the "base" configuration for each event and each differing observed configuration as an "alternate" configuration of one of the eight events.

These alternate configurations arise by three distinct mechanisms. Most frequently, alternate configurations arise through the introduction of a new event entity that does not change the relation among the previously identified entities that are native to the event. Less frequently, one of the event entities proves to have a dual relation with another event entity and this dual relation requires description by distinct associated thematic roles. In this case, the base configuration of the event accounts only for one element of the dual relation and the alternate configuration for the other. Least frequently, one entity native to the event undergoes bifurcation into constituent elements that require notation by an alternate configuration. Both the base and alternate configuration[s] of the event have the same event designation and italicized abbreviated event designation but require description by differing configurations of their constituent event entities.

The following discussion develops the three mechanisms in relation to three features of the conceptualization of events, that is, three event features: "entity incorporation," "entity reinterpretation," and "entity bifurcation." These event features when applied to eight events account for seventeen alternate configurations of entities for these events.

4. Event Feature: Entity Incorporation

Alternate configurations of a base event through entity incorporation are possible only when (1) the base event contains only two or three entities and (2) the incorporation of the third or fourth entity in no way changes the relation between the two or among the three entities native to the event. For two-entity events, the first requirement ensures that predicators, which are restricted to raising at most three event entities as arguments (§1.2), can raise all entities of the expanded conceptualization of the event as arguments. For both two- and three-entity base events, the second requirement ensures that the defining relations between or among the entities native to the event in no way are modified, which would result in the establishment of a distinct event. The following discussion considers the introduction into base events of entities associated with the Agent (A), Locative (L), Benefactive (B), Current (Cur) and Topic (T) thematic roles and concludes with a table of the configurations of all events characterized by entity incorporation. The three-letter abbreviation for the Current thematic role (Cur) indicates that the one-letter abbreviation of a thematic role starting with "c" already has been assigned (to the Content thematic role).

a. Incorporation of an Entity Associated with the Agent Thematic Role

The event feature "entity incorporation" introduces an entity associated with an Agent thematic role into five events: benefaction (*Ben.*), instrumentality (*Ins.*), materiality (*Mat.*), modification (*Mod.*), and capacity (*Cap.*). These events natively contain an entity associated with a Patient thematic role, PB (*Ben.*), PI (*Ins.*), PM (*Mat.*), and PR (*Mod.*), or an Occurrence thematic role, UO (*Cap.*). Since verb predicators that grammaticalize the expanded events consistently raise the newly incorporated entity associated with the Agent thematic role as first argument, the configurations of the expanded events have the Agent entity (A) in first position: APB (*Ben.*), API (*Ins.*), APM (*Mat.*), APR (*Mod.*), and AUO (*Cap.*). Note that, since the incorporation of this entity does not change the relation between the entities of the base configuration, the alternate configurations have the same event designation and italicized event designation abbreviation. The incorporation of this entity produces an agentive conceptualization of events that previously were non-agentive.

For example, γίνομαι (become) grammaticalizes the event of modification (*Mod.*) with its base configuration PR by raising respectively the entities associated with the Patient (P) and the Resultative (R) thematic roles as first and second argument; whereas στρέφω (turn) grammaticalizes the event of modification (*Mod.*) with its alternate configuration through entity incorporation, APR, by raising respectively the entities the Agent (A), Patient (P), and Resultative (R) as first, second, and third argument. The translation of the second example (11:6) introduces in double brackets, [[ ]], the contextual referent (them) of the unrealized Agent argument.

PR ἐγένετο τὸ τρίτον τῆς θαλάσσης αἷμα (8:8)
    [A third of the sea (1/Pat)] became (γίνομαι) [blood (2/Rst)].

APR   ἐξουσίαν ἔχουσιν ἐπὶ τῶν ὑδάτων στρέφειν αὐτὰ εἰς αἷμα (11:6)
They have authority over the waters to [[them (1/Agt)]] turn (στρέφω) [them (2/Pat)] [into blood (3/Rst)].

Since the predicators that grammaticalize the base configuration of entities and the alternate configuration of entities raise all event entities as arguments, the associated Valence Descriptions require no further notations to clarify the operation of entity incorporation.

	γίνομαι (8:8) <Mod.>		στρέφω (11:6) <Mod.>		
syn.	1	2	1	2	3
sem.	Pat	Rst	Agt	Pat	Rst
lex.	N	N+1	N	N+acc	P/εἰς

b. Incorporation of an Entity Associated with the Locative Thematic Role
The event feature "entity incorporation" introduces an entity associated with the Locative thematic role into the events of benefaction (*Ben.*) and communion (*Com.*). These events natively contain entities associated with Patient and Benefactive thematic roles, PB (*Ben.*), and Patient and Comitative thematic roles, PCom (*Com.*). The active participle predicator and the verb predicator that grammaticalize these respective expanded events raise the incorporated entity as third argument. As a consequence, the configurations of the expanded events place the entity associated with the Locative (L) thematic role in third position: BPL (*Ben.*) and PComL (*Com.*). Since both of these alternate configurations receive grammaticalization in only one occurrence, and there are differing complications that attend these grammaticalizations, these alternate configurations receive full explication and illustration in the discussions of predicator usages (§6.1e and §6.2a).

c. Incorporation of an Entity Associated with the Benefactive Thematic Role
The event feature incorporation introduces an entity associated with a Benefactive thematic role into the event of communication, ACE (*Cmm.*), and the configuration of the expanded event has the entity associated with the Benefactive (B) thematic role in fourth position, ACEB (*Cmm.*).[2] As with the four-entity base events of delegation (AOSG) and transference (AΘSG), this expanded configuration poses complications for grammaticalization, and the manner in which the predicator raises three of the four entities as arguments receives clarification in the discussion of usage features (§3.6e).

---

[2]   A partial description of the probable historical development of this alternate conceptualization of communication appears in Joseph H. Thayer, *Greek-English Lexicon of the New Testament: Coded with Strong's Concordance Numbers* (Edinburgh: T. & T. Clark, 1908), 63, 129, and Rutger J. Allan, *The Middle Voice in Ancient Greek: A Study in Polysemy* (ASCP 11; Amsterdam: Giessen, 2003), 109–10.

d. Incorporation of an Entity Associated with the Current Thematic Role

The event feature "entity incorporation" introduces an entity associated with the Current thematic role into the event of experience, EC (*Exp.*). The verb predicator that grammaticalizes this expanded event raises the Current entity (Cur) as third argument. As a consequence, the configuration of the expanded event places the entity associated with the Current (Cur) thematic role in third position: ECCur (*Exp.*).

For example, the verb predicator βλέπω (see) grammaticalizes the event of experience (*Exp.*) with its base configuration EC by raising the entities associated with the Experiencer (E) and Content (C) thematic roles as first and second argument; whereas the verb predicator εὑρίσκω (find) grammaticalizes the expanded event of experience with the alternate configuration ECCur by raising the entities associated with the Experiencer (E), Content (C), and Current (Cur) thematic roles as first, second, and third argument.

 EC βλέπωσιν τὸν καπνὸν τῆς πυρώσεως αὐτῆς (18:9)
  [They (1/Exp)] see (βλέπω) [the smoke of her fire (2/Con)].

 ECCur εὗρες αὐτοὺς ψευδεῖς (2:2)
  [You (1/Exp)] found (εὑρίσκω) [them (2/Con)] [false (3/Cur)].

Since the predicators that grammaticalize the base configuration of entities and the expanded configuration of entities raise all event entities as arguments, the associated Valence Descriptions require no further notations to clarify the operation of entity incorporation.

	βλέπω (18:9) <*Exp.*>		εὑρίσκω (2:2) <*Exp.*>		
syn.	1	2	1	2	3
sem.	Exp	Con	Exp	Con	Cur
lex.	N	N+acc	N	N+acc	Adj+2

e. Incorporation of an Entity Associated with the Topic Thematic Role

The event feature "entity incorporation" introduces an entity associated with a Topic thematic role into the event of experience (*Exp.*). The verb predicator that grammaticalizes the expanded event consistently raises the newly incorporated entity associated with the Topic thematic role as third argument, ECT (*Exp.*)

For example, ἔχω (hold) grammaticalizes the event of experience (*Exp.*) with its base configuration EC by raising the entities associated with the Experiencer (E) and Content (C) thematic roles as first and second argument and the event of experience with the alternate configuration ECT by raising the entities associated with the Experiencer (E), Content (C), and Topic (T) thematic roles as first, second, and third argument.

 EC ὅσοι οὐκ ἔχουσιν τὴν διδαχὴν ταύτην (2:24)
  [As many as (1/Exp)] do not hold (ἔχω) [this teaching (2/Con)].

ECT   ἔχω κατὰ σοῦ ὅτι τὴν ἀγάπην σου τὴν πρώτην ἀφῆκες (2:4)
[I (Exp)] hold (ἔχω) [against/concerning you (3/Top)] [that you left behind your first love (2//Con)].

Since the predicator that grammaticalizes the base configuration of entities and the alternate configuration of entities raises all event entities as arguments, the associated Valence Descriptions require no further notations to clarify the operation of entity incorporation.

	ἔχω (2:24) <Exp.>		ἔχω (2:4) <Exp.>		
syn.	1	2	1	2	3
sem.	Exp	Con	Exp	Con	Top
lex.	N	N+acc	N	V+ὅτι	P/κατά [+gen]

5. Event Feature: Entity Reinterpretation

The event feature "entity reinterpretation" is a function of Greek (and English) grammar that imposes the interpretation that the entity making, changing, or otherwise exerting influence over another entity has benefaction of the entity being made, changed, or otherwise influenced.[3] As a consequence, the event entity associated with the Agent (A) thematic role simultaneously is associated with the Benefactive (B) thematic role in relation to another event entity. The other event entity is associated with either the Content or the Patient thematic role. In English, this "agentive" Benefactive function is apparent in the fact that "I spoke to the assembly about fire safety" implies "my speech to the assembly about fire safety" and "I fought against this amendment" implies "my fight against this amendment."

This dual (Agent/Benefactive) relation with another entity has implications for the grammaticalization of an event because only verb, participle, and complex participle predicators are able to license as an argument an event entity associated with the Agent thematic role. As a consequence, when other categories of predicators grammaticalize the same event, they license as an argument the entity associated with the Benefactive thematic role. In the text of Revelation, entity reinterpretation has implications for the events of communication, benefaction, instrumentality, and materiality with the following configurations: ACE (*Cmm.*), APB (*Ben.*), API (*Ins.*), and APM (*Mat.*). When grammaticalized by a predicator that cannot license an Agent entity as an argument, entity reinterpretation changes these configurations respectively to BCE (*Cmm.*), BPB (*Ben.*), BPI (*Ins.*), and BPM (*Mat.*). The configurations of the events of benefaction, instrumentality, and materiality resulting from entity reinterpretation clarify that the event features incorporation and reinterpretation may be applied in sequence: through incorporation, the base configurations of entities of benefaction (PB), instrumentality

---

[3] This phenomenon, along with other examples of the dual relation imposed on specific event entities, appears in the discussion of "default Benefactive relationships" in Paul L. Danove, "A Comparison of the Usages of δίδωμι and δίδωμι Compounds in the Septuagint and New Testament," in *The Language of the New Testament: Context, History, and Development* (ed. Stanley E. Porter and Andrew W. Pitts; LBS 6; Leiden: Brill, 2013), 365–400.

(PI), and materiality (PM) becomes APB, API, and APM, and then through entity reinterpretation, these configurations become BPB, BPI, and BPM.

Entity reinterpretation is especially common with verb/noun cognates, as in the following examples of λέγω (say) and λόγος (word) that grammaticalize the event of communication (*Cmm.*) with the entity configurations, ACE and BCE, and of γεμίζω (fill) and γόμος (cargo) that grammaticalize the event of materiality (*Mat.*) with the entity configurations, APM and BPM. The translations introduce in double brackets, [[ ]], the contextual referent (you/the members of the church in Philadelphia) of the DNC Experiencer in the second example (3:10) and the contextual referent (the merchants) of the DNC Benefactive in the fourth example (18:12) and places in braces, { }, the never-realized Patient argument that is co-referential to its licensing predicator (§1.2c).

ACE ἐγὼ ἐρῶ σοι τὸ μυστήριον τῆς γυναικὸς... (17:7b)
[I (1/Agt)] will say (λέγω) [to you (3/Exp)] [the mystery of the woman... (2/Con)].

BCE τὸν λόγον τῆς ὑπομονῆς μου (3:10)
[My (1/Ben)] word (λόγος) [of endurance (2/Con)] [[to you/the members of the church in Philadelphia (3/Exp)]].

APM ἐγέμισεν αὐτὸν ἐκ τοῦ πυρὸς τοῦ θυσιαστηρίου (8:5)
[He (1/Agt)] filled (γεμίζω) [it (2/Pat)] [with the fire of the altar (3/Mat)].

BPM γόμον χρυσοῦ καὶ ἀργύρου καὶ... (18:12)
[[Merchants' (1/Ben)]] cargo (γόμος) {cargo (2/Pat)} [of gold and silver and... (3/Mat)].

Valence Descriptions specify the syntactic function of the never-realized Patient argument of γόμος in braces, { }, and list the lexical realization of this never-realized argument as {N} (§1.4a). Since the predicators that grammaticalize the configurations of entities raise all event entities as arguments, the associated Valence Descriptions require no further notations to clarify the operation of entity reinterpretation.

	λέγω (17:7b) <Cmm.>			λόγος (3:10) <Cmm.>		
syn.	1	2	3	1	2	[3]
sem.	Agt	Con	Exp	Ben	Con	Exp
lex.	N	N+acc	N+dat	N	N+acc	DNC

	γεμίζω (8:5) <Mat.>			γόμος (18:12) <Mat.>		
syn.	1	2	3	[1]	{2}	3
sem.	Agt	Pat	Mat	Ben	Pat	Mat
lex.	N	N+acc	P/ἐκ	DNC	{N}	N+gen

6. Event Feature: Entity Bifurcation

The event feature "entity bifurcation" arises when Greek grammar separates one event entity into two components that accommodate first a general and then a specific conceptualization of the entity. In the text of Revelation, bifurcation occurs only with verb predicators, impacts only the entities associated with the Content and Patient thematic roles, and requires that the Content entity and Patient entity appear in second position in the configurations of event entities. Through entity bifurcation, the events of experience and benefaction with the configurations, EC (*Exp.*), ECT (*Exp.*), and PB (*Ben.*), become configurations, EC^1/C^2 (*Exp.*), EC^1/C^{2}T (*Exp.*), and BP^1/P^2 (*Ben.*). As the second example of bifurcation with the event of experience indicates, the event features incorporation and bifurcation may be applied in sequence: through incorporation, the base configuration of event entities (EC) becomes ECT, and then through bifurcation, this configuration becomes EC^1/C^{2}T. The reversal of event entities in the configuration of event of benefaction, from the base configuration, PB, to the noted configuration, BP, receives explanation in the discussion of usage features (§3.8d).

Verb predicators license the bifurcated entity as a single argument with the same thematic role but two lexical realizations. The following examples of the verb predicators οἶδα (know) and ἔχω (have) illustrate the grammaticalization first of the events of experience and benefaction with their base configurations, EC and PB, and then with their configurations through bifurcation, EC^1/C^2 and BP^1/P^2, which separate the bifurcated event entities by a slash, /. The translations distinguish the bifurcated complements by placing superscripted numerals "1" and "2" after their thematic roles.

EC   οἶδα τὰ ἔργα σου... (2:2)
      [I (1/Exp)] know (οἶδα) [your works... (2/Con)].

EC^1/C^2 οἶδά σου τὰ ἔργα ὅτι ὄνομα ἔχεις ὅτι ζῇς (3:1)
      [I (1/Exp)] know (οἶδα) [your works (2/Con^1)] [that you have a reputation that you are alive (2/Con^2)].

BP   ἐπὶ τούτων ὁ δεύτερος θάνατος οὐκ ἔχει ἐξουσίαν (20:6b)
      [The second death (1/Ben)] does not have (ἔχω) [authority over them (2/Pat)].

BP^1/P^2 τοῦτο ἔχεις, ὅτι μισεῖς τὰ ἔργα τῶν Νικολαϊτῶν ἃ κἀγὼ μισῶ (2:6)
      [You (1/Ben)] have (ἔχω) [this (2/Pat^1)] [that you hate the works of the Nocolaitans which I also hate (2/Pat^2)].

Valence Descriptions assign both elements of the bifurcated arguments the same syntactic function (2), note the semantic function twice with superscripted numerals "1" and "2" separated by a slash, /, and list the lexical realizations of both elements separated by a slash, /. Since the predicators that grammaticalize the two configurations of entities raise all event entities as arguments and incorporate notations specific to bifurcation, the associated Valence Descriptions require no further notations to clarify the operation of entity bifurcation.

	οἶδα (2:2) <*Exp.*>		οἶδα (3:1) <*Exp.*>	
syn.	1	2	1	2
sem.	Exp	Con	Exp	Con^1/Con^2
lex.	N	N+acc	N	N+acc/V+ὅτι

	ἔχω (20:6b) <*Ben.*>		ἔχω (2:6) <*Ben.*>	
syn.	1	2	1	2
sem.	Ben	Pat	Ben	Pat^1/Pat^2
lex.	N	N+acc	N	N+acc/V+ὅτι

7. The Three Non-Events Grammaticalized in the Text of Revelation

In addition to the twenty-three events in their base and alternate configurations, predicators in the text of Revelation grammaticalize three non-events that do not satisfy the defining characteristic of an event, the setting of two or more entities in specific relation. These three non-events, qualification, coordination, and specification receive four-letter italicized abbreviations, *Qual.*, *Coor.*, and *Spec.*, to distinguish them from the previously developed three-letter abbreviations for events.

a. Qualification (Qual.)

In qualification, a predicator licenses a single argument that references what the predicator qualifies or "modifies." This single argument receives realization as the predicator's sole required complement. As a consequence, predication does not satisfy the defining requirement of an event, the setting of two or more entities in specific relation. The single argument may be associated with the Patient or the Occurrence thematic role, indicating that this non-event has two possible configurations, P or O. All one-place predicators grammaticalize the non-event of qualification, as illustrated in the following examples of the one-place verb predicator ζάω (live, be alive) and the one-place adjective predicator λευκός (white).

ἔζησεν (2:8)
[He (1/Pat)] was alive (ζάω).

ἔριον λευκὸν (1:14b)
White (λευκός) [wool (1/Pat)].

Since the predicators grammaticalize the two base configurations with one Patient or Occurrence entity as an argument, the associated Valence Descriptions require no further notations to clarify the configuration of the non-event entity.

	ζάω (2:8) <Qual.>	λευκός (1:14b) <Qual.>
syn.	1	1
sem.	Pat	Pat
lex.	N	N

b. Coordination (Coor.)

In coordination, a conjunction predicator licenses and coordinates two arguments that receive realization as the predicators' two required complements. Despite the presence of two arguments, coordination does not satisfy the defining characteristic of an event, the setting of these two entities in specific relation. This is readily apparent in the fact that conjunction predicators are able to coordinate maximal verb phrases (independent clauses and sentences) that do not admit to description by thematic roles. In all other occurrences, conjunction predicators coordinate phrasal elements whose specific relation is set by predicators other than the conjunctions themselves. Special notations (— and ---) replace the thematic role abbreviations for the arguments of coordination predicators. The former notation (—), which denotes the absence of a thematic role (§1.3), is used with maximal verb phrases that are not licensed by another predicator to indicate that there is no associated thematic role. The latter notation (---), which denotes the presence of a thematic role, is used with all other coordinated elements to indicate that a predicator other than the conjunction sets the relation of the coordinated entities. This proposes two possible configurations for the non-event of coordination: — — and --- ---.

The following examples of the conjunction predicator καί (and) with the configurations — — and --- --- illustrate first the coordination of maximal verb phrases (V+) that do not admit to description by a thematic role and then the coordination of noun phrase complements whose thematic role is set by a predicator other than the conjunction. In the second example (1:9d), the thematic role (Cause) of the two arguments of καί is set by the preceding preposition predicator διά [+acc] (because of).

— —   εἶδον θρόνους καὶ ἐκάθισαν ἐπ' αὐτοὺς (20:4b)
      [I saw thrones (1/—)] and (καί) [they sat on them (2/—)].

--- ---   διὰ τὸν λόγον τοῦ θεοῦ καὶ τὴν μαρτυρίαν Ἰησοῦ (1:9d)
      Because of [[the word of God (1/---)] and (καί) [the testimony of Jesus (2/---)]].

Valence Descriptions note the lack of the imposition of a specific relation on the predicator's two arguments by — when there is no thematic role and by --- when the thematic role is set by another predicator. For ease of reference, the lexical realizations in the Valence Descriptions distinguish complex participle phrases (Complex Part) and complex adjective phrases (Complex Adj) from all other categories of maximal verb phrases (V+). Since the conjunction predicators grammaticalize the two base configurations of entities as arguments, the associated Valence Descriptions require no further notations to clarify the configuration of non-event entities.

	καί (20:4b) <Coor.>		καί (1:9d) <Coor.>	
syn.	1	2	1	2
sem.	—	—	---	---
lex.	V+	V+	N+acc	N+acc

c. Specification (Spec.)

In specification, a predicator requires completion by no arguments but permits the licensing of adjuncts. Specification characterizes only zero-place noun predicators or noun phrase predicators formed by nominalizing adjective predicators through determination by the definite article. The notation for the absence of a thematic role (—) appears where the description of the thematic roles of the arguments typically appears. This proposes the following configuration for the non-event of specification: —. The noun and noun phrase predicators that grammaticalize this non-event generally do not license adjuncts but may do so in specific circumstances, as illustrated in the following examples of the noun predicator θηρίον (beast) and the noun phrase predicator τὸ ἀκάθαρτον (the unclean thing).

— τῶν θηρίων τῆς γῆς (6:8)
 The beasts (θηρίον) [of the earth (C/Ben)].

— τὰ ἀκάθαρτα τῆς πορνείας αὐτῆς (17:4)
 The unclean things (τὸ ἀκάθαρτον) [of her sexual immorality (C/Ben)].

Valence Descriptions assign "0" (zero) as the syntactic function of the lacking argument, note the absence of a thematic role by —, leave the lexical realization of the lacking argument blank, and list the adjunct in the usual fashion. Since the predicators that grammaticalize the base configuration raise no arguments, as apparent in having "0" (zero) as their syntactic function, the associated Valence Descriptions require no further notations to clarify the configuration of non-event entities.

	θηρίον (6:8) <Spec.>			τὸ ἀκάθαρτον (17:4) <Spec.>		
syn.	0	|	C	0	|	C
sem.	—	|	Ben	—	|	Ben
lex.		|	N+gen		|	N+gen

8. Event and Non-Event Configurations

The following table presents from left to right the complete list of event or non-event designations and their italicized abbreviations and the base configurations of events or non-events followed by the configurations of the events characterized by entity incorporation (inco.), entity reinterpretation (rein.), and entity bifurcation (bifu.). Since there are no non-event features, all non-events have base configuration[s]. These forty configurations of events and five configurations of non-events describe the twenty-three events and three non-events grammaticalized by predicators in the text of Revelation. For ease of reference, the table appears in the appendix.

event	base	inco.	rein.	bifu.
authority (*Aut.*)	BOL			
benefaction (*Ben.*)	PB	APB, BPL	BPB	BP^1/P^2
capacity (*Cap.*)	UO	AUO		
causation (*Cau.*)	PCau			
communication (*Cmm.*)	ACE	ACEB	BCE	
communion (*Com.*)	PCom	PComL		
comparison (*Cmp.*)	PCmp			
compulsion (*Cpl.*)	APO			
delegation (*Del.*)	AOSG			
disposition (*Dis.*)	AΘO			
effect (*Eff.*)	AP			
experience (*Exp.*)	EC	ECT, ECCur		EC^1/C^2, EC^1/C^{2}T
instrumentality (*Ins.*)	PI	API	BPI	
location (*Loc.*)	ΘL			
materiality (*Mat.*)	PM	APM	BPM	
measurement (*Mea.*)	PMea			
modification (*Mod.*)	PR	APR		
motion (*Mot.*)	ΘSG			
necessity (*Nec.*)	OI			
partition (*Par.*)	PPar			
separation (*Sep.*)	APS			
temporality (*Tem.*)	PTem			
transference (*Tra.*)	AΘSG			

non-event	base
qualification (*Qual.*)	P, O
coordination (*Coor.*)	— —, --- ---
specification (*Spec.*)	—

Three clarifications are appropriate here. First, since Valence Descriptions contain all the information necessary to distinguish the alternate conceptualizations of the same event arising through event features, they require no further notations concerning event features. Second, all configurations of event entities derived by event features from the same base configuration of the event are referenced by the same event designation and event designation abbreviation. Thus the event designation "benefaction" (*Ben*.) applies to the event with the configurations, PB, APB, BPB, BPL, and BP^1/P^2. Third, in all subsequent discussions, the word "event" is used to reference both the base configuration and, where present, its alternate configurations of entities, and "non-event" is used to reference both base configurations of qualification and coordination. That is, hereafter, discussions will reference as the event of benefaction all observed configurations of entities (PB, APB, BPB, BPL, and BP^1/P^2) without specifying whether this constitutes a base or alternate configuration of its event entities and will reference the non-event of qualification (*Qual*.) by P or O and the non-event of coordination (*Coor*.) by — — or --- --- without further comment.

9. Applications of Events, Event Features, and Non-Events

The event and non-event designations and their configurations introduced in this chapter are foundational to further developments in this study. Subsequent presentations will utilize the event and non-event designations and configurations to specify general qualifications of the conceptualizations grammaticalized by predicators (Chapter 3) and the conceptualizations of polysemous occurrences (Chapter 4), to label the ninety-two distinct predicator usages (Chapters 5 and 6), and to clarify distinctive grammatical characteristics of the text of Revelation (Chapter 7). All of the grammatical information in Valence Descriptions noted by event and non-event designations and configurations then receives restatement according to protocols (Chapter 8) into the lexicon entries for predicators (Chapter 9).

3

USAGES AND USAGE FEATURES

This chapter redefines the concept "usage," develops the concept "usage feature," and specifies the usage features that account for the fact that predicators are able to grammaticalize multiple distinct usages of a particular event with a given event configuration. The discussion explains and then illustrates through predicator occurrences the contribution of each category of usage feature and indicates the manner in which Valence Descriptions incorporate information about the features. The following presentation considers only those usage features necessary to distinguish the usages grammaticalized by predicators in the text of Revelation.

1. Usages and Their Conceptualization

Whereas event features describe the mechanisms by which an event may come to have alternate configurations of event entities, usage features describe the differing conceptualizations of a configuration of event entities that predicators are able to grammaticalize. Thus, although the event of transference (*Tra.*) does not admit to alternate configurations by event features and so presents only one configuration of event entities (AΘSG), usage features that qualify the conceptualization of this event in different ways permit predicators in the text of Revelation to grammaticalize thirteen distinct usages of transference. This permits the redefinition of a predicator usage as "all occurrences of predicators that grammaticalize the same event with the same configuration of event entities and the same set of usage features."[1] Just as only eight of the twenty-three events admit to alternate configurations of entities through event features, only specific configurations of events admit to grammaticalization by multiple usages described by usage features. The following discussions develop these usage features in relation to the event[s] to which they apply.

---

[1] A more detailed discussion of the usage features for predicators of transference appears in Paul L. Danove, *Grammatical and Exegetical Study of New Testament Verbs of Transference: A Case Frame Guide to Interpretation and Translation* (SNTG 13; LNTS 329; London: T&T Clark, 2009), 21–32.

2. Usage Features for the Events of Transference and Delegation

This discussion develops the six usage features required to distinguish the thirteen usages of transference (AΘSG) and the single usage of delegation (AOSG) in the text of Revelation: perspective, subject affectedness, focus, impetus, functionality of the Goal, and argument promotion. Since these usage features receive full illustration only in relation to transference, the development of the usage features uses examples only of predicators that grammaticalize transference. The discussion then identifies the usage features that describe the single usage of delegation. The concluding discussion illustrates the contribution of usage features to distinguishing among usages of the same event.

a. Usage Feature: Perspective

Description of usages of transference and delegation by the usage feature perspective is essential because this feature specifies the manner in which predicators grammaticalize conceptualizations of these four-entity events by raising only three of their event entities as arguments. In these events, the Agent initiates the actual movement of the Theme of transference/the metaphorical movement of the Occurrence of delegation, and the Theme/Occurrence moves along a continuous actual/metaphorical path from the Source to the Goal where movement ceases.[2] As the following occurrences of predicators of transference illustrate, these events do not specify uniquely the locale of the Agent, which may be at the Source (I will cast her onto a bed, 2:22) or at the Goal (the ones summoned to the wedding dinner, 19:9), or in motion (he carried me off to a deserted place, 17:3):

(Agent)
(Agent) Source/Theme ————————> Goal/Theme (Agent)
(Agent) Source/Occurrence ————————> Goal/Occurrence (Agent)

Since these events include two "fixed" entities, the Source and Goal, they may be resolved into two segments: initial, which includes the path of the Theme/Occurrence from the point where it is coincident with the Source, and terminal, which includes the path of the Theme/Occurrence to the point at which it is coincident with the Goal. For the purpose of this study, the transition from the initial to the terminal segment of the event may occur at any point along the path.

The verb and participle predicators that grammaticalize transference address the disparity between the number of event entities of transference and delegation (four) and the number of entities that they are able to raise as arguments (three) by assuming one of two perspectives on the initiation of the events. With the first perspective, predicators grammaticalize a conceptualization of transference or delegation in which the Agent initially is coincident with or at least proximate to the Source. With the

---

[2] Further discussion of the event of transference appears in Ray S. Jackendoff, "The Proper Treatment of Measuring Out, Telicity, and Perhaps Even Quantification in English," *Natural Language and Linguistic Theory* 11 (1996): 317–18.

second perspective, predicators grammaticalize a conceptualization of transference (never of delegation) in which the Agent initially is coincident with or in the direction of the Goal. With these perspectives, predicators do not raise either the coincident/proximate Source (S=A) or the coincident/co-directional Goal (G=A) that can be retrieved from the Agent at the initiation of the events and raise the remaining three event entities as arguments. These two possible perspectives receive illustration in the following occurrences of δίδωμι (give) and λαμβάνω (take). The translations introduce in double brackets, [[ ]], the unlicensed coincident/proximate Source or coincident/co-directional Goal.

S=A δώσω σοι τὸν στέφανον τῆς ζωῆς (2:10)
[I (1/Agt)] will give (δίδωμι) [to you (3/Goa)] [[from me (S=A)]] [the crown of life (2/Thm)].

G=A ἔλαβον τὸ βιβλαρίδιον ἐκ τῆς χειρὸς τοῦ ἀγγέλου (10:10)
[I (1/Agt)] took (λαμβάνω) [the little book (2/Thm)] [from the hand of the angel (3/Sou)] [[to myself (G=A)]].

Valence Descriptions specify the usage feature perspective in a usage label that appears at the top after the predicator, citation, and within the chevrons, < >, immediately after the italicized three-letter designation abbreviation of the event. The usage label consists of the event configuration (AΘSG for transference and AOSG for delegation) followed by notations about the usage features. The notation for the usage feature perspective places the entity not raised as an argument in brackets, [ ], to indicate that its referent is retrievable, followed by the event entity to which it is co-referential in brackets, [S=A] or [G=A]. When the inclusion of the usage label inordinately lengthens the top of the Valence Description, it may be split in the most convenient fashion into two or more rows above the notations for syntactic functions, semantic functions, and lexical realizations, as in the following Valence Descriptions.

	δίδωμι (2:10) <Tra. AΘ[S]G [S=A]>			λαμβάνω (10:10) <Tra. AΘS[G] [G=A]>		
syn.	1	2	3	1	2	3
sem.	Agt	Thm	Goa	Agt	Thm	Sou
lex.	N	N+acc	N+dat	N	N+acc	P/ἐκ

b. Usage Feature: Subject Affectedness

The verb and participle predicators of transference appear with active base forms (active usages) and, as previously discussed (§1.2d), may appear with passive forms through passivization. Verb predicators, however, also present passive occurrences that admit to a reflexive interpretation in which the Agent transfers itself. The following study interprets such passive occurrences of verb predicators to exhibit passive base forms and to grammaticalize passive usages of transference. This establishes two possibilities for subject affectedness with verbs that grammaticalize transference in the text of Revelation: active base forms (act.) are interpreted to provide no guidance in determining whether or not the action of the Agent affects the Agent, and the passive base forms (pass.) are interpreted to signal that the Agent transfers and so affects itself.[3]

The verb predicator occurrences that admit to interpretation with a passive usage of transference simultaneously admit to interpretation with a passivized active usage of transference. This polysemy arises because verbs with passive usages consistently and verbs with passivized active usages typically realize only two of their arguments. As previously discussed (§1.5c), Greek grammar permits verbs that grammaticalize a passivized active usage of a predicator to leave the Agent argument unrealized and to have no definite referent, that is, to be an indefinite null complement (INC). In fact, predicators with passivized active usages typically appear with only the Theme and either the Goal or the Source arguments realized as complements. Greek grammar also restricts predicators that grammaticalize a passive usage of transference to realizing only the Agent and either the Source or the Goal as complements, apparently because the passive base forms signal that the missing Theme argument is co-referential to the Agent. Thus the interpretation that a verb is grammaticalizing a passive usage of transference/a passivized active usage of transference becomes possible whenever the grammatical context (1) identifies no definite referent for a possible Agent with a referent distinct from the Theme and (2) the Agent admits to interpretation as transferring itself.

The distinction between the passivized active usages and the passive usages of transference receives illustration in the following occurrence of συνάγω (gather). The translations introduce in double brackets, [[ ]], the referents of null required complements with each of the possible interpretations.

συνάχθητε εἰς τὸ δεῖπνον τὸ μέγα τοῦ θεοῦ ἵνα φάγητε... (19:17-18)
act.   [You (2/Thm)] be gathered (συνάγω) [[by someone (1/Agt)]] [to the great dinner of God (3/Goa)] [so that you may eat... (C/Pur)].
pass. [You (1/Agt)] gather (συνάγω) [[yourselves (2/Thm)]] [to the great dinner of God (3/Goa)] [so that you may eat... (C/Pur)].

Since predicators in the text of Revelation consistently grammaticalize transference with active base forms outside the context of the polysemous occurrences, usage labels include a notation about subject affectedness (pass.) only when the subject admits to interpretation as affected. The label for the passive usage places the Theme argument in brackets, [ ], to signal that it never is realized as a complement but has a retrievable referent, signals that the referent of the unrealized Theme argument is retrievable from the Agent, [Θ=A], immediately after the configuration of arguments, and incorporates the notation about affectedness (pass.) after the perspective notation. Valence

---

[3] J. Lyons, *Introduction to Theoretical Linguistics* (London: Cambridge University Press, 1969), 373, discusses the nature of this affectedness; cf. Allan, *Middle Voice*, 19-20. Saeed, *Semantics*, 162-65, considers various categories of affectedness. The text of Revelation presents no verbs that grammaticalize transference with middle base forms.

Descriptions set the syntactic function of the Theme argument of the passive usage in double brackets, [[ ]], to signal that the argument never is realized but has a definite referent (retrievable from the Agent) and note the lexical realization of the never-realized Theme complement by [N]. As previously discussed (§1.5c), Case Frame analysis uses the passivization construction to transform the occurrence of a predicator with the interpretation of a passivized active usage (the Valence Description on the left below) into its active counterpart and analyzes it accordingly.

	συνάγω (19:17-18) <Tra. AΘ[S]G [S=A]>					συνάγω (19:17-18) <Tra. A[Θ][S]G [Θ=A] [S=A] pass.>				
syn.	1	2	3	|	C	1	[[2]]	3	|	C
sem.	Agt	Thm	Goa	|	Pur	Agt	Thm	Goa	|	Pur
lex.	N	N+acc	P/εἰς	|	V+ἵνα	N	[N]	P/εἰς	|	V+ἵνα

c. Usage Feature: Focus

Predicators grammaticalize conceptualizations of transference that bring into focus either both segments of the event or only the segment containing the Agent at the initiation of transference. Thus there are no usages of transference in which the conceptualization focuses only on the segment not containing the Agent at initiation. Grammaticalizations of conceptualizations that focus on both segments of the event result in primary (pri.) usages that permit the retrieval of referents for all four entities of the event; whereas those that focus only on one segment containing the Agent at initiation result in secondary (sec.) usages that do not permit retrieval of a referent for the Source or Goal in the segment that is not in focus. Secondary usages highlight the initial locale of the Agent.

The primary (pri.)/secondary (sec.) contrast receives illustration in the following examples of φέρω (bring) and κινέω (move). The translations introduce in double brackets, [[ ]], the definite referent of the coincident/proximate Source (where they are/the earth) in the first example (21:24) and the indefinite but circumscribed referent of the INC Agent (someone) in the second example (6:14) and in double parentheses, (( )), the irretrievable referent of the coincident/codirectional Goal in the second example (6:14). In the second example (6:14), the passivization construction (not a usage feature) permits the Agent argument of the passivized verb predicator to be an indefinite null complement (INC).

    pri.   οἱ βασιλεῖς τῆς γῆς φέρουσιν τὴν δόξαν αὐτῶν εἰς αὐτήν (21:24)
            [The kings of the earth (1/Agt)] bring (φέρω) [their glory (2/Thm)]
            [into it (3/Goa)] [[from where they are/from the earth (S=A)]].

    sec.   πᾶν ὄρος καὶ νῆσος ἐκ τῶν τόπων αὐτῶν ἐκινήθησαν (6:14)
            [Every mountain and island (2/Thm)] was moved (κινέω) [[by someone
            (1/Agt)]] [from their places (3/Sou)] ((to wherever they went/to an
            unspecified place)).

The usage label for the primary usage (21:24) is constructed in the manner of the labels for the primary usages considered in §3.2a: the Source appears in brackets, [ ], to signal that it is not raised as an argument but has a retrievable referent, and the following notation in brackets indicates that the referent of the Source is retrievable from the Agent at the initiation of transference, [S=A]. The label for the secondary usage (6:14) places in parentheses, ( ), the Goal entity of the segment that is not in focus and so has no retrievable referent. The Valence Description for the same example (6:14) uses the passivization construction to transform the occurrence into its active counterpart (§1.5c).

	φέρω (21:24) <Tra. AΘ[S]G [S=A]>			κινέω (6:14) <Tra. AΘS(G)>		
syn.	1	2	3	1	2	3
sem.	Agt	Thm	Goa	Agt	Thm	Sou
lex.	N	N+acc	P/εἰς	N	N+acc	P/ἐκ

d. Usage Feature: Impetus

In the conceptualization of transference, the Agent provides either an initial discrete impetus that sets the Theme in motion or a continuous impetus that sets the Theme in motion and sustains its motion throughout the transference. Since Greek and English do not mark impetus explicitly on predicators, it must be determined from the nature of the action designated by the predicator. In the following examples, βάλλω (cast) is characterized by a discrete impetus (–imp.) and κινέω (move) by a continuous impetus (+imp.):

–imp. ἔβαλεν αὐτὸν εἰς τὴν ἄβυσσον (20:3)
[He (1/Agt)] cast (βάλλω) [it (2/Thm)] [into the abyss (3/Goa)].

+imp. κινήσω τὴν λυχνίαν σου ἐκ τοῦ τόπου αὐτῆς, ἐὰν μὴ μετανοήσῃς (2:5)
[I (1/Agt)] will move (κινέω) [your lampstand (2/Thm)] [from its place (3/Sou)] [if you do not repent (C/Cnd)].

Usage labels note discrete impetus (–imp.) or continuous impetus (+imp.) at the very end of their statements, after all other usage feature notations.

	βάλλω (20:3) <Tra. AΘ[S]G [S=A] –imp.>			κινέω (2:5) <Tra. AΘS(G) +imp.>				
syn.	1	2	3	1	2	3	|	C
sem.	Agt	Thm	Goa	Agt	Thm	Sou	|	Cnd
lex.	N	N+acc	P/εἰς	N	N+acc	P/ἐκ	|	V+ἐάν

e. Usage Feature: Functionality of the Goal

Predicators of transference are able to grammaticalize a conceptualization of transference in which the entity toward which the Theme moves (Goal) takes on the interpretation of the abiding locale of the Theme at the termination of its transference (Locative). The change in functionality from Goal to Locative (G→L) produces Goal and Locative usages of transference that differ only in this usage feature, as illustrated in the following examples of τίθημι (place). The translation of the first example (11:9) introduces in double brackets, [[ ]], the indefinite but circumscribed referent of the INC Agent (someone) which is permissibly omitted by the passivization construction.

G   τὰ πτώματα αὐτῶν...τεθῆναι εἰς μνῆμα (11:9)
     [Their corpses (2/Thm)]...to be placed (τίθημι) [[by someone (1/Agt)]] [into a tomb (3/Goa)].

G→L ἔθηκεν τὸν πόδα αὐτοῦ τὸν δεξιὸν ἐπὶ τῆς θαλάσσης (10:2)
     [He (1/Agt)] placed (τίθημι) [his right foot (2/Thm)] [on the sea (3/Loc)].

Usage labels note a change in functionality of the Goal, G→L, after the perspective description. The Valence Description for the first example (11:9) uses the passivization construction to transform the occurrence into its active counterpart (§1.5c).

	τίθημι (11:9) <Tra. AΘ[S]G [S=A] +imp.>			τίθημι (10:2) <Tra. AΘ[S]G [S=A] G→L +imp.>		
	1	2	3	1	2	3
syn.	Loc	Thm	Goa	Agt	Thm	Loc
sem.	N	N+acc	P/εἰς	N	N+acc	P/ἐπὶ [+gen]

f. Usage Feature: Argument Promotion

Only the conceptualizations of transference grammaticalized by passivized participle predicators require description by the usage feature argument promotion. As previously discussed (§1.2c), these predicators, like adjective predicators, raise the argument associated with the modified entity, always the Theme, as their first argument, as illustrated in the following examples of ἀπεσταλμένος (sent) and βεβαμμένος (dipped). The translations introduce in double brackets, [[ ]], the contextual referent of the DNC Agent (God) in 5:6 and the indefinite but circumscribed referent of the INC Agent (someone) in 19:13.

τὰ [ἑπτὰ] πνεύματα τοῦ θεοῦ ἀπεσταλμένοι εἰς πᾶσαν τὴν γῆν (5:6)
[The [seven] spirits of God (1/Thm)] sent (ἀπεσταλμένος) [[by God (2/Agt)]] [into all the earth (3/Goa)].

ἱμάτιον βεβαμμένον αἵματι (19:13)
[A garment (1/Thm)] dipped (βεβαμμένος) [[by someone (2/Agt)]] [in blood (3/Loc)].

Usage labels note argument promotion by listing the event entities in the order of their grammaticalization, ΘASG.

	ἀπεσταλμένος (5:6) <Tra. ΘA[S]G [S=Θ] –imp.>			βεβαμμένος (19:13) <Tra. ΘA[S]G [S=Θ] G→L +imp.>		
syn.	1	[2]	3	1	(2)	3
sem.	Thm	Agt	Goa	Thm	Agt	Loc
lex.	N	DNC	P/εἰς	N	INC	N+dat

g. The Usage Features of the Usage of Delegation

Only δίδωμι (give) grammaticalizes a single usage of delegation with the perspective that the Source and Agent are coincident/proximate at the initiation of delegation [S=A], with no guidance concerning the affectedness of the Agent (act.), with a focus on both segments of the event (pri.), with a continuous impetus (+imp.), with no change in the functionality of the Goal (G=G), and with no argument promotion.

G τῷ νικῶντι δώσω αὐτῷ φαγεῖν ἐκ τοῦ ξύλου τῆς ζωῆς (2:7)
[To the one conquering, to him (3/Goa)] [I (1/Agt)] will give (δίδωμι) [to eat from the tree of life (2/Occ)].

	δίδωμι (2:7) <Del. AO[S]G [S=A] +imp.>		
syn.	1	2	3
sem.	Agt	Occ	Goa
lex.	N	V-i3	N+dat

h. The Contribution of Usage Features

Usage features provide a precise specification of the conceptualization of events with each predicator usage. As represented in usage labels, this specification accommodates the disambiguation of usages that otherwise would have exactly the same representation of required complements in Valence Descriptions. For example, the Valence Descriptions of the following examples of λαμβάνω (take), ἐμέω (spit [out]), and κινέω (move), present identical syntactic, semantic, and lexical information even though these verb predicators grammaticalize three distinct usages of transference, as clarified by the usage labels. The translations introduce in double brackets, [[ ]], the definite contextual referent of the Agent (I) which is retrievable from the verb μέλλω (be about to) which licenses ἐμέω (spit) in the second example (3:16) and the indefinite but circumscribed referent of the INC Agent (someone) in the third example (6:14).

ἔλαβον τὸ βιβλαρίδιον ἐκ τῆς χειρὸς τοῦ ἀγγέλου (10:10)
[I (1/Agt)] took (λαμβάνω) [the little book (2/Thm)] [from the hand of the angel (3/Sou)].

σε ἐμέσαι ἐκ τοῦ στόματός μου (3:16)
[[I (1/Agt)]] to spit (ἐμέω) [you (2/Thm)] [out of my mouth (3/Sou)].

πᾶν ὄρος καὶ νῆσος ἐκ τῶν τόπων αὐτῶν ἐκινήθησαν (6:14)
[Every mountain and island (2/Thm)] was moved (κινέω) [[by someone (1/Agt)]] [from their places (3/Sou)].

For ease of comparison, the following Valence Descriptions place the usage labels beneath the verb, citation, and italicized abbreviation of the event designation.

	λαμβάνω (10:10) <*Tra*. AΘS[G] [G=A] +imp.>			ἐμέω (3:16) <*Tra*. AΘS(G) –imp.>		
	1	2	3	1	2	3
syn.						
sem.	Agt	Thm	Sou	Agt	Thm	Sou
lex.	N	N+acc	P/ἐκ	N	N+acc	P/ἐκ

	κινέω (6:14) <*Tra*. AΘS(G) + imp.>		
	1	2	3
syn.			
sem.	Agt	Thm	Sou
lex.	N	N+acc	P/ἐκ

3. Usage Features for the Event of Motion: Part 1

The predicators that grammaticalize the event of motion (ΘSG) resolve into two unequal groups. The first group includes verb and participle predicators with active and middle base forms, preposition predicators, and complex predicators that incorporate these participle and preposition predicators as a component. The following discussions develop the four usage features that characterize the conceptualizations of motion grammaticalized by the first group of predicators: perspective, focus, functionality of the Goal, and argument promotion. The concluding discussion offers a clarification concerning preposition predicators.

a. Usage Feature: Perspective

In the conceptualization of the event of motion (ΘSG), the Theme moves along a continuous path from the Source to the Goal where motion ceases.

Source/Theme ————————> Goal/Theme

Since this event contains two fixed entities, the Source and the Goal, it may be resolved into two segments, initial and terminal. Although this event contains only three event entities (ΘSG), the predicators in the first group consistently assume the perspective that the Theme and Source are coincident/proximate at the initiation of motion and, in all but one usage, omit consideration of the Source which can be retrieved from the initially coincident/proximate Theme, S=Θ, and raise only the Theme and Goal as arguments (Θ[S]G). In the remaining usage, however, verb and participle predicators raise all three entities as arguments (ΘSG), despite the fact that the Theme and Source are conceptualized as initially coincident/proximate. The consistent perspective that the Theme and Source initially are coincident/proximate receives illustration in the following examples of πίπτω (fall) and its licensed prepositional phrase. As these examples indicate, the verb predicator that licenses the P/εἰς Goal and the preposition predicator set the Theme and Goal entities in the same relationship.

S=Θ   οἱ ἀστέρες τοῦ οὐρανοῦ ἔπεσαν εἰς τὴν γῆν, ὡς συκῆ βάλλει τοὺς ὀλύνθους αὐτῆς ὑπὸ ἀνέμου μεγάλου σειομένη (6:13)
[The stars of the sky (1/Thm)] fell (πίπτω) [to the earth (2/Goa)] [like a fig tree being shaken by great wind casts its figs (C/Cmp)].

S=Θ   οἱ ἀστέρες τοῦ οὐρανοῦ…εἰς τὴν γῆν (6:13)
[The stars of the sky (1/Thm)]…to (εἰς) [the earth (2/Goa)].

Usage labels specify the feature perspective at the top after the predicator, citation, and within the chevrons, < >, immediately after the italicized three-letter designation abbreviation of the event. The usage label consists of the configuration of event entities (ΘSG) plus a notation about the usage feature. The notation for the usage feature perspective places the Source entity not raised as an argument in brackets, [ ], to indicate that its referent is retrievable, followed by the event entity to which it is co-referential in brackets, [S=Θ].

	πίπτω (6:13) <*Mot.* Θ[S]G [S=Θ]>			εἰς (6:13) <*Mot.* Θ[S]G [S=Θ]>	
syn.	1	2	|	1	2
sem.	Thm	Goa	| C / Cmp	Thm	Goa
lex.	N	P/εἰς	| V+ὡς	N	N+acc

b. Usage Feature: Focus

Predicators in the first group grammaticalize conceptualizations of motion that bring into focus either both segments of the event (primary usage), only the initial segment that contains the Theme at the initiation of motion (secondary usage), or only the initial moment of motion at which the Theme and Source are strictly coincident (tertiary usage). The following descriptions enclose in brackets, [], the content of the progressively narrowing conceptualization of the event of motion associated with primary (pri.), secondary (sec.), and tertiary (ter.) usages.

pri. [Source/Theme ————————> Goal/Theme]
sec. [Source/Theme ————]—————> Goal/Theme
ter. [Source/Theme] —————————> Goal/Theme

Grammaticalizations of the conceptualization that focuses on both segments of the event result in a primary (pri.) usage that permits the retrieval of referents for all three entities of the event, and predicators raise the Theme and Goal entities as arguments and realize the Theme and Goal arguments as complements. Grammaticalizations of the conceptualization that focuses only on the initial segment of the event result in a secondary (sec.) usage that permits retrieval of referents for the Theme and Source but not for the Goal, and predicators raise the Theme and Source entities as arguments and realize the Theme and Source arguments as complements. Grammaticalization of the conceptualization that focuses only on the initial moment of motion results in a tertiary usage (ter.) that permits retrieval of referents for the Theme and its strictly coincident Source but not for the Goal. Predicators with this usage raise the Theme and Source entities as arguments and realize as a complement only the Theme argument from which the referent of the strictly coincident Source may be retrieved. The three categories of focus receive illustration in the following examples of ἀπέρχομαι (go away) and ὑπάγω (go forth). The translations of the verbs with the secondary and tertiary usages introduce in double brackets, [[ ]], the retrievable referents of the unrealized arguments and in double parentheses, (( )), the irretrievable referents of the event entities not raised as arguments.

pri. ἀπῆλθα πρὸς τὸν ἄγγελον (10:9)
[I (1/Thm)] went away (ἀπέρχομαι) [to the angel (2/Goa)] [[from where I was (S=Θ)]].

pri. εἰς ἀπώλειαν ὑπάγει (17:8)
[He (1/Thm)] goes forth (ὑπάγω) [to destruction (2/Goa)] [[from where he is (S=Θ)]].

sec. ἡ ὀπώρα σου τῆς ἐπιθυμίας τῆς ψυχῆς ἀπῆλθεν ἀπὸ σοῦ (18:14)
[The fruit of your life's desire (1/Thm)] went away (ἀπέρχομαι) [from you (2/Sou)] ((to some unspecified place)).

ter. ὕπαγε (10:8)
[You (1/Thm)] go (ὑπάγω) [[from where you are (2/Sou)]] ((to some unspecified place)).

Usage labels specify that the primary usage permits retrieval of a referent for the Source, Θ[S]G [S=Θ], that the secondary usage does not permit retrieval of a referent for the Goal, ΘS(G), and that the tertiary usage permits retrieval of a referent for the strictly coincident Source but not for the Goal, Θ[S](G) [S=Θ]. The Valence Description for the example in 10:8 places the syntactic function of the never-realized

Source argument of the tertiary usage in double brackets, [[ ]], and notes its lexical realization as [N].

	ἀπέρχομαι (10:9) <Mot. Θ[S]G [S=Θ]>		ὑπάγω (17:8) <Mot. Θ[S]G [S=Θ]>	
syn.	1	2	1	2
sem.	Thm	Goa	Thm	Goa
lex.	N	P/πρός [+acc]	N	P/εἰς

	ἀπέρχομαι (18:14) <Mot. ΘS(G)>		ὑπάγω (10:8) <Mot. Θ[S](G) [S=Θ]>	
syn.	1	2	1	[[2]]
sem.	Thm	Sou	Thm	Sou
lex.	N	P/ἀπό	N	[N]

c. Usage Feature: Functionality of the Goal

Predicators in the first group are able to grammaticalize a conceptualization of motion in which the entity toward which the Theme moves (Goal) takes on the interpretation of the abiding locale of the Theme at the termination of its motion (Locative). The change in functionality from Goal to Locative (G→L) produces primary usages of motion that differ only in this feature, as illustrated in the following examples of εἰσέρχομαι (come [to]). Since English verbs of motion that grammaticalize motion to a Goal typically do not also grammaticalize motion terminating in a Locative, the translation of the second example (11:11) introduces in brackets, [ ], "terminating" before the preposition to maintain the Locative interpretation of the second complement.[4]

    G   οὐ μὴ εἰσέλθῃ εἰς αὐτὴν πᾶν κοινὸν καὶ [ὁ] ποιῶν βδέλυγμα καὶ ψεῦδος εἰ μὴ οἱ γεγραμμένοι... (21:27)
        [Every common thing and one doing a detestable thing and a lie (1/Thm)] may not come (εἰσέρχομαι) [into it (2/Goa)] [except the ones written... (C/Mea)].

    G→L   μετὰ τὰς τρεῖς ἡμέρας καὶ ἥμισυ πνεῦμα ζωῆς ἐκ τοῦ θεοῦ εἰσῆλθεν ἐν αὐτοῖς (11:11)
        [After three and a half days (C/Tem)] [a spirit of life from God (1/Thm)] came (εἰσέρχομαι) [[terminating] in them (2/Loc)].

Usage labels note a change in functionality of the Goal, G→L, after the perspective description.

---

[4] English verbs of transference and motion natively grammaticalize only two usages of transference and motion. The possible usage combinations permitted by English grammar are transference and motion (1) to a Goal (primary)/from a Source (secondary), (2) from a Source (primary)/to a Goal (secondary), and (3) terminating in a Locative (primary)/to a Goal (secondary). Further discussion of the constraints of English grammar on the grammaticalization of transference and motion appear in Danove, *Verbs of Transference*, 36–37.

	εἰσέρχομαι (21:27) <Mot. Θ[S]G [S=Θ]>			εἰσέρχομαι (11:11) <Mot. Θ[S]G [S=Θ] G→L>		
syn.	1	2	C	1	2	C
sem.	Thm	Goa	Mea	Thm	Loc	Tem
lex.	N	P/εἰς	V+εἰ μή	N	P/ἐν	P/μετά [+acc]

d. Usage Feature: Argument Promotion

Although participles of motion in the first group do not admit to passivization, two verb predicators and one participle predicator grammaticalize a conceptualization of motion that promotes the Goal entity as the first (subject) argument, the Theme entity as second argument, and the Source entity as third argument. The perspective is that the Theme and Source are coincident/proximate at the initiation of motion, and the Theme argument must have a definite referent, that is, null Theme complements must be DNC. In the following examples of κληρονομέω (inherit) and λαβών (receiving), the translations introduce in double brackets, [[ ]], the contextual referent of the DNC Source in (the one sitting on the throne, cf. 21:5) in the first example (21:7) and the indefinite but circumscribed referent of the INC Source (someone) in the second example (19:20).

ὁ νικῶν κληρονομήσει ταῦτα (21:7)
[The one conquering (1/Goa)] will inherit (κληρονομέω) [these things (2/Thm)] [[from the one sitting on the throne (3/Sou)]].

τοὺς λαβόντας τὸ χάραγμα τοῦ θηρίου (19:20)
[The ones (1/Goa)] receiving (λαβών) [the mark of the beast (2/Thm)] [[from someone (3/Sou)]].

The usage labels note argument promotion by listing the event entities in their grammaticalized order, GΘS.

	κληρονομέω (21:7) <Mot. GΘS S=Θ>			λαβών (19:20) <Mot. GΘS S=Θ>		
syn.	1	2	[3]	1	2	(3)
sem.	Goa	Thm	Sou	Goa	Thm	Sou
lex.	N	N+acc	DNC	N	N+acc	INC

e. Preposition Predicators

Preposition predicators consistently raise two event entities as arguments. In the grammaticalization of motion, verb and participle predicators raise the entity in motion (Theme) and a local entity (Goal, Locative, or Source) as arguments, and, if the verb, participle, or complex participle predicator licenses a preposition phrase to realize the local argument, the prepositional predicator of that phrase raises as arguments the same two entities as its licensing verb or participle predicator. When the verb, participle, or complex participle predicators of transference license a prepositional phrase to realize the local (Goal, Locative, or Source) argument, however, the preposition predicator of the phrase is able to raise only the Theme and local entity as arguments. As a consequence, the conceptualization grammaticalized by the preposition predicator concerns only the motion of the Theme, as illustrated in the previously considered occurrences of λαμβάνω (take) and τίθημι (place). The examples present consecutively the verb predicators of transference and their licensed preposition predicators of motion.

AΘS[G] [G=A] ἔλαβον τὸ βιβλαρίδιον ἐκ τῆς χειρὸς τοῦ ἀγγέλου (10:10)
[I (1/Agt)] took (λαμβάνω) [the little book (2/Thm)] [from the hand of the angel (3/Sou)].

ΘS[G] [G=Θ]   τὸ βιβλαρίδιον ἐκ τῆς χειρὸς τοῦ ἀγγέλου (10:10)
[The little book (1/Thm)] from (ἐκ) [the hand of the angel (2/Sou)].

AΘ[S]G [S=A] G→L   ἔθηκεν τὸν πόδα αὐτοῦ τὸν δεξιὸν ἐπὶ τῆς θαλάσσης (10:2)
[He (1/Agt)] placed (τίθημι) [his right foot (2/Thm)] [on the sea (3/Loc)].

Θ[S]G [S=Θ] G→L   τὸν πόδα αὐτοῦ τὸν δεξιὸν ἐπὶ τῆς θαλάσσης (10:2a)
[His right foot (1/Thm)] on (ἐπί) [the sea (2/Loc)].

Usage labels for preposition predicators note only the usage of motion.

	λαμβάνω (10:10) <Tra. AΘS[G] [G=A] +imp.>			ἐκ (10:10) <Mot. ΘS[G] [G=Θ]>	
syn.	1	2	3	1	2
sem.	Agt	Thm	Sou	Thm	Sou
lex.	N	N+acc	P/ἐκ	N	N+gen

	τίθημι (10:2) <Tra. AΘ[S]G [S=A], G→L +imp.>			ἐπί (10:2a) <Mot. Θ[S]G [S=Θ] G→L>	
syn.	1	2	3	1	2
sem.	Agt	Thm	Loc	Thm	Loc
lex.	N	N+acc	P/ἐπί [+gen]	N	N+gen

4. Usage Features for the Event of Motion: Part 2

The second group of predicators that grammaticalize the event of motion are those that also admit to interpretation as grammaticalizing the event of transference with passive base forms (§3.2b). On the one hand, all occurrences of these predicators that admit to interpretation as grammaticalizing a passive usage of transference simultaneously admit to grammaticalizing a passive usage of motion. On the other hand, other passive occurrences of these predicators are restricted to interpretation as grammaticalizing only a passive usage of motion. In order to highlight the dependence of passive usages of motion on predicators that also (and most frequently) grammaticalize the event of transference, the labels for the passive usages of motion use the configuration of the entities of the event of transference, AΘSG, with the Agent entity in parentheses, ( ), to indicate that the referent of the Agent is irretrievable, (A)ΘSG. Although the conceptualizations of the passive usages of motion require description by four usage features (perspective, subject affectedness, focus, and functionality of the Goal), the usage features perspective and subject affectedness are linked in a specific way.

a. Usage Features: Perspective and Subject Affectedness

In the conceptualization of motion with predicators in the second group, the Theme again moves along a continuous path from the Source to the Goal, and, since the event contains two fixed entities, the Source and the Goal, it may be resolved into two segments, initial and terminal. In the occurrences that admit to interpretation with the passive usages of motion, however, the perspective changes to the termination of motion at which the Theme and Goal are strictly coincident and the motion of the Theme ceases (G=Θ). At this point, the cessation of the motion of the Theme receives interpretation as the Theme being affected. Since the Theme is the first (subject) argument and is affected, the predicators adopt passive base forms, and the usage labels note the passive usages by placing "pass." at the end. The text of Revelation presents no occurrences in which the predicators raise the Theme and Source as arguments for the purpose of illustration, and the examples from the following discussions illustrate the observed usages that raise the Theme and Goal event entities as arguments.

b. Usage Feature: Focus

Verb and participle predicators that admit to interpretation as grammaticalizing a passive usage of motion have three possible categories of focus: a focus on both segments of the event (primary), a focus only on the terminal segment of the event (secondary), and a focus only on the terminal moment of the event at which the Theme and Goal are strictly coincident (tertiary). The following descriptions enclose in brackets, [ ], the content of the progressively narrowing conceptualization of the event of motion associated with primary, secondary, and tertiary passive usages.

    pri. pass.   [Source/Theme ————————> Goal/Theme]
    sec. pass.   Source/Theme ————[——————> Goal/Theme]
    ter. pass.   Source/Theme ——————————> [Goal/Theme]

The text of Revelation, however, presents only grammaticalizations of conceptualizations that focus on the terminal segment (sec.) and on the terminal moment of motion (ter.).[5] The conceptualizations of the resulting secondary usages permit retrieval of

---

[5] Although absent from the text of Revelation, the primary passive usage of motion from a Source, (A)ΘS[G] [G=Θ] pass., appears elsewhere in the NT with verb predicators: ἀνάγω (Acts 13:13; 16:11; 18:21; 27:12, 21), ἀναλαμβάνω (Acts 1:11), ἀποστάω (Luke 22:41; Acts 21:1), διασῴζω (Acts 28:4), and φέρω (2 Pet 1:18).

referents for the Theme and Goal but not for the Source, and the predicators raise the Theme and Goal entities as arguments and realize the Theme and the Goal arguments as complements. The conceptualization of the tertiary usage also permits retrieval of a referent for the Theme and its strictly coincident Goal but not for the Source, and the predicators raise the Theme and Goal entities as arguments and realize only the Theme argument as a complement. Only the secondary passive usage of motion to a Goal can receive illustration in the following occurrences of συνάγω (come together) because the remaining secondary usage and the tertiary usage also involve a change in the functionality of the Goal, which receives investigation in the next section.

The occurrence of συνάγω (gather [together]) that admits to interpretation with the secondary passive usage of motion to a Goal also admits to interpretation with a passivized primary active usage of transference to a Goal and a primary passive usage of transference to a Goal. As previously discussed (§3.1b), this polysemy arises because predicators that grammaticalize the passive usage of motion to a Goal and the passive usages of transference to a Goal consistently realize only two entities (Theme/Agent and Goal) as arguments, and predicators with passivized active usages of transference typically realize only the Theme and Goal arguments as complements because Greek grammar permits predicators that grammaticalize a passivized active usage of transference to leave the Agent argument unrealized and to have no definite referent (§1.5c). As a consequence, predicators with passivized active usages typically appear with only the Theme and the local argument realized as complements. Thus the interpretation that a predicator is grammaticalizing a passive usage of motion to a Goal/a passivized active usage of transference to a Goal/a passive usage of transference to a Goal becomes possible whenever the grammatical context (1) identifies for a possible Agent no definite referent that is distinct from the referent of the Theme and (2) the Agent admits to interpretation as transferring itself.

Since the illustrative verb with the secondary passive usage of motion, συνάγω, admits to three possible interpretations, all three are given. The translations introduce in double brackets, [[ ]], the retrievable referents of the unrealized arguments and in double parentheses, (( )), the irretrievable referents of the event entities not raised as arguments. Since English verbs of transference typically do not also designate motion, the translation of συνάγω with the secondary usage of motion uses the verb of motion "come together."

     συνάχθητε εἰς τὸ δεῖπνον τὸ μέγα τοῦ θεοῦ ἵνα φάγητε... (19:17-18)
Mot. pass. [You (1/Thm)] come together (συνάγω) ((from an unspecified locale)) to the great dinner of God (2/Goa)] [so that you may eat... (C/Pur)].
Tra. act. [You (2/Thm)] be gathered (συνάγω) [[by someone (1/Agt)]] [to the great dinner of God (3/Goa)] [[from where you are (S=A)]] [so that you may eat... (C/Pur)].
Tra. pass. [You (1/Agt)] gather (συνάγω) [[yourselves (2/Thm)]] [to the great dinner of God (3/Goa)] [[from where you are (S=A)]] [so that you may eat... (C/Pur)].

3. Usages and Usage Features

Usage labels specify that the secondary usage of motion does not permit retrieval of a referent for the Source, (A)Θ(S)G. The Valence Description for the interpretation with the passivized active usage of transference uses the passivization construction to transform the occurrence into its active counterpart (§1.5c), and the Valence Description for the interpretation with the passive usage of transference places the syntactic function of the never-realized Theme in double brackets, [[ ]], and notes its lexical realization by [N]. The usage label for the passive usage of motion introduces the notation "pass." at the end to clarify that the first argument is affected.

	συνάγω (19:17-18) <Mot. (A)Θ(S)G G=Θ pass.>				συνάγω (19:17-18) <Tra. AΘ[S]G [S=A] +imp.>				
syn.	1	2		C	1	2	3		C
sem.	Thm	Goa		Pur	Agt	Thm	Goa		Pur
lex.	N	P/εἰς		V+ἵνα	N	N+acc	P/εἰς		V+ἵνα

	συνάγω (19:17-18) <Tra. A[Θ][S]G [Θ=A] [S=A] pass. +imp.>			
syn.	1	[[2]]	3	C
sem.	Agt	Thm	Goa	Pur
lex.	N	[N]	P/εἰς	V+ἵνα

c. Usage Feature: Functionality of the Goal

Predicators of the second group are able to grammaticalize conceptualizations of motion in which the entity toward which the Theme moves (Goal) takes on the interpretation of the abiding locale of the Theme at the termination of its motion (Locative). The change in functionality from Goal to Locative (G→L) produces a secondary passive usage of motion terminating in a Locative that differs only in this feature from the secondary passive usage of motion to a Goal as well as a tertiary passive usage that conceptualizes the final moment of motion at which the Theme and Locative are strictly coincident and motion ceases. The tertiary passive usage of motion typically receives reference as the usage of "state."[6]

The conceptualization of the secondary usage of motion terminating in a Locative permits the retrieval of referents for the Theme and Locative but not the Source, and the predicator with this usage raises the Theme and Locative entities as arguments and realizes the Theme and Locative arguments as complements. The verb predicator that admits to interpretation with the secondary passive usage of motion terminating in a Locative also admits to interpretation with a passivized primary active usage of transference terminating in a Locative and with a primary passive usage of transference terminating in a Locative. As previously discussed (§3.1b), this polysemy arises because verbs with the passive usage of motion terminating in a Locative and a passive usage of transference terminating in a Locative consistently and verbs with the passivized active usage of transference terminating in a Locative typically realize

---

[6] See Leonard Talmy, "Lexicalization Patterns: Semantic Structure in Lexical Forms," in T. Shopen (ed.), *Language Typology and Syntactic Distinction*. Vol. 3, *Grammatical Categories and the Lexicon* (Cambridge: Cambridge University Press, 1985), 50–61, and Goddard, *Semantic Analysis*, 197–98.

only two of their arguments: Theme/Locative, Agent/Locative, and Agent/Locative respectively. Thus the interpretation that a verb is grammaticalizing the secondary passive usage of motion terminating in a Locative/a passivized primary active usage of transference terminating in a Locative/a primary passive usage of transference terminating in a Locative becomes possible whenever the grammatical context (1) identifies for a possible Agent no definite referent that is distinct from the referent of the Theme and (2) the Agent admits to interpretation as transferring itself.

The following occurrence of ἵστημι (stand, station) illustrates the distinctions among the secondary passive usage of motion, the passivized primary active usage of transference, and the primary passive usage of transference. The translations introduce in double brackets, [[ ]], the retrievable referents of the unrealized arguments and in double parentheses, (( )), the irretrievable referents of the event entities not raised as arguments.

ἐστάθη ἐπὶ τὴν ἄμμον τῆς θαλάσσης (12:18)

Mot. pass. [It (1/Thm)] stood (ἵστημι) [on the sand of the sea (2/Loc)] ((from an unspecified locale)).

Tra. act. [It (2/Thm)] was stationed (ἵστημι) [[by someone (1/Agt)]] [on the sand of the sea (3/Loc)] [[from where it was (S=A)]].

Tra. pass. [It (1/Agt)] stationed (ἵστημι) [[itself (2/Thm)]] [on the sand of the sea (3/Loc)] [[from where it was (S=A)]].

Usage labels specify that the secondary passive usage of motion terminating in a Locative does not permit retrieval of a referent for the Source, (A)Θ(S)G, has a Goal that functions as a Locative, G→L, and has an affected Theme (pass.). The Valence Description for the interpretation with the passivized primary active usage of transference uses the passivization construction to transform the occurrence into its active counterpart (§1.5c). The Valence Description for the interpretation with the primary passive usage of transference places the syntactic function of the never-realized Theme in double brackets, [[ ]], and notes its lexical realization by [N].

	ἵστημι (12:18) <Mot. (A)Θ(S)G G→L pass.>		ἵστημι (12:18) <Tra. AΘ(S)G [S=A] G→L –imp.>		
syn.	1	2	1	2	3
sem.	Thm	Loc	Agt	Thm	Loc
lex.	N	P/ἐπί [+acc]	N	N+acc	P/ἐπί [+acc]

	ἵστημι (12:18) <Tra. A[Θ](S)G [Θ=A] S=A G→L pass. –imp.>		
syn.	1	[[2]]	3
sem.	Agt	Thm	Loc
lex.	N	[N]	P/ἐπί [+acc]

The conceptualization of the tertiary passive usage of motion (i.e., the passive usage of state) permits the retrieval of referents for the Theme and the strictly coincident Locative but not the Source, and the predicators raise the Theme and Locative as arguments but realize only the Theme argument as a complement, while the Locative argument retrieves its referent from the strictly coincident Theme, L=Θ. Elsewhere in the NT, occurrences that admit to interpretation with the tertiary passive usage of motion terminating in a Locative (the passive usage of state) frequently admit to interpretation with a passivized primary active usage of transference terminating in a Locative and a primary passive usage of transference terminating in a Locative. These alternate interpretations of transference, however, never are viable in the text of Revelation. This is the case because the alternate conceptualizations of transference permit their Locative complements to remain unrealized only when they have a definite referent retrievable from the context, that is, when they are DNC. In all occurrences attributed to the passive usage of state in the text of Revelation, however, the contexts present no retrievable definite contextual referent for a possible Locative of transference. With the passive usage of state, however, the Locative retrieves its referent directly from the Theme and requires no separate retrievable contextual referent. The tertiary passive usage of motion terminating in a Locative/the passive usage of state receives illustration in the following example of ἵστημι (stand). The translation places in double brackets, [[ ]], the definite referent of the never-realized, strictly coincident Locative.

τίς…σταθῆναι (6:17)
[Who (1/Thm)]…to stand (ἵστημι) [[where he is/at the locale where his motion ceases]].

Usage labels specify that the tertiary usage does not permit retrieval of the Source, (A) Θ(S)G, has a Goal that functions as a Locative, G→L, requires retrieval of a referent for the strictly coincident Locative from the Theme, L=Θ, and has an affected Theme (pass.). The Valence Description places the syntactic function of the never-realized Locative in double brackets, [[ ]], and notes its lexical realization by [N].

	ἵστημι (6:17) <*Mot.* (A)Θ(S)[G] [G→L] [L=Θ] pass.>	
syn.	1	[[2]]
sem.	Thm	Loc
lex.	N	[N]

5. Usage Feature for the Event of Location

The predicators that grammaticalize the event of location (*Loc.*) consistently raise both event entities (Theme and Locative) as arguments but assume two distinct conceptualizations of the Locative that receive description by the usage feature focus. Verb, participle, preposition, complex participle, and complex preposition predicators grammaticalize the conceptualization of location with the primary focus (pri.) in which the Theme and Locative are proximate but not strictly coincident, most frequently in the sense that they are not coterminous. The conceptualization of the usage with the primary focus permits the retrieval of distinct referents for the

Theme and Locative, and the predicators raise both entities as arguments and realize both arguments as complements whenever the context does not permit the retrieval of a definite referent for the null Locative. Complex adverb predicators, in contrast, grammaticalize the conceptualization of location with the secondary focus (sec.) in which the Theme and Locative are strictly coincident/coterminous. The conceptualization of the usage with the secondary focus permits the retrieval of a referent for the Theme which then is retrieved as the referent for the Locative, and the complex adverb predicators raise both the Theme and Locative as arguments, realize only the Theme argument as a complement, and draw the referent of the Locative directly from the adverb component of the complex predicator. The primary and secondary usages of location receive illustration in the following examples of ἵστημι (stand) and ὧδε + [εἰμί] (be here). The translation of the second example (13:10) introduces in double brackets, [[ ]], the definite contextual referent of the never-realized Locative (here).

    pri.   ἕστηκα ἐπὶ τὴν θύραν (3:20)
           [I (1/Thm)] stand (ἵστημι) [before the door (2/Loc)].

    sec.   ὧδέ ἐστιν ἡ ὑπομονὴ καὶ ἡ πίστις τῶν ἁγίων (13:10)
           Here is (ὧδε + [εἰμί]) [the endurance and the faith of the holy ones (1/ Thm)] [[here (2/Loc)]].

The usage label of the secondary usage places the strictly coincident/coterminous and never-realized Locative entity in brackets, [ ], and signals that its referent is retrievable from the Theme, L=Θ, and its Valence Description places the syntactic function of the Locative argument in double brackets, [[ ]], to indicate that it never is realized as a complement but has a retrievable referent and notes the lexical realization of the never-realized complement by [N].

	ἵστημι (3:20)		ὧδε + [εἰμί] (13:10)	
	<Loc. ΘL>		<Loc. Θ[L] [L=Θ]>	
syn.	1	2	1	[[2]]
sem.	Thm	Loc	Thm	Loc
lex.	N	P/ἐπὶ [+acc]	N	[N]

6. Usage Features for the Event of Communication

This discussion develops the five usage features required to distinguish the nine usages of communication (*Cmm.*) in the text of Revelation: secondary emphasis, suppression, functionality of the Content, argument promotion, and subject affectedness.

a. Usage Feature: Secondary Emphasis

Predicators that grammaticalize the event of communication consistently raise the Agent or agentive Benefactive as first argument. The selection of the second argument, however, depends on the relative emphasis that each predicator places on the Content

3. Usages and Usage Features

and Experiencer in its conceptualization of communication. In the text of Revelation, forty verb, active participle, complex active participle, and noun predicators place secondary emphasis on the Content and raise the Content as second argument, and two verb predicators present distinct usages with secondary emphasis on the Content and on the Experiencer. Secondary emphasis on the Content highlights the production and transmission of the Content and has the implication that the Agent/agentive Benefactive causes the message to go to the Experiencer. Secondary emphasis on the Experiencer, in contrast, highlights the reception and interpretation of the Content and has the implication that the Agent causes the Experiencer to receive the message.[7] Predicators that grammaticalize both possibilities of secondary emphasis also impose on the usage with secondary emphasis on the Experiencer the interpretation that the Content is interpreted successfully.[8] Secondary emphasis on the Content (C) and on the Experiencer (E) receives illustration in the following occurrences of λέγω (say) and διδάσκω (teach).

C εἶπέν μοι ὁ ἄγγελος· διὰ τί ἐθαύμασας; (17:7a)
   [The angel (1/Agt)] said (λέγω) [to me (3/Exp)] ["Why were you amazed?" (2/Con)].

E διδάσκει...τοὺς ἐμοὺς δούλους πορνεῦσαι καὶ φαγεῖν εἰδωλόθυτα (2:20)
   [She (1/Agt)] teaches (διδάσκω)...[my slaves (2/Exp)] [to engage in sexual immorality and to eat what is offered to idols (3/Con)].

As with argument promotion, usage labels note secondary emphasis by listing the event entities in the order of their grammaticalization, ACE or AEC.

	λέγω (17:7a) <Cmm. ACE>			διδάσκω (2:20) <Cmm. AEC>		
syn.	1	2	3	1	2	3
sem.	Agt	Con	Exp	Agt	Exp	Con
lex.	N	V+quo	N+dat	N	N+acc	V-i2

---

[7] Most frequently, discussions of the Content/Experiencer secondary emphasis employ a movement (cause to go)/possession (cause to have) distinction; cf. Steven Pinker, *Learnability and Cognition: The Acquisition of Argument Structure* (Cambridge, MA: MIT Press, 1987), 48, 63; Margaret Speas, *Phrase Structure in Natural Language* (Nordrecht: Kluwer, 1990), 87–89; David Pesetsky, *Zero Syntax: Experiencers and Cascades* (Cambridge, MA: MIT Press, 1995), 135–38; and Malka Rappaport Hovav and Beth Levin, "The English Dative Alternation: the Case for Verb Sensitivity," *JLing* 44 (2008): 134. The movement (cause to go)/reception (cause to receive) distinction, however, better explains the implication that the emphasized Experiencer successfully interprets the Content/message; cf. Adele Goldberg, "The Inherent Semantics of Argument Structure: The Case of the English Ditransitive Construction," *CogLing* 3-1 (1992): 46, 49–52. Although these authors are concerned with "dative alternation" among various classes of English verbs (X tells Y Z/X tells Z to Y), the movement/reception constraints on the English verbs appear to parallel exactly those of Greek verbs of communication.

[8] Adrienne Lehrer, "Checklist for Verbs of Speaking," *Acta Linguistica Hungarica* 38, nos. 1–4 (1988): 155; cf. Danove, *Verbs of Communication*, 28.

b. Usage Feature: Suppression of the Content

Predicators are able to grammaticalize conceptualizations of communication by placing a definite semantic referent directly onto the Content argument, suppressing the Content complement, and licensing only the Agent (or agentive Benefactive) and Experiencer as complements. Suppression of the Content differs from the omission of complements whose definite referent may be retrieved from the context (DNC), whose referent is indefinite but circumscribed (INC), and whose definite referent may be retrieved from another entity of the event (pass.) because the referent of the Content is not derived from the context but directly from the predicator itself. In the text of Revelation, all verb and participle predicators that suppress the Content complement have cognate nouns that could fulfill the role of the suppressed Content complement: αἴνεσις and αἶνος (praise) for αἰνέω (praise, speak {praise}), εὐαγγέλιον (gospel, good news) for εὐαγγελίζω (tell {good news}), προφητεία (prophecy) for προφητεύω (prophesy, speak {prophecy}), and ψεῦδος (lie) for ψεύδομαι (lie, speak {a lie}).[9] The following examples of αἰνέω (speak {praise}) and εὐαγγελίζω (tell {good news}) illustrate suppression of the Content. The translations introduce in braces, { }, the referents of the suppressed Content complements ("praise" in 19:5 and "good news" in 10:7).

αἰνεῖτε τῷ θεῷ ἡμῶν πάντες οἱ δοῦλοι αὐτοῦ [καὶ] οἱ φοβούμενοι αὐτόν, οἱ μικροὶ καὶ οἱ μεγάλοι (19:5)
[You (1/Agt)] speak (αἰνέω) {praise (2/Con)} [to our God (3/Exp)] [all his slaves and the ones fearing him, the small and the great (C/Voc)]!

εὐηγγέλισεν τοὺς ἑαυτοῦ δούλους τοὺς προφήτας (10:7)
[He (1/Agt)] told (εὐαγγελίζω) [his own slaves the prophets (2/Exp)] {good news (3/Con)}.

Usage labels note suppression of the Content by placing braces, { }, around the Content entity, and Valence Descriptions place double braces, {{ }}, around the syntactic function of the suppressed Content and note its lexical realization as {N}.

	αἰνέω (19:5) <Cmm. A{C}E>				εὐαγγελίζω (10:7) <Cmm. AE{C}>		
syn.	1	{{2}}	3	C	1	2	{{3}}
sem.	Agt	Con	Exp	Voc	Agt	Exp	Con
lex.	N	{N}	N+dat	N+voc	N	N+acc	{N}

c. Usage Feature: Functionality of the Content

Predicators are able to grammaticalize conceptualizations of communication in which the Content entity takes on the interpretation of information about the Content

---

[9] As the proposed translations of these Greek predicators indicate, suppression of the Content also characterizes many English verbs of communication: αἰνέω (praise), προφητεύω (prophesy), and ψεύδομαι (lie).

3. Usages and Usage Features 69

(Topic). The change in functionality from Content to Topic (C→T) produces usages of communication that differ only in this feature, as illustrated in the following examples of συμβουλεύω (recommend) with no change in the functionality of the Content (C=C) and προφητεύω (prophesy) with a change in functionality of the Content to a Topic (C→T). In the second example (10:11), the translation introduces in double brackets, [[ ]], the contextual referent of the DNC Experiencer (the churches).

C   συμβουλεύω σοι ἀγοράσαι παρ' ἐμοῦ χρυσίον πεπυρωμένον ἐκ πυρὸς ἵνα πλουτήσῃς (3:18)
[I (1/Agt)] recommend (συμβουλεύω) [to you (3/Exp)] [to buy from me gold burned with fire (2/Con)] [so that you may be rich (C/Pur)].

C→T   σε πάλιν προφητεῦσαι ἐπὶ λαοῖς καὶ ἔθνεσιν καὶ γλώσσαις καὶ βασιλεῦσιν πολλοῖς (10:11)
[You (1/Agt)] [again (C/Mea)] to prophesy (προφητεύω) [about many peoples and nations and tongues and kings (2/Top)] [[to the churches (3/Exp)]].

Usage labels note a change in the functionality of the Content to a Topic by introducing C→T after the notation for secondary emphasis.

	συμβουλεύω (3:18) < Cmm. ACE>				προφητεύω (10:11) < Cmm. ACE C→T>			
syn.	1	2	3	C	1	2	3	C
sem.	Agt	Con	Exp	Pur	Agt	Top	Exp	Mea
lex.	N	V-i3	N+dat	V+ἵνα	N	P/ἐπί [+dat]	DNC	A/πάλιν

d. Usage Feature: Argument Promotion

The complex predicator προσευχή + εἰμί (be a prayer) promotes its Content entity to first argument, as illustrated in the following occurrence in which the translation introduces in double brackets, [[ ]], the referent of the DNC Experiencer (God; cf. §1.5a).

αἵ εἰσιν αἱ προσευχαὶ τῶν ἁγίων (5:8)
[Which (1/Con)] are the prayers (προσευχή + εἰμί) [of the holy ones (2/Ben)] [[to God (3/Exp)]].

The usage label notes argument promotion by listing the event entities in the order of their grammaticalization, CBE.

	προσευχή + εἰμί (5:8) <Cmm. CBE>		
syn.	1	2	[3]
sem.	Con	Ben	Exp
lex.	N	N+gen	DNC

e. Usage Feature: Subject Affectedness

The verb predicator ἀποκρίνομαι (reply, respond) grammaticalizes event ACEB by imposing the interpretation that the Agent and Benefactive entities are co-referential.[10] With this interpretation, the verb omits consideration of the co-referential Benefactive entity and raises the event entities associated with the Agent, Content, and Experiencer thematic roles as first, second, and third argument. Since the Agent and Benefactive entities are co-referential, the action of the Agent affects itself, and the Agent is characterized by subject affectedness. As in the grammaticalization of subject affectedness with predicators of transference (§3.1b), the verb uses passive base forms to indicate this fact, as in the following example of the verb in 7:13. The translation introduces in double brackets, [[ ]], the contextual referent of the DNC Content (these wrapped in white robes, who are they?) and of the DNC Experiencer (me).

ἀπεκρίθη εἷς ἐκ τῶν πρεσβυτέρων (7:13)
[One of the elders (1/Agt)] responded (ἀποκρίνομαι) [[to me (3/Exp)]] [["These wrapped with white robes, who are they and from where did they come?" (2/Con)]].

The usage label sets the Benefactive entity in brackets, [ ], to clarify that it is not raised as an argument and that its referent is retrievable, specifies in brackets that the Benefactive entity is co-referential to the Agent entity, [B=A], and notes the use of passive base forms (pass.) at the end.

	ἀποκρίνομαι (7:13) <Cmm. ACE[B] [B=A] pass.>		
syn.	1	[2]	[3]
sem.	Agt	Con	Exp
lex.	N	DNC	DNC

7. Usage Features for the Event of Experience

This discussion develops the three usage features required to distinguish the seven usages of experience (EC) in the text of Revelation: suppression of the Content, functionality of the Content, and argument promotion. The concluding discussion offers a clarification concerning preposition predicators.

a. Usage Feature: Suppression of the Content

The participle predicator ὠδίνων (suffering {birth pains}) grammaticalizes a concepp tualization of experience by placing a definite semantic referent onto the Content argument, suppressing the Content complement, and licensing only the Experiencer

---

[10] A detailed proposal concerning the development of the ACEB conceptualization of the event of communication with ἀποκρίνομαι and one other predicator appears in Danove, *Verbs of Communication*, 35–37.

3. *Usages and Usage Features* 71

as a complement. This predicator also has a cognate noun that could fulfill the role of the suppressed Content complement, ὠδίν (birth pains). The translation of the following example introduces in braces, { }, the definite referent of the suppressed Content (birth pains).

ὠδίνουσα (12:2)
[She (1/Exp)] suffering (ὠδίνων) {birth pains (2/Con)}.

The usage label notes suppression of the Content by placing braces, { }, around the Content entity, and the Valence Description places double braces, {{ }}, around the syntactic function of the Content and notes its lexical realization as {N}.

	ὠδίνων (12:2) <Exp. E{C}>	
syn.	1	{{2}}
sem.	Exp	Con
lex.	N	{N}

b. Usage Feature: Functionality of the Content

Specific verb, participle, adjective, preposition, noun, and complex adjective predicators grammaticalize conceptualizations of experience in which the Content entity takes on the interpretation of information about the Content and so functions as a Topic (C→T). This change in functionality produces usages of experience that differ only in this feature. The change in functionality receives illustration in the following examples of χαίρω (rejoice), ἐπί [+dat] (at, concerning), and πιστός (faithful).

> C→T   οἱ κατοικοῦντες ἐπὶ τῆς γῆς χαίρουσιν ἐπ' αὐτοῖς...ὅτι οὗτοι οἱ δύο προφῆται ἐβασάνισαν τοὺς κατοικοῦντας ἐπὶ τῆς γῆς (11:10)
> [The ones dwelling on the earth (1/Exp)] rejoice (χαίρω) [concerning them (2/Top)]...[because these two prophets tormented the ones dwelling on the earth (C/Cau)].

> C→T   οἱ κατοικοῦντες ἐπὶ τῆς γῆς...ἐπ' αὐτοῖς (11:10b)
> [The ones dwelling on the earth (1/Exp)]...concerning (ἐπί) [them (2/Top)].

> C→T   ὁ μάρτυς μου ὁ πιστός μου (2:13)
> [My witness (1/Exp)] faithful (πιστός) [concerning me (2/Top)].[11]

Usage labels note a change in the functionality of the Content to a Topic by introducing C→T at the end.

---

[11] This example admits to polysemous interpretation and receives further consideration in §4.6.

	χαίρω (11:10) <Exp. EC C→T>			ἐπί (11:10b) <Exp. EC C→T>	
syn.	1	2	C	1	2
sem.	Exp	Top	Cau	Exp	Top
lex.	N	P/ἐπί [+dat]	V+ ὅτι	N	N+dat

	πιστός (2:13) <Exp. EC C→T>	
syn.	1	2
sem.	Exp	Top
lex.	N	N+gen

c. Usage Feature: Argument Promotion

Specific participle, adjective, preposition, noun, and complex adjective and noun predicators promote their Content entity to first argument, as illustrated in the following examples of ἐλεεινός + εἰμί (be pitiable) and θαυμαστός (marvelous). In both examples, the translations introduce in double brackets, [[ ]], the contextual referent of the DNC Experiencer (the speaker of the statement/Jesus or John).

σὺ εἶ ὁ...ἐλεεινὸς (3:17)
[You (1/Con)] are...pitiable (ἐλεεινός + εἰμί) [[to the speaker of the statement/ to Jesus (2/Exp)]].

σημεῖον...θαυμαστόν (15:1)
[A sign 1/Con)]...marvelous (θαυμαστός) [[to the speaker of the statement/ to John (2/Exp)]].

Usage labels note argument promotion by listing the event entities in the order of their grammaticalization, CE.

	ἐλεεινός + εἰμί (3:17) <Exp. CE>		θαυμαστός (15:1) <Exp. CE>	
syn.	1	[2]	1	[2]
sem.	Con	Exp	Con	Exp
lex.	N	DNC	N	DNC

d. Preposition Predicators

When a predicator of experience raises an argument realized by a prepositional phrase, the preposition predicator of that phrase grammaticalizes the same conceptualization of experience as its licensing predicator. Thus the licensing predicator of experience and the licensed preposition predicator receive description by the same usage label. When a predicator of communication raises an argument realized by a prepositional phrase, however, the preposition predicator is able to raise only two of the three event entities of communication as arguments. As with predicators of transference (§3.3c), the preposition predicators licensed by predicators of communication exclude the first (Agent or agentive Benefactive) argument of the licensing predicator of communication and raise the remaining arguments of the licensing predicator as arguments according to the rule for preposition predicators (§1.2c): the argument referencing the entity set in relation to the object of the preposition has syntactic function "1" and the argument referencing the object of the preposition has syntactic function "2."

Examples of the restriction on preposition predicators appear in 10:11 in which προφητεύω (prophesy) with usage ACE C→T of communication licenses the preposition predicator ἐπί [+dat] (at, concerning) with usage EC C→T of experience and in 14:6 in which εὐαγγελίζω (proclaim [as good news]) with usage ACE of communication licenses preposition predicator ἐπί [+acc] (to) with usage CE of experience. The translations introduce in double brackets, [[ ]], the contextual referent of the DNC Experiencer (churches) in 10:11 and of the DNC Agent (the angel) and DNC Content (everlasting good news) in 14:6. The examples present consecutively the verb predicators of communication and their licensed preposition predicators of experience.

ACE C→T   σε πάλιν προφητεῦσαι ἐπὶ λαοῖς καὶ...πολλοῖς (10:11)
[You (1/Agt)] [again (C/Mea)] to prophesy (προφητεύω) [[to the churches (3/Exp)]] [concerning many peoples and... (2/Top)].

EC C→T   ἐπὶ λαοῖς καὶ ἔθνεσιν καὶ γλώσσαις καὶ βασιλεῦσιν πολλοῖς (10:11)
[[The churches (1/Exp)]] about (ἐπί) [many peoples and nations and tongues and kings (2/Top)].

ACE   εὐαγγελίσαι ἐπὶ τοὺς καθημένους ἐπὶ τῆς γῆς... (14:6)
[[Another angel (1/Agt)]] to proclaim (εὐαγγελίζω) [[everlasting good news (2/Con)]] [to the ones dwelling on the earth... (3/Exp)].

CE   ἐπὶ τοὺς καθημένους ἐπὶ τῆς γῆς... (14:6a)
[[Everlasting good news (1/Con)]] to (ἐπί) [the ones dwelling on the earth... (3/Exp)].

Valence Descriptions for preposition predicators note only the usage of experience.

	προφητεύω (10:11) <Cmm. ACE C→T>					ἐπί (10:11) <Exp. EC C→T>	
	1	2	[3]	|	C	[1]	2
syn.							
sem.	Agt	Top	Exp	|	Mea	Exp	Top
lex.	N	P/ἐπί [+dat]	DNC	|	A/πάλιν	N	N+acc

	εὐαγγελίζω (14:6) <Cmm. ACE>			ἐπί (14:6a) <Exp. CE>	
	1	[2]	3	[1]	2
syn.					
sem.	Agt	Con	Exp	Con	Exp
lex.	N	DNC	P/ἐπί [+acc]	DNC	N+gen

8. Usage Features for Events Containing a Patient Entity

This discussion considers the usage features for all events containing a Patient entity. Considering these events simultaneously is possible because there are no significant differences in the features across events as there were, for example, with the feature focus in reference to the events of transference, motion, and location and because the only two categories of usage features that are relevant for events containing a Patient entity, suppression of required complements and argument promotion, have received extensive previous illustration. The following discussion identifies the events or event to which the usage features pertain and provides examples that illustrate the usage features and the manner in which they are noted in usage labels.

a. Usage Feature: Suppression of the Patient

When grammaticalizing the events of benefaction with the configurations APB and BPB, of effect with the configuration AP, and of instrumentality with the configuration API, specific verb and participle predicators place a definite referent directly onto the Patient argument and suppress the Patient complement. The verb and participle predicators that suppress the Patient complement in the text of Revelation have cognate nouns that could fulfill the role of the suppressed Patient complement: βλασφημία (blasphemy) for βλασφημέω (blaspheme, speak {blasphemy}), βοηθεία (aid) for βοηθέω (aid, provide {aid}), πόλεμος (battle) for πολεμέω (battle, make {war}), and κατηγορία (accusation) for κατηγορῶν (accusing, making {an accusation}) when grammaticalizing benefaction; κραυγή (shout) for κράζω (shout, make {a shout}), μύκημα (roar) for μυκάομαι (roar, make {a roar}), σάλπιγξ (trumpet) for σαλπίζω (trumpet, blow {a trumpet}), κιθάρα (harp) for κιθαρίζων (playing {a harp}), ποίησις (action, deed) and ποίημα (deed, work) for ποιέω (act, do, work), and πλοῖον (boat) for πλέων (sailing {a boat}) when grammaticalizing effect, and πορνεία (sexual immorality) for πορνεύω (engage in {sexual immorality}) and πορνεύσας (engaging in {sexual immorality}) and μοιχεία (adultery) for μοιχεύων (committing {adultery}) when grammaticalizing instrumentality.[12] Suppression of the Patient receives illustration in the following examples of βοηθέω (provide {aid}) and σαλπίζω (blow {a trumpet}). The translations introduce in braces, { }, the definite referents of the suppressed required Patient complements.

A{P}B ἐβοήθησεν ἡ γῆ τῇ γυναικί (12:16)
[The earth (1/Agt)] provided (βοηθέω) {aid (2/Pat)} [for the woman (3/Ben)].

A{P} ὁ πρῶτος ἐσάλπισεν (8:7)
[The first one (1/Agt)] blew (σαλπίζω) {a trumpet (2/Pat)}.

---

[12] As the proposed translations of these Greek predicators indicate, suppression of the required Patient complement also characterizes many English verbs that grammaticalize various events: βλασφημέω (blaspheme), βοηθέω (aid), πολεμέω (battle), and κατηγορῶν (accusing) when grammaticalizing benefaction, and κράζω (shout), μυκάομαι (roar), and σαλπίζω (trumpet) when grammaticalizing effect.

Usage labels note suppression of the Patient by placing braces, { }, around the Patient entity, and Valence Descriptions place double braces, {{ }}, around the syntactic function of the Patient and note its lexical realization as {N}.

	βοηθέω (12:16) <*Ben.* A{P}B>			σαλπίζω (8:7) <*Eff.* A{P}>	
syn.	1	{{2}}	3	1	{{2}}
sem.	Agt	Pat	Ben	Agt	Pat
lex.	N	{N}	N+dat	N	{N}

b. Usage Feature: Suppression of the Instrument

When grammaticalizing the event of instrumentality with the configuration API and PI, the verb predicator ποτίζω (provide {with a cup [of something able to be drunk]}) and the adjective predicator ποταμοφόρητος (swept away {by a river}) place a definite referent directly onto the Instrument argument and suppress the Instrument complement. The verb and adjective predicators have the cognate nouns ποτήριον (cup) and ποταμός (river) that could fulfill the role of the suppressed Instrument complements. The translations introduce in braces, { }, the definite referents of the suppressed required Instrument complements. In the first example (14:8), the suppressed Instrument is able to license the Material complement (of the wine of the passion of her sexual immorality), and, in the second example (12:15), the translation introduces in double brackets, [[ ]], the contextual referent of the DNC Patient (her/the woman).

ἣ ἐκ τοῦ οἴνου τοῦ θυμοῦ τῆς πορνείας αὐτῆς πεπότικεν πάντα τὰ ἔθνη (14:8)
[Who (1/Agt)] has provided (ποτίζω) [all the nations (2/Pat)] {with a cup [of the wine of the passion of her sexual immorality] (3/Ins)}.

ποταμοφόρητον (12:15)
[[Her/the woman (1/Pat)]] swept away (ποταμοφόρητος) {by a river (2/Ins)}.

Usage labels note suppression of the Instrument by placing braces, { }, around the Instrument entity, and Valence Descriptions place double braces, {{ }}, around the syntactic function of the Instrument and note its lexical realization as {N}.

	ποτίζω (14:8) <*Ins.* AP{I}>			ποταμοφόρητος (12:15) <*Ins.* P{I}>	
syn.	1	2	{{3}}	[1]	{{2}}
sem.	Agt	Pat	Ins	Pat	Ins
lex.	N	N+acc	{N}	DNC	{N}

c. Usage Feature: Suppression of the Resultative (with Argument Promotion)

When grammaticalizing the event of modification with the configuration APR, which through the usage feature argument promotion yields usage PAR, specific verb and participle predicators place a definite referent directly onto the Resultative argument and suppress the Resultative complement. The verb and participle predicators that suppress the Resultative complement have cognate adjectives that could fulfill the role of the suppressed Resultative complement: ἔρημος (desolate) for ἐρημόω (desolate, make {desolate}) and ἠρημωμένος (desolated, made {desolate}), λευκός (white) for λευκαίνω (whiten, make {white}), πικρός (bitter) for πικραίνω (make {bitter}), and σκοτεινός (dark) for σκοτίζω (darken, make {dark}), σκοτόω (darken, make {dark}), and ἐσκοτωμένος (darkened, made {dark}).[13] Suppression of the Resultative receives illustration in the following examples of πικραίνω (make {bitter}) and ἐσκοττωμένος (made {dark}). The translations introduce in braces, { }, the referents of the suppressed required Resultative complements. In the second example (16:10), the translation introduces in double brackets, [[ ]], the contextual referent of the unrealized Agent (the fifth angel [and his action]).

AP{R}   πικρανεῖ σου τὴν κοιλίαν (10:9)
        [It (1/Agt)] makes (πικραίνω) [your stomach (2/Pat)] {bitter (3/Rst)}.

PA{R}   ἡ βασιλεία αὐτοῦ ἐσκοτωμένη (16:10)
        [His kingdom (1/Pat)] made (ἐσκοτωμένος) {dark (3/Rst)} [[by the fifth angel [and his action] (2/Agt)]].

Usage labels note suppression of the Resultative by placing braces, { }, around the Resultative entity, and Valence Descriptions place double braces, {{ }}, around the syntactic function of the Resultative and note its lexical realizations as {Adj+2} and {Adj+1}.

	πικραίνω (10:9) <Mod. AP{R}>			ἐσκοτωμένος (16:10) <Mod. PA{R}>		
syn.	1	2	{{3}}	N	[2]	{{3}}
sem.	Agt	Pat	Rst	Pat	Agt	Rst
lex.	N	N+acc	{Adj+2}	N	DNC	{Adj+1}

d. Usage Feature: Suppression of the Patient (with Argument Promotion)

All noun predicators that raise but never realize a Patient argument that is co-referential to the predicators themselves (§1.2c) are attributed with argument suppression. These noun predicators grammaticalize either usages derived directly from alternate configurations of the events of benefaction (BPB), instrumentality (BPI), and materiality (BPM) or usages derived from events through the usage feature argument promotion: benefaction (PB), communion (ComPL), and partition (ParP). The linkage of argument promotion and suppression with noun predicators receives illustration in the following examples of πληγή (wound) and πηγή (spring). The translation of the

---

[13] As the proposed translations of these Greek predicators indicate, suppression of the required Resultative complement characterizes many English predicators of modification: ἐρημόω (desolate), ἠρημωμένος (desolated), λευκαίνω (whiten), σκοτίζω (darken), σκοτόω (darken), and ἐσκοτωμένος (darkened).

first example (13:12) clarifies that, when predicators license two Benefactive complements, English typically realizes the Benefactive first (personal) complement by a possessive adjective or a noun in the possessive case ('s or s') and the Benefactive third complement by an "of" prepositional phrase. The translations introduce in braces, { }, the definite referents of the suppressed required Patient complements.

B{P}B   οὗ...ἡ πληγὴ τοῦ θανάτου αὐτοῦ (13:12)
[Whose (1/Ben)]...wound (πληγή) {wound (2/Pat)} [of his death (3/Ben)].

M{P}   τὰς πηγὰς τῶν ὑδάτων (8:10)
The springs (πηγή) [of waters (1/Mat)] {springs (2/Pat)}.

Usage labels note suppression of the Patient by placing braces, { }, around the Patient entity, and Valence Descriptions place double braces, {{ }}, around the syntactic function of the suppressed Patient and note its lexical realization as {N}.

	πληγή (13:12) <Ben. B{P}B>			πηγή (8:10) <Mat. M{P}>	
syn.	1	{{2}}	3	1	{{2}}
sem.	Ben	Pat	Ben	Mat	Pat
lex.	N+gen	{N}	N+gen	N+gen	{N}

e. Usage Feature: Suppression of the Benefactive (with Suppression of the Patient)

Two noun predicators that raise but never realize a Benefactive argument that is co-referential to the predicators are attributed with argument suppression. These predicators grammaticalize usages derived from the base (PB) and an alternate (APB) configuration of benefaction through argument promotion (BP and PAB). The first example (2:14) presents suppression of the required Benefactive complement, and the second example (6:15) presents suppression of both the required Benefactive complement and the required Patient complement. The latter is possible because the noun predicator itself is a composite of two predicators, with the first component supplying the referent for the Benefactive and the second component supplying the referent of the Patient. The translations introduce in braces, { }, the definite referents of the suppressed required complements. In the first example (2:14), the translation introduces in double brackets, [[ ]], the definite referents of the DNC Patient (foods [as opposed to other possible objects of dedication]) and the indefinite but circumscribed referent of the INC Agent (someone).

PA{B}   εἰδωλόθυτα (2:14)
[[Foods (1/Pat)]] sacrificed (εἰδωλόθυτος) [[by someone (2/Agt)]] {to idols (3/Ben)}.

{B}{P}   οἱ χιλίαρχοι (6:15)
The commanders (χιλίαρχος) {of a thousand (1/Ben)} {commanders (2/Pat)}.

The usage labels note suppression of the Benefactive in 2:14 and of both the Benefactive and the Patient in 6:15 by placing braces, { }, around these arguments, and the Valence Descriptions place double braces, {{ }}, around the syntactic function of the suppressed complements and note their lexical realizations as {N}.

	εἰδωλόθυτος (2:14)			χιλίαρχος (6:15)	
	<Ben. PA{B}>			<Ben. {B}{P}>	
syn.	[1]	(2)	{{3}}	{{1}}	{{2}}
sem.	Pat	Agt	Ben	Ben	Pat
lex.	DNC	INC	{N}	{N}	{N}

9. Applications of Usages and Usage Features

The redefinition of "usage," the specification of the features of the conceptualizations of the event associated with each usage, the generation of labels for usages derived by usage features and specified in relation to the configurations of event entities, and the incorporation of usage labels into Valence Descriptions are foundational to the following study and complete the development of the concepts and procedures required to describe all usages grammaticalized by predicators in the text of Revelation. These concepts and procedures clear the way for the development of notations that impact only specific Valence Descriptions (Chapter 4), permit the formulation of a unique description of each of the ninety-two usages that predicators grammaticalize in the text of Revelation (Chapters 5 and 6) and distinguish the text's distinctive grammatical characteristics (Chapter 7). All of the grammatical information in Valence Descriptions noted by usage features then receives restatement according to protocols (Chapter 8) into the lexicon entries for predicators (Chapter 9).

4

THE FURTHER SPECIFICATION OF VALENCE
DESCRIPTIONS

This chapter develops five further specifications for the row of lexical realizations (lex.) in Valence Descriptions and describes the manner in which the Case Frame study addresses polysemous occurrences of predicators. The first three specifications describe direct intrusions of Greek grammar that constrain the lexical realizations and interpretations of specific predicator complements. The fourth specification clarifies the manner of noting in Valence Description occurrences in which two complements with the same syntactic function, semantic function, and lexical realization redundantly realize an argument or adjunct of a predicator. The fifth specification clarifies the manner of noting in Valence Descriptions that indeclinable Greek noun phrases realize arguments and adjuncts and so do not appear with the expected syntactic case endings. The discussion of polysemous occurrences clarifies the conditions under which polysemy may arise and the manner of representing polysemous occurrences in Valence Descriptions. The concluding discussion then develops the contribution of these developments to the following study.

1. Semantic Feature: ±Animate

Greek Grammars frequently employ the distinctions, person/thing or personal/impersonal, to describe the function and interpretation of the complements of preposition and verb predicators. For example, the BDF discussion of P/παρά provides the following notes on usage: for P/παρά [+acc], "in the local sense, 'never used with persons'"; for P/παρά [+dat], "'by, near, beside' answering the question 'where?' only with persons"; and for P/παρά [+gen], "'from the side of' only with persons."[1] Again, Smyth's discussion of ἀκούω (hear) begins, "*To hear a thing* is usually ἀκούειν τι."[2] These distinctions appeal to a semantic feature in Greek grammar that characterizes

---

[1] BDF 122–124: cf. Herbert Weir Smyth, *Greek Grammar* (Cambridge, MA: Harvard University Press, 1959), 381–83; Antonius Nicholas Janneris, *An Historical Greek Grammar* (London: MacMillan, 1897), 83; and Daniel B. Wallace, *Greek Grammar Beyond the Basics: With Scripture, Subject, and Greek Word Indexes* (Grand Rapids: Zondervan, 1996), 376.
[2] Herbert Weir Smyth, *Greek Series for Colleges and Schools* (New York: American Book Company, 1906), 322; cf. BDF, 24.

entities as either animate (+animate) or inanimate (-animate).[3] In the NT, Greek grammar attributes as +animate those arguments and adjuncts that reference divine beings (God, the Holy Spirit, angels), demonic beings (demons, the devil, Satan), heavenly bodies (sun, moon), natural forces (wind, fire), and living human beings and animals.[4] All other arguments and adjuncts, including those that reference dead human beings and animals, body parts, concepts, places, and artifacts made by human beings, are -animate.

The ±animate distinction has direct implication for the lexical realizations of specific arguments and adjuncts of predicators and so for interpreting the function of the complements that realize these arguments and adjuncts. For example, verb and participle predicators that grammaticalize usages of transference most frequently raise the Goal entity as third argument. Greek grammar imposes the restriction that the Goal with these predicators can have an N+dat lexical realization only when its referent is +animate. All -animate referents of the Goal of transference, in contrast, are introduced by preposition predicators. This distinction receives illustration in the following examples of πέμπω (send) with +animate (+an) and of βάλλω (cast) with -animate (-an) referents of the Goal (Goa) complements.

+an Goa   δῶρα πέμψουσιν ἀλλήλοις, ὅτι οὗτοι οἱ δύο προφῆται ἐβασάνισαν
          τοὺς κατοικοῦντας ἐπὶ τῆς γῆς (11:10)
          [They (1/Agt)] will send (πέμπω) [gifts (2/Thm)] [to one another (3/
          Goa)] [because these two prophets tormented the ones dwelling on the
          earth (C/Cau)].

-an Goa   ἔβαλεν αὐτοὺς εἰς τὴν γῆν (12:4)
          [It (1/Agt)] cast (βάλλω) [them (2/Thm)] [to the earth (3/Goa)].

Valence Descriptions note the ±animate distinction of the referent of an argument or adjunct by placing the abbreviation "+an" or "-an" in brackets, [ ], after the lexical realization of the associated complement.

	πέμπω (11:10) <Tra. AΘ[S]G [S=A] -imp.>				βάλλω (12:4) <Tra. AΘ[S]G [S=A] -imp.>		
syn.	1	2	3	C	1	2	3
sem.	Agt	Thm	Goa	Cau	Agt	Thm	Goa
lex.	N	N+acc	N+dat [+an]	V+ὅτι	N	N+acc	P/εἰς [-an]

The ±animate semantic feature also distinguishes the use of the N+dat realization of the +animate Goal of transference from the N+dat realization of the -animate Locative of transference, as illustrated in the following occurrences of δίδωμι (give)

---

[3] An introduction to the semantic feature ±animate appears in Paul L. Danove, "Distinguishing Goal and Locative Complements of New Testament Verbs of Transference," *FN* 39–40 (2007): 51–68, and *idem*, "A Comparison of the Usage of ἀκούω and ἀκούω-Compounds in the Septuagint and New Testament," *FN* 14 (2001): 65–85.

[4] Danove, "Δίδωμι and δίδωμι-Compounds," 365–400.

4. Further Specification of Valence Description

and βεβαμμένος (dipped).[5] The translation of the second example (19:13) introduces in double brackets, [[ ]], the indefinite but circumscribes referent of the INC Agent (someone).

+an Goa   δώσω σοι τὸν στέφανον τῆς ζωῆς (2:10)
           [I (1/Agt)] will give (δίδωμι) [to you (3/Goa)] [the crown of life (2/Thm)].

−an Loc   ἱμάτιον βεβαμμένον αἵματι (19:13)
           [A garment (1/Thm)] dipped (βεβαμμένος) [[by someone (2/Agt)]] [in blood (3/Loc)].

The Valence Descriptions note the ±animate distinction of the referent of these arguments by placing the abbreviation "+an" or "−an" in brackets, [ ], after the lexical realization of the associated complement.

	δίδωμι (2:10) <Tra. AΘ[S]G [S=A] +imp.>			βεβαμμένος (19:13) <Tra. ΘA[S]G [S=A] G→L +imp.>		
syn.	1	2	3	1	(2)	3
sem.	Agt	Thm	Goa	Thm	Agt	Loc
lex.	N	N+acc	N+dat [+an]	N	INC	N+dat [−an]

Greek grammar also imposes ±animate constraints on the use of particular preposition predicators and on the syntactic case that particular preposition predicators may license. An example of the former with predicators of transference is P/πρός [+acc] which licenses Goal (Goa) complements only when the referent of its second argument is +animate (+an) and Locative (Loc) complements only when the referent of its second argument is −animate (−an), as in the following examples of πίπτω (fall) and ἀπέρχομαι (go forth). The translations present in sequence each verb predicator and its licensed preposition predicator. For both occurrences of the preposition predicators, the referents of the first argument are supplied by the governing verb.

+an Goa   ἀπῆλθα πρὸς τὸν ἄγγελον (10:9)
           [I (1/Thm)] went forth (ἀπέρχομαι) [to the angel (2/Goa)].

+an Goa   πρὸς τὸν ἄγγελον (10:9)
           [I (1/Thm)] to (πρός) [the angel (2/Goa)].

−an Loc   ὅτε εἶδον αὐτόν, ἔπεσα πρὸς τοὺς πόδας αὐτοῦ ὡς νεκρός (1:17)
           [When I saw him (C/Tem)] [I (1/Thm)] fell (πίπτω) [at his feet (2/Loc)] [like a dead [man] (C/Cmp)].

---

[5] This rare use of the N+dat [−an] Locative with predicators of transference also appears with ἐπιτίθημι (John 19:2), παραδίδωμι (Luke 20:20; 23:25), προσφέρω (John 19:29), and ὑψόω (Acts 2:33; 5:31).

–an Loc πρὸς τοὺς πόδας αὐτοῦ (1:17)
[I (1/Thm)] at (πρός) [his feet (2/Loc)].

When preposition predicators license complements with two or three possible syntactic case lexical realizations, Valence Descriptions note the ±animate notation after the syntactic case notation separated by a comma.

	ἀπέρχομαι (10:9) <Mot. Θ[S]G [S=Θ]>		πρός (10:9) <Mot. Θ[S]G [S=Θ]>	
syn.	1	2	1	2
sem.	Thm	Goa	Thm	Goa
lex.	N	P/πρός [+acc, +an]	N	N+acc [+an]

	πίπτω (1:17) <Mot. Θ[S]G [S=Θ] G→L>			C	C
syn.	1	2		C	C
sem.	Thm	Loc		Cmp	Tem
lex.	N	P/πρός [+acc, –an]		A/ὡς Adj+1	V+ὅτε

	πρός (1:17) <Mot. Θ[S]G [S=Θ] G→L>	
syn.	1	2
sem.	Thm	Loc
lex.	N	N+acc [–an]

Valence Descriptions incorporate into the row of lexical realizations notations on the ±animate distinction only when this distinction identifies a salient characteristic of the function and interpretation of particular lexical realizations of complements. Non-salient characteristics would include the introduction of [+an] after P/ὑπό which consistently licenses a +animate genitive case noun phrase complement and so requires no distinction from the –animate accusative case noun phrase complements that do not appear in the text of Revelation. Also non-salient would be to classify V+ complements as –animate, since all V+ complements are –animate.

The following table details all occurrences of noun phrase and prepositional phrase complements for which the ±animate distinction is salient. The table lists the lexical realization (Lex.) of the noun phrase (N) or preposition phrase (P/) according to its syntactic case (Case), the ±animate distinction (±An), thematic role of the complement (Role), translation (Trans.), and an illustrative example (Example).

Lex.	Case	±An.	Role	Trans.	Example
N	+dat	+an	Ben	for	Rev 14:4
N	+dat	+an	Con	---	Rev 4:10
N	+dat	+an	Exp	to	Rev 19:5
N	+dat	+an	Goa	to	Rev 14:4
N	+dat	–an	Loc	in, with	Rev 18:4
P/εἰς	+acc	–an	Ben	for	Rev 13:6

P/εἰς	+acc	−an	Goa	to, into	Rev 11:12b
P/ἐπί	+gen	+an	Loc	before	Rev 1:20
P/παρά	+gen	+an	Sou	from	Rev 2:28
P/πρός	+acc	+an	Ben	for	Rev 13:6
P/πρός	+acc	+an	Goa	to	Rev 10:9
P/πρός	+acc	−an	Loc	on, at	Rev 12:5b
P/πρός	+dat	−an	Loc	on, at	Rev 1:13

A further contribution of the semantic feature ±animate appears in the following discussion of the semantic feature ±response.

2. Semantic Feature: ±Response

In the text of Revelation, the semantic feature ±response (±resp) pertains only to the verb predicator ἀκούω (hear, listen to) and to its associated participle and complex participle predicators.[6] This semantic feature specifies whether [+resp] or not [−resp] the referent of the Experiencer (first) argument of ἀκούω, ἀκούων, and ἀκούων + εἰμί is attributed with an explicit response or reaction to what is heard. In the text of Revelation, this response appears in the following context and most frequently involves the referent of the Experiencer of ἀκούω referencing the Agent argument of a following verb predicator, as illustrated in the following [+resp] examples of ἀκούω.[7] As these examples illustrate, the response may be only potential (3:20) or commanded (10:4). What is crucial is the fact that the referent of the Experiencer of ἀκούω appears as the referent of the first argument of a verb predicator that designates a real or potential response. The translations highlight the response in bold print.

+resp ἐάν τις ἀκούσῃ τῆς φωνῆς μου καὶ ἀνοίξῃ τὴν θύραν... (3:20)
If [someone (1/Exp)] hears (ἀκούω) [my voice (2/Con)] and [he/she (1/Agt)] **opens** (ἀνοίγω) [the door (2/Pat)]...

+resp ἤκουσα φωνὴν ἐκ τοῦ οὐρανοῦ λέγουσαν· σφράγισον ἃ ἐλάλησαν αἱ ἑπτὰ βρονταί, καὶ μὴ αὐτὰ γράψῃς (10:4)
[I (1/Exp)] heard (ἀκούω) [a voice from heaven (2/Con)] saying, "[You (1/Agt)] **seal** (σφραγίζω) [the things which the seven thunders spoke (2/Pat)] and [you (1/Agt)] **do not write** (γράφω) [them (2/Pat)]!"

---

[6] An introduction to the semantic feature ±response appears in Paul L. Danove, "The Grammatical Uses of ἀκούω in the Septuagint & the New Testament," *Forum: A Journal of the Foundations and Facets of Western Culture* (New Series) 2, no. 2 (1999): 239–61.
[7] Although the responding action typically appears in the immediately following clause, it may appear several clauses into the following context. In such cases, the appeal to semantic considerations in contexts of extension greater than a clause or verb phrase is similar to that required for the analysis of anaphora; cf. Fillmore, "Zero Anaphora," 95–107.

Frequently, however, no response [−resp] of the referent of the Experiencer appears in the immediately following context, as illustrated in the following occurrences in which the description of hearing continues without a noted response (14:2a) or the narration switches to another topic without noting a response (6:3-4a).

−resp ἤκουσα φωνὴν ἐκ τοῦ οὐρανοῦ ὡς φωνὴν ὑδάτων πολλῶν καὶ ὡς φωνὴν βροντῆς μεγάλης, καὶ ἡ φωνὴ ἣν ἤκουσα... (14:2a)
[I (1/Exp)] heard (ἀκούω) [a voice from heaven like a sound of many waters and like a sound of great thunder (2/Con)] and the voice which I heard...

−resp ὅτε ἤνοιξεν τὴν σφραγῖδα τὴν δευτέραν, ἤκουσα τοῦ δευτέρου ζῴου λέγοντος· ἔρχου. καὶ ἐξῆλθεν ἄλλος ἵππος πυρρός (6:3-4a)
[When he opened the second seal (C/Tem)], [I (1/Exp)] heard (ἀκούω) [the second living creature (2/Con)] saying, "Come!" And another horse came out, a red one.

The semantic features ±response and ±animate permit the formulation of a descriptive rule that accounts for the fact that ἀκούω and its associated participle and complex participle predicators appear with two possible lexical realizations of their noun phrase Content (second) argument. As illustrated in the previous examples, these possible noun phrase realizations are N+acc (10:4; 14:2a) and N+gen (3:20; 6:3-4a). In the following descriptive rule, "ἀκούω" references both the verb predicator and its associated participle and complex participle predicators. The descriptive rule is hierarchical, so that an occurrence accounted for by a previous subgrouping is eliminated from consideration in all following subgroupings.[8]

Except for occasions of the attraction of noun phrase realizations of the second (Content) complement to the case of their antecedent, the noun phrase lexical realization of the second complement of ἀκούω is[9]

1. N+acc when ἀκούω grammaticalizes usage EC C→T
2. N+gen when ἀκούω grammaticalizes usage EC and the referent of the Content (second) argument is +animate
3. N+acc when ἀκούω grammaticalizes usage EC and the referent of the Experiencer (first) argument is −response
4. N+acc or N+gen when ἀκούω grammaticalizes usage EC and the referent of the Experiencer (first) argument is +response.

---

[8] The original proposal of this descriptive rule using ±impact for the semantic feature ±response appears in Paul L. Danove, "The Theory of Construction Grammar and its Application to New Testament Greek," in *Biblical Greek Language and Linguistics: Open Questions in Current Research* (ed. Stanley E. Porter and Don Carson; JSNTSup 80; Sheffield: Sheffield Academic Press, 1993), 8–36.

[9] Discussion of the attraction of the relative pronoun to the syntactic case of its antecedent receives consideration in BDF, 153–54, and Smyth, *Greek Grammar*, 536 (§1457).

The following non-hierarchical statement of this descriptive rule highlights the semantic features ±response and ±animate.

Except for occasions of the attraction of relative pronoun realizations of the second (Content) complement to the case of their antecedent, the noun phrase lexical realization of the second complement of ἀκούω is

1. N+acc with usage EC C→T (E [±resp], T [±an])
2. N+gen with usage EC (E [±resp], C [+an])
3. N+acc with usage EC (E [-resp], C [-an])
4. N+acc or N+gen with usage EC (E [+resp], C [-an]).

Valence Descriptions incorporate into the row of lexical realizations notations on the semantic features ±response and ±animate for all occurrences of ἀκούω and its associated predicators with noun phrase realizations of the Content complement, as in the four previously considered occurrences.

	ἀκούω (3:20) <Exp. EC>		ἀκούω (10:4) <Exp. EC>	
syn.	1	2	1	2
sem.	Exp	Con	Exp	Con
lex.	N [+resp]	N+gen [-an]	N [+resp]	N+acc [-an]

	ἀκούω (14:2a) <Exp. EC>		ἀκούω (6:3-4a) <Exp. EC>			
syn.	1	2	1	2	|	C
sem.	Exp	Con	Exp	Con	|	Tem
lex.	N [-resp]	N+acc [-an]	N [-resp]	N+gen [+an]	|	V+ὅτε

The previously stated descriptive rule accounts in a straightforward way for the noun phrase lexical realizations of the second argument for all but two of the 380 occurrences of ἀκούω and its associated predicators in the NT.[10] The two apparent exceptions appear in the text of Revelation and receive consideration in the discussion of novel lexical realizations of required complements (§7.2h).

3. Licensing Alignment: Λέγω Melding

In the text of Revelation, λέγω melding permits the participle predicator λέγων (saying) when grammaticalizing the event of communication with the configuration

---

[10] As a consequence, the proposed descriptive rule provides a more rigorous explanation of the syntactic case of noun phrase second complements than the classical rules cited and/or adapted in Smyth, *Greek Series*, 322; BDF, 95, Maximilian Zerwick, *Biblical Greek: Illustrated by Examples* (trans. Joseph Smith; 2nd edn.; Rome: Scripti Pontificium Institutum Biblicum, 1985), 24; Nigel Turner, *A Greek Grammar of the New Testament*. Vol. III, *Syntax* (Edinburgh: T. & T. Clark, 1963), 233–34; R. Kühner and B. Gerth, *Ausführliche Grammatik der Griechische Sprache*. Teil II (Munich: Max Hueber, 1963), 357–59; Smyth, *Greek Grammar*, 324; and Stanley E. Porter, *Idioms of the Greek New Testament* (Sheffield: Sheffield Academic Press, 1992), 97; cf. A. T. Robertson, *A Short Grammar of the New Testament* (New York: Hodder & Stoughton, 1908), 448–49.

ACE to intrude between both a preceding verb or active participle predicator grammaticalizing the event of communication with configurations ACE or ACEB and the preceding verb or participle predicator's second (Content) required complement or second (Content) and third (Experiencer) required complements.[11]

In λέγω melding, a predicator grammaticalizing the event of communication and a following λέγων join to license the same Content complement. The Content complement always is a quotation realized by a maximal verb phrase (V+quo). Λέγω melding is restricted to verb phrases in which (1) a predicator of communication (ACE) is followed by λέγων, (2) the predicators are not coordinated by a conjunction, and (3) λέγων realizes the Content complement.[12]

Λέγω melding imposes the added restriction that, among melded predicators with the same lexical realization for required Experiencer complements, only one of the predicators may realize this complement. Since λέγων realizes its +animate Experiencer complements by N+dat in the text of Revelation, when λέγω melding links λέγων and the preceding predicator that realizes its +animate Experiencer complement by N+dat, the preceding predicator and λέγων jointly realize at most one N+dat [+an] Experiencer complement.

This and following discussions reference λέγω melding by the abbreviation, "LM" in brackets, [ ], after the citation of the initial predicator. Since the second predicator in λέγω melding in the text of Revelation always is the participle λέγων, the notation [LM] has the interpretation [λέγω melding with λέγων as second predicator]. Λέγω melding receives illustration in the following examples of λαλέω (speak) and φωνέω (call). The translations introduce in double brackets, [[ ]], the contextual referents of the DNC Experiencer (me) in 17:1 and of the DNC Experiencer (the one having the sharp sickle) in 14:18.

ἐλάλησεν μετ' ἐμοῦ λέγων· δεῦρο (17:1 [LM])
[He (1/Agt)] spoke (λαλέω) [with me (3/Exp)] saying (λέγων) [[to me (3/Exp)]] ["Come..." (2/Con)].

ἐφώνησεν φωνῇ μεγάλῃ τῷ ἔχοντι τὸ δρέπανον τὸ ὀξὺ λέγων, πέμψον σου τὸ δρέπανον τὸ ὀξὺ... (14:18 [LM])
[He (1/Agt)] called (φωνέω) [with a loud voice (C/Ins)] [to the one having the sharp sickle (3/Exp)] saying (λέγων) [[to the one having the sharp sickle (3/Exp)]] ["Send your sharp sickle..." (2/Con)].

Valence Descriptions place the notation [LM] within the parentheses, ( ), surrounding the citation of the preceding predicator and attribute the Content complement only to λέγων. There is no special notation for the definite null Content complement of the preceding predicator.

---

[11] This and following discussions summarize, adapt, and develop elements of the presentation in Paul L. Danove, "Λέγω Melding in the Septuagint and New Testament," *FN* 16 (2003): 19–31, and *idem*, "A Reconsideration of Λέγω Melding in the New Testament," *FN* 27–28 (2015–16): 92–108.

[12] For a general discussion of λέγων, εἰπών, ἀποκριθείς and other participles of verbs of speaking and their relation to coordination, see BDF 216–17.

	λαλέω (17:1 [LM]) <Cmm. ACE>			λέγων (17:1) <Cmm. ACE>		
syn.	1	[2]	3	1	2	[3]
sem.	Agt	Con	Exp	Agt	Con	Exp
lex.	N	DNC	P/μετά [+gen]	N	V+quo	DNC

	φωνέω (14:18 [LM]) <Cmm. ACE>					λέγων (14:18) <Cmm. ACE>		
syn.	1	[2]	3	|	C	1	2	[3]
sem.	Agt	Con	Exp	|	Ins	Agt	Con	Exp
lex.	N	DNC	N+dat [+an]	|	N+dat	N	V+quo	DNC

4. Redundant Complements

The text of Revelation presents examples of the grammaticalization of redundant complements, that is, two complements with identical referents and semantic functions. In most cases, a redundant personal pronoun reprises the referent of a previously introduced noun phrase, as in the following examples of δίδωμι (give) and ἔχω (have). The translations highlight this phenomenon by placing both the initial noun phrase and the redundant personal pronoun in bold print. In the translation of the first example (7:2), English grammar avoids raising the complex subject complement (to harm the sea and the land) by extraposing the semantically empty "it" in subject position. The translation of the second example (2:17a) introduces in double brackets, [[ ]], the indefinite but circumscribed referent of the INC Agent (someone). The third example (12:6) clarifies that a redundant adverb also may reprise a previously introduced adverb.

οἷς ἐδόθη αὐτοῖς ἀδικῆσαι τὴν γῆν καὶ τὴν θάλασσαν (7:2)
[**To whom** (3/Goa)] it was given (δίδωμι) [**to them** (3/Goa)] [[by someone (1/Agt)]] [to harm the land and the sea (2/Occ)].

τῷ νικῶντι δώσω αὐτῷ τοῦ μάννατοῦ κεκρυμμένου (2:17a)
[**To the one conquering** (3/Goa)] [I (1/Agt)] will give (δίδωμι) [**to him/her** (3/Goa)] [some of the hidden manna (2/Thm)].

ὅπου ἔχει ἐκεῖ τόπον ἡτοιμασμένον ἀπὸ τοῦ θεοῦ (12:6)
[**Where** (C/Loc)] [she (1/Ben)] has (ἔχω) [**there** (C/Loc)] [a place prepared by God (2/Pat)].

Valence Descriptions indicate redundant personal pronouns that have the same lexical realization and redundant adverbs by a notation that places "red.," an abbreviation for "redundant," in brackets, [red.], into the lexical realization row. Since the redundant personal pronouns recorded in this way have the same syntactic, semantic, and lexical description as their initial co-referential noun phrases, this information need not be repeated, and the notation [red.] appears immediately after the lexical realization of the initial co-referential complement. Adverbs, in contrast, consistently have different lexical realizations. As a consequence, both adverbs receive representation in

Valence Descriptions, and the second, that is, the redundant adverb, has the notation [red.] immediately after its lexical realization. As previously discussed (§1.5c), Case Frame analysis uses the passivization construction to transform the passivized verb predicator in the first example (7:2) to its non-passivized form and analyzes the verb accordingly.

	δίδωμι (7:2) <Del. AO[S]G [S=A]>			δίδωμι (2:17a) <Tra. AΘ[S]G [S=A] +imp.>	
syn.	1	2	3	1	2	3
sem.	Agt	Occ	Goa	Agt	Thm	Goa
lex.	N	V-i3	N+dat [+an] [red.]	N	N+gen	N+dat [+an] [red.]

	ἔχω (12:6) <Ben. BP>			
syn.	1	2	C	C
sem.	Ben	Pat	Loc	Loc
lex.	N	N+acc	A/ὅπου	A/ἐκεῖ [red.]

5. Indeclinable Greek Noun Phrases

The text of Revelation presents two Greek noun phrases that do not decline to mark syntactic case.[13] The first, ὁ ὢν καὶ ὁ ἦν καὶ ὁ ἐρχόμενος (the one being and the one that was and the one coming, 1:4), is a title for God, and the second, Ἀντιπᾶς (Antipas, 2:13), is the name of a member of the community in Pergamum (2:12). The apparent lexical realization of the title in 1:4 and the name in 2:13 is N+nom. The noun phrase in 1:4 is deemed indeclinable because its licensing preposition predicator ἀπό (from) is coordinated by καί (and) with two other occurrences of ἀπό that license N+gen complements, and elsewhere in the text of Revelation this predicator consistently realizes its Source argument by N+gen.[14]

χάρις...καὶ εἰρήνη ἀπὸ ὁ ὢν καὶ ὁ ἦν καὶ ὁ ἐρχόμενος... (1:4)
[Grace...and peace (1/Thm)] from (ἀπό) [the one being and the one that was and the one coming (2/Sou)]....

The analysis also deems the name Antipas in 2:13 indeclinable because Benefactive adjuncts of ἡμέρα (day) elsewhere in the text of Revelation consistently receive realization by N+gen, whereas the form Ἀντιπᾶς appears to be N+nom.[15]

ταῖς ἡμέραις Ἀντιπᾶς (2:13)
The days (ἡμέρα) [of Antipas (C/Ben)].

---

[13] This discussion does not develop notations for non-Greek noun phrases (e.g., Μιχαήλ) that have not been regularized into the Greek declensional system (as have Ἰησοῦς and Ἰωάννης) because such noun phrases typically are indeclinable and so do not exhibit endings that may cause confusion.
[14] N+gen Source complements of ἀπό: 1:4b, 5; 3:12; 6:16a, 16b; 7:2; 9:6; 12:14; 14:3, 4, 20; 16:12, 17; 18:10, 14a, 14b, 15b, 17; 19:5; 20:11; 21:2, 10; 22:19a.
[15] N+gen Benefactive complements of ἡμέρα: 2:13; 6:17; 10:7; 11:6; 16:14.

The presence of these indeclinable noun phrases with what appear to be nominative syntactic case endings could cause confusion. As a consequence, the Valence Descriptions for their licensing predicators retain the expected syntactic case of their complements, N+gen, in the lexical realization row and introduce after it and in brackets, [ ], the notation "ind. N+nom," which specifies that the following indeclinable noun phrase complements appear with nominative syntactic case endings.

	ἀπό (1:4a) <Mot. ΘS(G) [S=Θ]>			ἡμέρα (2:13) <Spec.>	
syn.	1	2	0		C
sem.	Thm	Sou	—		Ben
lex.	N	[ind. N+nom]			N+gen [ind. N+nom]

6. Polysemous Occurrences

The previous discussion (§3.4) considered the possibility of polysemy with verb and participle predicators that grammaticalize the event of transference with passive forms. Polysemy also is possible for noun predicators that grammaticalize the event of communication with the configuration BCE (§2.5) because they realize both their agentive Benefactive first required complement and their Content second required complement by N+gen. As a consequence, polysemy can arise whenever such a noun predicator realizes only one N+gen complement and the context provides guidance for interpreting this complement as either an agentive Benefactive or a Content or the context provides insufficient guidance for determining one or the other interpretation.

Examples of contextual information that guides a dual interpretation appear in 1:1 with ἀποκάλυψις Ἰησοῦ Χριστοῦ (revelation of Jesus Christ) and in 1:2 with μαρτυρίαν Ἰησοῦ Χριστοῦ (testimony of Jesus Christ). In 1:1, the statement that God gave the revelation to Jesus to show God's servants what must happen soon casts Jesus as the one showing or revealing the revelation and recommends an agentive Benefactive interpretation for "of Jesus Christ"; whereas the following narration places greater emphasis on revealing information about Jesus and recommends a Content interpretation for "of Jesus Christ."[16] Again, in 1:2 the following context first identifies Jesus as a faithful witness (1:5), recommending an agentive Benefactive interpretation for "of Jesus Christ" and then moves immediately to commentary that concerns Jesus' action of making John's addressees into a kingdom of priests for God (1:6), recommending a Content interpretation for "of Jesus Christ." The dual interpretations receive illustration in the following translations with first the agentive Benefactive and then the Content interpretation. The translations follow the English practice of realizing the agentive Benefactive by a possessive case noun phrase ('s or s') and the Content by an "of" prepositional phrase. The translations of 1:1 introduce in double brackets, [[ ]], the contextual referent of the DNC Content (what will happen soon) with the first interpretation and of the DNC Agentive Benefactive (John) with the second

---

[16] See Louis A. Brighton, *Revelation* (Concordia Commentary; St. Louis, MO: Concordia, 1999), 33, and John Paul Heil, *The Book of Revelation: Worship for Life in the Spirit of Prophecy* (Cascade Books; Eugene, OR: Wipf & Stock, 2014), 18.

interpretation. The translations of 1:2 introduce the contextual referent of the DNC Content (what pertains to the revelation, cf. 1:1) with the first interpretation and of the DNC agentive Benefactive (John) with the second interpretation. For both examples, the referent of the DNC Experiencer is "John's addressees."

ἀποκάλυψις Ἰησοῦ Χριστοῦ (1:1)
[Jesus Christ's (1/Ben)] revelation (ἀποκάλυψις) [[of what will happen soon (2/Con)]] [[to John's addressees (3/Exp)]].
[[John's (1/Ben)]] revelation (ἀποκάλυψις) [of Jesus Christ (2/Con)] [[to John's addressees (3/Exp)]].

τὴν μαρτυρίαν Ἰησοῦ Χριστοῦ (1:2)
[Jesus Christ's (1/Ben)] testimony (μαρτυρία) [[of what pertains to the revelation (2/Con)]] [[to John's addressees [[3/Exp)]].
[[John's (1/Ben)]] testimony (μαρτυρία) [of Jesus Christ (2/Con)] [[to John's addressees (3/Exp)]].

The examples of ἀποκάλυψις and μαρτυρία with this two-fold interpretation receive description by composite Valence Descriptions that have at the top a single specification of the predicator, its location in parentheses, ( ), and usage label in chevrons, < >, and the rows of syntactic functions, semantic functions, and lexical realizations for each interpretation separated by double vertical lines, ||.

ἀποκάλυψις (1:1) <Cmm. BCE>

syn.	1	[2]	[3]				[1]	2	[3]
sem.	Ben	Con	Exp				Ben	Con	Exp
lex.	N+gen	DNC	DNC				DNC	N+gen	DNC

μαρτυρία (1:2) <Cmm. BCE>

syn.	1	[2]	[3]				[1]	2	[3]
sem.	Ben	Con	Exp				Ben	Con	Exp
lex.	N+gen	DNC	DNC				DNC	N+gen	DNC

An example of insufficient information to determine the function of the N+gen complement appears in 2:13 with ὁ μάρτυς μου ὁ πιστός μου (my witness, my faithful one). This admits to dual interpretation because the context does not specify whether the first person pronoun references Jesus as the agentive Benefactive who appointed Antipas as witness or as the Content of the testimony given by Antipas. The same polysemy attends the other occurrences of μάρτυς with a single N+gen complement realized in the text of Revelation. As a consequence, this and other occurrences of μάρτυς require description by two linked Valence Descriptions. With the former interpretation, the referent of the DNC Content apparently would be something along the lines of "the word of God and the testimony of Jesus" (1:2, 9); with the latter interpretation, the referent of the DNC agentive Benefactive is "the church in Pergamum" (2:12), and with both interpretations, the referent of the DNC Experiencer includes those who dwell where Satan's throne is (2:1). The translations introduce in double brackets, [[ ]], the referents of the DNC complements with both translations and follow the English practice of realizing the agentive Benefactive personal pronoun by a possessive adjective and the Content by an "of" prepositional phrase.

ὁ μάρτυς μου ὁ πιστός μου (2:13)
[My (1/Ben)] witness (μάρτυς) [[of the word of God and the testimony of Jesus (2/Con)]] [[to those where Satan's throne is (3/Exp)]].
[[The church in Pergamum's (1/Agt)]] witness (μάρτυς) [of Jesus (2/Con)] [[to those where Satan's throne is (3/Exp)]].

The composite Valence Description for this and other occurrences of μάρτυς similarly has at the top a single specification of the predicator, its location in parentheses, ( ), and usage label in chevrons, < >, and the rows of syntactic functions, semantic functions, and lexical realizations for each interpretation separated by double vertical lines, ||.

	μάρτυς (2:13) <Cmm. BCE>					
syn.	1	[2]	[3]	||	[1]	2	[3]
sem.	Ben	Con	Exp	||	Ben	Con	Exp
lex.	N+gen	DNC	DNC	||	DNC	N+gen	DNC

7. Applications of the Further Specifications

The discussions of the semantic features ±animate and ±response, λέγω melding, redundant complements, and indeclinable Greek noun phrases complete the development for notations in the lexical realization row of Valence Descriptions, and the concluding discussion describes the method of linking the Valence Descriptions of predicators that admit to polysemous interpretation. These developments provide all of the descriptive notations and procedures required to identify, describe, and represent the licensing properties of predicators that grammaticalize the ninety-two usages in the text of Revelation (Chapters 5 and 6), distinguish the text's distinctive grammatical characteristics (Chapter 7), and re-present all of the grammatical information in the Valence Descriptions of all predicator occurrences according to protocols (Chapter 8) into lexicon entries (Chapter 9).

Part II

USAGES AND PREDICATORS

5

USAGES OF EVENTS WITH A THEME (Θ), EXPERIENCER (E), OR OCCURRENCE (O)

Predicators in the text of Revelation grammaticalize forty-seven usages of the eleven previously identified events (§2.2) that contain entities associated with the Theme, Experiencer, or Occurrence thematic roles. The following presentations introduce each event with a specification of its entities and, if applicable, a discussion of the event features that account for its various configurations and of the usage features that distinguish the conceptualizations being grammaticalized.

The discussion of each usage specifies its usage label, identifies the categories of predicators that grammaticalize the usage, incorporates lists of the predicators in each category, proposes a capitalized descriptive designation for the usage, describes the usage features of its conceptualization, provides illustrative examples of the usage with each observed category of predicator, and generates the Valence Description for each illustrative example. Beginning with this chapter, the usage labels in Valence Descriptions introduce at the end and in brackets, [ ], the sectional heading of the discussion in which the usage receives specification and illustration.

When only one predicator grammaticalizes a particular usage, it is listed in the text of the discussion of that usage. In all other cases, the predicators are listed according to their category in the footnotes. These listings introduce a numeric (1, 2, ...) or an alphanumeric (1a, 1b, ...) specification in parentheses, ( ), after predicators that grammaticalize more than one usage in the text of Revelation. These specifications are linked to the subdivisions of their associated lexicon entries (Chapter 9) which distinguish the events grammaticalized under separate numeric headings (1, 2, ...) and the different usages of the same event under alphanumeric sub-headings (1a, 1b, ...). To avoid ambiguity, this and following discussions avoid the use of alphanumeric listings ending in the letter "l" so that a specification ending in "k" is followed by a specification ending in "m." The following discussion reintroduces illustrative examples from previous discussions (most frequently from Chapter 3) whenever only one predicator in a single occurrence grammaticalizes the usage or the occurrence most clearly exemplifies the licensing properties of its class of predicator, typically by realizing all or most required complements. For ease of interpretation, the translations of the illustrative examples introduce in double brackets, [[ ]], the retrievable contextual referents of definite null complements (DNCs) and the indefinite but circumscribed referents of indefinite null complements (INCs).

1. Usages of Transference (Tra.)

The event of transference (*Tra.*) contains four entities that are associated with the Agent (A), Theme (Θ), Source (S), and Goal (G) thematic roles. This base configuration of transference (AΘSG) does not admit to alternate formulation by event features. The differing conceptualizations of the base configuration of transference grammaticalized by predicators require description by six usage features: perspective (§3.2a), subject affectedness (§3.2b), focus (§3.2c), impetus (§3.2d), functionality of the Goal (§3.2e), and, in the case of passive participle predicators, argument promotion (§3.2f). These usage features distinguish the conceptualizations of the thirteen usages of the event of transference in the text of Revelation. The following discussion describes and provides illustrative examples of each of the thirteen observed usages of transference by the categories of predicators.

a. Usage AΘ[S]G [S=A] +Imp.

Only verb predicators grammaticalize the Primary Active Usage of Transference to a Goal with a Continuous Impetus, AΘ[S]G [S=A] +imp.[1] The conceptualization of transference with this usage has the Agent and Source initially coincident/proximate (S=A), an unaffected Agent (act.), a focus on both segments of the event (pri.), a continuous impetus (+imp.), no change in the functionality of the Goal (G=G), and no argument promotion. The predicators raise the Agent entity as first argument, the Theme entity as second argument, and the Goal entity as third argument.

ἀπήνεγκέν με εἰς ἔρημον ἐν πνεύματι (17:3)
[He (1/Agt)] brought [me (2/Thm)] away (ἀποφέρω) [in spirit (C/Man)] [to a deserted place (3/Goa)].

ἔδωκεν αὐτῷ ὁ δράκων τὴν δύναμιν αὐτοῦ καὶ τὸν θρόνον αὐτοῦ καὶ ἐξουσίαν μεγάλην (13:2)
[The dragon (1/Agt)] gave (δίδωμι) [to it (3/Goa)] [his power and his throne and great authority (2/Thm)].

	ἀποφέρω (17:3) <*Tra.* AΘ[S]G [S=A] +imp. [§5.1a]>				δίδωμι (13:2) <*Tra.* AΘ[S]G [S=A] +imp. [§5.1a]>		
syn.	1	2	3	C	1	2	3
sem.	Agt	Thm	Goa	Man	Agt	Thm	Goa
lex.	N	N+acc	P/εἰς [–an]	P/ἐν	N	N+acc	N+dat [+an]

b. Usage AΘ[S]G [S=A] G→L +Imp.

Only verb predicators grammaticalize the Primary Active Usage of Transference Terminating in a Locative with a Continuous Impetus, AΘ[S]G [S=A] G→L +imp.[2]

---

[1] Usage AΘ[S]G [S=A] +imp.: verbs, ἀποδίδωμι (1), ἀποφέρω, ἁρπάζω (1a), δίδωμι (1), ἐκχέω (1), κρύπτω (1a), ὁδηγέω, συνάγω (1), συνάγω (2), τίθημι (1a), φέρω.
[2] Usage AΘ[S]G [S=A] G→L +imp.: verbs, ἁρπάζω (1b), ἐπιτίθημι, τίθημι (1b).

5. Events with Theme (Θ), Experiencer (E), or Occurrence (O)

The conceptualization of transference with this usage has the Agent and Source initially coincident/proximate (S=A), an unaffected Agent (act.), a focus on both segments of the event (pri.), a continuous impetus (+imp.), a change in the functionality of the Goal to a Locative (G→L), and no argument promotion. The predicators raise the Agent entity as first argument, the Theme entity as second argument, and the Locative entity as third argument.

ἔθηκεν τὸν πόδα αὐτοῦ τὸν δεξιὸν ἐπὶ τῆς θαλάσσης (10:2)
[He (1/Agt)] placed (τίθημι) [his right foot (2/Thm)] [on the sea (3/Loc)].

ἐάν τις ἐπιθῇ ἐπ' αὐτά, ἐπιθήσει ὁ θεὸς ἐπ' αὐτὸν τὰς πληγὰς τὰς γεγραμμένας ἐν τῷ βιβλίῳ τούτῳ (22:18b)
[If anyone adds on these (C/Cnd)] [God (1/Agt)] will add (ἐπιτίθημι) [on him (3/Loc)] [the plagues written in this book (2/Thm)].

	τίθημι (10:2) <Tra. AΘ[S]G [S=A] G→L +imp. [§5.1b]>			ἐπιτίθημι (22:18b) <Tra. AΘ[S]G [S=A] G→L +imp. [§5.1b]>				
syn.	1	2	3	1	2	3		C
sem.	Agt	Thm	Loc	Agt	Thm	Loc		Cnd
lex.	N	N+acc	P/ἐπί [+gen]	N	N+acc	P/ἐπί [+acc]		V+ ἐάν

c. Usage AΘS[G] [G=A] +Imp.

Only verb predicators grammaticalize the Primary Active Usage of Transference from a Source with a Continuous Impetus, AΘS[G] [G=A] +imp.[3] The conceptualization of transference with this usage has the Agent and Goal initially coincident/co-directional (G=A), an unaffected Agent (act.), a focus on both segments of the event (pri.), a continuous impetus (+imp.), no change in the functionality of the Goal (G=G), and no argument promotion. The predicators raise the Agent entity as first argument, the Theme entity as second argument, and the Source entity as third argument. The translations introduce in double brackets, [[ ]], the contextual referent of the DNC Agent (the one sitting on the red horse) in 6:4 and of the DNC Source (the earth) in 14:19.

λαβεῖν τὴν εἰρήνην ἐκ τῆς γῆς (6:4)
[[The one sitting in the red horse (1/Agt)]] to take (λαμβάνω) [peace (2/Thm)] [from the earth (3/Sou)].

ἐτρύγησεν τὴν ἄμπελον τῆς γῆς (14:19)
[He (1/Agt)] gathered (τρυγάω) [the vineyard of the earth (2/Thm)] [[from the earth (3/Sou)]].

---

[3] Usage AΘS[G] [G=A] +imp.: verbs, ἀφαιρέω, λαμβάνω (1), τρυγάω.

	λαμβάνω (6:4) <Tra.			τρυγάω (14:19) <Tra.		
	AΘS[G] [G=A] +imp. [§5.1c]>			AΘS[G] [G=A] +imp. [§5.1c]>		
syn.	1	2	3	1	2	[3]
sem.	Agt	Thm	Sou	Agt	Thm	Sou
lex.	N	N+acc	P/ἐκ	N	N+acc	DNC

d. Usage AΘS(G) S=A +Imp.

Only verb predicators grammaticalize the Secondary Active Usage of Transference from a Source with a Continuous Impetus, AΘS(G) S=A +imp.[4] The conceptualization of transference with this usage has the Agent and Source initially coincident/proximate (S=A), an unaffected Agent (act.), a focus only on the segment of the event containing the Agent at the initiation of transference (sec.), a continuous impetus (+imp.), an irretrievable Goal, and no argument promotion. The predicators raise the Agent entity as first argument, the Theme entity as second argument, and the Source entity as third argument.

κινήσω τὴν λυχνίαν σου ἐκ τοῦ τόπου αὐτῆς, ἐὰν μὴ μετανοήσῃς (2:5)
[I (1/Agt)] will move (κινέω) [your lampstand (2/Thm)] [from its place (3/Sou)] [if you do not repent (C/Cnd)].

κρύψατε ἡμᾶς ἀπὸ προσώπου τοῦ καθημένου ἐπὶ τοῦ θρόνου καὶ ἀπὸ τῆς ὀργῆς τοῦ ἀρνίου, ὅτι ἦλθεν ἡ ἡμέρα ἡ μεγάλη τῆς ὀργῆς αὐτῶν (6:16-17)
[You (1/Agt)] hide (κρύπτω) [us (2/Thm)] [from the face of the one sitting on the throne and from the wrath of the lamb (3/Sou)] [because the great day of their wrath came (C/Cau)].

	κινέω (2:5) <Tra.				κρύπτω (6:16-17) <Tra.			
	AΘS(G) S=A +imp. [§5.1d]>				AΘS(G) S=A +imp. [§5.1d]>			
syn.	1	2	3	C	1	2	3	C
sem.	Agt	Thm	Sou	Cnd	Agt	Thm	Sou	Cau
lex.	N	N+acc	P/ἐκ	V+ἐάν	N	N+acc	P/ἀπό	V+ὅτι

e. Usage A[Θ][S]G [Θ=A] [S=A] Pass. +Imp.

Only verb predicator συνάγω (2) (gather) in a single occurrence (19:17-18) admits to interpretation as grammaticalizing the Primary Passive Usage of Transference to a Goal with a Continuous Impetus, A[Θ][S]G [Θ=A] [S=A] pass. +imp. The conceptualization of transference with this usage has the Agent and Source initially coincident/proximate (S=A), an affected Agent insofar as the Agent and Theme are co-referential (Θ=A) and the Agent acts on itself (pass.), a focus on both segments of the event (pri.), a continuous impetus (+imp.), no change in the functionality of the Goal (G=G), and no argument promotion. The predicator raises the Agent entity as first argument, the

---

[4] Usage AΘS(G) S=A +imp.: verbs, κινέω, κρύπτω (1b).

5. Events with Theme (Θ), Experiencer (E), or Occurrence (O)   99

co-referential (to the Agent) Theme entity as the never-realized second argument, and the Goal entity as third argument. The example with this usage also admits to interpretation with passivized Usage AΘ[S]G [S=A] +imp. (§5.1a) and Usage (A)Θ(S)G G=Θ pass. (§5.2f) as illustrated in the three-fold translation of 19:17-18. The translations introduce in double brackets, [[ ]], the contextual referents of the never-realized co-referential Theme (yourself) with usage A[Θ][S]G [Θ=A] [S=A] pass. +imp. and the indefinite but circumscribed referent of the INC Agent (someone) with Usage AΘ[S]G [S=A] +imp.

συνάχθητε εἰς τὸ δεῖπνον τὸ μέγα τοῦ θεοῦ ἵνα φάγητε... (19:17-18)
A[Θ][S]G [Θ=A] [S=A] pass. +imp. [You (1/Agt)] gather (συνάγω) [[yourselves (2/Thm)]] [to the great dinner of God (3/Goa)] [so that you may eat... (C/Pur)].
AΘ[S]G [S=A] +imp. [You (1/Thm)] be gathered (συνάγω) [[by someone (2/Agt)]] [to the great dinner of God (3/Goa)] [so that you may eat... (C/Pur)].
(A)Θ(S)G G=Θ pass. [You (1/Thm)] come together (συνάγω) [to the great dinner of God (2/Goa)] [so that you may eat... (C/Pur)].

	συνάγω (19:17-18) <Tra. A[Θ][S]G [Θ=A] [S=A] pass. +imp. [§5.1e]>			
syn.	1	[[2]]	3	C
sem.	Agt	Thm	Goa	Pur
lex.	N	[N]	P/εἰς [–an]	V+ἵνα

	συνάγω (19:17-18) <Tra. AΘ[S]G [S=A] +imp [§5.1a]>			συνάγω (19:17-18) <Mot. (A)Θ(S)G G=Θ pass. [§5.2f]>		
syn.	1	2	3	C	1	2	C
sem.	Agt	Thm	Goa	Pur	Thm	Goa	Pur
lex.	N	N+acc	P/εἰς [–an]	V+ἵνα	N	P/εἰς [–an]	V+ἵνα

f. Usage ΘA[S]G [S=A] +Imp.

Only the participle predicator κεκρυμμένος (hidden) grammaticalizes the Passivized Primary Active Usage of Transference to a Goal with a Continuous Impetus, ΘA[S]G [S=A] +imp. The conceptualization of transference with this usage has promotion of the Theme (ΘASG), the Agent and Source initially coincident/proximate (S=A), an affected Theme insofar as it is acted on by the Agent (pass.), a focus on both segments of the event (pri.), a continuous impetus (+imp.), and no change in the functionality of the Goal (G=G). The predicator raises the Theme entity as (promoted) first argument, the Agent entity as second argument, and the Goal entity as third argument. The translation introduces in double brackets, [[ ]], the indefinite but circumscribed referents of the INC Agent (someone) and the INC Goal (somewhere).

τοῦ μάννα τοῦ κεκρυμμένου (2:17)
[The manna (1/Thm)] hidden (κεκρυμμένος) [[by someone (2/Agt)]] [[somewhere (3/Goa)]].

	κεκρυμμένος (2:17) <Tra. ΘA[S]G [S=A] +imp. [§5.1f]>		
syn.	1	(2)	(3)
sem.	Thm	Agt	Goa
lex.	N	INC	INC

g. Usage ΘA[S]G [S=A] G→L +Imp.

Only the participle predicator βεβαμμένος (dipped) grammaticalizes the Passivized Primary Active Usage of Transference Terminating in a Locative with a Continuous Impetus, ΘA[S]G [S=A] G→L +imp. The conceptualization of transference with this usage has promotion of the Theme (ΘASG), the Agent and Source initially coincident/proximate (S=A), an affected Theme insofar as it is acted on by the Agent (pass.), a focus on both segments of the event (pri.), a continuous impetus (+imp.), and a change in the functionality of the Goal to a Locative (G→L). The predicator raises the Theme entity as (promoted) first argument, the Agent entity as second argument, and the Locative entity as third argument. The translation introduces in double brackets, [[ ]], the indefinite but circumscribed referent of the INC Agent (someone).

ἱμάτιον βεβαμμένον αἵματι (19:13)
[A garment (1/Thm)] dipped (βεβαμμένος) [[by someone (2/Agt)]] [in blood (3/Loc)].

	βεβαμμένος (19:13) <Tra. ΘA[S]G [S=A] G→L +imp. [§5.1g]>		
syn.	1	(2)	3
sem.	Thm	Agt	Loc
lex.	N	INC	N+dat [–an]

h. Usage ΘA(S)G G=A +imp.

Only the participle predicator κεκλημένος (summoned) grammaticalizes the Passivized Secondary Active Usage of Transference to a Goal with a Continuous Impetus, ΘA(S)G G=A +imp. The conceptualization of transference with this usage has promotion of the Theme (ΘASG), the Agent and Goal initially coincident/co-directional (G=A), an affected Theme insofar as it is acted on by the Agent (pass.), a focus only on the segment of the event containing the Agent at the initiation of transference (sec.), a continuous impetus (+imp.), and no change in the functionality of the Goal (G=G). The predicator raises the Theme entity as (promoted) first argument, the Agent entity as second argument, and the Goal entity as third argument. The translation introduces in double brackets, [[ ]], the indefinite but circumscribed referent of the INC Agent (someone).

οἱ εἰς τὸ δεῖπνον τοῦ γάμου τοῦ ἀρνίου κεκλημένοι (19:9)
[The ones (1/Thm)] summoned (κεκλημένος) [[by someone (2/Agt))]] [to the dinner of the marriage of the lamb (3/Goa)].

	κεκλημένος (19:9) <Tra. ΘA(S)G G=A +imp. [§5.1h]>		
syn.	1	(2)	3
sem.	Thm	Agt	Goa
lex.	N	INC	P/εἰς [-an]

i. Usage AΘ[S]G [S=A] –Imp.

Verb and participle predicators grammaticalize the Primary Active Usage of Transference to a Goal with a Discrete Impetus, AΘ[S]G [S=A] –imp.[5] The conceptualization of transference with this usage has the Agent and Source initially coincident/proximate (S=A), an unaffected Agent (act.), a focus on both segments of the event (pri.), a discrete impetus (imp.), no change in the functionality of the Goal (G=G), and no argument promotion. The predicators raise the Agent entity as first argument, the Theme entity as second argument, and the Goal entity as third argument. The translation of 1:1 introduces in double brackets, [[ ]], the contextual referent of the DNC Theme (revelation).

verb βάλλω αὐτὴν εἰς κλίνην (2:22)
[I (1/Agt)] am casting (βάλλω) [her (2/Thm)] [onto a bed (3/Goa)].

part. ἀποστείλας διὰ τοῦ ἀγγέλου αὐτοῦ τῷ δούλῳ αὐτοῦ Ἰωάννῃ (1:1)
[He (1/Agt)] sending (ἀποστείλας) [[the revelation (2/Thm)]] [through his angel (C/Ins)] [to his slave John (3/Goa)].

	βάλλω (2:22) <Tra. AΘ[S]G [S=A] –imp. [§5.1i]>		
syn.	1	2	3
sem.	Agt	Thm	Goa
lex.	N	N+acc	P/εἰς [-an]

	ἀποστείλας (1:1) <Tra. AΘ[S]G [S=A] –imp. [§5.1i]>				
syn.	1	[2]	3	|	C
sem.	Agt	Thm	Goa	|	Ins
lex.	N	DNC	N+dat [+an]	|	P/διά [+gen]

j. Usage AΘ[S]G [S=A] G→L –Imp.

Only the verb predicator ἵστημι (1) (stand, station) in two occurrences (8:3; 12:18) grammaticalizes the Primary Active Usage of Transference Terminating in a Locative with a Discrete Impetus, AΘ[S]G [S=A] G→L –imp. The conceptualization of

---

[5] Usage AΘ[S]G [S=A] –imp.: verbs, βάλλω, ἐκβάλλω, πέμπω (1); and participle, ἀποστείλας (1).

transference with this usage has the Agent and Source initially coincident/proximate (S=A), an unaffected Agent (act.), a focus on both segments of the event (pri.), a discrete impetus (-imp.), a change in the functionality of the Goal to a Locative (G→L), and no argument promotion. The predicator raises the Agent entity as first argument, the Theme entity as second argument, and the Locative entity as third argument. Both examples with this usage also admit to interpretation with Usage A[Θ][S]G [Θ=A] [S=A] G→L pass. -imp. (§5.1k) and Usage (A)Θ(S)G G=Θ G→L pass. (§5.2g) as illustrated in the three-fold interpretation of 12:18. The translations introduce in double brackets, [[ ]], the indefinite but circumscribed referent of the INC Agent (someone) with passivized Usage AΘ[S]G [S=A] G→L -imp. and the contextual referent of the never-realized co-referential Theme with Usage A[Θ][S]G [Θ=A] [S=A] G→L pass. -imp. (§5.1k).

ἐστάθη ἐπὶ τὴν ἄμμον τῆς θαλάσσης (12:18)
AΘ[S]G [S=A] G→L -imp. [§5.1j] [It (2/Thm)] was stationed (ἵστημι) [[by someone (1/Agt)]] [on the sand of the sea (3/Loc)].
A[Θ][S]G [Θ=A] [S=A] G→L pass. -imp. [§5.1k] [It (1/Agt)] stationed (ἵστημι) [[itself (2/Thm)]] [on the sand of the sea (3/Loc)].
(A)Θ(S)G G=Θ G→L pass. [§5.2g] [It (1/Thm)] stood (ἵστημι) [on the sand of the sea (2/Loc)].

	ἵστημι (12:18) <Tra. AΘ[S]G [S=A] G→L -imp. [§5.1j]			
syn.	1	2	3	||
sem.	Agt	Thm	Loc	||
lex.	N	N+acc	P/ἐπί [+acc]	||

	ἵστημι (12:18) <Tra. A[Θ][S]G [Θ=A] [S=A] G→L pass. -imp. [§5.1k]			ἵστημι (12:18) <Mot. (A)Θ(S)G G=Θ G→L pass. [§5.2g]>	
syn.	1	[[2]]	3	1	2
sem.	Agt	Thm	Loc	Thm	Loc
lex.	N	[N]	P/ἐπί [+acc]	N	P/ἐπί [+acc]

k. Usage A[Θ][S]G [Θ=A] [S=A] G→L Pass. -Imp.

Only the verb predicator ἵστημι (stand, station) in two occurrences (8:3; 12:18) admits to interpretation as grammaticalizing the Primary Passive Usage of Transference Terminating in a Locative with a Discrete Impetus, A[Θ][S]G [Θ=A] [S=A] G→L pass. -imp. The conceptualization of transference with this usage has the Agent and Source initially coincident/proximate (S=A), an affected Agent insofar as the Agent and Theme are co-referential and the Agent acts on itself (pass.), a focus on both segments of the event (pri.), a discrete impetus (-imp.), a change in the functionality of the Goal to a Locative (G→L), and no argument promotion. The predicator raises the Agent entity as first argument, the co-referential (to the Agent) Theme entity as the never-realized second argument, and the Locative entity as third argument. Both examples of ἵστημι with this usage (8:3; 12:18) also admit to interpretation with passivized Usage AΘ[S]G [S=A] G→L –imp. [§5.1j] and with Usage (A)Θ(S)G G=Θ G→L pass. [§6.2g]. The translation and Valence Description of ἵστημι with this usage receive illustration in the discussion of §5.ij.[6]

m. Usage AΘS(G) S=A –Imp.

Only the verb predicator ἐμέω (spit [out]) grammaticalizes the Secondary Active Usage of Transference from a Source with a Discrete Impetus, AΘS(G) –imp. The conceptualization of transference with this usage has the Agent and Source initially coincident/proximate (S=A), an unaffected Agent (act.), a focus only on the segment containing the Agent at the initiation of transference (sec.), a discrete impetus (–imp.), no change in the functionality of the Goal (G=G), and no argument promotion. The predicator raises the Agent entity as first argument, the Theme entity as second argument, and the Source entity as third argument. The translation introduces in double brackets, [[ ]], the contextual referent of the Agent (I).

σε ἐμέσαι ἐκ τοῦ στόματός μου (3:16)
[[I (1/Agt)]] to spit (ἐμέω) [you (2/Thm)] [out of my mouth (3/Sou)].

	ἐμέω (3:16) <Tra. AΘS(G) S=A –imp. [§5.1m]>		
syn.	1	2	3
sem.	Agt	Thm	Sou
lex.	N	N+acc	P/ἐκ

n. Usage ΘA[S]G [S=A] –Imp.

Only the participle predicator ἀπεσταλμένος (sent) grammaticalizes the Passivized Primary Active Usage of Transference to a Goal with a Discrete Impetus, ΘA[S]G [S=A] –imp. The conceptualization of transference with this usage has promotion of the Theme (ΘASG), the Agent and Source initially coincident/proximate (S=A), an affected Theme insofar as it is acted on by the Agent (pass.), a focus on both segments of the event (pri.), a discrete impetus (–imp.), and no change in the functionality of the Goal (G=G). The predicator raises the Theme entity as (promoted) first argument, the Agent entity as second argument, and the Goal entity as third argument. The translation introduces in double brackets, [[ ]], the contextual referent of the DNC Agent (God). In this phrase, "sent" retrieves its gender from the preceding masculine relative pronoun, οἵ (which).

---

[6] The occurrence in 8:3 is coordinated by καί (and) with ἔρχομαι (come) which grammaticalizes a usage of motion, recommending the interpretation with the usage of motion.

τὰ [ἑπτὰ] πνεύματα τοῦ θεοῦ ἀπεσταλμένοι εἰς πᾶσαν τὴν γῆν (5:6)
[The [seven] spirits of God (1/Thm)] sent (ἀπεσταλμένος) [[by God (2/Agt)]] [into all the earth (3/Goa)].

	ἀπεσταλμένος (5:6) <*Tra.* ΘA[S]G [S=A] –imp. [§5.1n]>		
syn.	1	[2]	3
sem.	Thm	Agt	Goa
lex.	N	DNC	P/εἰς [–an]

2. Usages of Motion (Mot.)

The event of motion (*Mot.*) contains three entities that are associated with the Theme (Θ), Source (S), and Goal (G) thematic roles. This base configuration of motion (ΘSG) does not admit to alternate formulation by event features. The differing conceptualizations of the base configuration of motion grammaticalized by predicators that do not also grammaticalize transference require description by four usage features: perspective (§3.3a), focus (§3.3b), functionality of the Goal (§3.3c), and, with three predicators, argument promotion (§3.3d). The differing conceptualizations of the base configuration of transference grammaticalized by predicators that also grammaticalize motion require description by four usage features: linked perspective and subject affectedness (§3.4a), focus (§3.4b), and functionality of the Goal (§3.4c). These usage features distinguish the conceptualizations of the eight usages of the event of motion in the text of Revelation. The following discussion describes and provides illustrative examples of each of the eight observed usages of motion by the categories of predicators.

a. Usage Θ[S]G [S=Θ]

Verb, participle, complex noun, and preposition predicators grammaticalize the Primary Usage of Motion to a Goal, Θ[S]G [S=Θ].[7] The conceptualization of motion with this usage has the Theme and Source initially coincident/proximate (S=Θ), a focus on both segments of the event (pri.), no change in the functionality of the Goal (G=G), and no argument promotion. The predicators raise the Theme entity as first argument and the Goal entity as second argument. The translation of 3:20 introduces in double brackets, [[ ]], the contextual referent of the unrealized Theme (I) which is retrieved from the licensing verb predicator.

verb ἐκ τοῦ καπνοῦ ἐξῆλθον ἀκρίδες εἰς τὴν γῆν (9:3)
[Locusts (1/Thm)] came forth (ἐξέρχομαι) [out of the smoke (C/Sou)] [onto the land (2/Goa)].

---

[7] Usage Θ[S]G [S=Θ]: verbs, ἀκολουθέω, ἀναβαίνω (1a), ἀπέρχομαι (1a), διώκω, εἰσέρχομαι (1a), ἐκπορεύομαι (1a), ἐξέρχομαι (1a), ἐπιπίπτω, ἐπιστρέφω, ἔρχομαι (1a), ζητέω, ἥκω, καταβαίνω (1a), περιπατέω, πέτομαι, πίπτω (1b), ὑπάγω (1a), φεύγω (1a); participles, ἐπιστρέψας, ἐρχόμενος (1a), πεπτωκώς (1b), περιπατῶν, πετόμενος, τρέχων; complex predicators, ὁ ἀκολουθῶν + [εἰμί], ὁ ἐρχόμενος + εἰμί (1a); and prepositions, εἰς (1), ἐνώπιον (2a), ἐπί (2c), ὀπίσω (2), πρός (1a).

5. *Events with Theme (Θ), Experiencer (E), or Occurrence (O)* 105

part.   ἁρμάτων ἵππων πολλῶν τρεχόντων εἰς πόλεμον (9:9)
        [Many chariots of horses (1/Thm)] running (τρέχων) [into battle (2/Goa)].

cp-n   οὗτοι οἱ ἀκολουθοῦντες τῷ ἀρνίῳ ὅπου ἂν ὑπάγῃ (14:4)
        [These (1/Thm)] [are] the ones following (ὁ ἀκολουθῶν + [εἰμί]) [the lamb (2/Goa)] [wherever he goes (C/Loc)].

prep.   πρὸς αὐτὸν (3:20)
        [[I (1/Thm)]] to (πρός) [him (2/Goa)].

	ἐξέρχομαι (9:3) <Mot. Θ[S]G [S=Θ] [§5.2a]>			τρέχων (9:9) <Mot. Θ[S]G [S=Θ] [§5.2a]>	
syn.	1	2	C	1	2
sem.	Thm	Goa	Sou	Thm	Goa
lex.	N	P/εἰς [-an]	P/ἐκ	N	P/εἰς [-an]

	ὁ ἀκολουθῶν + [εἰμί] (14:4) <Mot. Θ[S]G [S=Θ] [§5.2a]>			πρός (3:20) <Mot. Θ[S]G [S=Θ] [§5.2a]>	
syn.	1	2	C	1	2
sem.	Thm	Goa	Loc	Thm	Goa
lex.	N	N+dat	V+ὅπου ἂν	N	N+acc [+an]

b. Usage Θ[S]G [S=Θ] G→L

Verb and preposition predicators grammaticalize the Primary Usage of Motion Terminating in a Locative, Θ[S]G [S=Θ] G→L.[8] The conceptualization of motion with this usage has the Theme and Source initially coincident/proximate (S=Θ), a focus on both segments of the event (pri.), a change in the functionality of the Goal to a Locative (G→L), and no argument promotion. The predicators raise the Theme entity as first argument and the Locative entity as second argument. As the first example (19:10) illustrates, if the English verb of motion that best translates the Greek verb of motion natively grammaticalizes motion terminating in a Locative as its primary usage, the translation is straightforward. As the second example (3:10a) illustrates, if the English verb of motion that best translates the Greek verb of motion natively grammaticalizes motion to a Goal as its primary usage, straightforward translation is impossible. To address this, the translation of the second verbal example introduces "terminating" before the Locative complement (§3.3c). The introduction of "terminating" into the translation permits the use of the same translation of verb and participle predicators with usages of motion to a Goal and terminating in a Locative. In the second example (3:10a), the licensing predicator ἔρχομαι (come) of the preposition (ἐπί [+gen]) imposes the requirement for the introduction of "terminating."

---

[8]   Usage Θ[S]G [S=Θ] G→L: verbs, γίνομαι (3), εἰσέρχομαι (1b), ἔρχομαι (1b), ἵστημι (2), καθίζω, πίπτω (1a), πνέω; and prepositions, ἔμπροσθεν (1), ἐν (5), ἐνώπιον (2b), ἐπί (2a), ἐπί (2b), πρός (1b).

verb   ἔπεσα ἔμπροσθεν τῶν ποδῶν αὐτοῦ προσκυνῆσαι αὐτῷ (19:10)
[I (1/Thm)] fell (πίπτω) [before his feet (2/Loc)] [in order to worship him (C/Pur)].

prep. τῆς ὥρας τοῦ πειρασμοῦ...ἐπὶ τῆς οἰκουμένης ὅλης (3:10a)
[The hour of testing (1/Thm)]...terminating on (ἐπί) [the whole world (2/Loc)].

	πίπτω (19:10) <Mot. Θ[S]G [S=Θ] G→L [§5.2b]>			ἐπί (3:10a) <Mot. Θ[S]G [S=Θ] G→L [§5.2b]>	
syn.	1	2	C	1	2
sem.	Thm	Loc	Pur	Thm	Loc
lex.	N	P/ἔμπροσθεν	V-i1	N	N+gen

c. Usage ΘS(G) S=Θ

Verb, participle, complex preposition, and preposition predicators grammaticalize the Secondary Usage of Motion from a Source, ΘS(G) S=Θ.[9] The conceptualization of motion with this usage has the Theme and Source initially coincident/proximate (S=Θ), a focus only on the segment of the event containing the Theme at the initiation of motion (sec.), an irretrievable Goal, and no argument promotion. The predicators raise the Theme entity as first argument and the Source entity as second argument. For clarity of presentation, the analysis in the translation of 16:13a ignores the contribution of the two occurrences of the conjunction predicator καί (and).

verb   ἡ ὀπώρα σου τῆς ἐπιθυμίας τῆς ψυχῆς ἀπῆλθεν ἀπὸ σοῦ (18:14)
[The fruit of your life's desire (1/Thm)] went forth (ἀπέρχομαι) [from you (2/Sou)].

part.   ἄλλον ἄγγελον ἰσχυρὸν καταβαίνοντα ἐκ τοῦ οὐρανοῦ (10:1)
[Another mighty angel (1/Thm)] coming down (καταβαίνων) [from heaven (2/Sou)].

cp-prep ἐκ τοῦ στόματος τοῦ δράκοντος καί...πνεύματα τρία ἀκάθαρτα ὡς βάτραχοι (16:13a)
[Three unclean spirits like frogs (1/Thm)] were out of (ἐκ + [εἰμί]) [the mouth of the dragon and... (2/Sou)].

prep.   παρ' ἐμοῦ χρυσίον πεπυρωμένον ἐκ πυρὸς (3:18)
[Gold burned by fire (1/Thm)] from (παρά) [me (2/Sou)].

[9] Usage ΘS(G) S=Θ: verbs, ἀναβαίνω (1b), ἀπέρχομαι (1b), ἐκπορεύομαι (1b), ἐξέρχομαι (1b), πίπτω (1c), φεύγω (1b); participles, ἀναβαίνων (1b), ἐκπορευόμενος (1b), ἐξελθών (1b), καταβαίνων (1b); complex predicator, ἐκ + εἰμί (1); and prepositions, ἀπό (1), ἐκ (1), παρά (1).

5. Events with Theme (Θ), Experiencer (E), or Occurrence (O)

	ἀπέρχομαι (18:14) <Mot. ΘS(G) S=Θ [§5.2c]>		καταβαίνων (10:1) <Mot. ΘS(G) S=Θ [§5.2c]>	
syn.	1	2	1	2
sem.	Thm	Sou	Thm	Sou
lex.	N	P/ἀπό	N	P/ἐκ

	ἐκ + [εἰμί] (16:13a) <Mot. ΘS(G) S=Θ [§5.2c]>		παρά (3:18) <Mot. ΘS(G) S=Θ [§5.2c]>	
syn.	1	2	1	2
sem.	Thm	Sou	Thm	Sou
lex.	N	P/ἐκ	N	N+gen [+an]

d. Usage Θ[S](G) [S=Θ]

Only verb predicators grammaticalize the Tertiary Usage of Motion from a Source, Θ[S](G) [S=Θ].[10] The conceptualization of motion with this usage has the Theme and Source initially strictly coincident (S=Θ), a focus only on initial moment of motion (ter.), an irretrievable Goal, and no argument promotion. The predicators raise the Theme entity as first argument and the strictly coincident Source entity as the never-realized second argument. The translations introduce in double brackets, [[ ]], the referent of the strictly coincident Source (from where you are). As the following examples illustrate, this usage appears only in commands in the text of Revelation.

ἔγειρε (11:1)
[You (1/Thm)] rise (ἐγείρω) [[from where you are (2/Sou)]]!

ὑπάγετε (16:1)
[You (1/Thm)] go (ὑπάγω) [[from where you are (2/Sou)]]!

	ἐγείρω (11:1) <Mot. Θ[S](G) [S=Θ] [§5.2d]>		ὑπάγω (16:1) <Mot. Θ[S](G) [S=Θ] [§5.2d]>	
syn.	1	[[2]]	1	[[2]]
sem.	Thm	Sou	Thm	Sou
lex.	N	[N]	N	[N]

e. Usage GΘS S=Θ/(A)GΘS S=Θ

Verb and participle predicators grammaticalize the Primary Usage of Receptive Motion to a Goal, GΘS S=Θ/(A)GΘS S=Θ.[11] As this usage label indicates, this usage occurs both with native predicators of motion, GΘS S=Θ, and with native predicators

---

[10] Usage Θ[S](G) [S=Θ]: verbs, ἐγείρω, ὑπάγω (1b).
[11] Usage GΘS S=Θ/(A)GΘS S=Θ: verbs, κληρονομέω/λαμβάνω (2); participles, ---/λαβών (2), λαμβάνων (2). The change in perspective for λαμβάνω with the usage of transference, G=Θ, and with this usage of motion, S=Θ, is a function of Greek grammar which imposes on predicators that grammaticalize both transference and motion the restriction that, when grammaticalizing motion,

of transference that also grammaticalize motion, (A)GΘS S=Θ. This convergence results from the fact that the loss of the Agent of transference leaves the exact entities of the event of motion. The conceptualization of receptive motion with this usage has promotion of the Goal (GΘS/(A)GΘS), the Theme and Source initially coincident/ proximate (S=Θ), a focus on both segments of the event (pri.), and no change in the functionality of the Goal (G=G). The predicators raise the Goal entity as (promoted) first argument, the Theme entity as second argument, and the Source entity as third argument. The translations introduce in double brackets, [[ ]], the contextual referent of the DNC Source (the one sitting on the throne) in 21:7 and of the DNC Theme (white stone) and DNC Source (the one having the two-edged sharp sword) in 2:17.

verb ὁ νικῶν κληρονομήσει ταῦτα (21:7)
[The one conquering (1/Goa)] will inherit (κληρονομέω) [these things (2/Thm)] [[from the one sitting on the throne (3/Sou)]].

part. ὁ λαμβάνων (2:17)
[The one (1/Goa)] receiving (λαμβάνων) [[the white stone (2/Thm)]] [[from the one having the two-edged sharp sword (3/Sou)]].

	κληρονομέω (21:7) <Mot. GΘS S=Θ [§5.1e]>			λαμβάνων (2:17) <Mot. (A)GΘS S=Θ [§5.1e]>		
syn.	1	2	[3]	1	[2]	[3]
sem.	Goa	Thm	Sou	Goa	Thm	Sou
lex.	N	N+acc	DNC	N	DNC	DNC

f. Usage (A)Θ(S)G G=Θ Pass.

Only the verb predicator συνάγω (2) (come together) in a single occurrence (19:17-18) admits to interpretation as grammaticalizing the Secondary Passive Usage of Motion to a Goal, (A)Θ(S)G G=Θ pass. The conceptualization of motion with this usage has the Theme and Goal coincident at the termination of motion (G=Θ), an affected Theme insofar as its motion ceases at the Goal (pass.), a focus only on the segment containing the Theme at the termination of motion (sec.), no change in the functionality of the Goal (G=G), an irretrievable Agent and Source, and no argument promotion. The predicator raises the Theme entity as first argument and the Goal entity as second argument. When admitting to interpretation with this usage, the verb predicator also admits to interpretation with the passivized Primary Active Usage of Transference to a Goal with a Continuous Impetus, AΘ[S]G [S=A] +imp. (§5.1a), and with the Primary Passive Usage of Transference to a Goal with a Continuous Impetus, A[Θ][S]G [Θ=A] [S=A] pass. +imp. (§5.1e). The translation and Valence Description of συνάγω with this usage receive illustration in the discussion of §5.1e.

---

the predicators use active base forms with the perspective S=Θ and passive base forms with the perspective G=Θ: cf. Danove, *Verbs of Transference*, 85.

g. Usage (A)Θ(S)G G=Θ G→L Pass.

Only the verb predicator ἵστημι (1) (stand) in two occurrences (8:3; 12:18) admits to interpretation as grammaticalizing the Secondary Passive Usage of Motion Terminating in a Locative, (A)Θ(S)G G=Θ G→L pass. The conceptualization of motion with this usage has the Theme and Goal coincident at the termination of motion (G=Θ), an affected Theme insofar as its motion ceases at the Goal (pass.), a focus only on the segment containing the Theme at the termination of motion (sec.), a change in the functionality of the Goal to a Locative (G→L), an irretrievable Agent and Source, and no argument promotion. The predicator raises the Theme entity as first argument and the Locative entity as second argument. When admitting to interpretation with this usage, the verb predicator also admits to interpretation with the passivized Primary Active Usage of Transference Terminating in a Locative with a Discrete Impetus, AΘ[S]G [S=A] G→L –imp. (§5.1j), and with the Primary Passive Usage of Transference Terminating in a Locative with a Discrete Impetus, A[Θ][S]G [Θ=A] [S=A] G→L pass. –imp. (§5.1k). The translation and Valence Description for ἵστημι with this usage receive illustration in the discussion of §5.1j.

h. Usage (A)Θ(S)[G] [G=Θ] [G→L] Pass.

Verb and participle predicators grammaticalize the Tertiary Passive Usage of State, (A)Θ(S)[G] [G=Θ] [G→L] pass.[12] The conceptualization of motion with this usage has the Theme and Goal strictly coincident (G=Θ) at the termination of motion, an affected Theme insofar as its motion ceases at the Goal (pass.), a focus only on the terminal moment of motion (ter.), a change in the functionality of the Goal to a Locative, (G→L), and an irretrievable Agent and Source.[13] The predicators raise the Theme entity as first argument and the strictly coincident Locative entity as the never-realized second argument. The translations introduce in double brackets, [[ ]], the referents of the strictly coincident and never-realized Locatives (where he is/at the locale where his motion ceases) in 6:17 and (where they are/at the locale where their motion ceased) in 19:19.

    verb   τίς...σταθῆναι; (6:17)
              [Who (1/Thm)]...to stand (ἵστημι) [[where he is/at the locale where his motion ceases (2/Loc)]]?

---

[12] Usage (A)Θ(S)[G] [G→L] [S=Θ] pass.: verb, ἵστημι (3); and participle, συνηγμένος (3). The rationale for interpreting the Usage of State as a grammaticalization of the event of motion appears in Talmy, "Lexicalization Patterns," 60-61, and Goddard, *Semantic Analysis*, 197–98.

[13] As previously discussed (§3.4c), the predicator occurrences assigned to this usage do not admit to further (polysemous) interpretation with a passivized form of the Primary Active Usage of Transference Terminating in a Locative with a Discrete Impetus, AΘ[S]G [S=A] G→L –imp. (§5.1j), or a form of the Primary Passive Usage of Transference Terminating in a Locative with a Discrete Impetus, A[Θ][S]G [Θ=A] [S=A] G→L pass. –imp. (§5.1k), because the latter usages of transference require that unrealized Locative complements have a definite referent that is retrievable from the context and this is not possible in these occurrences.

part. τὸ θηρίον τοὺς βασιλεῖς τῆς γῆς καὶ τὰ στρατεύματα αὐτῶν συνηγμένα ποιῆσαι τὸν πόλεμον μετὰ τοῦ καθημένου ἐπὶ τοῦ ἵππου καὶ μετὰ τοῦ στρατεύματος αὐτοῦ (19:19)
[The beast and kings of the earth and their armies (1/Thm)] having come together (συνηγμένος) [[where they are/at the locale where their motion ceased (2/Loc)]] [to make war against the one sitting on the horse and against his army (C/Pur)].

	ἵστημι (6:17) <Mot. (A)Θ(S)[G] [G=Θ] [G→L] pass. [§5.2h]>		συνηγμένος (19:19) <Mot. (A)Θ(S)[G] [G=Θ] [G→L] pass. [§5.2h]>		
syn.	1	[[2]]	1	[[2]]	C
sem.	Thm	Loc	Thm	Loc	Pur
lex.	N	[N]	N	[N]	V-i1

3. Usages of Location (Loc.)

The event of Location (*Loc.*) contains two entities that are associated with the Theme (Θ) and Locative (L) thematic roles. The base configuration of the event (ΘL) does not admit to alternate formulation by event features. The differing conceptualizations of the base configuration of Location grammaticalized by predicators in the text of Revelation require description only by the usage feature focus (§3.5). The following discussion describes and provides illustrative examples of each of the two observed usages of location by the categories of predicators.

a. Usage ΘL

Verb, participle, complex preposition, and preposition predicators grammaticalize the Primary Usage of Location, ΘL.[14] The conceptualization of location with this usage has a focus on the Theme and Locative which are proximate but not strictly coincident or coterminous. The predicators realize both the Theme and Locative as complements whenever the context does not permit retrieval of a definite referent for the Locative and raise the Theme entity as first argument and the Locative entity as second argument.

verb θρόνος ἔκειτο ἐν τῷ οὐρανῷ (4:2)
[A throne (1/Thm)] lay (κεῖμαι) [in heaven (2/Loc)].

part. τοὺς ἐν τῷ οὐρανῷ σκηνοῦντας (13:6)
[The ones (1/Thm)] dwelling (σκηνῶν) [in heaven (2/Loc)].

[14] Usage ΘL: verbs, ἵστημι (4), κάθημαι, κατοικέω, κεῖμαι, μένω, σκηνόω; participles, ἑστηκώς (4), ἑστώς (4), καθήμενος, κατοικῶν, σκηνῶν; complex predicators, ἀπό + [εἰμί] (5), ἐν + [εἰμί] (1), ἐν μέσῳ + [εἰμί], ἐνώπιον + [εἰμί], ἐπί + [εἰμί] (1a), ἐπί + [εἰμί] (1c), ἑστώς + [εἰμί] (4), καθήμενος + [εἰμί], κυκλόθεν + [εἰμί], κύκλῳ + [εἰμί], μετά + [εἰμί], ὑποκάτω + [εἰμί]; and prepositions, ἀνὰ μέσον, ἀπό (5), ἄχρι (1), ἐν (1), ἐν μέσῳ, ἐνώπιον (1), ἔξωθεν (1), ἐπάνω, ἐπί (1a), ἐπί (1b), ἐπί (1c), κυκλόθεν (1), κύκλῳ, μετά (**1**), ὀπίσω (1), παρά (2), περί, πρός (2), ὑποκάτω.

5. Events with Theme (Θ), Experiencer (E), or Occurrence (O)   111

cp-prep ἡ σκηνὴ τοῦ θεοῦ μετὰ τῶν ἀνθρώπων (21:3)
[The dwelling of God (1/Thm)] is with (μετά + [εἰμί]) [human beings (2/Loc)].

prep.   περὶ τὰ στήθη ζώνας χρυσᾶς (15:6)
[Golden belts (1/Thm) around (περί) [their chests (2/Loc)].

	κεῖμαι (4:2) <Loc. ΘL [§5.3a]>		σκηνῶν (13:6) <Loc. ΘL [§5.3a]	
syn.	1	2	1	2
sem.	Thm	Loc	Thm	Loc
lex.	N	P/ἐν	N	P/ἐν

	μετά + [εἰμί] (21:3) <Loc. ΘL [§5.3a]>		περί (15:6) <Loc. ΘL [§5.3a]>	
syn.	1	2	1	2
sem.	Thm	Loc	Thm	Loc
lex.	N	N+gen	N	N+acc

b. Usage Θ[L] [L=Θ]

Only complex adverb predicators grammaticalize the Secondary Usage of Location, Θ[L] [L=Θ].[15] The conceptualization of location with this usage has a focus on the Theme and the strictly coincident/coterminous Locative. The predicators raise the Theme entity as first argument and the Locative entity as the never-realized second argument. The never-realized Locative retrieves its referent from the strictly coincident/coterminous Theme. The translations introduce in double brackets, [[ ]], the referents of the Locatives (outside) in 22:15 and (here) in 13:18.

ἔξω οἱ κύνες καὶ οἱ φάρμακοι καὶ οἱ πόρνοι καὶ... (22:15)
Outside are (ἔξω + [εἰμί]) [the dogs and the potion makers... (1/Thm)] [[outside (2/Loc)]].

ὧδε ἡ σοφία ἐστίν (13:18)
Here is (ὧδε + εἰμί) [wisdom (1/Thm)] [[here (2/Loc)]].

	ἔξω + [εἰμί] (22:15) <Loc. Θ[L] [L=Θ] [§5.6c]>		ὧδε + εἰμί (13:18) <Loc. Θ[L] [L=Θ] [§5.6c]>	
syn.	1	[[2]]	1	[[2]]
sem.	Thm	Loc	Thm	Loc
lex.	N	[N]	N	[N]

---

[15] Usage Θ[L] [L=Θ]: complex predicators, ἔξω + [εἰμί], ὅπου + [εἰμί], ὧδε + [εἰμί].

4. Usages of Communication (Cmm.)

The event of communication (*Cmm.*) contains three entities that are associated with the Agent, Content, and Experiencer thematic roles. This base configuration of the event (ACE) admits to alternate formulation by two event features: incorporation (§2.3) and reinterpretation (§2.4). Entity incorporation expands the configuration of the event through the addition of a Benefactive in fourth position (ACEB). Entity reinterpretation highlights the agentive Benefactive function of the first entity (BCE). The differing conceptualizations of the base and alternate configurations of communication grammaticalized by predicators require description by five usage features: secondary emphasis (§3.6a), suppression of the Content (§3.6b), functionality of the Content (§3.6c), argument promotion (§3.6d), and subject affectedness (§3.6e). These usage features distinguish the conceptualizations of the nine usages of the event of communication in the text of Revelation. The following discussion describes and provides illustrative examples of each of the nine observed usages of communication by the various categories of predicators. The translations of noun predicators follow the English practice of realizing the agentive Benefactive by a possessive adjective or a noun in the possessive case ('s or s') and the Content by an "of" prepositional phrase.

a. Usage ACE

Verb, participle, and complex participle predicators grammaticalize the Usage of Communication with an Emphasized Content, ACE.[16] The conceptualization of communication with this usage has secondary emphasis on the Content, no suppression of the Content, no change in the functionality of the Content (C=C), no argument promotion, and an unaffected Agent (act.). The predicators raise the Agent entity as first argument, the Content entity as second argument, and the Experiencer entity as third argument. The translation of 4:1b introduces in double brackets, [[ ]], the contextual referent of the DNC Experiencer (me/John).

verb   μαρτυρῶ ἐγὼ παντὶ τῷ ἀκούοντι τοὺς λόγους τῆς προφητείας τοῦ βιβλίου τούτου· ἐάν τις ἐπιθῇ ἐπ᾽ αὐτά, ἐπιθήσει ὁ θεὸς ἐπ᾽ αὐτὸν τὰς πληγὰς τὰς γεγραμμένας ἐν τῷ βιβλίῳ τούτῳ... (22:18)
[I (1/Agt)] testify (μαρτυρέω) [to everyone hearing the words of the prophecy of this book (3/Exp)] ["If anyone adds on them, God will add on him the plagues written in this book..." (2/Con)].

part.   τοῦ ἀγγέλου τοῦ δεικνύοντός μοι ταῦτα (22:8)
[The angel (1/Agt)] showing (δεικνύων) [these things (2/Con)] [to me (3/Exp)].

---

[16] Usage ACE: verbs, γράφω (1), δείκνυμι, διδάσκω (1a), εὐαγγελίζω (1a), κράζω (1), λαλέω, λέγω (1), μαρτυρέω, ὀμνύω, ὁμολογέω, σημαίνω, συμβουλεύω, φανερόω, φωνέω; participles, ἀναγινώσκων, δεικνύων, κηρύσσων, κράζων, λαλῶν, λέγων (1), μαρτυρῶν; and complex predicator, λέγων + [εἰμί].

cp-part ἡ φωνὴ ἡ πρώτη ἣν ἤκουσα ὡς σάλπιγγος λαλούσης μετ' ἐμοῦ λέγων·
ἀνάβα ὧδε, καὶ... (4:1b)
[The first voice which I heard as of a trumpet speaking with me (1/Agt)]
was saying (λέγων + [εἰμί]) [[to me/John (3/Exp)]] ["Come up here,
and..." (2/Con)].

	μαρτυρέω (22:18) <Cmm. ACE [§5.4a]>			δεικνύων (22:8) <Cmm. ACE [§5.4a]>		
syn.	1	2	3	1	2	3
sem.	Agt	Con	Exp	Agt	Con	Exp
lex.	N	V+quo	N+dat [+an]	N	N+acc	N+dat [+an]

	λέγων + [εἰμί] (4:1b) <Cmm. ACE [§5.4a]>		
syn.	1	2	[3]
sem.	Agt	Con	Exp
lex.	N	V+quo	DNC

b. Usage A{C}E

Only verb predicators grammaticalize the Usage of Communication with an Emphasized and Suppressed Content, A{C}E.[17] The conceptualization of communication with this usage has secondary emphasis on the Content, a suppressed Content {C} that never is realized as a complement and draws its referent from the predicator, no change in the functionality of the Content (C=C), no argument promotion, and an unaffected Agent (act.). The predicators raise the Agent entity as first argument, the Content entity as (suppressed) second argument, and the Experiencer entity as third argument. The illustrative examples provide two translations of each Greek verb predicator separated by a slash, /: the former introduces the referent of the suppressed Content complement in braces, { }, and the second provides an equivalent English verb predicator with a suppressed Content.

αἰνεῖτε τῷ θεῷ ἡμῶν πάντες οἱ δοῦλοι αὐτοῦ [καὶ] οἱ φοβούμενοι αὐτόν, οἱ μικροὶ καὶ οἱ μεγάλοι (19:5)
[You (1/Agt)] speak {praise (2/Con)} to/praise (αἰνέω) [our God (3/Exp)] [all his slaves and the ones fearing him, the small and the great (C/Voc)].

εὐχαριστοῦμέν σοι, κύριε ὁ θεὸς ὁ παντοκράτωρ, ὁ ὢν καὶ ὁ ἦν, ὅτι εἴληφας τὴν δύναμίν σου τὴν μεγάλην καὶ ἐβασίλευσας (11:17)
[We (1/Agt)] speak {thanks (2/Con)} to/thank (εὐχαριστέω) [you (3/Exp)] [Lord God Almighty, the One Being and That Was (C/Voc)] [because you took up your great power and ruled (C/Cau)].

---

[17] Usage A{C}E: verbs, αἰνέω, εὐχαριστέω, προφητεύω (1a), ψεύδομαι.

αἰνέω (19:5) <Cmm. A{C}E [§5.4b]>
syn.	1	{{2}}	3	|	C
sem.	Agt	Con	Exp	|	Voc
lex.	N	{N}	N+dat [+an]	|	N+voc

εὐχαριστέω (11:17) <Cmm. A{C}E [§5.4b]>
syn.	1	{{2}}	3	|	C	C
sem.	Agt	Con	Exp	|	Cau	Voc
lex.	N	{N}	N+dat [+an]	|	V+ὅτι	N+voc/nom

c. Usage ACE C→T

Only the verb predicator προφητεύω (1b) (prophesy) grammaticalizes the Usage of Communication with an Emphasized Topic, ACE C→T. The conceptualization of communication with this usage has secondary emphasis on the Content, no suppression of the Content, a change in the functionality of the Content to a Topic (C→T), no argument promotion, and an unaffected Agent (act.). The predicator raises the Agent entity as first argument, the Topic entity as second argument, and the Experiencer entity as third argument. The translation introduces in double brackets, [[ ]], the contextual referent of the DNC Experiencer (the churches).

σε πάλιν προφητεῦσαι ἐπὶ λαοῖς καὶ ἔθνεσιν καὶ γλώσσαις καὶ βασιλεῦσιν πολλοῖς (10:11)
[You (1/Agt)] [again (C/Mea)] to prophesy (προφητεύω) [[to the churches (3/Exp)]] [concerning many peoples and nations and tongues and kings (2/Top)].

προφητεύω (10:11) <Cmm. ACE C→T [§5.4c]>
syn.	1	2	[3]	|	C
sem.	Agt	Top	Top	|	Mea
lex.	N	P/ἐπί [+dat]	DNC	|	A/πάλιν

d. Usage AEC

Only the verb predicator διδάσκω (1b) (teach) grammaticalizes the Usage of Communication with an Emphasized Experiencer, AEC. The conceptualization of communication with this usage has secondary emphasis on the Experiencer, no suppression of the Content, no change in the functionality of the Content (C=C), no argument promotion, and an unaffected Agent (act.). The predicator raises the Agent entity as first argument, the Experiencer entity as second argument, and the Content entity as third argument.

διδάσκει...τοὺς ἐμοὺς δούλους πορνεῦσαι καὶ φαγεῖν εἰδωλόθυτα (2:20)
[She (1/Agt)] teaches (διδάσκω)...[my slaves (2/Exp)] [to engage in sexual immorality and to eat what is offered to idols (3/Con)].

5. *Events with Theme (Θ), Experiencer (E), or Occurrence (O)*   115

	διδάσκω (2:20) <*Cmm.* AEC [§5.4d]>		
syn.	1	2	3
sem.	Agt	Exp	Con
lex.	N	N+acc	V-i2

e. Usage AE{C}

Only the verb predicator εὐαγγελίζω (1b) (tell {good news}) grammaticalizes the Usage of Communication with an Emphasized Experiencer and a Suppressed Content, AE{C}. The conceptualization of communication with this usage has secondary emphasis on the Experiencer, a suppressed Content {C} that never is realized as a complement and draws its referent from the predicator, no change in the functionality of the Content (C=C), no argument promotion, and an unaffected Agent (act.). The predicator raises the Agent entity as first argument, the Experiencer entity as second argument, and the Content entity as (suppressed) third argument. The translation introduces the referent of the suppressed Content complement in braces, { }.

εὐηγγέλισεν τοὺς ἑαυτοῦ δούλους τοὺς προφήτας (10:7)
[He (1/Agt)] told (εὐαγγελίζω) [his own slaves the prophets (2/Exp)] {good news (3/Con)}.

	εὐαγγελίζω (10:7) <*Cmm.* AE{C} [§5.4e]>		
syn.	1	2	{{3}}
sem.	Agt	Exp	Con
lex.	N	N+acc	{N}

f. Usage BCE

Only noun predicators grammaticalize the Nominal Usage of Communication with an Emphasized Content, BCE.[18] The conceptualization of communication with this usage has secondary emphasis on the Content, no suppression of the Content, no change in the functionality of the Content (C=C), and no argument promotion. The predicators raise the agentive Benefactive entity as first argument, the Content entity as second argument, and the Experiencer entity as third argument. The translations introduce in double brackets, [[ ]], the contextual referent of the DNC Experiencer (you/the members of the church in Philadelphia; cf. 3:7) in 3:10 and of the DNC Content (to cast a stumbling stone before the sons of Israel) and DNC Experiencer (Balak) in 2:14.

τὸν λόγον τῆς ὑπομονῆς μου (3:10)
[My (1/Ben)] word (λόγος) [of endurance (2/Con)] [[to you/the members of church in Philadelphia (3/Exp)]].

---

[18] Usage BCE: nouns, ἀποκάλυψις, διδαχή, ἐντολή, εὐαγγέλιον, λόγος, μαρτυρία, μαρτύριον, μάρτυς, προσευχή, προφητεία, σημεῖον, ψεῦδος.

τὴν διδαχὴν Βαλαάμ (2:14)
[Balaam's (1/Ben)] teaching (διδαχή) [[to Balak (3/Exp)]] [[to eat a stumbling stone before the sons of Israel (2/Con)]].

	λόγος (3:10) <Cmm. BCE [§5.4f]>			διδαχή (2:14) <Cmm. BCE [§5.4f]>		
syn.	1	2	[3]	1	[2]	[3]
sem.	Ben	Con	Exp	Ben	Con	Exp
lex.	N+gen	N+gen	DNC	N+gen	DNC	DNC

g. Usage B{C}E

Only the noun predicator εὐχαριστία (thanks) grammaticalizes the Nominal Usage of Communication with an Emphasized and Suppressed Content, B{C}E. The conceptualization of communication with this usage has secondary emphasis on the Content, a suppressed Content {C} that never is realized as a complement and draws its referent from the predicator, no change in the functionality of the Content (C=C), and no argument promotion. The predicator raises the agentive Benefactive entity as first argument, the Content entity as (suppressed) second argument, and the Experiencer entity as third argument. The translation introduces in double brackets, [[ ]], the contextual referent of the DNC agentive Benefactive (the living creatures) and the DNC Experiencer (the one sitting on the throne living into the ages of ages) and in braces, { }, the referent of the suppressed Content complement.

εὐχαριστίαν (4:9)
[[The living creatures' (1/Ben)]] thanks (εὐχαριστία) {thanks (2/Con)} [[to the one sitting on the throne living into the ages of ages (3/Exp)]].

	εὐχαριστία (4:9) <Cmm. B{C}E [§5.4g]>		
syn.	[1]	{{2}}	[3]
sem.	Ben	Con	Exp
lex.	DNC	{N}	DNC

h. Usage CBE

Only the complex predicator προσευχή + εἰμί (be a prayer) grammaticalizes the Usage of Communication with a Promoted Content, CBE. The conceptualization of communication with this usage has a promoted Content, no suppression of the Content, and no change in the functionality of the Content (C=C). The predicator raises the Content entity as (promoted) first argument, the agentive Benefactive entity as second argument, and the Experiencer entity as third argument. The translation introduces in double brackets, [[ ]], the contextual referent of the DNC Experiencer (God; cf. §1.5a).

5. Events with Theme (Θ), Experiencer (E), or Occurrence (O)

αἵ εἰσιν αἱ προσευχαὶ τῶν ἁγίων (5:8)
[Which (1/Con)] are [the holy ones' (2/Ben)] prayers (προσευχή + εἰμί) [[to God (3/Exp)]].

	προσευχή + εἰμί (5:8) <Cmm. CBE [§5.4h]>		
syn.	1	2	[3]
sem.	Con	Ben	Exp
lex.	N	N+gen	DNC

i. Usage ACE[B] [B=A] Pass.

Only the verb predicator ἀποκρίνομαι (respond) grammaticalizes the Passive Usage of Communication with an Emphasized Content, ACE[B] [B=A] pass. The conceptualization of communication with this usage has secondary emphasis on the Content, no suppression of the Content, no change in the functionality of the Content (C=C), no argument promotion, and an affected Agent insofar as the Agent and omitted Benefactive are coreferential and the Agent acts for itself (pass.). The predicator raises the Agent entity as first argument, the Content entity as second argument, and the Experiencer entity as third argument. Since the sole occurrence of this predicator (7:13) participates in λέγω Melding with both the Content and the Experiencer arguments realized by the following λέγων (saying), the translation introduces in double brackets, [[ ]], the contextual referent of the DNC Content ("These wrapped with white robes, who are they and from where did they come?") and the DNC Experiencer (me).

ἀπεκρίθη εἷς ἐκ τῶν πρεσβυτέρων (7:13)
[One of the elders (1/Agt)] responded (ἀποκρίνομαι) [[to me (3/Exp)]] [["These wrapped with white robes, who are they and from where did they come?" (2/Con)]].

	ἀποκρίνομαι (7:13 [LM]) <Cmm. ACE[B] [B=A] pass. [§5.4i]>		
syn.	1	[2]	[3]
sem.	Agt	Con	Exp
lex.	N	DNC	DNC

5. Usages of Experience (Exp.)

The event of experience (*Exp.*) contains two entities that are associated with the Experiencer and Content thematic roles. The base configuration of this event (EC) admits to alternate formulation by two event features: incorporation (§2.3) and bifurcation (§2.5). Entity incorporation expands the configuration of the event through the addition of a Current (ECCur) or a Topic (ECT) in third position. Entity bifurcation imposes on the Content entity a composite interpretation that is constituted by a general and a specific conceptualization of the Content (EC¹/C²). The two event features in succession impose a composite interpretation of the Content of ECT (EC¹/C²T). The differing conceptualizations of the base and alternate configurations of experience grammaticalized by predicators require description by three usage features: suppression of the Content (§3.7a), functionality of the Content (3.7b), and argument promotion (§3.7c). These usage features distinguish the conceptualizations of the eight usages of the event of experience in the text of Revelation. The following discussion describes and provides illustrative examples of each of the eight observed usages of experience by the categories of predicators. The translations of noun predicators follow the English practice of realizing the Experiencer by a possessive adjective or a noun in the possessive case ('s or s') and the Content by an "of" prepositional phrase.

a. Usage EC

Verb, participle, preposition, noun, and complex noun predicators grammaticalize the Usage of Experience of a Content, EC.[19] The conceptualization of experience with this usage has no suppression of the Content, no change in the functionality of the Content (C=C), and no argument promotion. The predicators raise the Experiencer entity as first argument and the Content entity as second argument. Since English grammar does not tolerate a Content complement introduced by the preposition as in the third example (1:7), the preposition in this example is left untranslated, as indicated by ---. The translation of the example of the noun predicator in 18:10 introduces in double brackets, [[ ]], the contextual referent of the DNC Experiencer (the kings [of the earth]; cf. 18:9).

    verb   οἶδά σου τὴν θλῖψιν καὶ τὴν πτωχείαν (2:9)
                  [I (1/Exp)] know (οἶδα) [your oppression and poverty (2/Con)].

    part.   βλέποντες τὸν καπνὸν τῆς πυρώσεως αὐτῆς (18:18)
                  [They (1/Exp)] seeing (βλέπων) [the smoke of her burning (2/Con)].

    prep.   ἐπ' αὐτὸν πᾶσαι αἱ φυλαὶ τῆς γῆς (1:7)
                  [All the tribes of the earth (1/Exp)] --- (ἐπί) [her 2/Con)].

    noun   τὸν φόβον τοῦ βασανισμοῦ αὐτῆς (18:10)
                  [The kings' (1/Exp)] fear (φόβος) [of her torments (2/Con)].

    cp-n   εἰμι ὁ ἐραυνῶν νεφροὺς (2:23)
                  [I (1/Exp)] am the one searching (ὁ ἐραυνῶν + εἰμί) [kidneys/hearts (2/Con)].

---

[19] Usage EC: verbs, ἀγαπάω, ἀκούω, βαστάζω (1), βλέπω, γινώσκω, ἐπιθυμέω, ζηλεύω, θέλω, θεωρέω, κόπτω, μανθάνω, μιμνήσκομαι, μισέω, μνημονεύω, οἶδα (1a), ὁράω, πάσχω, προσκυνέω, φιλέω, φοβέομαι; participles, ἀγαπῶν, ἀκούων, βλέπων, εἰδώς, θέλων, θεωρῶν, ἰδών, προσκυνῶν, φιλῶν, φοβούμενος; prepositions, ἐκ (5), ἐπί (3a); nouns, ἀγάπη, ἐπιθυμία, θυμός, μυστήριον, ὄνομα (2), ὅρασις, φόβος, χρεία; and complex predicators, ὁ ἀκούων + [εἰμί], ὁ βλέπων + [εἰμί], ὁ ἐραυνῶν + εἰμί.

5. Events with Theme (Θ), Experiencer (E), or Occurrence (O)

	οἶδα (2:9) <*Exp*. EC [§5.5a]>		βλέπων (18:18) <*Exp*. EC [§5.5a]>		ἐπί (1:7) <*Exp*. EC [§5.5a]>	
syn.	1	2	1	2	1	2
sem.	Exp	Con	Exp	Con	Exp	Con
lex.	N	N+acc	N	N+acc	N	N+acc

	φόβος (18:10) <*Exp*. EC [§5.5a]>		ὁ ἐραυνῶν + εἰμί (2:23) <*Exp*. EC [§5.5a]>	
syn.	[1]	2	1	2
sem.	Exp	Con	Exp	Con
lex.	DNC	N+gen	N	N+acc

b. Usage E{C}

Only the participle predicator ὠδίνων (suffer {birth pains}) grammaticalizes the Usage of Experience with a Suppressed Content, E{C}. The conceptualization of experience with this usage has a suppressed Content {C} that never is realized as a complement and draws its referent from the predicator, no change in the functionality of the Content (C=C), and no argument promotion. The predicator raises the Experiencer entity as first argument and the Content entity as (suppressed) second argument. The translation introduces the referent of the suppressed Content complement in braces, { }.

ὠδίνουσα (12:2)
[She (1/Exp)] (ὠδίνων) suffering {birth pains (2/Con)}.

	ὠδίνων (12:2) <*Exp*. E{C} [§5.5b]>	
syn.	1	{{2}}
sem.	Exp	Con
lex.	N	{N}

c. Usage EC C→T

Verb, participle, complex adjective, adjective, preposition, and noun predicators grammaticalize the Usage of Experience of a Topic, EC C→T.[20] The conceptualization of experience with this usage has no suppression of the Content, a change in the functionality of the Content to a Topic (C→T), and no argument promotion. The predicators raise the Experiencer entity as first argument and the Topic entity as second argument. The translations introduce in double brackets, [[ ]], the contextual referent of the DNC Topic (her/Babylon the Great; cf. 18:2) in 18:15, of the DNC Topic

[20] Usage EC C→T: verbs, ἀγαλλιάω, διψάω, εὐφραίνω, θαυμάζω, μετανοέω, ὀργίζω, πεινάω, πενθέω, χαίρω; participles, διψῶν, πενθῶν; complex predicators, πιστός + [εἰμί], ταλαίπωρος + εἰμί; adjectives, ἄπιστος, πιστός; prepositions, ἐπί (3b), κατά (1); and nouns, αἰσχύνη, ἀσχημοσύνη, γνώμη, θαῦμα, λιμός, ὀργή, πένθος, πίστις, σοφία.

(God/God and Jesus) in 17:14, of the Experiencer (you) drawn from the licensing predicator in 18:20, and of the DNC Experiencer (you) in 3:18.

    verb   ὠργίσθη ὁ δράκων ἐπὶ τῇ γυναικὶ (12:17)
             [The dragon (1/Exp)] was angry (ὀργίζω) [at/concerning the woman (2/Top)].

    part.   οἱ ἔμποροι τούτων…πενθοῦντες (18:15)
             [The merchants of these things (1/Exp)]…mourning (πενθῶν) [[concerning her/Babylon the Great (2/Top)]].

    cp-adj οἱ μετ' αὐτοῦ…πιστοί (17:14)
             [The ones with him (1/Exp)]…are faithful (πιστός + [εἰμί]) [[concerning God/God and Jesus (2/Top)]].

    adj.   ὁ μάρτυς μου ὁ πιστός μου (2:13)
             [My witness (1/Exp)]] faithful (πιστός) [concerning me (2/Top)].

    prep.   ἐπ' αὐτῇ (18:20)
             [[You (1/Exp)]] concerning (ἐπί) [her (2/Top)].

    noun   ἡ αἰσχύνη τῆς γυμνότητός σου (3:18)
             [[Your (1/Exp)]] shame (αἰσχύνη) [concerning/at your nakedness (2/Con)].

	ὀργίζω (12:17) <Exp. EC C→T [§5.5c]>		πενθῶν (18:15) <Exp. EC C→T [§5.5c]>	
syn.	1	2	1	[2]
sem.	Exp	Top	Exp	Top
lex.	N	P/ἐπί [+dat]	N	DNC

	πιστός + [εἰμί] (17:14) <Exp. EC C→T [§5.5c]>		πιστός (2:13) <Exp. EC C→T [§5.5c]>	
syn.	1	[2]	1	2
sem.	Exp	Top	Exp	Top
lex.	N	DNC	N	N+gen

	ἐπί (18:20) <Exp. EC C→T [§5.5c]>		αἰσχύνη (3:18) <Exp. EC C→T [§5.5c]>	
syn.	1	2	1	2
sem.	Exp	Top	Exp	Top
lex.	N	N+dat	DNC	N+gen

d. Usage ECT

Verb, participle, and noun predicators grammaticalize the Usage of Experience with an Incorporated Topic, ECT.[21] The conceptualization of experience with this usage has no suppression of the Content, no change in the functionality of the Content (C=C), no argument promotion, and an incorporated Topic. The predicator raises the Experiencer entity as first argument, the Content entity as second argument, and the Topic entity as third argument. The translations introduce in double brackets, [[ ]], the contextual referent of the DNC Content (her works) in 18:8 and the DNC Content (the sword and being killed) and the DNC Topic (their faith) in 13:10.

verb ἔχω κατὰ σοῦ ὅτι τὴν ἀγάπην σου τὴν πρώτην ἀφῆκες (2:4)
[I (1/Exp)] hold (ἔχω) [against/concerning you (3/Top)] [that you left your earlier love (2/Con)].

part. κύριος ὁ θεὸς ὁ κρίνας αὐτήν (18:8)
[The Lord God (1/Exp)] judging (κρίνας) [her (2/Con)] [[concerning her works (3/Top)]].

noun ἡ ὑπομονὴ... τῶν ἁγίων (13:10)
[The holy ones' (1/Exp)]...endurance (ὑπομονή) [[of the sword and being killed (2/Con)]] [[concerning their faith (3/Top)]].

	ἔχω (2:4) <*Exp.* ECT [§5.5d]>			κρίνας (18:8) <*Exp.* ECT [§5.5d]>		
syn.	1	2	3	1	2	[3]
sem.	Exp	Con	Top	Exp	Con	Top
lex.	N	V+ὅτι	P/κατά [+gen]	N+nom	N+acc	DNC

	ὑπομονή (13:10) <*Exp.* ECT [§5.5d]>		
syn.	1	[2]	[3]
sem.	Exp	Con	Top
lex.	N+gen	DNC	DNC

e. Usage EC¹/C²

Only the verb predicator οἶδα (1b) (know) grammaticalizes the Usage of Experience with a Bifurcated Content, EC¹/C². The conceptualization of experience with this usage has no suppression of the Content, no change in the functionality of the Content (C=C), a bifurcated Content (C¹/C²), and no argument promotion. The predicator raises the Experiencer entity as first argument and the (bifurcated) Content entity as second argument.

---

[21] Usage ECT: verbs, ἔχω (2a), κρίνω; participle, κρίνας; and nouns, κρίμα, κρίσις, ὑπομονή.

οἶδά σου τὰ ἔργα ὅτι οὔτε ψυχρὸς εἶ οὔτε ζεστός (3:15)
[I (1/Exp)] know (οἶδα) [your works (2/Con¹)] [that you are neither cold nor hot (2/Con²)].

	οἶδα (3:15) <*Exp*. EC¹/C² [§5.5e]>	
syn.	1	2
sem.	Exp	Con¹/Con²
lex.	N	N+acc/V+ὅτι

f. Usage EC¹/C² T

Only the verb predicator ἔχω (2b) (hold) grammaticalizes the Usage of Experience with a Bifurcated Content and an Incorporated Topic, EC¹/C² T. The conceptualization of experience with this usage has no suppression of the Content, no change in the functionality of the Content (C=C), a bifurcated Content (C¹/C²), no argument promotion, and an incorporated Topic. The predicator raises the Experiencer entity as first argument, the (bifurcated) Content entity as second argument, and the Topic entity as third argument.

ἔχω κατὰ σοῦ ὀλίγα ὅτι ἔχεις ἐκεῖ κρατοῦντας τὴν διδαχὴν Βαλαάμ (2:14a)
[I (1/Exp)] hold (ἔχω) [concerning/against you (3/Top)] [a few things (2/Con¹)] [that you have there ones holding the teaching of Balaam (2/Con²)].

	ἔχω (2:14a) <*Exp*. EC¹/C²T [§5.5f]>		
syn.	1	2	3
sem.	Exp	Con¹/Con²	Top
lex.	N	N+acc/V+ ὅτι	P/κατά [+gen]

g. Usage ECCur

Only the verb predicator εὑρίσκω (2) (find) grammaticalizes the Usage of Experience with an Incorporated Current, ECCur. The conceptualization of experience with this usage has no suppression of the Content, no change in the functionality of the Content (C=C), no argument promotion, and an incorporated Current. The predicator raises the Experiencer entity as first argument, the Content entity as second argument, and the Current entity as third argument.

οὐ γὰρ εὕρηκά σου τὰ ἔργα πεπληρωμένα ἐνώπιον τοῦ θεοῦ μου (3:2)
For [I (1/Exp)] did not find (εὑρίσκω) [your works (2/Con)] [fulfilled before my God (3/Cur)].

	εὑρίσκω (3:2) <*Exp*. ECCur [§5.5g]>		
syn.	1	2	3
sem.	Exp	Con	Cur
lex.	N	N+acc	Adj+2

h. Usage CE

Participle, complex adjective, adjective, and preposition predicators grammaticalize the Usage of Experience with a Promoted Content, CE.[22] The conceptualization of experience with this usage has no suppression of the Content, no change in the functionality of the Content (C=C), and promotion of the Content. The predicators raise the Content entity as (promoted) first argument and the Experiencer entity as second argument. The translations introduce in double brackets, [[ ]], the indefinite but circumscribed referent of the INC Experiencer (people) in 18:2 and the contextual referents of the DNC Experiencer (you/John) in 10:9, and of the DNC Experiencer (the speaker of the statement/John) in 15:1.

part. παντὸς θηρίου...μεμισημένου (18:2)
[Every beast (1/Con)]...hated (μεμισημένος) [[by people (2/Exp)]].

cp-adj ἐν τῷ στόματί σου ἔσται γλυκὺ ὡς μέλι (10:9a)
[In your mouth (C/Loc)] [it (1/Con)] will be sweet (γλυκύς + εἰμί) [[to you/John (2/Exp)]] [like honey (C/Cmp)].

adj. σημεῖον...θαυμαστόν (15:1)
[A sign 1/Con)]...marvelous (θαυμαστός) [[to the speaker of the statement/to John (2/Exp)]].

prep. σάλπιγγος...μετ' ἐμοῦ (4:1b)
[A trumpet (1/Con)]...with (μετά) [me (2/Exp)].

	μεμισημένος (18:2) <Exp. CE [§5.5h]>		γλυκύς + εἰμί (10:9a) <Exp. CE [§5.5h]>			
syn.	1	(2)	1	[2]	C	C
sem.	Con	Exp	Con	Exp	Cmp	Loc
lex.	N	INC	N	DNC	V+ὡς	P/ἐν

	θαυμαστός (15:1) <Exp. CE [§5.5h]>		μετά (4:1b) <Exp. CE [§5.5h]>	
syn.	1	[2]	1	2
sem.	Con	Exp	Con	Exp
lex.	N	DNC	N	N+gen

6. Usages of Capacity (Cap.)

The event of capacity (Cap.) contains two entities that are associated with the Unspecified (U) and Occurrence (O) thematic roles. The base configuration of this event (UO) admits to alternate formulation by the event feature incorporation which

---

[22] Usage CE: participles, ἠγαπημένος, μεμισημένος; complex predicators, γλυκύς + εἰμί, ἐλεεινός + εἰμί, θαυμαστός + [εἰμί]; adjectives, δειλός, θαυμαστός; and prepositions, ἐπί (3c), μετά (3).

expands the event to include an Agent in first position (AUO). The differing conceptualizations of the base and alternate configurations of capacity grammaticalized by predicators do not require description by usage features. The following discussion describes and provides illustrative examples of the two observed usages of capacity by the categories of predicators in the text of Revelation.

a. Usage AUO

Only the verb predicator ἀφίημι (1) (permit) grammaticalizes the Usage of Agentive Capacity, AUO. The conceptualization of capacity with this usage has an incorporated Agent. The predicator raises the Agent entity as first argument, the Unspecified entity as second argument, and the Occurrence entity as third argument. Note that the Unspecified complement coinstantiates the subject (second) complement of the passivized verb of the Occurrence complement which functions as a Theme.

> τὰ πτώματα αὐτῶν οὐκ ἀφίουσιν τεθῆναι εἰς μνῆμα (11:9)
> [They (1/Agt)] do not permit (ἀφίημι) [their corpses (2/Uns)] [to be placed into a tomb (3/Occ)].

	ἀφίημι (11:9) <Cap. AUO [§5.6a]>		
syn.	1	2	3
sem.	Agt	Uns	Occ
lex.	N	N+acc	V-i2

b. Usage UO

Verb, participle, complex adjective, and adjective predicators grammaticalize the Usage of Capacity, UO.[23] The predicators raise the Unspecified entity as first argument and the Occurrence entity as second argument. Note that the Unspecified complement coinstantiates the subject (first) complement of the predicator of the Occurrence complement which functions as a Theme (6:17; 3:10), a Goal (5:12), and an Agent and Experiencer (5:4).

> verb   τίς δύναται σταθῆναι; (6:17)
> [Who (1/Uns)] is able (δύναμαι) [to stand (2/Occ)]?

> part.   τῆς ὥρας τοῦ πειρασμοῦ τῆς μελλούσης ἔρχεσθαι ἐπὶ τῆς οἰκουμένης ὅλης (3:10)
> [The hour of testing (1/Uns)] being about (μέλλων) [to come on the whole world (2/Occ)].

---

[23] Usage UO: verbs, δύναμαι, μέλλω: participle, μέλλων; complex predicator, ἄξιος + [εἰμί]; and adjective, ἄξιος.

cp-adj ἄξιόν ἐστιν τὸ ἀρνίον τὸ ἐσφαγμένον λαβεῖν τὴν δύναμιν καὶ πλοῦτον καὶ σοφίαν καὶ ἰσχὺν καὶ τιμὴν καὶ δόξαν καὶ εὐλογίαν (5:12)
Worthy is (ἄξιος + εἰμί) [the slain lamb (1/Uns)] [to receive power and riches and wisdom and might and honor and glory and blessing (2/Occ)].

adj. οὐδεὶς ἄξιος...ἀνοῖξαι τὸ βιβλίον οὔτε βλέπειν αὐτό (5:4)
[No one (1/Uns)] worthy (ἄξιος)...[to open the book or look at it (2/Occ)].

	δύναμαι (6:17) <Cap. UO [§5.6b]>		μέλλων (3:10) <Cap. UO [§5.6b]>	
syn.	1	2	1	2
sem.	Uns	Occ	Uns	Occ
lex.	N	V-il	N	V-il

	ἄξιος + εἰμί (5:12) <Cap. UO [§5.6b]>		ἄξιος (5:4) <Cap. UO [§5.6b]>	
syn.	1	2	1	2
sem.	Uns	Occ	Uns	Occ
lex.	N	V-il	N	V-il

7. Events with Only One Usage

The remaining five events (disposition, compulsion, delegation, necessity, and authority) contain an event entity associated with the Theme or Content or Occurrence thematic role and present only one usage in the text of Revelation. The following discussions describe and provide illustrative examples of each observed usage by the category or categories of predicators.

a. Usage AΘO

The event of disposition (*Dis.*) contains three entities that are associated with the Agent (A), Theme (Θ), and Occurrence (O) thematic roles. This base configuration of disposition (AΘO) does not admit to alternate formulation by event features, and the conceptualization of the base configuration of disposition grammaticalized by predicators does not require description by usage features. Only verb predicators grammaticalize the event of disposition with the Usage of Disposition, AΘO.[24] The predicators raise the Agent entity as first argument, the Theme entity as second argument, and the Occurrence entity as third argument.

---

[24] Usage AΘO: verbs, ἀποστέλλω (2), δίδωμι (4), πέμπω (2), πλανάω (1).

126   *A Case Frame Grammar and Lexicon for the Book of Revelation*

ὁ κύριος ὁ θεὸς τῶν πνευμάτων τῶν προφητῶν ἀπέστειλεν τὸν ἄγγελον αὐτοῦ δεῖξαι τοῖς δούλοις αὐτοῦ ἃ δεῖ γενέσθαι ἐν τάχει (22:6)
[The Lord, the God of the spirits of the prophets (1/Agt)] sent (ἀποστέλλω) [his angel (2/Thm)] [to show to his slaves the things which are necessary to happen quickly (3/Occ)].

πλανᾷ τοὺς ἐμοὺς δούλους πορνεῦσαι καὶ φαγεῖν εἰδωλόθυτα (2:20)
[She (1/Agt)] misleads (πλανάω) [my slaves (2/Thm)] [to commit sexual immorality and to eat what is offered to idols (3/Occ)].

	ἀποστέλλω (22:6) <Dis. AΘO [§5.7a]>			πλανάω (2:20) <Dis. AΘO [§5.7a]>		
syn.	1	2	3	1	2	3
sem.	Agt	Thm	Occ	Agt	Thm	Occ
lex.	N	N+acc	V-i2	N	N+acc	V-i2

b. Usage APO

The event of compulsion (*Cpl.*) contains three entities that are associated with the Agent (A), Patient (P), and Occurrence (O) thematic roles. The base configuration of compulsion (APO) does not admit to alternate formulation by event features, and the conceptualization of the base configuration of compulsion grammaticalized by the predicator does not require description by usage features. Only the verb predicator ποιέω (4) (make) grammaticalizes the event of compulsion with the Usage of Compulsion, APO. The predicator raises the Agent entity as first argument, the Patient entity as second argument, and the Occurrence entity as third argument.

ποιεῖ τὴν γῆν καὶ τοὺς ἐν αὐτῇ κατοικοῦντας ἵνα προσκυνήσουσιν τὸ θηρίον τὸ πρῶτον (13:12b)
[It (1/Agt)] makes (ποιέω) [the earth and the ones dwelling in it (2/Pat)] [that they worship the first beast (3/Occ)].

	ποιέω (13:12b) <Cpl. APO [§5.7b]>		
syn.	1	2	3
sem.	Agt	Pat	Occ
lex.	N	N+acc	V+ἵνα

c. Usage AO[S]G [S=A] +Imp.

The event of delegation (*Del.*) contains four entities that are associated with the Agent (A), Occurrence (O), Source (S), and Goal (G) thematic roles. This base configuration of delegation (AOSG) does not admit to alternate formulation by event features. The conceptualization of the base configuration grammaticalized by the predicator requires description by five usage features: perspective (§3.2a), subject affectedness (§3.2b), focus (§3.2c), impetus (§3.2d), and functionality of the Goal (3.2e). Only the verb predicator δίδωμι (3) (give, delegate) grammaticalizes the event of delegation with the Usage of Delegation to a Goal, AO[S]G [S=A] +imp. The conceptualization of delegation with this usage has the Agent and Source initially coincident/proximate (S=A), an unaffected Agent (act.), a focus on both segments of the event (pri.), a continuous impetus (+imp.), and no change in the functionality of the Goal (G=G). The verb predicator with this usage raises the Agent entity as first argument, the Occurrence entity as second argument, and the Goal entity as third argument. The introductory articular participle that is co-referential to the Goal is attributed to an intruding grammatical construction, perhaps that governing *casus pendens*, and so is not licensed by the predicator or included among its complements.

ὁ νικῶν δώσω αὐτῷ καθίσαι μετ' ἐμοῦ ἐν τῷ θρόνῳ μου, ὡς κἀγὼ ἐνίκησα καὶ ἐκάθισα μετὰ τοῦ πατρός μου ἐν τῷ θρόνῳ αὐτοῦ (3:21)
The one conquering [to him (3/Goa)] [I (1/Agt)] will give/delegate (δίδωμι) [to sit with me on my throne (2/Occ)] [just as I also conquered and sat with my Father on his throne (C/Man)].

	δίδωμι (3:21) <*Del.* AO[S]G [S=A] +imp. [§5.7c]>				
syn.	1	2	3	|	C
sem.	Agt	Occ	Goa	|	Man
lex.	N	V-i3	N+dat [+an]	|	V+ὡς

d. Usage OI

The event of necessity (*Nec.*) contains two entities that are associated with the Occurrence (O) and Instrument (I) thematic roles. The base configuration of the event of necessity (OI) does not admit to alternate formulation by event features, and the conceptualization of the base configuration of necessity grammaticalized by one predicator does not require description by usage features. Only the verb predicator δεῖ (be necessary) grammaticalizes this event with the Usage of Necessity, OI. The predicator with this usage raises the Occurrence entity as first argument and the Instrument entity as second argument. The translation introduces in double brackets, [[ ]], the referent of the DNC Instrument (God's will/God's plan) which is assumed to be supplied directly by the interpreter (§1.5a).[25] The first translation captures the actual grammar of the Greek phrase whereas the second presents the more usual manner in which English grammar avoids an overly complex subject complement by extraposing an empty subject (here, "it") as the verb predicator's first complement and realizing the actual first complement after the verb predicator.[26]

---

[25] Walter Grundmann, "δεῖ, δέον ἐστί," *TDNT* 2:22.
[26] A discussion of "it" extraposition appears in Laurel J. Brinton, *The Structure of Modern English: A Linguistic Introduction* (Amsterdam/Philadelphia: Benjamins, 2000), 218–20.

δεῖ σε πάλιν προφητεῦσαι ἐπὶ λαοῖς καὶ ἔθνεσιν καὶ γλώσσαις καὶ βασιλεῦσιν πολλοῖς (10:11)
[That you again prophesy concerning many peoples and nations and tongues and kings (1/Occ)] is necessary (δεῖ) [[by God's will/God's plan (2/Ins)]].
It is necessary (δεῖ) [[by God's will/God's plan (2/Ins)]] [that you again prophesy concerning many peoples and nations and tongues and kings (1/Occ)].

	δεῖ (10:11) <Nec. OI [§5.7d]>	
syn.	1	[2]
sem.	Occ	Ins
lex.	V+i	DNC

e. Usage BOL

The event of authority (*Aut.*) contains three entities that are associated with the Benefactive (B), Occurrence (O), and Locative (L) thematic roles. The base configuration of authority (BOL) does not admit to alternate formulation by event features, and the conceptualization of the base configuration of authority grammaticalized by one predicator does not require description by usage features. Only the noun predicator ἐξουσία (authority) grammaticalizes this event with the Usage of Authority, BOL. The predicator with this usage raises the Benefactive entity as first argument, the Occurrence entity as second argument, and the Locative entity as third argument. The translation introduces in double brackets, [[ ]], the contextual referent of the DNC Benefactive (the two witnesses, cf. 11:3). The translation of the noun predicator follows the English practice of realizing the +animate Benefactive by the possessive case (s').

ἐξουσίαν...ἐπὶ τῶν ὑδάτων στρέφειν αὐτὰ εἰς αἷμα (11:6b)
[[The two witnesses' (1/Ben)]] authority (ἐξουσία)...[over the waters (3/Loc)] [to turn them into blood (2/Occ)].

	ἐξουσία (11:6b) <Aut. BOL [§5.7e]>		
syn.	[1]	2	3
sem.	Ben	Occ	Loc
lex.	DNC	V-il	P/ἐπί [+gen]

6

PREDICATOR USAGES OF OTHER EVENTS AND OF THREE NON-EVENTS

Predicators in the text of Revelation grammaticalize forty usages of the twelve remaining events (§2.2), and the following presentations extend the definition of "usage" to include the grammaticalizations of the entities in the five configurations of the three non-events (§2.7). The presentations introduce each event and non-event with a specification of its entities. If applicable to the events, the presentation clarifies the event features that account for its various configurations and of the usage features that distinguish the conceptualizations being grammaticalized. If applicable to non-events, the presentation clarifies the non-events' differing configurations.

The discussion of each usage specifies its usage label, identifies the categories of predicators that grammaticalize the usage, incorporates lists of the predicators in each category, proposes a capitalized descriptive designation for the usage, describes the usage features of its conceptualization, provides illustrative examples of the usage with each observed category of predicator, and generates the Valence Description for each illustrative example. The usage labels in Valence Descriptions introduce at the end and in brackets, [ ], the sectional heading of the discussion in which the usage receives specification and illustration.

When only one predicator grammaticalizes a particular usage, it is listed in the text of the discussion of that usage. In all other cases, the predicators are listed according to their category in the footnotes. These listings introduce a numeric (1, 2, ...) or an alphanumeric (1a, 1b, ...) specification in parentheses, ( ), after predicators that grammaticalize more than one usage in the text of Revelation. These specifications are linked to the subdivisions of their associated lexicon entries (Chapter 9) which distinguish the events grammaticalized under separate numeric headings (1, 2, ...) and the different usages of the same event under alphanumeric sub-headings (1a, 1b, ...). The following discussion reintroduces illustrative examples from previous discussions (most frequently from Chapter 3) whenever only one predicator in a single occurrence grammaticalizes the usage under study or the occurrence most clearly exemplifies the licensing properties of its class of predicator (typically by realizing all or most required complements). For ease of interpretation, the translations of the illustrative examples introduce in double brackets, [[ ]], the retrievable contextual referents of definite null complements (DNCs) and the indefinite but circumscribed referents of indefinite null complements (INCs).

1. Usages of Benefaction (Ben.)

The event of Benefaction (*Ben.*) contains two entities that are associated with the Patient (P) and Benefactive (B) thematic roles. The base configuration of benefaction (PB) admits to alternate formulation by three event features: incorporation (§2.3), reinterpretation (§2.4), and bifurcation (§2.5). Entity incorporation expands the base configuration of the event through the addition of an Agent (A) in first position (APB) or a Locative in third position (BPL). Entity reinterpretation highlights the agentive Benefactive function of the Agent entity of event APB (BPB). Entity bifurcation imposes on the Patient entity a composite interpretation that is constituted by a general and a specific conceptualization of the Patient of event BP (BP^1/P^2). The differing conceptualizations of the base and alternate configurations of benefaction grammaticalized by predicators require description by three usage features: suppression of the Patient (§3.8a), argument promotion (§3.8d), and suppression of the Benefactive (§3.8e). These usage features distinguish the conceptualizations of the ten usages of the event of benefaction in the text of Revelation. The following discussion describes and provides illustrative examples of each of the ten observed usages of benefaction by the categories of predicators. Except in the context of countervailing grammatical considerations, the translations of noun predicators follow the English practice of realizing the agentive Benefactive by a possessive adjective or a noun in the possessive case ('s or s').

a. Usage APB

Only verb predicator ποιέω (3) (make) grammaticalizes event APB with the Usage of Agentive Benefaction, APB. The conceptualization of benefaction with this usage has no suppression of the Patient, no argument promotion, and no suppression of the Benefactive. The predicator raises the Agent entity as first argument, the Patient entity as second argument, and the Benefactive entity as third argument. Although the first complement of the infinitive is coinstantiated by the first complement of the licensing predicator δύναμαι (be able) and so is not realized as a complement within the infinitive phrase, the Valence Description follows the convention (§1.4) of listing the first complement of the infinitive verb predicator with the syntactic function as "1" (no brackets) and the lexical realization "N." In 11:7 and similar occurrences (12:7, 17; 13:7; 16:14; 19:19) in which ποιέω licenses a second argument realized by the noun predicator πόλεμος (war, battle), both ποιέω with Usage APB [§6.1a] and πόλεμος with Usage B{P}B [§6.1h] can license a third argument Benefactive that is realized by P/μετά [+gen] (against). In order to avoid duplicate references to the P/μετά [+gen] complement, the prepositional phrase is attributed only to the licensing properties of ποιέω.[1] The translation introduces in double brackets, [[ ]], the contextual referent of the coinstantiated Agent (the ones dwelling on the earth).

---

[1] As a consequence, the occurrences of πόλεμος when licensed by ποιέω and accompanied by P/μετά [+gen] complement consistently are listed as having a DNC third argument whose referent is retrieved from the third argument of ποιέω.

ποιῆσαι εἰκόνα τῷ θηρίῳ (13:14b)
[[The ones dwelling on the earth (1/Agt)]] to make (ποιέω) [an image (2/Pat)] [for the beast (3/Ben)].

ὅταν τελέσωσιν τὴν μαρτυρίαν αὐτῶν, τὸ θηρίον τὸ ἀναβαῖνον ἐκ τῆς ἀβύσσου ποιήσει μετ' αὐτῶν πόλεμον (11:7)
[When they complete their testimony (C/Tem)] [the beast coming up from the abyss (1/Agt)] will make (ποιέω) [war (2/Pat)] [against them (3/Ben)].

	ποιέω (13:14b) <*Ben.* APB [§6.1a]>		
syn.	1	2	3
sem.	Agt	Pat	Ben
lex.	N	N+acc	N+dat [+an]

	ποιέω (11:7) <*Ben.* APB [§6.1a]>				
syn.	1	2	3	|	C
sem.	Agt	Pat	Ben	|	Tem
lex.	N	N+acc	P/μετά [+gen]	|	V+ὅταν

b. Usage A{P}B

Verb and participle predicators grammaticalize event APB with the Usage of Agentive Benefaction with a Suppressed Patient, A{P}B.[2] The conceptualization of benefaction with this usage has a suppressed Patient {P} that never is realized as a complement and draws its referent from the predicator, no argument promotion, and no suppression of the Benefactive. The predicators raise the Agent entity as first argument, the Patient entity as (suppressed) second argument, and the Benefactive entity as third argument. The following examples provide two translations of each Greek predicator separated by a slash, /: the former introduces the referents of the suppressed Patient complements in braces, { }, and the second provides an equivalent English predicator with a suppressed Patient complement.

verb   οὗτοι μετὰ τοῦ ἀρνίου πολεμήσουσιν (17:14)
        [These (1/Agt)] make {war (2/Pat)}/battle (πολεμέω) [against the lamb (3/Ben)].

part.   ὁ κατηγορῶν αὐτοὺς ἐνώπιον τοῦ θεοῦ ἡμῶν ἡμέρας καὶ νυκτός (12:10)
        [The one (1/Agt)] making {accusations (2/Pat)} against/accusing (κατηγορῶν) [them (3/Ben)] [before God (C/Loc)] [day and night (C/Tem)].

---

[2] Usage A{P}B: verbs, βλασφημέω, βοηθέω, πολεμέω; and participle, κατηγορῶν.

	πολεμέω (17:14) <Ben. A{P}B [§6.1b]>		
syn.	1	{{2}}	3
sem.	Agt	Pat	Ben
lex.	N	{N}	P/μετά [+gen]

	κατηγορῶν (12:10) <Ben. A{P}B [§6.1b]>					
syn.	1	{{2}}	3	|	C	C
sem.	Agt	Pat	Ben	|	Loc	Tem
lex.	N	{N}	N+acc	|	P/ἐνώπιον	N+gen

c. Usage BP

Verb, participle, and complex predicators grammaticalize event PB with the Usage of Benefaction of a Patient, BP.[3] The conceptualization of benefaction with this usage has no suppression of the Patient, a promoted Benefactive, and no suppression of the Benefactive. The predicators raise the Benefactive entity as first argument and the Patient entity as second argument.

    verb   ὑπομονὴν ἔχεις (2:3)
              [You (1/Ben)] have (ἔχω) [endurance (2/Pat)].

    part.   ἄλλον ἄγγελον...ἔχοντα ἐξουσίαν μεγάλην (18:1)
              [Another angel (1/Ben)]...having (ἔχων) [great authority (2/Pat)].

    cp-part τὸ τεῖχος τῆς πόλεως ἔχων θεμελίους δώδεκα (21:14)
              [The wall of the city (1/Ben)] is having (ἔχων + [εἰμί]) [twelve foundations (2/Pat)].

	ἔχω (2:3) <Ben. BP [§6.1c]>		ἔχων (18:1) <Ben. BP [§6.1c]>		ἔχων + [εἰμί] (21:14) <Ben. BP [§6.1c]>	
syn.	1	2	1	2	1	2
sem.	Ben	Pat	Ben	Pat	Ben	Pat
lex.	N	N+acc	N	N+acc	N	N+acc

d. Usage BP/¹P²

Only verb predicator ἔχω (1b) (have) grammaticalizes event BP¹/P² with the Usage of Benefaction with a Bifurcated Patient, BP¹/P². The conceptualization of benefaction with this usage has no suppression of the Patient, a promoted Benefactive, no suppression of the Benefactive, and a bifurcated Patient. The predicator raises the Benefactive entity as first argument and the bifurcated Patient entity as second argument.

---

[3] Usage BP: verb, ἔχω (1a); participle, ἔχων (1a); and complex predicator, ἔχων + [εἰμί] (1a).

τοῦτο ἔχεις, ὅτι μισεῖς τὰ ἔργα τῶν Νικολαϊτῶν ἃ κἀγὼ μισῶ (2:6)
[You (1/Ben)] have (ἔχω) [this (2/Pat¹)] [that you hate the works of the Nicolaitans which I also hate (2/Pat²)].

	ἔχω (2:6) <Ben. BP¹/P² [§6.1d]>	
syn.	1	2
sem.	Ben	Pat¹/Pat²
lex.	N	N+acc/V+ὅτι

e. Usage B[P]L

Only participle predicator ἔχων (1c) (having) grammaticalizes event BPL with the Usage of Benefaction of an Idiomatic Patient with a Locative, B[P]L. The conceptualization of benefaction with this usage has no suppression of the Patient, omission of the Patient with an idiomatic (i.e., not predictable from the predicator) referent (child), promotion of the Benefactive, and no suppression of the Benefactive. The predicator raises the Benefactive entity as first argument, the idiomatic Patient entity as second (unrealized) argument, and the Locative entity as third argument. In this example, the translation introduces in double brackets, [[ ]], the idiomatic referent of the unrealized Patient complement (a child).

γυνὴ...ἐν γαστρὶ ἔχουσα (12:2)
[A woman (1/Ben)]...having (ἔχων) [[a child (2/Pat)]] [in the womb (3/Loc)].

	ἔχων (12:2) <Ben. B[P]L [§6.1e]>		
syn.	1	[[2]]	3
sem.	Ben	Pat	Loc
lex.	N	[N]	P/ἐν

f. Usage PB

Verb, complex noun, and preposition predicators grammaticalize event PB with the Usage of Simple Benefaction, PB.[4] The conceptualization of benefaction with this usage has no suppression of the Patient, no argument promotion, and no suppression of the Benefactive. The predicators raise the Patient entity as first argument and the Benefactive entity as second argument. As the second example (7:10) with permissibly omitted εἰμί (2) (be [for]) and the third example (21:7) with υἱός + εἰμί (be a

---

[4] Usage PB: verbs, βασιλεύω, εἰμί (2), λατρεύω; complex predicators, ἄγγελος + εἰμί, [ἀπόστολος] + εἰμί, ἀρχή + [εἰμί], [βασιλεύς] + εἰμί, γένος + εἰμί, γλῶσσα + εἰμί, δικαίωμα + εἰμί, ἔθνος + εἰμί, εἰς + [εἰμί] (2), ἐκκλησία + εἰμί, θάνατος + εἰμί, θεός + εἰμί, ἱερεύς + εἰμί, κύριος + εἰμί, λαός + εἰμί, λυχνία + εἰμί, λύχνος + [εἰμί], μεγιστάν + εἰμί, [μέτρον] + εἰμί, ναός + εἰμί, ὄνομα + [εἰμί], πνεῦμα + εἰμί, πόλις + εἰμί, ῥίζα + εἰμί, συναγωγή + [εἰμί], σύνδουλος + εἰμί, τέλος + [εἰμί], υἱός + εἰμί, χήρα + εἰμί; and prepositions, εἰς (2), μετά (2), πρός (3).

son) indicate, this usage encompasses predicators characterized by the "dative of possession."[5]

verb λατρεύουσιν αὐτῷ ἡμέρας καὶ νυκτὸς ἐν τῷ ναῷ αὐτοῦ (7:15)
[They (1/Pat)] are servants (λατρεύω) [of/for him (2/Ben)] [day and night (C/Tem)] [in his temple (C/Loc)].

verb ἡ σωτηρία τῷ θεῷ ἡμῶν τῷ καθημένῳ ἐπὶ τῷ θρόνῳ καὶ τῷ ἀρνίῳ (7:10)
[Salvation (1/Pat)] is (εἰμί) [of our God sitting on the throne and of the lamb (2/Ben)].

cp-n αὐτὸς ἔσται μοι υἱός (21:7)
[He (1/Pat)] will be a son (υἱός + εἰμί) [of/for me (2/Ben)].

prep. ἵπποις…εἰς πόλεμον (9:7)
[Horses (1/Pat)]…for (εἰς) [war (2/Ben)].

	λατρεύω (7:15) <Ben. PB [§6.1f]>			εἰμί (7:10) <Ben. PB [§6.1f]>	
syn.	1	2	C C	1	2
sem.	Pat	Ben	Loc Tem	Pat	Ben
lex.	N	N+dat [+an]	P/ἐν N+gen	N	N+dat [+an]

	υἱός + εἰμί (21:7) <Ben. PB [§6.1f]>		εἰς (9:7) <Ben. PB [§6.1f]>	
syn.	1	2	1	2
sem.	Pat	Ben	Pat	Ben
lex.	N	N+dat [+an]	N	N+acc

g. Usage B{P}

Only noun predicators grammaticalize event PB with the Usage of Benefaction with a Suppressed Patient and a Promoted Benefactive, B{P}.[6] The conceptualization of benefaction with this usage has a suppressed Patient {P} that never is

---

[5] The dative of possession receives discussion in BDF 102 (§§189–190) and Smyth, *Greek Grammar*, 242 (§935).

[6] Usage B{P}: nouns, ἄγγελος, ἀδελφός, αἷμα, ἄλυσις, ἄμπελος, ἀνάπαυσις, ἀνάστασις, ἀνατολή, ἀνήρ, ἀπόστολος, ἀριθμός, ἅρμα, ἀρχή, ἄρχων, αὐλή, βασιλεία, βασιλεύς, βδέλυγμα, βιβλαρίδιον, βιβλίον, βίβλος, γάμος, γαστήρ, γλῶσσα, γυμνότης, γυνή (1), γωνία, δάκρυον, δεσπότης, διάδημα, δικαιοσύνη, δικαίωμα, δόξα, δοῦλος, δρέπανον, δύναμις, ἔθνος, ἐκκλησία, ἕλκος, ἐνδώμησις, ἔργον, ἐχθρός, ζυγός, ζωή, ζώνη, θεός, θρίξ, θρόνος, θύρα, θώραξ, ἱερεύς, ἱμάτιον, ἰσχύς, καιρός, καρδία, καρπός, κατήγωρ, κατοικητήριον, κέντρον, κέρας, κεφαλή, κιβωτός, κιθάρα, κλίνη, κοιλία, κολλούριον, κόπος, κράτος, κραυγή, κτίσις, κυβερνήτης, κύριος, λαός, ληνός, λιβανωτός, λίνον, λυχνία, λύχνος, μαστός, μάχαιρα, μεγιστάν, μέτρον, μέτωπον, μῆκος, μηρός, μήτηρ, μνῆμα, μύλος, ναός, νεφρός, νοῦς, νύμφη, νυμφίος, ὀδούς, ὄλυνθος, ὁμοίωμα, ὄνομα (1), οὐαί, οὐρά, οὖς, ὀφθαλμός, ὄψις, παρεμβολή, πατήρ, πλατεῖα, πλάτος, πλοῖον, πλοῦτος, πνεῦμα (1), πόλις, πόνος, ποτήριον, πούς, πρόσωπον, προφῆτις, πτέρυξ, πτῶμα, πτωχεία, πυλών, ῥάβδος, ῥίζα, ρομφαία, σάκκος, σάλπιγξ, σάρξ, σκηνή, σπέρμα, στέφανος, στῆθος, στολή, στόμα, στράτευμα, στρῆνος, συναγωγή, σύνδουλος, σφραγίς, τεῖχος, τέκνον, τέλος, τέχνη, τεχνίτης, τιμή, τιμιότης, τόξον, τόπος, υἱός, ὕψος, φαρμακεία, φάρμακον, φιάλη, φονεύς, φρέαρ, φυλή, φύλλον, φωνή, φῶς, φωστήρ, χείρ, Χριστός, ψευδοπροφήτης, ψυχή, ᾠδή.

realized as a complement and draws its referent from the predicator, promotion of the Benefactive, and no suppression of the Benefactive. The predicators raise the Benefactive entity as first argument and the Patient entity as (suppressed) second argument. The translations introduce the referents of the suppressed Patient complements in braces, { }.

τῷ αἵματί σου (5:9)
[Your (1/Ben)] blood (αἷμα) {blood (2/Pat)}.

ὁ υἱὸς τοῦ θεοῦ (2:18)
[God's (1/Ben)] son (υἱός) {son (2/Pat)}.

	αἷμα (5:9) <Ben. B{P} [§6.1g]>		υἱός (2:18) <Ben. B{P} [§6.1g]>	
syn.	1	{{2}}	1	{{2}}
sem.	Ben	Pat	Ben	Pat
lex.	N+gen	{N}	N+gen	{N}

h. Usage B{P}B

Only noun predicators grammaticalize event BPB with the Usage of Double Benefaction with a Suppressed Patient, B{P}B.[7] The conceptualization of benefaction with this usage has a suppressed Patient {P} that never is realized as a complement and draws its referent from the predicator, promotion of the agentive Benefactive, and no suppression of either Benefactive. The predicators raise the agentive Benefactive entity as first argument, the Patient entity as (suppressed) second argument, and the remaining Benefactive entity as third argument. The translation of 1:5 introduces in double brackets, [[ ]], the definite referent of the DNC second Benefactive (God), which is assumed to be supplied by the interpreter (§1.5a), and follows the English practice of realizing the second Benefactive by a prepositional phrase, in this case headed by "against."[8] The translation of 13:3, however, appears in two forms. The first follows the English practice of realizing the agentive Benefactive by a noun in the possessive case ('s) and the remaining Benefactive by an "of" prepositional phrase, and the second follows a competing English practice of realizing the +animate and personal Benefactive by a noun in the possessive case ('s) and the non-personal agentive Benefactive by a "by" (sometimes "of") prepositional phrase. The translations introduce the referents of the suppressed Patient complements in braces, { }.

---

[7] Usage B{P}B: nouns, ἀδίκημα, αἰχμαλωσία, ἁμαρτία, ἀπαρχή, ἀπώλεια, βασανισμός, βλασφημία, δεῖπνον, διαθήκη, διακονία, δῶρον, εἰκών, εὐλογία, θεμέλιος, θεραπεία, θερισμός, θλῖψις, θυσιαστήριον, καταβολή, κλείς, κλέμμα, μισθός, ὁδός, πληγή, πόλεμος, πύρωσις, σωτηρία, φόνος, φυλακή, χαλινός, χάραγμα, χάρις.
[8] This discussion interprets "sins" as covenantal violations that make the sinner indebted to God as Benefactive; cf. Paul L. Danove, "The Action of Forgiving in the New Testament," in *Forgiveness: Selected Papers from the 2008 Annual Conference of the Villanova University Theology Institute* (ed. Darlene Fozard Weaver and Jeffrey S. Mayer; Villanova, PA: Villanova University Press, 2008), 41–2.

τῶν ἁμαρτιῶν ἡμῶν (1:5)
[Our (1/Ben)] sins (ἁμαρτία) {sins (2/Pat)} [[against God (3/Ben)]].

ἡ πληγὴ τοῦ θανάτου αὐτοῦ (13:3)
[Death's (1/Ben)] wound (πληγή) {wound (2/Pat)} [of him (2/Ben)].
[His (2/Ben)] wound (πληγή) {wound (2/Pat)} [by death (1/Ben)].

	ἁμαρτία (1:5) <Ben. B{P}B p§6.1h]>			πληγή (13:3) <Ben. B{P}B p§6.1h]>		
syn.	1	{{2}}	[3]	1	{{2}}	3
sem.	Ben	Pat	Ben	Ben	Pat	Ben
lex.	N+gen	{N}	DNC	N+gen	{N}	N+gen

i. Usage PA{B}

Only the adjective predicator εἰδωλόθυτος (sacrificed {to idols}) grammaticalizes event APB with the Usage of Agentive Benefaction with a Promoted Patient and a Suppressed Benefactive, PA{B}. The conceptualization of benefaction with this usage has a suppressed Benefactive {B} that never is realized as a complement and draws its referent from the predicator, promotion of the Patient, and no suppression of the Patient. The predicator raises the Patient entity as first argument, the Agent entity as second argument, and the Benefactive entity as (suppressed) third argument. The translation introduces in double brackets, [[ ]], the definite referent of the DNC Patient (foods) and indefinite but circumscribed referent of the INC Agent (someone) and introduces the referent of the never-realized and suppressed Benefactive complement in braces, { }.

εἰδωλόθυτα (2:14)
[[Foods (1/Pat)]] sacrificed (εἰδωλόθυτος) [[by someone (2/Agt)]] {to idols (3/Ben)}.

	εἰδωλόθυτος (2:14) <Ben. PA{B} {§6.1i]>		
syn.	[1]	(2)	{{3}}
sem.	Pat	Agt	Ben
lex.	DNC	INC	{N}

j. Usage {B}{P}

Only the noun predicator χιλίαρχος ({commander} {of a thousand}) grammatiŧ calizes event PB with the Usage of Benefaction with a Suppressed Benefactive and a Suppressed Patient, {B}{P}. The conceptualization of benefaction with this usage has a suppressed Benefactive {B} that is not realized as a complement and draws its referent from the predicator, a suppressed Patient {P} that never is realized as a complement and draws its referent from the predicator, and promotion of the Benefactive. The predicator raises the Benefactive entity as (suppressed) first argument and the Patient entity as the (suppressed) second argument. The translation introduces the referents of the suppressed complements in braces, { }.

οἱ χιλίαρχοι (6:15)
The commanders (χιλίαρχος) {of a thousand (1/Ben)} {commanders (2/Pat)}.

	χιλίαρχος (6:15) <Ben. {B}{P} [§6.1j]>	
syn.	{{1}}	{{2}}
sem.	Ben	Pat
lex.	{N}	{N}

2. Usages of Communion (Com.)

The event of communion (*Com.*) contains two entities that are associated with the Patient (P) and Comitative (Com) thematic roles. The base configuration of communion (PCom) admits to alternate formulation by the event feature incorporation (§2.3) by the addition of a Locative entity in third position (PComL). The differing conceptualizations of the base and alternate configurations of communion grammaticalized by predicators require description by two usage features: suppression of the Patient (§3.8a) and argument promotion (§3.8d). These usage features distinguish the conceptualizations of the three observed usages of the event of communion in the text of Revelation. The following discussion describes and provides illustrative examples of each of the three observed usages of communion by the categories of predicators.

a. Usage PComL

Only the verb predicator συγκοινωνέω (be a partner) grammaticalizes event PComL with the Usage of Communion in a Location, PComL. The conceptualization of communion with this usage has no suppression of the Patient and no argument promotion. The predicator raises the Patient entity as first argument, the Comitative entity as second argument, and the Locative entity as third argument. The translation introduces in double brackets, [[ ]], the contextual referent of the DNC Comitative (her/Babylon the Great, cf. 13:2).

μὴ συγκοινωνήσητε ταῖς ἁμαρτίαις αὐτῆς (18:4)
[You (1/Pat)] may not be a partner (συγκοινωνέω) [[with her/Babylon the Great (2/Com)]] [in her sins (3/Loc)].

	συγκοινωνέω (18:4) <*Com.* PComL [§6.2a]>		
syn.	1	[2]	3
sem.	Pat	Com	Loc
lex.	N	DNC	N+dat [+an]

b. Usage Com{P}L

Only the noun predicator συγκοινωνός (partner) grammaticalizes event PComL with the Usage of Communion in a Location with a Promoted Comitative and a Suppressed Patient, Com{P}L. The conceptualization of communion with this usage has a suppressed Patient {P} that never is realized as a complement and draws its referent from the predicator and promotion of the Comitative. The predicator raises the Comitative entity as (promoted) first argument, the Patient entity as (suppressed) second argument, and the Locative entity as third argument. The translation uses a possessive adjective for the animate personal pronoun realization of the Comitative complement and introduces the referent of the suppressed Patient complements in braces, { }.

ὑμῶν καὶ συγκοινωνὸς ἐν τῇ θλίψει καὶ βασιλείᾳ καὶ ὑπομονῇ ἐν Ἰησοῦ (1:9)
And [your (1/Com)] partner (συγκοινωνός) {partner (2/Pat)} [in the oppression and the kingdom and the endurance (3/Loc)] [in Jesus (C/Loc)].

	συγκοινωνός (1:9) <Com. Com{P}L [§6.2b]>				
syn.	1	{{2}}	3	|	C
sem.	Com	Pat	Loc	|	Loc
lex.	N+gen	{N}	P/ἐν	|	P/ἐν

c. Usage PCom

Only the preposition predicator μετά (5) ([together] with) grammaticalizes event PCom with the Usage of Communion, PCom. The conceptualization of communion with this usage has no suppression of the Patient and no argument promotion. The predicator raises the Patient entity as first argument and the Comitative entity as second argument.

οἱ ἄγγελοι αὐτοῦ μετ᾽ αὐτοῦ (12:9)
[His angels (1/Pat)] [together] with (μετά) [him (2/Com)].

	μετά (12:9) <Com. PCom [§6.2c]>	
syn.	1	2
sem.	Pat	Com
lex.	N	N+gen

3. Usages of Effect (Eff.)

The event of effect (*Eff.*) contains two entities that are associated with the Agent (A) and Patient (P) thematic roles. The base configuration of effect (AP) does not admit to alternate formulation by event features. The differing conceptualizations of the base configuration of effect grammaticalized by predicators require description by two usage features: suppression of the Patient (§3.8a), and argument promotion (§3.8d).

6. *Predicator Usages of Other Events and Non-Events* 139

These usage features distinguish the conceptualizations of the three usages of the event of effect in the text of Revelation. The following discussion describes and provides illustrative examples of each of the three observed usages of effect by the categories of predicators.

a. Usage AP

Verb, participle, and complex participle predicators grammaticalize event AP with the Usage of Effect, AP.[9] The conceptualization of effect with this usage has no suppression of the Patient and no argument promotion. The predicators raise the Agent entity as first argument and the Patient entity as second argument.

verb κατέφαγον αὐτό (10:10)
      [I (1/Agt)] ate (κατεσθίω) [it (2/Pat)].

part. τοὺς διαφθείροντας τὴν γῆν (11:18b)
      [The ones (1/Agt)] destroying (διαφθείρων) [the earth (2/Pat)].

cp-part ὁ καθήμενος ἐπ' αὐτὸν ἔχων τόξον (6:2)
        [The one sitting on it (1/Agt)] was holding (ἔχων + [εἰμί]) [a bow (2/Pat)].

	κατεσθίω (10:10)		διαφθείρων (11:18b)		ἔχων + [εἰμί] (6:2)	
	<*Eff.* AP [§6.3a]>		<*Eff.* AP [§6.3a]>		<*Eff.* AP [§6.3a]>	
syn.	1	2	1	2	1	2
sem.	Agt	Pat	Agt	Pat	Agt	Pat
lex.	N	N+acc	N	N+acc	N	N+acc

b. Usage A{P}

Verb and participle predicators grammaticalize event AP with the Usage of Effect with a Suppressed Patient, A{P}.[10] The conceptualization of effect with this usage has a suppressed Patient {P} that never is realized as a complement and draws its referent from the predicator and no argument promotion. The predicators raise the Agent entity as first argument and the Patient entity as (suppressed) second argument. The translations introduce the referents of the suppressed Patient complements in braces, { }.

---

[9] Usage AP: verbs, ἀδικέω, ᾄδω, αἴρω, ἀνοίγω, ἀποκτείνω, ἀπόλλυμι, ἀριθμέω, ἀρνέομαι, ἀφίημι (2), βασανίζω, γράφω (2), δειπνέω, δέω, διαφθείρω, δίδωμι (2), διπλόω, δοξάζω, ἐκκεντέω, ἐκχέω (2), ἐλέγχω, ἐργάζομαι, ἐσθίω, ἑτοιμάζω, εὑρίσκω (1), ἔχω (3), θεραπεύω, θερίζω, κατακαίω, καταπίνω, κατεσθίω, καυματίζω, κεράννυμι, κλείω, κολλάω, κρατέω, κρούω, κτίζω, κυκλεύω, λαμβάνω (3), μασάομαι, μεθύσκω, μετρέω, μολύνω, νικάω, ξηραίνω, παιδεύω, παίω, πατάσσω, πατέω, πειράζω, πιάζω, πίνω, πλανάω (2), πληρόω, πλήσσω, πλύνω, ποιέω (1a), ποιμαίνω, σταυρόω, στηρίζω, συντρίβω, σύρω, σφάζω, σφραγίζω, τελέω, τηρέω (1), τίκτω, τρέφω, φθείρω, φωτίζω, χορτάζω, ψηφίζω; participles, ἀδικῶν, ἀνοίγων, ἀποδιδούς (2), βαστάζων (2), διαφθείρων, ἔχων (3), κλείων, κρατῶν, νικῶν, πλανῶν (2), πλύνων, ποιήσας (1a), ποιῶν (1a), τηρῶν (1); and complex predicator, ἔχων + [εἰμί] (3).

[10] Usage A{P}: verbs, κράζω (2), μυκάομαι, ποιέω (1b), σαλπίζω; and participles, κιθαρίζων, πλέων.

140   *A Case Frame Grammar and Lexicon for the Book of Revelation*

verb σαλπίσωσιν (8:6)
[They (1/Agt)] might blow (σαλπίζω) {the trumpets (2/Pat)}.

part. κιθαρῳδῶν κιθαριζόντων ἐν ταῖς κιθάραις αὐτῶν (14:2)
[Harpists (1/Agt)] playing (κιθαρίζων) {harps (2/Pat)} [by means of their harps (C/Ins)].

	σαλπίζω (8:6) <*Eff.* A{P} [§6.3b]>		κιθαρίζων (14:2) <*Eff.* A{P} [§6.3b]>		
syn.	1	{{2}}	1	{{2}}	| C
sem.	Agt	Pat	Agt	Pat	| Ins
lex.	N	{N}	N	{N}	| P/ἐν

c. Usage PA

Verb, participle, complex noun (passive infinitive), and preposition predicators grammaticalize event AP with the usage of Effect by an Agent, PA.[11] The conceptualization of effect with this usage has no suppression of the Patient and promotion of the Patient. The predicators raise the Patient entity as (promoted) first argument and the Agent entity as second argument. The translations introduce in double brackets, [[ ]], the contextual referent of the DNC Agent (God) in 21:6 and of the indefinite but circumscribed referent of the INC Agent (someone) in 13:10.

verb γέγοναν (21:6)
[They (1/Pat)] have come to be (γίνομαι) [[by God (2/Agt)]].

part. τόπον ἡτοιμασμένον ἀπὸ τοῦ θεοῦ, ἵνα ἐκεῖ τρέφωσιν αὐτὴν ἡμέρας χιλίας διακοσίας ἑξήκοντα (12:6)
[A place (1/Pat)] prepared (ἡτοιμασμένος) [by God (2/Agt)] [so that they might feed her there for one thousand two hundred sixty days (C/Pur)].

cp-n τις ἐν μαχαίρῃ ἀποκτανθῆναι (13:10a)
[Someone (1/Pat)] is to be killed (ἀποκτανθῆναι + [εἰμί]) [by/with a sword (C/Ins)] [[by someone (2/Agt)]].

prep. τόπον...ἀπὸ τοῦ θεοῦ (12:6)
[A place (1/Pat)]...by (ἀπό) [God (2/Agt)].

---

[11] Usage PA: verb, γίνομαι (2); participles, βασανιζόμενος, γεγραμμένος (2), δεδεμένος, ἐλισσόμενος, ἐπιγεγραμμένος (2), ἐσφαγμένος, ἐσφραγισμένος, ἠνεῳγμένος, ἡτοιμασμένος, κατεσφραγισμένος, κεκερασμένος, κεκοσμημένος, πεπελεκισμένος, πεπληρωμένος, πεπυρωμένος, σειόμενος; complex predeicators, ἀποκτανθῆναι...αὐτὸν + [εἰμί], ἐκλεκτός + [εἰμί], ἠνεῳγμένος + [εἰμί], κεκοσμημένος + [εἰμί], κλητός + [εἰμί]; and prepositions, ἀπό (2), ὑπό.

	γίνομαι (21:6)			ἠτοιμασμένος (12:6)	
	<Eff. PA [§6.3c]>			<Eff. PA [§6.3c]>	
syn.	1	[2]	1	2	C
sem.	Pat	Agt	Pat	Agt	Pur
lex.	N	DNC	N	P/ἀπὸ	V+ἵνα

	ἀποκτανθῆναι + [εἰμί] (13:10a)			ἀπό (12:6)	
	<Eff. PA [§6.3c]>			<Eff. PA [§6.3c]>	
syn.	1	(2)	C	1	2
sem.	Pat	Agt	Ins	Pat	Agt
lex.	N	INC	P/ἐν	N	N+gen

4. Usages of Instrumentality (Ins.)

The event of Instrumentality (*Ins.*) contains two entities that are associated with the Patient (P) and Instrument (I) thematic roles. The base configuration of instrumentality (PI) admits to alternate formulation by two event features: incorporation (§2.3) and reinterpretation (§2.4). Entity incorporation expands the base configuration of the event by the addition of an Agent in first position (API). Entity reinterpretation highlights the agentive Benefactive function of the Agent entity of event API (BPI). The differing conceptualizations of the base and alternate configurations of instrumentality grammaticalized by predicators require description by three usage features: suppression of the Patient (§3.8a), suppression of the Instrument (§3.8b), and argument promotion (3.8d). These usage features distinguish the conceptualizations of the seven usages of the event of instrumentality in the text of Revelation. The following discussion describes and provides illustrative examples of each of the seven observed usages of instrumentality by the categories of predicators.

a. Usage API

Only verb predicators grammaticalize event API with the Usage of Agentive Instrumentality, API.[12] The conceptualization of instrumentality with this usage has no suppression of the Patient, no suppression of the Instrument, and no argument promotion. The predicators raise the Agent entity as first argument, the Patient entity as second argument, and the Instrument entity as third argument. The translations introduce in double brackets, [[ ]], the referent of the coinstantiated Agent (you) and the contextual referent of the DNC Instrument (salve) in 3:18 and the indefinite but circumscribed referent of the INC Agent (someone) in 3:5. Although the first complement of the infinitive in 3:18 ultimately is coinstantiated by the second complement of συμβουλεύω (recommend) and so is not realized as a complement within the infinitive phrase, the Valence Description for this example follows the convention (§1.4) of listing the first complement of the infinitive verb predicator with the syntactic function as "1" (no brackets) and the lexical realization "N."

---

[12] Usage API: verbs, ἐγχρίω, περιβάλλω.

ἐγχρῖσαι τοὺς ὀφθαλμούς σου ἵνα βλέπῃς (3:18)
[[You (1/Agt)]] to anoint (ἐγχρίω) [your eyes (2/Pat)] [[with salve (3/Ins)]] [so that you may see (C/Pur)].

ὁ νικῶν οὕτως περιβαλεῖται ἐν ἱματίοις λευκοῖς (3:5)
[The one conquering (2/Pat)] [thus (C/Man)] will be wrapped (περιβάλλω) [[by someone (1/Agt)]] [by/with white garments (3/Ins)].

	ἐγχρίω (3:18) <Ins. API [§6.4a]>				περιβάλλω (3:5) <Ins. API [§6.4a]>			
syn.	1	2	[3]	| C	1	2	3	| C
sem.	Agt	Pat	Ins	| Pur	Agt	Pat	Ins	| Man
lex.	N	N+acc	DNC	| V+ἵνα	N	N+acc	P/ἐν	| A/οὕτως

b. Usage A{P}I

Verb and participle predicators grammaticalize event API with the Usage of Agentive Instrumentality with a Suppressed Patient, A{P}I.[13] The conceptualization of instrumentality with this usage has a suppressed Patient {P} that never is realized as a complement and draws its referent from the predicator, no suppression of the Instrument, and no argument promotion. The predicators raise the Agent entity as first argument, the Patient entity as (suppressed) second argument, and the Instrument entity as third argument. The translations introduce the referents of the suppressed Patient complements in braces, { }.

verb   οἱ βασιλεῖς τῆς γῆς μετ' αὐτῆς ἐπόρνευσαν (18:3)
[The kings of the earth (1/Agt)] engaged in {sexual immorality (2/Pat)} (πορνεύω) [with/by her (3/Ins)].

part.   τοὺς μοιχεύοντας μετ' αὐτῆς (2:22)
[The ones (1/Agt)] committing {adultery (2/Pat)} (μοιχεύων) [with/by her (3/Ins)].

	πορνεύω (18:3) <Ins. A{P}I [§6.4b]>			μοιχεύων (2:22) <Ins. A{P}I [§6.4b]>		
syn.	1	{{2}}	3	1	{{2}}	3
sem.	Agt	Pat	Ins	Agt	Pat	Ins
lex.	N	{N}	P/μετά [+gen]	N	{N}	P/μετά [+gen]

c. Usage AP{I}

Only the verb predicator ποτίζω (provide {with a cup [of something able to be drunk]}) grammaticalizes event API with the Usage of Agentive Instrumentality with

---

[13] Usage A{P}I: verb, πορνεύω; and participles, μοιχεύων, πορνεύσας.

a Suppressed Instrument, AP{I}. The conceptualization of instrumentality with this usage has no suppression of the Patient, a suppressed Instrument {I} that never is realized as a complement and draws its referent from the predicator, and no argument promotion. The predicator raises the Agent entity as first argument, the Patient entity as second argument, and the Instrument entity as (suppressed) third argument. The translation interprets the phrase "of the wine of the passion of her sexual immorality" as the Material complement of the suppressed Instrument and introduces the referent of the suppressed Instrument complement in braces, { }.

ἣ ἐκ τοῦ οἴνου τοῦ θυμοῦ τῆς πορνείας αὐτῆς πεπότικεν πάντα τὰ ἔθνη (14:8)
[Who (1/Agt)] has provided (ποτίζω) [all the nations (2/Pat)] {with a cup [of the wine of the passion of her sexual immorality] (3/Ins)}.

	ποτίζω (14:8) <Ins. AP{I} [§6,4c]>		
syn.	1	2	{{3}}
sem.	Agt	Pat	Ins
lex.	N	N+acc	{N}

d. Usage PAI

Participle and complex participle predicators grammaticalize event API with the Usage of Instrumentality by an Agent, PAI.[14] The conceptualization of instrumentality with this usage has no suppression of the Patient, no suppression of the Instrument, and promotion of the Patient. The predicators raise the Patient entity as (promoted) first argument, the Agent entity as second argument, and the Instrument entity as third argument. The translations introduce in double brackets, [[ ]], the indefinite but circumscribed referent of the INC Agent (someone).

part. υἱὸν ἀνθρώπου ἐνδεδυμένον ποδήρη (1:13)
[A son of man (1/Pat)] clothed (ἐνδεδυμένος) [[by someone (2/Agt)]] [with/by a robe to the feet (3/Ins)].

cp-part ἡ γυνὴ ἦν...κεχρυσωμένη χρυσίῳ καὶ λίθῳ τιμίῳ καὶ μαργαρίταις (17:4)
[The woman (1/Pat)]...was encrusted (κεχρυσωμένος + εἰμί) [[by someone (2/Agt)]] [with/by gold and precious stone and pearls (3/Ins)].

	ἐνδεδυμένος (1:13) <Ins. PAI [§6.4d]>			κεχρυσωμένος + εἰμί (17:4) <Ins. PAI [§6.4d]>		
syn.	1	(2)	3	1	(2)	3
sem.	Pat	Agt	Ins	Pat	Agt	Ins
lex.	N	INC	N+acc	N	INC	N+dat [−an]

---

[14] Usage PAI: participles, ἐνδεδυμένος, κεχρυσωμένος, μεμιγμένος, περιβεβλημένος, περιεζωσμένος; and complex predicators, κεχρυσωμένος + εἰμί, περιβεβλημένος + [εἰμί].

e. Usage PI

Only preposition predicators grammaticalize event PI with the Usage of Instrumentality, PI.[15] The conceptualization of instrumentality with this usage has no suppression of the Patient, no suppression of the Instrument, and no argument promotion. The predicators raise the Patient entity as first argument and the Instrument entity as second argument.

τὰ ἔθνη διὰ τοῦ φωτὸς αὐτῆς (21:24)
[The nations (1/Pat)] by means of (διά) [its light (2/Ins)].

τὰ τέκνα αὐτῆς...ἐν θανάτῳ (2:23)
[Her children (1/Pat)]...by [means of] (ἐν) [death (2/Ins)].

	διά (21:24) <*Ins.* PI [§6.4e]>		ἐν (2:23) <*Ins.* PI [§6.4e]>	
syn.	1	2	1	2
sem.	Pat	Ins	Pat	Ins
lex.	N	N+gen	N	N+dat

f. Usage B{P}I

Only the noun predicator πορνεία (sexual immorality) grammaticalizes event BPI with the Nominal Usage of Instrumentality by a Benefactive, B{P}I. The conceptualization of instrumentality with this usage has a suppressed Patient {P} that never is realized as a complement and draws its referent from the predicator, no suppression of the Instrument, and no argument promotion. The predicator raises the agentive Benefactive entity as first argument, the Patient entity as (suppressed) second argument, and the Instrument entity as third argument. The translation introduces in double brackets, [[ ]], the contextual referent of the DNC Instrument (the kings of the earth), follows the English practice of realizing the agentive Benefactive by a possessive adjective, and introduces the referent of the suppressed Patient complement in braces, {}.

τῆς πορνείας αὐτῆς (17:2)
[Her (1/Ben)] sexual immorality (πορνεία) {sexual immorality (2/Pat)} [[with/by the kings of the earth (3/Ins)]].

	πορνεία (17:2) <*Ins.* B{P}I [§6.4f]>		
syn.	1	{{2}}	[3]
sem.	Ben	Pat	Ins
lex.	N	{N}	DNC

---

[15] Usage PI: prepositions, ἀπό (3), διά (1), ἐκ (3), ἐν (2), μετά (4).

g. Usage P{I}

Only the participle predicator ποταμοφόρητος (swept away {by a river}) grammaticalizes event PI with the Usage of Instrumentality by a Suppressed Instrument. The conceptualization of instrumentality with this usage has a suppressed Instrument {I} that never is realized as a complement and draws its referent from the predicator, no suppression of the Patient, and no argument promotion. The predicator raises the Patient entity as first argument and the Instrument entity as (suppressed) second argument. The translation introduces in double brackets, [[ ]], the contextual referent of the DNC Patient (her/the woman) and the referent of the suppressed Instrument complement in braces, { }.

ποταμοφόρητον (12:15)
[[Her/the woman (1/Pat)]] swept away (ποταμοφόρητος) {by a river (2/Ins)}.

	ποταμοφόρητος (12:15) <Ins. P{I} [§6.4g]>	
syn.	[1]	{2}
sem.	Pat	Ins
lex.	DNC	{N}

5. Usages of Materiality (Mat.)

The event of materiality (*Mat.*) contains two entities that are associated with the Patient (P) and Material (M) thematic roles. The base configuration of materiality (PM) admits to alternate formulation by two event features: incorporation (§2.3) and reinterpretation (§2.4). Entity incorporation expands the configuration of the base event through the addition of an Agent (A) in first position (APM). Entity reinterpretation highlights the agentive Benefactive function of the first entity of event APM (BPM). The differing conceptualizations of the base and alternate configurations of materiality grammaticalized by predicators require description by two usage features: suppression of the Patient (§3.8a) and argument promotion (§3.8d). These usage features distinguish the conceptualizations of the four usages of the event of materiality in the text of Revelation. The following discussion describes and provides illustrative examples of each of the four observed usages of materiality by the categories of predicators.

a. Usage APM

Only the verb predicator γεμίζω (fill) grammaticalizes event APM with the Usage of Agentive Materiality, APM. The conceptualization of materiality with this usage has no suppression of the Patient and no argument promotion. The predicator raises the Agent entity as first argument, the Patient entity as second argument, and the Material entity as third argument.

ἐγέμισεν αὐτὸν ἐκ τοῦ πυρὸς τοῦ θυσιαστηρίου (8:5)
[He (1/Agt)] filled (γεμίζω) [it (2/Pat)] [with the fire of the altar (3/Mat)].

	γεμίζω (8:5) <Mat. APM [§6.5a]>		
syn.	1	2	3
sem.	Agt	Pat	Mat
lex.	N	N+acc	P/ἐκ

b. Usage PM

Participle, complex noun, and preposition predicators grammaticalize event PM with the Usage of Materiality, PM.[16] The conceptualization of materiality with this usage has no suppression of the Patient and no argument promotion. The predicators raise the Patient entity as first argument and the Material entity as second argument.

part. φιάλας χρυσᾶς γεμούσας θυμιαμάτων (5:8)
[Golden bowls (1/Pat)] being full (γέμων) [of incenses (2/Mat)].

cp-n ἦν ὁ ἀριθμὸς αὐτῶν μυριάδες μυριάδων (5:11)
[Their number (1/Pat)] was ten-thousand-member groups (μυρίας + εἰμί) [of ten-thousand-member groups (2/Mat)].

prep. πᾶν σκεῦος ἐκ ξύλου τιμιωτάτου (18:12)
[Every vessel (1/Pat)] of (ἐκ) [precious wood (2/Mat)].

	γέμων (5:8) <Mat. PM [§6.5b]>		μυρίας + εἰμί (5:11) <Mat. PM [§6.5b]>	
syn.	1	2	1	2
sem.	Pat	Mat	Pat	Mat
lex.	N	N+gen	N	N+gen

	ἐκ (18:12) <Mat. PM [§6.5b]>	
syn.	1	2
sem.	Pat	Mat
lex.	N	N+gen

c. Usage M{P}

Only noun predicators grammaticalize event PM the Nominal Usage of Materiality, M{P}.[17] The conceptualization of materiality with this usage has a suppressed Patient {P} that never is realized as a complement and draws its referent from the predicator

---

[16] Usage PM: participle, γέμων; complex predicators, δισμυριάς + [εἰμί], ἐκ + [εἰμί] (4), μυρίας + εἰμί, χιλιάς + εἰμί; and preposition, ἐκ (4).
[17] Usage M{P}: nouns, αἰών, ἔμπορος, λαμπάς, μυριάς, πηγή, ποταμός, στῦλος, φλόξ, χιλιάς, χοῖνιξ.

and promotion of the Material. The predicators raise the Material entity as (promoted) first argument and the Patient entity as (suppressed) second argument. The translations introduce the referents of the never-realized Patient complements in braces, { }.

ζωῆς πηγὰς ὑδάτων (7:17)
Springs (πηγή) [of the waters of life (1/Mat)] {springs (2/Pat)}.

χοῖνιξ σίτου (6:6a)
A quart (χοῖνιξ) [of wheat (1/Mat)] {quart (2/Pat)}.

	πηγή (7:17) <Mat. M{P} [§6.5c]>		χοῖνιξ (6:6a) <Mat. M{P} [§6.5c]>	
syn.	1	{{2}}	1	{{2}}
sem.	Mat	Pat	Mat	Pat
lex.	N	{N}	N	{N}

d. Usage B{P}M

Only noun predicators grammaticalize event BPM with the Nominal Usage of Materiality with a Benefactive, B{P}M.[18] The conceptualization of materiality with this usage has a suppressed Patient {P} that never is realized as a complement and draws its referent from the predicator and no argument promotion. The predicators raise the agentive Benefactive entity as first argument, the Patient entity as (suppressed) second argument, and the Material entity as third argument. The translations introduce in double brackets, [[ ]], the contextual referent of the DNC Benefactive (merchants), follow the English practice of realizing the agentive Benefactive by a noun in the possessive case (s'), and introduce the referents of the suppressed Patient complements in braces, { }.

γόμον χρυσοῦ καὶ ἀργύρου καὶ... (18:12)
[[Merchants' (1/Ben)]] cargo (γόμος) {cargo (2/Pat)} [of gold and silver and... (3/Mat)].

σκεῦος ἐκ ξύλου τιμιωτάτου καὶ χαλκοῦ καὶ σιδήρου καὶ μαρμάρου (18:12b)
[[Merchants' (1/Ben)]] vessels (σκεῦος) {vessels (2/Pat)} [of precious wood and bronze and iron and marble (3/Mat)].

	γόμος (18:12) <Mat. B{P}M [§6.5d]>			σκεῦος (18:12b) <Mat. B{P}M [§6.5d]>		
syn.	[1]	{{2}}	3	[1]	{{2}}	3
sem.	Ben	Pat	Mat	Ben	Pat	Mat
lex.	DNC	{N}	N+gen	DNC	{N}	P/ἐκ

---

[18] Usage B{P}M: nouns, γόμος, σκεῦος.

6. Usages of Modification (Mod.)

The event of modification (*Mod.*) contains two entities that are associated with the Patient (P) and Resultative (R) thematic roles. This base configuration of modification (PR) admits to alternate formulation by the event feature incorporation (§2.3). This event feature expands the conceptualization of the event through the addition of an Agent entity in first position (APR). The differing conceptualizations of the base and alternate configurations of modification grammaticalized by predicators require description by two usage features: suppression of the Resultative (§3.8c) and argument promotion (§3.8d). These usage features distinguish the conceptualizations of the five usages of the event of modification in the text of Revelation. The following discussion describes and provides illustrative examples of the five observed usages of modification by the categories of predicators.

a. Usage APR

Verb and participle predicators grammaticalize event APR with the Usage of Agentive Modification, APR.[19] The conceptualization of modification with this usage has no suppression of the Resultative and no argument promotion. The predicators raise the Agent entity as first argument, the Patient entity as second argument, and the Resultative entity as third argument.

    verb   ἠρημωμένην ποιήσουσιν αὐτήν (17:16)
             [They (1/Agt)] will make (ποιέω) [her (2/Pat)] [desolated (3/Rst)].

    part.   ἡ λέγουσα ἑαυτὴν προφῆτιν (2:20)
             [The one (1/Agt)] calling (λέγων) [herself (2/Pat)] [a prophet (3/Rst)].

	ποιέω (17:16) <Mod. APR [§6.6a]>			λέγων (2:20) <Mod. APR [§6.6a]>		
syn.	1	2	3	1	2	3
sem.	Agt	Pat	Rst	Agt	Pat	Rst
lex.	N	N+acc	Adj+2	N	N+acc	N+2

b. Usage AP{R}

Only verb predicators grammaticalize event APR with the Usage of Modification with a Suppressed Resultative, AP{R}.[20] The conceptualization of modification with this usage has a suppressed Resultative {R} that never is realized as a complement and draws its referent from the predicator and no argument promotion. The predicators raise the Agent entity as first argument, the Patient entity as second argument, and the Resultative entity as (suppressed) third argument. The translations introduce the referents of the suppressed Resultative complements in braces { }.

---

[19] Usage APR: verbs, καλέω (1), λέγω (2), ποιέω (2), στρέφω; and participle, λέγων (2).
[20] Usage AP{R}: verbs, ἁγιάζω, ἐρημόω, λευκαίνω, πικραίνω, σκοτίζω, σκοτόω.

ἐλεύκαναν αὐτὰς ἐν τῷ αἵματι τοῦ ἀρνίου (7:14)
[They (1/Agt)] made (λευκαίνω) [them (2/Pat)] {white (3/Rst)} [by the blood of the lamb (C/Ins)].

πικρανεῖ σου τὴν κοιλίαν (10:9)
[It (1/Agt)] will make (πικραίνω) [your stomach (2/Pat)] {bitter (3/Rst)}.

	λευκαίνω (7:14) <Mod. AP{R} [§6.6b]>				πικραίνω (10:9) <Mod. AP{R} [§6.6b]>		
syn.	1	2	{{3}}	C	1	2	{{3}}
sem.	Agt	Pat	Rst	Ins	Agt	Pat	Rst
lex.	N	N+acc	{N}	P/ἐν	N	N+acc	{N}

c. Usage PAR

Only the participle predicator καλούμενος (being called) grammaticalizes event APR with the Usage of Modification by an Agent, PAR. The conceptualization of modification with this usage has no suppression of the Resultative and promotion of the Patient. The predicator raises the Patient entity as (promoted) first argument, the Agent entity as second argument, and the Resultative entity as third argument. The translation introduces in double brackets, [[ ]], the indefinite but circumscribed referent of the INC Agent (people).

ὁ καλούμενος Διάβολος καὶ ὁ Σατανᾶς (12:9)
[The one (1/Pat)] being called (καλούμενος) [[by people (2/Agt)]] [Devil and Satan (3/Rst)].

	καλούμενος (12:9) <Mod. PAR [§6.6c]>		
syn.	1	(2)	3
sem.	Pat	Agt	Rst
lex.	N	INC	N+1

d. Usage PA{R}

Only participle predicators grammaticalize event APR with the Usage of Modification by an Agent with a Suppressed Resultative PA{R}.[21] The conceptualization of modification with this usage has a suppressed Resultative {R} that never is realized as a complement and draws its referent from the predicator and promotion of the Patient. The predicators raise the Patient entity as (promoted) first argument, the Agent entity as second argument, and the Resultative entity as (suppressed) third argument. The translations introduce in double brackets, [[ ]], the contextual referent of the DNC Agent (the fifth angel who poured out the contents of the fifth bowl) in 16:10 and of

---

[21] Usage PA{R}: participles, ἐσκοτωμένος, ἠρημωμένος.

the DNC Agent (the ten horns and the beast) in 17:16 and introduce the referents of the suppressed Resultative complements in braces, { }.

ἡ βασιλεία αὐτοῦ ἐσκοτωμένη (16:10)
[Its kingdom (1/Pat)] made {dark (3/Rst)} (ἐσκοτωμένος) [[by the fifth angel who poured out the contents of the fifth bowl (2/Agt)]].

ἠρημωμένην...αὐτὴν (17:16)
[Her (1/Pat)]...made {desolated (3/Rst)} (ἠρημωμένος) [[by the ten horns and the beast (2/Agt)]].

	ἐσκοτωμένος (16:10) <Mod. PA{R} [§6.6d]>			ἠρημωμένος (17:16) <Mod. PA{R} [§6.6d]>		
syn.	1	[2]	{{3}}	1	[2]	{{3}}
sem.	Pat	Agt	Rst	Pat	Agt	Rst
lex.	N	DNC	{N}	N	DNC	{N}

e. Usage PR

Verb and preposition predicators grammaticalize event PR with the Usage of Modification, PR.[22] The conceptualization of modification with this usage has no suppression of the Resultative and no argument promotion. The predicators raise the Patient entity as first argument and the Resultative entity as second argument.

verb ἐγένετο τὸ τρίτον τῆς θαλάσσης αἷμα (8:8)
[A third of the sea (1/Pat)] became (γίνομαι) [blood (2/Rst)].

prep. αὐτὰ εἰς αἷμα (11:6)
[Them (1/Pat)] into (εἰς) [blood (2/Rst)].

	γίνομαι (8:8) <Mod. PR [§6.6e]>		εἰς (11:6) <Mod. PR [§6.6e]>	
syn.	1	2	1	2
sem.	Pat	Rst	Pat	Rst
lex.	N	N+1	N	N+acc

7. Usages of Partition (Par.)

The event of partition (*Par.*) contains two entities that are associated with the Patient (P) and Partitive (Par) thematic roles. The base configuration of partition (PPar) does not admit to alternate formulation by event features. The differing conceptualizations of the base configuration of partition grammaticalized by predicators require

---

[22] Usage PR: verb, γίνομαι (1); and prepositions, εἰς (3), ἐν (3).

description by two usage features: suppression of the Patient (§3.8a) and argument promotion (§3.8d). These usage features distinguish the conceptualizations of the two usages of the event of partition in the text of Revelation. The following discussion describes and provides illustrative examples of each of the two observed usages of partition by the categories of predicators.

a. Usage PPar

Complex adjective, adjective, and preposition predicators grammaticalize event PPar with the Usage of Partition, PPar.[23] The conceptualization of partition with this usage has no suppression of the Patient and no argument promotion. The predicators raise the Patient entity as first argument and the Partitive entity as second argument. The translation of 17:11 introduces in double brackets, [[ ]], the contextual referent of the DNC Partitive (the kings, cf. 17:9).

cp-adj   αὐτὸς ὄγδοός ἐστιν (17:11)
         [He (1/Pat) is the eighth (ὄγδοος + εἰμί) [[of the kings (2/Par)]].

adj.   εἷς ἕκαστος τῶν πυλώνων (21:21)
         Each (ἕκαστος) [one (1/Pat)] [of the gates (2/Par)].

prep.   εἷς ἐκ τῶν ἑπτὰ ἀγγέλων τῶν ἐχόντων τὰς ἑπτὰ φιάλας... (21:9)
         [One (1/Pat)] of (ἐκ) [the seven angels having the seven bowls... (2/Par)].

	ὄγδοος + εἰμί (17:11) <Par. PPar [§6.7a]>		ἕκαστος (21:21) <Par. PPar [§6.7a]>		ἐκ (21:9) <Par. PPar [§6.7a]>	
syn.	1	[2]	1	2	1	2
sem.	Pat	Par	Pat	Par	Pat	Par
lex.	N	DNC	N	N+gen	N	N+gen

b. Usage Par{P}

Only the noun predicator μέρος (portion, part) grammaticalizes event PPar with the Nominal Usage of Partition with a Suppressed Patient, Par{P}. The conceptualization of partition with this usage has a suppressed Patient {P} that never is realized as a complement and draws its referent from the predicator and promotion of the Partitive. The predicator raises the Partitive entity as first argument and the Patient entity as (suppressed) second argument. The translation introduces the referent of the suppressed Patient complement in braces, { }.

---

[23] Usage PPar: complex predicators, ὁ ἔσχατος + [εἰμί], ὄγδοος + εἰμί, πρῶτος + [εἰμί], ὁ πρῶτος + [εἰμί]; adjectives, δέκατος, δεύτερος, δωδέκατος, ἕβδομος, εἷς (2), ἕκαστος, ἕκτος, ἔνατος, ἑνδέκατος, ἔσχατος, ἥμισυς (2), λοιπός, ὄγδοος, πέμπτος, πολύς (2), πρῶτος, πρωτότοκος, τέταρτος, τρίτος; and prepositions, ἀπό (4), ἐκ (2).

τὸ μέρος αὐτοῦ ἀπὸ τοῦ ξύλου τῆς ζωῆς... (22:19)
[His (C/Ben)] portion (μέρος) [of the tree of life... (1/Par)] {portion (2/Pat)}.

	μέρος (22:19) <Par. Par{P} [§6.7b]>		
syn.	1	{{2}}	C
sem.	Par	Pat	Ben
lex.	P/ἀπό	{N}	N+gen

8. Usages of Separation (Sep.)

The event of separation (*Sep.*) contains three entities that are associated with the Agent (A), Patient (P), and Source (S) thematic roles. This base configuration of separation (APS) does not admit to alternate formulation by event features. The differing conceptualizations of the base configuration of separation grammaticalized by predicators require description by the usage feature argument promotion (§3.8d). This usage feature distinguishes the conceptualizations of the two usages of the event of separation in the text of Revelation. The following discussion describes and provides illustrative examples of each of the two observed usages of separation by the categories of predicators.

a. Usage APS

Verb and participle predicators grammaticalize event APS with the Usage of Separation, APS.[24] The conceptualization of separation with this usage has no argument promotion. The predicators raise the Agent entity as first argument, the Patient entity as second argument, and the Source entity as third argument.

ἐξεδίκησεν τὸ αἷμα τῶν δούλων αὐτοῦ ἐκ χειρὸς αὐτῆς (19:2)
[He (1/Agt)] exacted (ἐκδικέω) [the blood of his slaves (2/Pat)] [from her hands (3/Sou)].

τῷ...λύσαντι ἡμᾶς ἐκ τῶν ἁμαρτιῶν ἡμῶν ἐν τῷ αἵματι αὐτοῦ (1:5)
[The one (1/Agt)]...releasing (λύσας) [us (2/Pat)] [from our sins (3/Sou)] [by his blood (C/Ins)].

	ἐκδικέω (19:2) <Sep. APS [§6.8a]>			λύσας (1:5) <Sep. APS [§6.8a]>			
	1	2	3	1	2	3	C
syn.							
sem.	Agt	Pat	Sou	Agt	Pat	Sou	Ins
lex.	N	N+acc	P/ἐκ	N	N+acc	P/ἐκ	P/ἐν

[24] Usage APS: verbs, ἀγοράζω, ἀποχωρίζω, ἐκδικέω, ἐξαλείφω, λύω, τηρέω (2); and participle, λύσας.

b. Usage PAS

Only participle predicator ἠγορασμένος (bought) grammaticalizes event APS with the Usage of Separation by an Agent, PAS. The conceptualization of separation with this usage has promotion of the Patient entity. The predicator raises the Patient entity as (promoted) first argument, the Agent entity as second argument, and the Source entity as third argument. The translation introduces in double brackets, [[ ]], the contextual referent of the DNC Agent (the lamb/the blood of the lamb).

αἱ ἑκατὸν τεσσεράκοντα τέσσαρες χιλιάδες, οἱ ἠγορασμένοι ἀπὸ τῆς γῆς (14:3)
[The one hundred forty-four thousand (1/Pat)] bought (ἠγορασμένος) [from the earth (3/Sou)] [[by the lamb/the blood of the lamb (2/Agt)]].

	ἠγορασμένος (14:3) <Sep. PAS [§6.8b]>		
syn.	1	[2]	3
sem.	Pat	Agt	Sou
lex.	N	DNC	P/ἀπό

9. Events with Only One Usage

The remaining four events (causation, comparison, measurement, and temporality) contain an event entity associated with the Patient thematic role. In the text of Revelation, the base configurations of these events do not admit to alternate formulation by event features, the conceptualizations of their base configurations grammaticalized by predicators do not require description by usage features, and the events present only one usage. The following discussions describe and provide illustrative examples of each observed usage by the category or categories of predicators.

a. Usage PCau

The event of causation (*Cau.*) contains two entities that are associated with the Patient (P) and Cause (Cau) thematic roles. Only preposition predicators grammaticalize the Usage of Causation, PCau.[25] The predicators raise the Patient entity as first argument and the Cause entity as second argument.

ἐγὼ Ἰωάννης...διὰ τὸν λόγον τοῦ θεοῦ καὶ τὴν μαρτυρίαν Ἰησοῦ (1:9)
[I John (1/Pat)]...because of (διά) [the word of God and the testimony of Jesus (2/Cau)].

τὰς γλώσσας αὐτῶν ἐκ τοῦ πόνου (16:10)
[Their tongues (1/Pat)] because of (ἐκ) [the pain (2/Cau)].

---

[25] Usage PCau: prepositions, διά (2), ἐκ (6).

	διά (1:9)		ἐκ (16:10)	
	<Cau. PCau [§6.9a]		<Cau. PCau [§6.9a]>	
syn.	1	2	1	2
sem.	Pat	Cau	Pat	Cau
lex.	N	N+acc	N	N+gen

b. Usage PCmp

The event of comparison (*Cmp.*) contains two entities that are associated with the Patient (P) and Comparative (Cmp) thematic roles. Complex adjective, adjective, preposition, and adverb predicators grammaticalize the Usage of Comparison, PCmp.[26] The predicators raise the Patient entity as first argument and the Comparative entity as second argument.

cp-adj   οἱ πόδες αὐτοῦ ὅμοιοι χαλκολιβάνῳ (2:18)
          [His feet (1/Pat)] were like (ὅμοιος + [εἰμί]) [fine bronze (2/Cmp)].

adj.   τὸ μῆκος αὐτῆς ὅσον…τὸ πλάτος (21:16)
      [Its length (1/Pat)] as much as (ὅσος)…[its breadth (2/Cmp)].

prep.   ἕκαστος κατὰ τὰ ἔργα αὐτῶν (20:13)
       [Each one (1/Pat)] according to/in comparison to (κατά) [their works (2/Cmp)].

adv.   τοὺς ὀφθαλμοὺς αὐτοῦ ὡς φλόγα πυρός (2:18)
      [His eyes (1/Pat)] like (ὡς) [a flame of fire (2/Cmp)].

	ὅμοιος + [εἰμί] (2:18)		ὅσος (21:16)	
	<Cmp. PCmp [§6.9b]>		<Cmp. PCmp [§6.9b]>	
syn.	1	2	1	2
sem.	Pat	Cmp	Pat	Cmp
lex.	N	N+dat	N	N+l

	κατά (20:13)		ὡς (2:18)	
	<Cmp. PCmp [§6.9b]>		<Cmp. PCmp [§6.9b]>	
syn.	1	2	1	2
sem.	Pat	Cmp	Pat	Cmp
lex.	N	N+acc	N	N+l

---

[26] Usage PCmp: complex predicators, ἴσος + εἰμί, ὅμοιος + [εἰμί] (1), ὅσος + [εἰμί] (1), πλείων + [εἰμί], ὡς + [εἰμί] (1); adjectives, ὅμοιος (1), ὅσος (1), τιμιώτατος; preposition, κατά (2); and adverb, ὡς (1). See G. Messies, *The Morphology of Koine Greek, as Used in the Apocalypse of St. John: A Study in Bilingualism* (Supplements to Novum Testamentum 27; Leiden: Brill, 1971), 93, on the use of ὡς + [εἰμί].

c. Usage PMea

The event of measurement (*Mea.*) contains two entities that are associated with the Patient (P) and Measure (Mea) thematic roles. Only preposition predicators grammaticalize the Usage of Measurement, PMea.[27] The predicators raise the Patient entity as first argument and the Measure entity as second argument.

τὴν πόλιν...ἐπὶ σταδίων δώδεκα χιλιάδων (21:16)
[The city (1/Pat)]...at (ἐπί) [twelve thousand stadia (2/Mea)].

ἓν καθ' ἓν αὐτῶν (4:8)
[One (1/Pat)] by (κατά) [one of them (2/Mea)].

	ἐπί (21:16) <Mea. PMea [§6.9c]>		κατά (4:8) <Mea. PMea [§6.9c]>	
syn.	1	2	1	2
sem.	Pat	Mea	Pat	Mea
lex.	N	N+gen	N	N+acc

d. Usage PTem

The event of temporality (*Tem.*) contains two entities that are associated with the Patient (P) and Temporal (Tem) thematic roles. Complex preposition and preposition predicators grammaticalize the Usage of Temporality, PTem.[28] The predicators raise the Patient entity as first argument and the Temporal entity as second argument. The translation of 22:10 introduces in double brackets, [[ ]], the contextual referent of the DNC Temporal (now/today).

cp-a   ὁ καιρὸς γὰρ ἐγγύς ἐστιν (22:10)
       For [the time (1/Pat)] is near (ἐγγύς + εἰμί) [[to now/today (2/Tem)]].

prep. δόξαν καὶ τιμὴν καὶ εὐχαριστίαν...εἰς τοὺς αἰῶνας τῶν αἰώνων (4:9)
       [Glory and honor and thanksgiving (1/Pat)]...into (εἰς) [the ages of the ages (2/Tem)].

	ἐγγύς + εἰμί (22:10) <Tem. PTem [§6.9d]>		εἰς (4:9) <Tem. PTem [§6.9d]>	
syn.	1	[2]	1	2
sem.	Pat	Tem	Pat	Tem
lex.	N	DNC	N	N+acc

---

[27] Usage PMea: prepositions, ἐπί (4), κατά (3).
[28] Usage PTem: complex predicators, ἐγγύς + [εἰμί], ἐν + [εἰμί] (4); and prepositions, ἀπό (6), ἄχρι (2), εἰς (4), ἐν (4), μετά (6), ὡς (2).

10. Usages of the Non-Event Qualification (Qual.)

The non-event of qualification (*Qual.*) contains a single entity that is associated with either the Patient (P) or the Occurrence (O) thematic role. The two base configurations of qualification (P and O) grammaticalized by predicators in the text of Revelation do not require description by usage features.

a. Usage P

Verb, participle, complex, and adjective predicators grammaticalize non-event P with the Usage of Qualification of a Patient, P. Given the large number of predicators with this usage, the discussion provides two illustrative examples of each category of predicator, and the Valence Descriptions appear immediately beneath the translations.

Seventeen verb predicators grammaticalize usage P.[29]

ἀπέθανεν τὸ τρίτον τῶν κτισμάτων τῶν ἐν τῇ θαλάσσῃ τὰ ἔχοντα ψυχὰς (8:9)
[A third of the creatures in the seas having lives (1/Pat)] died (ἀποθνῄσκω).

πεπλούτηκα (3:17)
[I (1/Pat)] have been rich (πλουτέω).

	ἀποθνῄσκω (8:9) <*Qual.* P [§6.10a]>	πλουτέω (3:17) <*Qual.* P [§6.10a]>
syn.	1	1
sem.	Pat	Pat
lex.	N	N

Eleven participle predicators grammaticalize usage P.[30]

ὄρος μέγα πυρὶ καιόμενον (8:8)
[A great mountain (1/Pat)] burning (καιόμενος) [with fire (C/Ins)].

τὴν γυναῖκα μεθύουσαν ἐκ τοῦ αἵματος τῶν ἁγίων καὶ ἐκ τοῦ αἵματος τῶν μαρτύρων Ἰησοῦ (17:6)
[The woman (1/Pat)] being drunk (μεθύων) [with/by the blood of the holy ones and by the blood of the witnesses to Jesus (C/Ins)].

	καιόμενος (8:8) <*Qual.* P [§6.10a]>		μεθύων (17:6) <*Qual.* P [§6.10a]	
syn.	1	| C	1	| C
sem.	Pat	| Ins	Pat	| Ins
lex.	N	| N+dat	N	| P/ἐκ

---

[29] Usage P: verbs, ἀκμάζω, ἀναπαύω, ἀποθνῄσκω, βρέχω, γίνομαι (4), γρηγορέω, εἰμί (1), ζάω, ἰσχύω, κλαίω, κοπιάω, πάρειμι, πίπτω (2), πλουτέω, ῥυπαίνω, στρηνιάω, φαίνω.
[30] Usage P: participles, ἀποθνῄσκων, ἐβδελυγμένος, γρηγορῶν, ζῶν, καιόμενος, κλαίων, κρυσταλλίζων, μεθύων, πλουτήσας, στρηνιάσας, ὤν (1).

6. Predicator Usages of Other Events and Non-Events

Forty-eight complex participle, adjective, and noun predicators grammaticalize usage P.[31]

cp-part ζῶν εἰμι εἰς τοὺς αἰῶνας τῶν αἰώνων (1:18b)
[I 1/Pat)] am living (ζῶν + εἰμι) [into the ages of ages (C/Tem)].

cp-adj σὺ εἶ...τυφλός (3:17)
[You (1/Pat)] are...blind (τυφλός + εἰμί).

cp-n ὅς ἐστιν Διάβολος (20:2)
[Who (1/Pat)] is [the] Devil (Διάβολος + εἰμί)

	ζῶν + εἰμί (1:18) <Qual. P [§6.10a]>		τυφλός + εἰμί (3:17) <Qual. P [§6.10a]>
syn.	1	C	1
sem.	Pat	Tem	Pat
lex.	N	P/εἰς	N

	Διάβολος + εἰμί (20:2) <Qual. P [§6.10a]>
syn.	1
sem.	Pat
lex.	N

Ninety-two adjective predicators grammaticalize usage P.[32]

τὴν πόλιν τὴν ἁγίαν (11:2)
The holy (ἅγιος) [city (1/Pat)].

πᾶσαν φυλὴν καὶ λαὸν καὶ γλῶσσαν καὶ ἔθνος (13:7)
Every (πᾶς) [tribe and people and tongue and nation (1/Pat)].

[31] Usage P: complex predicators, ἅγιος + [εἰμί], ἀληθινός + [εἰμί], τὸ ἄλφα + εἰμί, ἀμέθυστος + [εἰμί], ἄμωμος + εἰμί, βήρυλλος + [εἰμί], γυμνός + εἰμί, Διάβολος + εἰμί, δίκαιος + [εἰμί], ἐλαία + εἰμί, ἑξακόσιοι ἑξήκοντα ἕξ + [εἰμί], ζεστός + εἰμί, ζῶν + εἰμί, ὁ ζῶν + εἰμί, ἴασπις + [εἰμί], [Ἰουδαῖος] + εἰμί, ἰσχυρός + [εἰμί], καιόμενος + [εἰμί], [λαμπρός] + [εἰμί], λευκός + [εἰμί], μακάριος + [εἰμί], μαργαρίτης + [εἰμί], μέγας + [εἰμί], [μέλας] + [εἰμί], νεκρός + εἰμί, ὅμοιος + [εἰμί] (2), ὄρος + εἰμί, ὅσιος + [εἰμί], ὄχλος + εἰμί, παρθένος + εἰμί, πλούσιος + εἰμί, πτωχός + εἰμί, σάπφιρος + [εἰμί], σάρδιον + [εἰμί], σαρδόνυξ + [εἰμί], Σατανᾶς + εἰμί, σμάραγδος + [εἰμί], τηλικοῦτος + [εἰμί], τίς + εἰμί, τοπάζιον + [εἰμί], τυφλός + εἰμί, ὑάκινθος + [εἰμί], χαλκηδών + [εἰμί], χλιαρός + εἰμί, χρυσίον + [εἰμί], χρυσόλιθος + [εἰμί], χρυσόπρασος + [εἰμί], ψυχρός + εἰμί, τὸ ὦ + εἰμί.
[32] Usage P: adjectives, ἅγιος, αἰώνιος, ἀληθινός, ἄλλος, ἀργυροῦς, ἄρσην, ἀρχαῖος, βύσσινος, γυμνός, δέκα, δεξιός, διακόσιοι, διαυγής, δίκαιος, διπλοῦς, δίστομος, δύο, δώδεκα, εἴκοσι, εἷς (1), ἑκατόν, ἐλεύθερος, ἐλεφάντινος, Ἑλληνικός, ἐμός, ἑξακόσιοι, ἑξήκοντα, ἑπτά, ἔρημος, εὐώνυμος, ἥμισυς (1), θειώδης, θύϊνος, Ἰουδαῖος, ἰσχυρός, καθαρός, καινός, κακός, κεραμικός, κοινός, κόκκινος, κυριακός, λαμπρός, λευκός, λίθινος, λιπαρός, μέγας, μέλας, μηδείς, μικρός, μόνος, μουσικός, μύλινος, νεκρός, ξύλινος, ὀλίγος, ὅλος, ὅμοιος (2), ὀξύς, ὅσιος, ὅσος, οὐδείς, οὗτος, πᾶς, πέντε, πλούσιος, ποῖος, πολύς (1), πονηρός, πορφυροῦς, πρωϊνός, πτωχός, πύρινος, πυρρός, ῥυπαρός, σιδηροῦς, σιρικός, ταλαντιαῖος, τεσσεράκοντα, τέσσαρες, τετράγωνος, τίμιος, τοσοῦτος, τρεῖς, τρίχινος, ὑακίνθινος, ὑάλινος, ὑψηλός, χαλκοῦς, χίλιοι, χλωρός, χρυσοῦς.

	ἅγιος (11:2)	πᾶς (13:7)
	<Qual. P [§6.10a]>	<Qual. P [§6.10a]>
syn.	1	1
sem.	Pat	Pat
lex.	N	N

b. Usage O

Only interjection predicators grammaticalize the non-event O with the Usage of Qualification of an Occurrence, O.[33] The predicators raise the Occurrence entity as first argument.

ναί, ἔρχομαι ταχύ (22:20)
Yes (ναί), [I am coming quickly (1/Occ)].

δεῦρο, δείξω σοι τὴν νύμφην τὴν γυναῖκα τοῦ ἀρνίου (21:9)
Come (δεῦρο), [I will show to you the bride, the wife of the lamb (1/Occ)].

	ναί (22:20)	δεῦρο (21:9)
	<Qual. O [§6.10b]>	<Qual. O [§6.10b]>
syn.	1	1
sem.	Occ	Occ
lex.	V+	V+

11. Usages of the Non-Event Coordination (Coor.)

The non-event of coordination (*Coor.*) contains two entities that either do not admit to description by thematic roles (—) or are associated with specific thematic roles not set by the conjunction predicators themselves (---). The two base configurations of the non-event of coordination clarify whether the coordinated entities do not admit to description by thematic roles (— —) or admit to description by thematic roles that are set by a predicator other than the licensing conjunction predicators (--- ---). The conceptualization of coordination grammaticalized by conjunction predicators does not require description by usage features. The conjunction predicators do not license adjuncts.

a. Usage — —

Only conjunction predicators grammaticalize non-event — — with the Usage of Coordination of Entities without Thematic Roles, — —.[34]

---

[33] Usage O: interjections, ἁλληλουϊά, ἀμήν, δεῦρο, δεῦτε, ἰδού, ναί, ὄφελον.
[34] Usage — —: conjunctions, ἀλλά (1a), γάρ, δέ, ἤ (1a), καί (1a), οὐδέ (1a), οὐδέ…οὐδέ (1a), οὔτε…οὔτε (1a).

οἶδά σου τὴν θλῖψιν καὶ τὴν πτωχείαν, ἀλλὰ πλούσιος εἶ (2:9a)
[I know your struggle and poverty (1/—)] but (ἀλλά) [you are rich (2/—)].

ἕστηκα ἐπὶ τὴν θύραν καὶ κρούω (3:20a)
[I stand at the gate (1/—)] and (καί) [I knock (2/—)].

	ἀλλά (2:9a)		καί (3:20a)	
	<Coor. — — [§6.11a]>		<Coor. — — [§6.11a]>	
syn.	1	2	1	2
sem.	—	—	—	—
lex.	V+	V+	V+	V+

b. Usage --- ---

Only conjunction predicators grammaticalize non-event --- --- with the Usage of Coordination of Entities with Thematic Roles, --- ---.[35] Note that predicators other than the conjunction predicators set the thematic roles of the arguments (§2.7b).

ἐπὶ τῆς χειρὸς αὐτῶν τῆς δεξιᾶς ἢ ἐπὶ τὸ μέτωπον αὐτῶν (13:16)
[On their right hand (1/---)] or (ἤ) [on their forehead (2/---)].

τὸν χόρτον τῆς γῆς οὐδὲ πᾶν χλωρὸν (9:4a)
[The grass of the earth (1/---)] nor (οὐδέ) [any green [plant] (2/---)].

	ἤ (13:16)		οὐδέ (9:4a)	
	<Coor. --- --- [§6.11b]>		<Coor. --- --- [§6.11b]>	
syn.	1	2	1	2
sem.	---	---	---	---
lex.	P/ἐπί [+gen]	P/ἐπί [+acc]	N	N

12. Usage of the Non-Event Specification (Spec.)

The non-event of specification (*Spec.*) contains no entities that are raised as arguments. The base configuration of the event of specification (—) characterizes all zero-place predicators that license only adjuncts as complements. Noun and noun phrase predicators grammaticalize non-event — with the Usage of Specification with a Realized Adjunct, —.[36]

---

[35] Usage --- --- conjunctions, ἀλλά (1b), ἤ (1b), καί (1b), μήτε...μήτε (1), οὐδέ (1b), οὔτε, οὔτε...οὔτε (1b), τε καί.
[36] Usage —: nouns and noun phrases, τὸ ἀκάθαρτον, ἄμμος, ἄνεμος, ἀρνίον, ἀστήρ, τὸ βαθύ, βότρυς, ἡμέρα, θηρίον, Ἶρις, καπνός, κτίσμα, λέων, λίθος, λίμνη, ξύλον, οἶνος, ὄχλος, πέτρα, πῦρ, σκορπίος, σταφυλή, ὕδωρ, χόρτος, ὥρα.

τὸ ἀρνίον τὸ ἀνὰ μέσον τοῦ θρόνου (7:17)
The lamb (ἀρνίον) [in the middle of the throne (C/Loc)].

τὰς πέτρας τῶν ὀρέων (6:15)
The rocks (πέτρα) [of the mountains (C/Ben)].

	ἀρνίον (7:17) <Spec. — [§6.12]>		πέτρα (6:15) <Spec. — [§6.12]>	
syn.	0	C	0	C
sem.	—	Loc	—	Ben
lex.		P/ἀνὰ μέσον		N+gen

13. Applications of the Ninety-Two Usages

The description and illustration of the ninety-two usages of predicators in the text of Revelation (Chapters 5 and 6) complete the analysis required to identify the distinctive characteristics of the text's predicators (Chapter 7) and accommodate the restatement of all of the grammatical information in the Valence Descriptions of all predicator occurrences according to protocols (Chapter 8) into lexicon entries (Chapter 9).

7

DISTINCTIVE GRAMMATICAL CHARACTERISTICS OF THE TEXT OF REVELATION

This chapter develops distinctive grammatical characteristics of the text of Revelation. These characteristics are deemed grammatical because they fall within the range of grammatical phenomena observed elsewhere in the LXX and NT. The characteristics are distinctive, however, because they introduce predicator usages and lexical realizations of required complements that are not observed elsewhere in the NT or they utilize particular resources of Greek grammar with a disproportionately greater frequency than other NT texts. The following discussions develop the novel predicator usages, novel lexical realizations of required complements, occurrences of disharmonious coordination by one conjunction predicator, the frequency of the omission of εἰμί (be) and of other predicators in the text, and the frequency of distant predicator retrieval. Since Valence Descriptions automatically incorporate information concerning these distinctive characteristics, the lexicon entries (Chapter 9) clearly distinguish all occurrences of them. As a consequence, the following discussions offer only illustrative examples of predicators with the distinctive grammatical characteristics with their Valence Descriptions. The concluding discussions develop the contribution of the presentation on distinctive grammatical characteristics and review the accomplishments of the Case Frame study.

1. Novel Predicator Usages

The first distinctive characteristic concerns predicators that occur in the text of Revelation and elsewhere in the NT but exhibit novel usages in the text of Revelation. These novel usages are deemed grammatical whenever (1) other predicators in the NT grammaticalize a similar distribution of usages or (2) the contexts of their occurrences offer specific motivations for the usages or (3) the same predicator grammaticalizes the same usage in the LXX or (4) a cognate predicator (noun for verb) grammaticalizes a parallel usage. Appeals to the LXX are assumed appropriate, given the frequent allusions to the LXX in the text of Revelation.[1] The following discussion introduces the novel usages in the order of their initial presentation (in Chapters 5 and 6) and illustrates their representation in Valence Descriptions.

---

[1] See the discussion in Stephen S. Smalley, *The Revelation of John: A Commentary on the Text of the Apocalypse* (Downers Grove, IL: Intervarsity, 2005), 8–10.

a. Usage AΘ[S]G [S=A] +Imp.[§5.1a] with Κρύπτω

The verb predicator κρύπτω (hide) grammaticalizes the Primary Active Usage of Transference to a Goal with a Continuous Impetus, AΘ[S]G [S=A] +imp. [§5.1a], only in 6:15. Elsewhere in the NT, this predicator grammaticalizes only the Primary Usage of Transference Terminating in a Locative with a Continuous Impetus, AΘ[S]G [S=A] G→L +imp. [§5.1b], and the Secondary Usage of Transference from a Source with a Continuous Impetus, AΘS(G) [S=A] +imp. [§5.1d].[2] This distinctive usage is deemed grammatical because a verb predicator that grammaticalizes one of these three usages of transference has the potential to grammaticalize the other two, given the appropriate contextual motivation.[3] The potential is realized in the LXX where κρύπτω with Usage AΘ[S]G [S=A] +imp. [§5.1a] appears with the P/εἰς realization of the Goal (Job 40:13; Isa 2:10; Jer 4:29).

οἱ βασιλεῖς τῆς γῆς καὶ...πᾶς δοῦλος καὶ ἐλεύθερος ἔκρυψαν ἑαυτοὺς εἰς τὰ σπήλαια καὶ εἰς τὰς πέτρας τῶν ὀρέων (6:15)
[The kings of the earth and...every slave or free person (1/Agt)] hid (κρύπτω) [themselves (2/Thm)] [into the caves and into the rocks of mountains (3/Goa)].

	κρύπτω (6:15) <(Tra.) AΘ[S]G [S=A] +imp. [§5.1a]>		
syn.	1	2	3
sem.	Agt	Thm	Goa
lex.	N	N+acc	P/εἰς

b. Usage AΘ[S]G [S=A] G→L +imp. [§5.1b] with Ἁρπάζω

The verb predicator ἁρπάζω (carry off) grammaticalizes the Primary Active Usage of Transference Terminating in a Locative with a Continuous Impetus, AΘ[S]G [S=A] G→L +imp. [§5.1b], only in 12:5. Elsewhere in the NT, this verb predicator grammaticalizes only the Primary Usage of Transference to a Goal with a Continuous Impetus, AΘ[S]G [S=A] +imp. [§5.1a], and the Secondary Usage of Transference from a Source with a Continuous Impetus, AΘS(G) [S=A] +imp. [§5.1d].[4] As previously discussed (§7.1a), this novel usage is deemed grammatical because a verb predicator that grammaticalizes one of these three usages of transference has the potential to grammaticalize the other two, given the appropriate contextual motivation. In 12:5, the verb predicator grammaticalizes both the Primary Usage of Transference to a Goal with a Continuous Impetus and the Primary Usage of Transference Terminating in a

---

[2] Κρύπτω with Usage AΘ[S]G [S=A] G→L +imp. [§5.1b]: Matt 5:14; 13:35, 44a, 44b; 25:18, 25; John 8:59; 19:38; Col 3:3; 1 Tim 5:25; Heb 11:23; Rev 2:17. Κρύπτω with Usage AΘS(G) [S=A] +imp. [§5.1d]: Matt 11:25; Luke 18:34; 19:42; John 12:36; Rev 6:16.
[3] See Danove, *Verbs of Transference*, 70–71.
[4] Ἁρπάζω with Usage AΘ[S]G [S=A] +imp. [§5.1a]: 2 Cor 12:2, 4; 1 Thes 4:17; Rev 12:5. Ἁρπάζω with Usage AΘS(G) [S=A] +imp. [§5.1d]: Matt 12:29; 13:19; John 10:28, 29; Acts 8:39; 23:10; Jude 23.

Locative with a Continuous Impetus. The translation introduces in double brackets, [[ ]], the indefinite but circumscribed referent of the INC Agent (someone).

ἡρπάσθη τὸ τέκνον αὐτῆς πρὸς τὸν θεὸν καὶ πρὸς τὸν θρόνον αὐτοῦ (12:5)
[Her child (2/Thm)] was carried off (ἁρπάζω) [[by someone (1/Agt)]] [to God (3/Goa)] and [[terminating] at his throne (3/Loc)].

	ἁρπάζω (12:5) <Tra. AΘ[S]G [S=A] +imp. [§5.1a]>		
syn.	1	2	3
sem.	Agt	Thm	Goa
lex.	N	N+acc	P/πρός [+acc, +an]

	ἁρπάζω (12:5) <Tra. AΘ[S]G [S=A] G→L +imp. [§5.1b]>		
syn.	1	2	3
sem.	Agt	Thm	Loc
lex.	N	N+acc	P/πρός [+acc, -an]

c. Usage ACE [§5.4a] with Διδάσκω and Εὐαγγελίζω

The verb predicator διδάσκω (teach) grammaticalizes the Usage of Communication with an Emphasized Content, ACE [§5.4a], only in 2:14, and the verb predicator εὐαγγελίζω (proclaim [as good news]) grammaticalizes the same usage with active base forms only in 14:6. Elsewhere in the NT, διδάσκω grammaticalizes only the Usage of Communication with an Emphasized Experiencer, AEC [§5.4d], or the Usage of Communication about a Topic with an Emphasized Experiencer, AET (which is not grammaticalized in the text of Revelation), and εὐαγγελίζω grammaticalizes Usage ACE [§5.4a] only with middle base forms.[5]

The apparent motivation for the novel usage of διδάσκω in 2:14 is the contextual focus on what is being taught (Content) rather than on those being taught (Experiencer). This focus dictates a usage of communication with secondary emphasis on the Content rather than on the Experiencer (§3.6a).[6] Supporting the grammaticality of διδάσκω with Usage ACE [§5.4a] is the fact that its cognate noun διδαχή (teaching)

---

[5] Διδάσκω with Usage AEC [§5.4d]: Matt 4:23; 5:2, 19a, 19b; 7:29; 9:35; 11:1; 13:54; 15:9; 21:23; 22:16; 26:55; 28:15, 20; Mark 1:21, 22; 2:13; 4:1, 2; 6:2, 6, 30, 34; 7:7; 8:31; 9:31; 10:1; 11:17; 12:14, 35; 14:49; Luke 4:15, 31; 5:3, 17; 6:6; 11:1a, 1b; 12:12; 13:10, 22, 26; 19:47; 20:1, 21a, 21b; 21:37; 23:5; John 6:59; 7:14, 28, 35; 8:2, 20, 28; 9:34; 14:26; 18:20; Acts 1:1; 4:2, 18; 5:21, 25, 28, 42; 11:26; 15:1, 35; 18:11, 25; 20:20; 21:21, 28; 28:31; Rom 2:21a, 21b; 12:7; 1 Cor 4:17; 11:14; Gal 1:12; Eph 4:21; Col 1:28; 2:7; 3:16; 2 Thes 2:15; 1 Tim 2:12; 4:11; 6:2; 2 Tim 2:2; Tit 1:11; Heb 5:12; 8:11; 1 John 2:27a, 27c; Rev 2:20. Διδάσκω with Usage AET [not in Revelation]: 1 John 2:27b. Εὐαγγελίζομαι with Usage ACE [§5.4a] with middle base form: Luke 1:19; 2:10; 4:43; 8:1; 9:6; 16:16; Acts 5:42; 8:4, 35; 10:36; 11:20; 15:35; 17:18; Rom 10:15; 1 Cor 15:1, 2; 2 Cor 11:7; Gal 1:8a, 8b, 11, 16, 23; Eph 2:17; 3:8; 1 Thes 3:6; 1 Pet 1:25; 4:6.

[6] Alternate proposals for explaining the occurrence of διδάσκω (teach) with Usage ACE in 2:14 receive review in Laurentiu Florentin Mot, *Morphological and Syntactic Irregularities in the Book of Revelation: A Greek Hypothesis* (LBS 11; Leiden: Brill, 2013), 147-49.

in Tit 1:9 grammaticalizes the parallel Nominal Usage of Communication with an Emphasized Content, BCE [§5.4f].

The apparent motivation for the active base form with εὐαγγελίζω in 14:6 is more complex. Elsewhere in the NT, the referent of the Agent argument of this predicator consistently is portrayed as commissioned or obliged to proclaim good news by some external force.[7] Greek grammar interprets this commission or obligation as a constraint that affects the subject/Agent and signals the resulting subject affectedness by the use of middle base forms on the verb predicator.[8] In the text of Revelation, in contrast, the angel that references the Agent in 14:6 is not portrayed as commissioned or under obligation to proclaim good news. As a consequence, this is the only NT occurrence of the verb predicator with this usage that does not require middle base forms. Εὐαγγελίζων also has active base forms with Usage ACE [§5.4a] in the LXX (2 Sam 18:19). The translation of 14:6 introduces in double brackets, [[ ]], the referent of the coinstantiated Agent (another angel) and the contextual referent of the DNC Content (everlasting good news).

ὃς ἐδίδασκεν τῷ Βαλὰκ βαλεῖν σκάνδαλον ἐνώπιον τῶν υἱῶν Ἰσραὴλ φαγεῖν εἰδωλόθυτα καὶ πορνεῦσαι (2:14)
[Who (1/Agt)] was teaching (διδάσκω) [to Balak (3/Exp)] [to cast a stumbling block before the children of Israel to eat what is sacrificed to idols and to commit sexual immorality (2/Con)].

εὐαγγελίσαι ἐπὶ τοὺς καθημένους ἐπὶ τῆς γῆς καὶ ἐπὶ πᾶν ἔθνος καὶ φυλὴν καὶ γλῶσσαν καὶ λαόν (14:6)
[[Another angel (1/Agt)]] to proclaim (εὐαγγελίζω) [[everlasting good news (2/Con)]] [to the ones dwelling on the earth and to every nation and tribe and tongue and people (3/Exp)].

Although the first complement of the infinitive in 14:6 is coinstantiated by the first complement of licensing predicator ἔχων (having) and so is not realized as a complement within the infinitive phrase, the Valence Description follows the convention

[7] For example, in Luke/Acts, God sends (ἀποστέλλω) Gabriel (Luke 1:19) and Jesus (Luke 4:43; Acts 10:36) to proclaim, and Jesus sends (ἀποστέλλω, Luke 9:2) his disciples to proclaim (Luke 9:6) and states that proclaiming is a necessity for him (Luke 4:43). In the Pauline Letters, God sends (ἀποστέλλω) Christian preachers to proclaim (Rom 10:15); God calls (καλέω, Gal 1:15) Paul and reveals (ἀποκαλύπτω, Gal 1:16) his son to Paul and gives Paul the grace (Eph 3:8) so that he may proclaim, and Paul too claims that proclaiming is a necessity for him (1 Cor 9:16). In 1 Peter, those proclaiming the good news do so by the Holy Spirit (1:12).

[8] See the discussion of εὐαγγελίζω in Paul L. Danove, "New Testament Verbs of Communication with Active and Middle Forms: The Distinction," in *In Mari Via Tua: Studies in Honor of Antonio Piñero* (ed. Jesús Peláez and Israel Muñoz Gallarte; Estudios de Filología Neotestamentaria 11; Córdoba: El Almendro, 2016), 133–56. Discussion of the subject affectedness associated specifically with middle base forms appears in Allan, *Middle Voice*, 112–14; Albert Rijksbaron, *The Syntax and Semantics of the Verb in Classical Greek: An Introduction*, 3rd edn. (Linguistic Contributions to the Study of Greek Literature; Amsterdam: Giessen, 2002), 147–50; and Egbert Bakker, "Voice, Aspect, and Aktionsart: Middle and Passive in Ancient Greek," in *Voice: Form and Function* (ed. Barbara Fox and Paul J. Hopper; Typological Studies in Language; Amsterdam/Philadelphia: Benjamins, 1994), 36.

(§1.4) of listing the first complement of the infinitive verb predicator with the syntactic function as "1" (no brackets) and the lexical realization as "N." The form of the predicator (active) in the Valence Description for the example in 14:6 clarifies the active base forms of the predicator.

	διδάσκω (2:14) <Cmm. ACE [§5.4a]>			εὐαγγελίζω (14:6) <Cmm. ACE [§5.4a]>		
syn.	1	2	3	1	[2]	3
sem.	Agt	Con	Exp	Agt	Con	Exp
lex.	N	V-i3	N+dat [+an]	N	DNC	P/ἐπί [+acc]

d. Usage AE{C} [§3.4e] with Εὐαγγελίζω

The verb predicator εὐαγγελίζω (tell {good news}) grammaticalizes with active base forms the Usage of Communication with an Emphasized Experiencer and a Suppressed Content, AE{C} [§3.4e], only in 10:7. Elsewhere in the NT, the predicator grammaticalizes this usage only with middle base forms.[9] As previously discussed (§7.1c), the referents of the Agent outside of the text of Revelation consistently are portrayed as commissioned or under obligation to tell good news, and Greek grammar interprets this commission or obligation as affecting the subject/Agent and signals this subject affectedness through the use of middle base forms. In 10:7, however, God, the referent of the Agent, is not subject to external constraints. As a consequence, this is the only NT occurrence of the verb predicator with this usage that does not require the use of middle base forms. The translation introduces in braces, { }, the referent of the suppressed Content (good news).

εὐηγγέλισεν τοὺς ἑαυτοῦ δούλους τοὺς προφήτας (10:7)
[He (1/Agt)] told (εὐαγγελίζω) [his own slaves the prophets (2/Exp)] {good news (3/Con)}.

The form of the predicator (active) in the Valence Description clarifies the predicator's active base form.

	εὐαγγελίζω (10:7) <Cmm. AE{C} [§3.4e]>		
syn.	1	2	{{3}}
sem.	Agt	Exp	Con
lex.	N	N+acc	{N}

e. Usage AΘO [§5.7a] with Πλανάω

The verb predicator πλανάω (mislead) grammaticalizes the Usage of Disposition, AΘO [§5.7a], only in the text of Revelation (2:20; 13:14; 18:23; 19:20; 20:3, 8).

---

[9] Εὐαγγελίζομαι with Usage AE{C} [§3.4e] with middle base forms: Matt 11:5; Luke 3:18; 7:22; 20:1; Acts 8:25, 40; 14:21; 16:10; Heb 4:2, 6; 1 Pet 1:12.

Elsewhere in the NT, πλανάω grammaticalizes only the Primary Usage of Motion to a Goal, Θ[S]G [S=Θ] [§5.2a], the Secondary Usage of Motion from a Source, ΘS(G) [S=Θ] [§5.2c], and the Usage of Effect, AP [§6.3a].[10] This distinctive usage is deemed grammatical because παραδίδωμι (hand over, come over) in the NT provides a precedent for grammaticalizing usages of motion, effect, and disposition.[11] Πλανάω also appears with Usage AΘO [§5.7a] in the LXX (2 Kgs 21:9; 2 Chr 33:9).

πλανᾷ τοὺς ἐμοὺς δούλους πορνεῦσαι καὶ φαγεῖν εἰδωλόθυτα (2:20)
[She (1/Agt)] misleads (πλανάω) [my slaves (2/Thm)] [to commit sexual immorality and to eat what is sacrificed to idols (3/Occ)].

	πλανάω (2:20) <Dis. AΘO [§5.7a]>		
syn.	1	2	3
sem.	Agt	Thm	Occ
lex.	N	N+acc	V-i2

f. Usage AP [§6.3a] with Σύρω

The verb predicator σύρω (drag away) grammaticalizes the Usage of Effect, AP [§6.3a], only in 12:4. Elsewhere in the NT, this predicator grammaticalizes only the Primary Usage of Transference to a Goal with a Continuous Impetus, AΘ[S]G [S=Θ] +imp. [§5.1a].[12] This distinctive usage is deemed grammatical because thirteen other NT predicators grammaticalize only this set of usages.[13] Σύρω also appears with Usage AP [§6.3a] in the LXX (Deut 32:24; Ode 2:24; Isa 3:16).

ἡ οὐρὰ αὐτοῦ σύρει τὸ τρίτον τῶν ἀστέρων τοῦ οὐρανοῦ (12:4)
[Its tail (1/Agt)] drags away (σύρω) [a third of the stars of the sky (2/Pat)].

	σύρω (12:4) <Eff. AP [§6.3a]>	
syn.	1	2
sem.	Agt.	Pat
lex.	N	N+acc

---

[10] Πλανάω with Usage Θ[S]G [S=Θ] [§5.2a]: Matt 18:12a, 12b, 13; Heb 11:38; 1 Pet 2:25; 2 Pet 2:15. Πλανάω with Usage ΘS(G) [S=Θ] [§5.2c]: Jas 5:19. Πλανάω with Usage AP [§6.3a]: Matt 22:29; 24:4, 5, 11, 24; Mark 12:24, 27; 13:5, 6; Luke 21:8; John 7:12, 47; 1 Cor 6:9; 15:33; Gal 6:7; 2 Tim 3:13; Tit 3:3; Heb 3:10; 5:2; Jas 1:16; 1 John 1:8; 2:26; 3:7.
[11] Παραδίδωμι with Usage (A)Θ(S)G G=Θ pass. [§5.2f]: Matt 17:22; 20:18; 26:2, 45; Mark 9:31; 10:33a; 14:41; Luke 9:44; 18:32; 24:7; Rom 4:25; 2 Cor 4:11. Παραδίδωμι with Usage Θ[S](G) [S=Θ] [§5.2d]: Mark 4:29. Παραδίδωμι with Usage AΘO [§5.7a]: Matt 4:12; 10:4; 24:10; 26:21, 23, 24, 25, 46; 27:3, 4; Mark 1:14; 3:19; 7:13; 14:18, 21, 42; Luke 22:21, 22, 48; John 6:64, 71; 12:4; 13:2, 11, 21; 18:2, 5; 21:20; Acts 3:13; 15:26; Rom 8:32; 1 Cor 11:23b; 13:3; Gal 2:20; Eph 5:2, 25.
[12] Σύρω with Usage AΘ[S]G [S=Θ] +imp. [§5.1a]: John 21:8; Acts 8:3; 14:19; 17:6.
[13] NT predicators that grammaticalize only Usages AP [§6.3a] and AΘ[S]G [S=Θ] +imp. [§5.1a]: ἀνταποδίδωμι, ἀπάγω, βυθίζω, διαδίδωμι, ἕλκω, ἐπιχορηγέω, κατευθύνω, μετάγω, μετατίθημι, ὁδηγέω, σωρεύω, ὑποτίθημι, and χαλάω.

7. Distinctive Grammatical Characteristics 167

g. Usage APR [§6.6a] with Στρέφω

The verb predicator στρέφω (turn) grammaticalizes the Usage of Agentive Modification, APR [§6.6a], only in 11:6. Elsewhere in the NT, this predicator grammaticalizes only the Primary Usage of Motion to a Goal, Θ[S]G [S=Θ] [§5.2a] and the Primary Usage of Transference to a Goal with a Continuous Impetus, AΘ[S]G [S=A] +imp. [§5.1a].[14] Although no other NT predicator grammaticalizes this exact set of usages, the example in 11:6 is deemed grammatical because the most frequently grammaticalized usage of στρέφω in the LXX is the Usage of Agentive Modification.[15] In this example, the first argument of ἔχω (have) coinstantiates the first argument of ἐξουσία (authority) which then coinstantiates the first argument of στρέφω (turn) and the translation introduces in double brackets, [[ ]], the referent of the coinstantiated Agent of στρέφω (the two witnesses, cf. 11:3).

στρέφειν αὐτὰ εἰς αἷμα (11:6)
[[The two witnesses (1/Agt)]] to turn (στρέφω) [them (2/Pat)] [into blood (3/Rst)].

Although the first complement of the infinitive is coinstantiated by the first complement of licensing predicator ἐξουσία (authority) and so is not realized as a complement within the infinitive phrase, the Valence Description follows the convention (§1.4) of listing the first complement of the infinitive verb predicator with the syntactic function as "1" (no brackets) and the lexical realization as "N."

	στρέφω (11:6) <Mod. APR [§6.6a]>		
syn.	1	2	3
sem.	Agt	Pat	Rst
lex.	N	N+acc	P/εἰς

h. Usage — [§6.12] with Noun Predicators

Eight nouns that occur elsewhere in the NT without licensing arguments or adjuncts and so might be assumed to be non-predicators license adjuncts in the text of Revelation and so prove to be zero-place noun predicators with the Usage of Specification, — [§6.12]: θηρίον (beast), καπνός (smoke), λέων (lion), ξύλον (wood, tree), οἶνος (wine), σκορπίος (scorpion), σταφυλή (bunch of grapes), and ὕδωρ (water).[16] In addition, the zero-place noun predicators ἀρνίον (lamb), κτίσμα (creature), λίθος (stone), and λίμνη (lake), which elsewhere in the NT license only Benefactive adjuncts with the Usage

---

[14] Στρέφω with Usage Θ[S]G [S=Θ] [§5.2a]: Matt 5:39; 7:6; 9:22; 16:23; 18:3; Luke 7:9, 44; 9:55; 10:23; 14:25; 22:61; 23:28; John 1:38; 12:40; 20:14, 16; Acts 7:39, 42; 13:46. Στρέφω with Usage AΘ[S]G [S=A] +imp. [§5.1a]: Matt 27:3.
[15] Στρέφω with Usages APR [§6.6a] in the LXX: Exod. 4:17; 7:15; 1 Sam 10:6; Neh 13:2; Esth 13:17; Tob 2:6; 1 Macc 1:39, 40; Pss 29:12; 32:4; 40:4; 77:9; 113:8; Sir 6:28; Isa 34:9; Jer 2:21; 37:6; 38:13; Lam 5:15.
[16] NT occurrences of the noted noun predicators with adjuncts (listed by thematic role and lexical realization): θηρίον, Rev 6:8 (Ben: N+gen); καπνός, Rev 8:4 (Ben: N+gen); 9:2b (Ben: N+gen), 2c (Ben: N+gen); 14:11 (Ben: N+gen); 15:8 (Sou: P/ἐκ); 18:9 (Ben: N+gen), 18 (Ben: N+gen); 19:3

of Specification, license adjuncts with novel thematic roles in the text of Revelation.[17] These novel occurrences clarify that the predicators permit the licensing of Benefactive (θηρίον, καπνός, ξύλον, σκορπίος, σταφυλή, ὕδωρ), Comparative (ἀρνίον, λίθος), Locative (ἀρνίον, κτίσμα), Material (λίμνη, οἶνος), and Source (καπνός, λέων) adjuncts with the Usage of Specification. Given the range of possible adjuncts available to noun predicators with the Usage of Specification, all of these adjuncts are deemed grammatical.

Ben   τῶν θηρίων τῆς γῆς (6:8)
      The beasts (θηρίον) [of the earth (C/Ben)].

Cmp   λίθον ὡς μύλινον μέγαν (18:21)
      A stone (λίθος) [like a great [stone] made of millstone (C/Cmp)].

Loc   τῶν κτισμάτων τῶν ἐν τῇ θαλάσσῃ (8:9)
      The creatures (κτίσμα) [in the sea C/Loc)]

Mat   τοῦ οἴνου τοῦ θυμοῦ τῆς ὀργῆς αὐτοῦ (16:19)
      The wine (οἶνος) [of the passion of his anger (C/Mat)].

Sou   ὁ λέων ὁ ἐκ τῆς φυλῆς Ἰούδα (5:5)
      The lion (λέων) [from the tribe of Judah (C/Sou)].

	θηρίον (6:8) <Spec. — [§6.12]>			λίθος (18:21) <Spec. — [§6.12]>		
syn.	0	|	C	0	|	C
sem.	—	|	Ben	—	|	Cmp
lex.		|	N+gen		|	A/ὡς DNC

	κτίσμα (8:9) <Spec. — [§6.12]>			οἶνος (16:19) <Spec. — [§6.12]>		
syn.	0	|	C	0	|	
sem.	—	|	Loc	—	|	Mat
lex.		|	P/ἐν		|	N+gen

	λέων (5:5) <Spec. — [§6.12]>		
syn.	0	|	C
sem.	—	|	Sou
lex.		|	P/ἐκ

(Ben: N+gen); λέων, Rev 5:5 (Sou: P/ἐκ); ξύλον, Rev 2:7 (Ben: N+gen); 22:2a (Ben: N+gen), 14 (Ben: N+gen), 19 (Ben: N+gen); οἶνος, Rev 14:8 (Mat: N+gen), 10 (Mat: N+gen); 16:19 (Mat: N+gen); 17:2 (Mat: N+gen); 18:3 (Mat: N+gen); 19:15 (Mat: N+gen); σκορπίος, Rev 9:3 (Ben: N+gen); σταφυλή, Rev 14:18 (Ben: N+gen); and ὕδωρ, Rev 7:17 (Ben: N+gen); 16:12 (Ben: N+gen); 21:6 (Ben: N+gen); 22:1 (Ben: N+gen), 17 (Ben: N+gen).

[17] NT occurrences of the noted noun predicators with adjuncts (listed by thematic role and lexical realization): ἀρνίον, John 21:15 (Ben: N+gen); Rev 5:6 (Cmp: A/ὡς DNC); 7:17 (Loc: P/ἀνὰ μέσον); κτίσμα, 1 Tim 4:4 (Ben: N+gen); Jas 1:18 (Ben: N+gen); Rev 8:9 (Loc: P/ἐν); λίθος; Rom 9:32 (Ben: N+gen); Rev 18:21 (Cmp: A/ὡς Adj+1); and λίμνη, Luke 5:1 (Ben: N+gen); Rev 19:20 (Mat: N+gen); 20:10 (Mat: N+gen), 14 (Mat: N+gen), 15 (Mat: N+gen).

2. Novel Realizations of Required Complements

Eight predicators in the text of Revelation have required complement realizations that differ from those found with the same predicators elsewhere in the NT. These novel realizations of required complements are deemed grammatical whenever (1) other predicators in the NT that grammaticalize the same usage realize the same arguments with these lexical realizations or (2) the same predicators in the LXX license the same arguments with these lexical realizations or (3) the contexts of their occurrences present specific motivations for the lexical realizations. The following discussion introduces the novel lexical realizations alphabetically by their thematic roles.

a. Novel Lexical Realizations of the Required Content Complement of Ἀκούω

The previous discussion (§4.2) proposed a descriptive rule that accounts for the lexical realization of all but two of the noun phrase required Content complements of ἀκούω (hear, listen to) with usage EC [§5.5a] in the LXX and NT. The following discussion proposes possible motivations for the two exceptions to this descriptive rule, both of which appear in the text of Revelation (5:13; 16:1).

The occurrence of ἀκούω in 5:13 violates the second subsection of the restated descriptive rule concerning the lexical realization of the noun phrase required Content complement (§4.2) which states, "The noun phrase lexical realization of the second argument of ἀκούω is N+gen with usage EC (E [±resp], C [+an])."

πᾶν κτίσμα ὃ ἐν τῷ οὐρανῷ καὶ ἐπὶ τῆς γῆς καὶ ὑποκάτω τῆς γῆς καὶ ἐπὶ τῆς θαλάσσης καὶ τὰ ἐν αὐτοῖς πάντα ἤκουσα λέγοντας... (5:13)
[I (1/Exp)] heard (ἀκούω) [every created thing that is in heaven and on earth and under the earth and on the sea and all the things in them saying... (2/Con)].

In this occurrence, the first (Experiencer) complement, "I," is characterized by the semantic feature –response, and the second (Content) complement, "every created thing...and all the things in them," initially is characterized by the semantic feature –animate. As a consequence, the descriptive rule would require that the noun phrase Content complement appear as N+acc. This is, in fact, its realization. The subsequent introduction of the masculine plural participle, "saying," however, then reinterprets the initially –animate "every created thing...and all the things in them" as +animate, insofar as the attribution of speech qualifies entities as +animate. Although the descriptive rule at this point would require the use of a genitive plural form of the participle (λεγόντων), the participle is N+acc (λέγοντας). Here, the apparent motivation for maintaining the N+acc realization of the participle predicator is to provide at least a continuity of syntactic case between the neuter (–animate) noun phrase and its following masculine (+animate) participle.[18]

---

[18] This interpretation receives the support of Maximilian Zerwick, *Analysis Philologica Novi Testamenti Graeci* (SPIB 107; Rome: Sumptibus Pontificii Instituti Biblici, 1966), 575.

The occurrence of ἀκούω in 16:1 violates the third subsection of the restated descriptive rule which states, "The noun phrase lexical realization of the second argument of ἀκούω is N+acc with usage EC (E [-resp], C [-an])."

ἤκουσα μεγάλης φωνῆς ἐκ τοῦ ναοῦ λεγούσης τοῖς ἑπτὰ ἀγγέλοις (16:1)
[I (1/Exp)] heard (ἀκούω) [a loud voice from the temple speaking to the seven angels (2/Con)].

In this occurrence, "voice" is intrinsically –animate, and the subsequent introduction of the participle, "saying" immediately reinterprets the initially –animate "voice" as +animate, insofar as the attribution of speech qualifies an entity as +animate. As opposed to the previously considered occurrence (5:13) in which the licensing verb (ἀκούω) separates the noun phrase and its participle and the noun phrase only subsequently is reinterpreted as +animate, in 16:1 the participle is integrated into its noun phrase and so immediately reinterprets it as +animate. As a consequence, the N+gen realization is deemed to anticipate the immediately following attribution of +animate status.

The third row of the Valence Descriptions clarifies the semantic features and lists the ±animate distinction as initially proposed by their syntactic case: –animate (N+acc) in 5:13 and +animate (N+gen) in 16:1.

	ἀκούω (5:13) <Exp. EC [§5.5a]>		ἀκούω (16:1) <Exp. EC [§5.5a]>	
syn.	1	2	1	2
sem.	Exp	Con	Exp	Con
lex.	N [-resp]	N+acc [-an]	N [-resp]	N+gen [+an]

b. Lexical Realization of the Required Goal Complement of Δίδωμι

The verb predicator δίδωμι (give, delegate) with the Usage of Delegation, AO[S]G [S=A] [§5.7c], realizes its required Goal –animate complement by P/εἰς [-an] (to) only in 17:17a. Elsewhere in the NT, the required Goal complement of this predicator consistently is +animate and realized by N+dat [+an].[19] Here the motivation for the novel lexical realization is the fact that N+dat is restricted to +animate Goal complements whereas P/εἰς is the most frequent realization of –animate Goal complements in the NT.

ὁ γὰρ θεὸς ἔδωκεν εἰς τὰς καρδίας αὐτῶν ποιῆσαι τὴν γνώμην αὐτοῦ καὶ ποιῆσαι μίαν γνώμην καὶ δοῦναι τὴν βασιλείαν αὐτῶν τῷ θηρίῳ ἄχρι τελεσθήσονται οἱ λόγοι τοῦ θεοῦ (17:17a)
For [God (1/Agt)] gave/delegated (δίδωμι) [to their hearts (3/Goa)] [to do his intent and to do one intent and to give their kingdom to the beast until the words of God are fulfilled (2/Occ)].

[19] N+dat [+an] realization of the required Goal complement of δίδωμι with Usage AO[S]G [S=A] +imp. [§5.7c]: Matt 13:11a, 11b; Mark 10:37; Luke 1:73-74; 8:10; John 5:26; Acts 4:29; Eph 3:16; 2 Tim 1:18; Rev 2:7; 3:21; 6:4a; 7:2; 9:5; 11:3; 13:7a, 15a; 16:8; 19:8.

	δίδωμι (17:17a) <*Del.* AO[S]G [S=A] [§5.7c]>		
syn.	1	2	3
sem.	Agt	Occ	Goa
lex.	N	V-i3	P/εἰς [-an]

c. Lexical Realizations of the Required Instrument Complements of Predicators

Three predicators, περιβάλλω (clothe, wrap), περιβεβλημένος (clothed, wrapped), and περιεζωσμένος (wrapped), exhibit novel realizations of their required Instrument complements. With the Usage of Agentive Instrumentality, API [§6.4a], περιβάλλω realizes its required Instrument complement by P/ἐν (by/with) in 3:5, whereas elsewhere in the NT, this predicator realizes its required Instrument complement by N+acc.[20] With the Usage of Instrumentality by an Agent, PAI [§6.4d], the required Instrument complement of περιβεβλημένος is P/ἐν (by/with) in 4:4 and of περιεζωσμένος is N+acc (with) in 1:13 and 15:6. Elsewhere in the NT, the realization of the required Instrument complement of περιβεβλημένος is N+acc and that of περιεζωσμένος is P/ἐν.[21] Since the LXX presents P/ἐν as the realization of the required Instrument complement of περιβάλλω (Deut 22:12; 1 Chr 21:16; Ps 147:8) and περιεζωσμένος (Ps 45:13) and N+acc as the realization of the required Instrument complement of περιεζωσμένος (Judg 18:16, 17; 1 Sam 2:4, 18; 20:8; 21:16; 2 Kgs 1:8; 3:2; Jdt 4:14; Joel 1:8), both are deemed grammatical. The translations introduce in double brackets, [[ ]], the indefinite but circumscribed referent of the INC Agent (someone).

ὁ νικῶν οὕτως περιβαλεῖται ἐν ἱματίοις λευκοῖς (3:5)
[The one conquering (2/Pat)] [thus (C/Man)] will be wrapped (περιβάλλω) [[by someone (1/Agt)]] [by/with white garments (3/Ins)].

εἴκοσι τέσσαρας πρεσβυτέρους...περιβεβλημένους ἐν ἱματίοις λευκοῖς (4:4)
[Twenty-four elders (1/Pat)]...wrapped (περιβεβλημένος) [[by someone (2/Agt)]] [by/with white garments (3/Ins)].

υἱὸν ἀνθρώπου...περιεζωσμένον πρὸς τοῖς μαστοῖς ζώνην χρυσᾶν (1:13)
[A son of man (1/Pat)]...wrapped (περιεζωσμένος) [[by someone (2/Agt)]] [at the breasts (C/Loc)] [with/by a golden belt (3/Ins)].

	περιβάλλω (3:5) <*Ins.* API [§6.4a]>				περιβεβλημένος (4:4) <*Ins.* PAI [§6.4d]>		
syn.	1	2	3	C	1	(2)	3
sem.	Agt	Pat	Ins	Man	Pat	Agt	Ins
lex.	N	N+acc	P/ἐν	A/οὕτως	N	INC	P/ἐν

[20] N+acc required Instrument complement of περιβάλλω with Usage API [§6.4a]: Matt 6:31; John 19:2; Acts 12:8; Rev 19:8; cf. the N+acc Instrument with περιβαλών with Usage API [§6.4a] in Luke 23:11.
[21] N+acc required Instrument complement of περιβεβλημένος with Usage PAI [§6.4d]: Mark 14:51; 16:5; Rev 7:9, 13; 10:1; 11:3; 12:1; 17:4; 18:16; 19:13. P/ἐν required Instrument complement of περιεζωσμένος with Usage PAI [§6.4d]: Eph 6:14.

περιεζωσμένος (1:13)
<Ins. PAI [§6.4d]>

syn.	1	(2)	3		C
sem.	Agt	Pat	Ins		Loc
lex.	N	INC	N+acc		P/πρός [+dat, –an]

d. Lexical Realization of the Required Occurrence Complement of Δίδωμι

The verb predicator δίδωμι (give, dispose) with the Usage of Disposition, AΘO [§5.7a], realizes its required Occurrence complement by V+ἵνα (that) in 3:9. Elsewhere in the NT, δίδωμι realizes this Occurrence complement by V-i2 (Luke 12:58; Acts 2:27; 10:40; 13:35; 14:3). The apparent motivation for the V+ἵνα realization of the Occurrence in 3:9 is the fact that δίδωμι is coordinated with a following ποιέω (make) with the Usage of Compulsion, APO [§5.7b], in licensing this Occurrence complement, and ποιέω, the predicator immediately preceding the V+ἵνα realization, elsewhere in Revelation most frequently realizes its Occurrence complement with the Usage of Compulsion by V+ἵνα (13:12b, 15, 16; cf. 13:13b for the one occurrence of V-i2). Thus this lexical realization is deemed grammatical in this context.

διδῶ ἐκ τῆς συναγωγῆς τοῦ σατανᾶ... ἵνα ἥξουσιν καὶ προσκυνήσουσιν ἐνώπιον τῶν ποδῶν σου καὶ γνῶσιν ὅτι ἐγὼ ἠγάπησά σε (3:9)
[I (1/Agt)] am giving/disposing (δίδωμι) [some of the synagogue of Satan (2/ Pat)]...[that they come and worship before your feet and know that I loved you (3/Occ)].

δίδωμι (3:9) <Dis. AΘO [§5.7a]>

syn.	1	2	3
sem.	Agt	Thm	Occ
lex.	N	P/ἐκ	V+ἵνα

e. Lexical Realizations of the Required Partitive Complements of Μέρος

The noun predicator μέρος (portion) with the Nominal Usage of Partition with a Never-Realized Patient, Par{P} [§6.7b], realizes its Partitive required complement by P/ἀπό (of) and P/ἐκ (of) in 22:19. Elsewhere in the NT, μέρος realizes the Partitive of Partition by N+gen (Luke 15:12; 24:42). The realizations in the text of Revelation are deemed grammatical because occurrences of μέρος in the LXX realize their required Partitive complements by P/ἀπό (1 Macc 9:15) and P/ἐκ (1 Kgs 12:31). The translation of 22:19 introduces the never-realized Patient complement in braces, { } and follows the English practice of realizing the +animate Benefactive by a possessive adjective. For clarity of presentation, the translation omits the contribution of the coordination predicator καί (and).

τὸ μέρος αὐτοῦ ἀπὸ τοῦ ξύλου τῆς ζωῆς καὶ ἐκ τῆς πόλεως τῆς ἁγίας τῶν γεγραμμένων ἐν τῷ βιβλίῳ τούτῳ (22:19)
[His (C/Ben)] portion (μέρος) [of the tree of life and of the holy city written in this book (1/Par)] {portion (2/Pat)}.

Two Valence Descriptions are required to clarify that the Partitive Complement is composite and coordinated by καί (and).

	μέρος (22:19a) <Par. Par{P} [§6.7b]>			μέρος (22:19b) <Par. Par{P} [§6.7b>		
syn.	1	{2}	C	1	{2}	C
sem.	Par	Pat	Ben	Par	Pat	Ben
lex.	P/ἀπό	{N}	N+gen	P/ἐκ	{N}	N+gen

f. Lexical Realizations of the Required Source Complement of Λύω

The verb predicator λύω (release) with the Usage of Separation, APS [§6.8a], realizes its Source required complement by P/ἐκ (from) in 1:5 and 20:7. Elsewhere in the NT, λύω realizes the Source of Separation by P/ἀπό (Luke 13:16; 1 Cor 7:27). The P/ἐκ realization in the text of Revelation is deemed grammatical because occurrences of λύω in the LXX realize their required Source complement by P/ἐκ (Josh 5:15; Job 5:20). The translation of 20:7 introduces in double brackets, [[ ]], the indefinite but circumscribed referent of the INC Agent (someone).

ὅταν τελεσθῇ τὰ χίλια ἔτη, λυθήσεται ὁ σατανᾶς ἐκ τῆς φυλακῆς αὐτοῦ (20:7)
[When the thousand years are completed (C/Tem)] [Satan (2/Pat)] will be released (λύω) [[by someone (1/Agt)]] [from his prison (3/Sou)].

	λύω (20:7) <Sep. APS [§6.8a]>				
syn.	1	2	3		C
sem.	Agt	Pat	Sou		Tem
lex.	N	N+acc	P/ἐκ		V+ὅταν

g. Lexical Realizations of the Required Topic Complements of Predicators

When grammaticalizing the Usage of Experience of a Topic, EC C→T [§5.5c], the verb predicator εὐφραίνω (rejoice) realizes its required Topic complement by P/ἐπί [+dat] (at/concerning) in 18:20, and the verb predicator ὀργίζω (be angry) also realizes its required Topic complement by P/ἐπί [+dat] (at/concerning) in 12:17. Elsewhere in the NT, εὐφραίνω realizes its required Topic complement by P/ἐν (Acts 7:41), and ὀργίζω realizes its required Topic complement by N+dat (Matt 5:22). The P/ἐπί [+dat] realization in the text of Revelation is deemed grammatical for both predicators because occurrences of εὐφραίνω and ὀργίζω in the LXX realize their required Topic complements by P/ἐπί [+dat].²²

εὐφραίνου ἐπ' αὐτῇ, οὐρανὲ καὶ οἱ ἅγιοι καὶ οἱ ἀπόστολοι καὶ οἱ προφῆται, ὅτι ἔκρινεν ὁ θεὸς τὸ κρίμα ὑμῶν ἐξ αὐτῆς (18:20)
[You (1/Exp)] rejoice (εὐφραίνω) [at/concerning her (2/Top)], [heaven and holy ones and apostles and prophets (C/Voc)], [because God judged your judgment of/against her (C/Cau)].

ὠργίσθη ὁ δράκων ἐπὶ τῇ γυναικὶ (12:17)
[The dragon (1/Exp)] was angry (ὀργίζω) [at/concerning the woman (2/Top)].

	εὐφραίνω (18:20) <Exp. EC C→T [§5.5c]>				ὀργίζω (12:17) <Exp. EC C→T [§5.5c]>	
syn.	1	2	C	C	1	2
sem.	Exp	Top	Cau	Voc	Exp	Top
lex.	N	P/ἐπί [+dat]	V+ὅτι	N+voc	N	P/ἐπί [+dat]

3. Disharmonious Coordination by Conjunction Predicators

As previously discussed (§6.11), the labels of the two usages of coordination clarify whether the coordination predicator relates two entities that do not admit to description by thematic roles (— —) or two entities whose thematic roles are set by a predicator other than the conjunction (--- ---). Conjunction predicators typically license complements with parallel lexical realizations (two maximal verb phrases, two prepositional phrases, two noun phrases, etc.), as in the following examples. The second example (13:16) introduces the entire verb phrase of the predicator that sets the relation of the coordinated complements of the conjunction predicator.

πικρανεῖ σου τὴν κοιλίαν, ἀλλ' ἐν τῷ στόματί σου ἔσται γλυκὺ ὡς μέλι (10:9)
[It will make your stomach bitter (1/—)] but (ἀλλά) [in your mouth it will be sweet like honey (2/—)].

δῶσιν αὐτοῖς χάραγμα ἐπὶ τῆς χειρὸς αὐτῶν τῆς δεξιᾶς ἢ ἐπὶ τὸ μέτωπον αὐτῶν (13:16)
[They (1/Agt)] give (δίδωμι) [to them (3/Goa)] [a mark (2/Thm)] [[on their right hand (1/---)] or (ἤ) [on their forehead (2/---)] (C/Loc)].

---

[22] The P/ἐπί [+dat] realization of the Topic in the LXX with εὐφραίνω: Deut 12:7; 28:63a, 63b; 30:9; 1 Macc 11:44; 12:12; 14:21; Pss 30:8; 39:17; 62:12; 63:11; 65:11; 69:5; 84:7; 96:12; 103:31, 34; 121:1; 149:2; Prov 2:14; 17:21; 23:24, 25; Job 31:25; Wis 7:12; Sir 16:1, 2; 18:32; 25:7; Amos 6:13; Joel 2:23; Isa 14:8; 25:9; 62:5a, 5b; 65:19; Bar 4:33. The P/ἐπί [+dat] realization of the Topic in the LXX with ὀργίζω: Gen 40:2; Num 31:14; 2 Chr 16:10; Eccl 5:5; Isa 57:6.

7. Distinctive Grammatical Characteristics

Valence Descriptions note that there is no thematic role by listing — in the semantic function row and that the thematic role is set by a predicator other than the conjunction by listing --- in the semantic function row. The Valence Description for δίδωμι (give) incorporates the coordinated Locative adjuncts separately to clarify that they have different lexical realization.

	ἀλλά (10:9)		ἤ (13:16)	
	<Coor. — — [§6.11a]>		<Coor. --- --- [§6.11b]>	
syn.	1	2	1	2
sem.	—	—	---	---
lex.	V+	V+	P/ἐπί [+gen]	P/ἐπί [+acc]

δίδωμι (13:16) <Tra. AΘ[S]G [S=A] +imp. [§5.1a]>

	1	2	3		C	C
syn.	1	2	3		C	C
sem.	Agt	Thm	Goa		Loc	Loc
lex.	N	N+acc	N+dat [+an]		P/ἐπί [+gen]	P/ἐπί [+acc]

What is distinctive about the text of Revelation is the presence of two sets of coordinated arguments that differ in lexical realization and/or the thematic roles set by a predicator other than the conjunction. These atypical occurrences are deemed to fall within the range of grammaticality because the NT presents other examples of disharmonious concord, as, for example, in John 20:18, where καί (and) coordinates a statement of direct discourse (V+quo) with a summary of indirect discourse (V+).

Μαριὰμ ἡ Μαγδαληνὴ ἀγγέλλουσα τοῖς μαθηταῖς ὅτι ἑώρακα τὸν κύριον, καὶ ταῦτα εἶπεν αὐτῇ (John 20:18)
[Mary the Magdalene (1/Agt)] announcing (ἀγγέλλων) [to the disciples (3/Exp)] ["I have seen the Lord" and he said these things to her (2/Con)].

ἑώρακα τὸν κύριον, καὶ ταῦτα εἶπεν αὐτῇ (John 20:18)
["I have seen the Lord" (1/---)] and (καί) [he said these things to her (2/---)].

The two sets of disharmonious coordination in the text of Revelation receive illustration in the following examples of ἐξέρχομαι (go forth) with the Primary Usage of Motion to a Goal, Θ[S]G [S=Θ] [§5.2a], and of καί (and) with the Usage of Coordination of Entities with Thematic Roles, --- --- [§6.11b]. Since the coordinated adjuncts in the first example (6:2) differ in thematic role and lexical realization, the typical means of resolving coordinated complements in the translations (by combining the coordinated phrases under the same thematic role) does not work. As a consequence, the translations incorporate further resolutions of the disharmoniously coordinated complements.

ἐξῆλθεν νικῶν καὶ ἵνα νικήσῃ (6:2)
[He (1/Thm)] went forth (ἐξέρχομαι) [[to some place (2/Goa)]] [[conquering (C/Cur)] and [in order that he might conquer (C/Pur)]].

νικῶν καὶ ἵνα νικήσῃ (6:2f)
[Conquering (1/---)] and (καί) [in order that he might conquer (2/---)].

οὐκ ἔχουσιν ἀνάπαυσιν ἡμέρας καὶ νυκτὸς οἱ προσκυνοῦντες τὸ θηρίον καὶ τὴν εἰκόνα αὐτοῦ καὶ εἴ τις λαμβάνει τὸ χάραγμα τοῦ ὀνόματος αὐτοῦ (14:11)
[[The ones worshipping the beast and its image] and [if someone receives the mark of its name (1/Cnd)]] do not have [rest (2/Pat)] [night and day (C/Tem)].

οἱ προσκυνοῦντες τὸ θηρίον καὶ τὴν εἰκόνα αὐτοῦ καὶ εἴ τις λαμβάνει τὸ χάραγμα τοῦ ὀνόματος αὐτοῦ (14:11b)
[The ones worshipping the beast and its image (1/---)] and (καί) [if someone receives the mark of its name (2/---)].

Valence Descriptions note the lack of thematic role concord by placing after the citation and in brackets, [ ], a note to confer (cf.) the governing predicator that sets the relation with its citation. Since the coordinated adjuncts in the first example (6:2) differ in thematic role and lexical realization, the Valence Description lists them separately.

	ἐξέρχομαι (6:2) <Mot. Θ[S]G [S=Θ] [§5.2a]>				καί (6:2f) [cf. ἐξέρχομαι, 6:2] <Coor. --- --- [§6.11b]	
syn.	1	(2)	C	C	1	2
sem.	Thm	Goa	Cur	Pur	---	---
lex.	N	INC	Part+1	V+ἵνα	Part+1	V+ἵνα

	ἔχω (14:11) <Ben. BP [§6.1c]>				καί (14:11d) [cf. ἔχω, 14:11] <Coor. --- --- [§6.11b]>	
syn.	1	2	C	C	1	2
sem.	Ben	Pat	Cnd	Tem	---	---
lex.	N	N+acc	V+εἴ	N+gen	N+nom	V+εἰ

4. The Omission of Εἰμί (Be)

Since Greek grammar, unlike English grammar, permits the omission of εἰμί (be) whenever its contribution can be deduced from the context, all such omissions are deemed grammatical.[23] What is distinctive about the omission of εἰμί in the text of Revelation is its frequency of occurrence both as a simple verb predicator and as a component of complex predicators.[24] The following examples illustrate the omission

---

[23] BDF, 70–71 (§§127–128).
[24] Mot, *Irregularities*, 116–28, considers the interpretation of the omission of the εἰμί component with various categories of complex predicators: e.g., ἔχων + [εἰμί] in 1:16 (116), ὡς + [εἰμί] in 16:13 (122), and ὅμοιος + [εἰμί] in 21:11 (128). Messies, *The Morphology of Koine Greek*, 324-25, attributes a

first of the verb εἰμί with the usage of Qualification of a Patient, P [§6.10a], and then of εἰμί as a component of a complex predicator πλείων + [εἰμί] (be greater) with the Usage of Comparison, PCmp [§6.9b]. The translations introduce the omitted forms of "be" in bold print.

ἵππος λευκός, (6:2a)
There **is** ([εἰμί]) [a white horse (1/Pat)].

τὰ ἔργα σου τὰ ἔσχατα πλείονα τῶν πρώτων (2:19)
[Your last works (1/Pat)] **are** greater (πλείων + [εἰμί]) [than the first (2/Cmp)].

Valence Descriptions note the omission of εἰμί by placing the citation and, in the case of complex predicators, the omitted εἰμί in brackets, [ ].

	εἰμί [6:2a] <Qual. P [§6.10a]>	πλείων + [εἰμί] [2:19] <Cmp. PCmp [§6.9b]>	
syn.	1	1	2
sem.	Pat	Pat	Cmp
lex.	N	N	N+gen

The recognition of the frequency of the omission of εἰμί in straightforward contexts like those in 6:2 and 2:19 encourages a reconsideration of numerous instances in which the motivation for N+nom noun phrases may not be readily apparent, as in the following examples of ἔχων + [εἰμί] (be holding) and ἰσχυρός + [εἰμί] (be strong). The translations introduce the proposed omitted forms of "be" in bold print.

ὁ καθήμενος ἐπ' αὐτὸν ἔχων ζυγὸν ἐν τῇ χειρὶ αὐτοῦ (6:5)
[The one sitting on it (1/Agt)] **was** holding (ἔχων + [εἰμί]) [a scale (2/Pat)] [in his hand (C/Loc)].

ἰσχυρὸς κύριος ὁ θεὸς ὁ κρίνας αὐτήν (18:8)
Strong **is** (ἰσχυρός + [εἰμί]) [the Lord God judging her (1/Pat)].

	ἔχων + [εἰμί] [6:5] <Ben. BP [§6.1c]>			ἰσχυρός + [εἰμί] [18:8] <Qual. P [§6.10a]>
syn.	1	2	C	1
sem.	Agt	Pat	Loc	Pat
lex.	N	N+acc	P/ἐν	N

majority of these complex participle predicators with omitted εἰμί, excepting most occurrences of ἔχων + [εἰμί], to Mishnaic Hebrew or Aramaic influence.

5. The Omission of Other Predicators

Since Greek grammar, like English grammar, permits the omission of predicators that can be retrieved from the context, all such omissions in the text of Revelation are deemed grammatical.[25] In general, predicator omission is restricted to occasions in which the same predicator appears in the immediately preceding context. Such proximate predicator omission occurs throughout the NT. What is distinctive about proximate predicator omission in the text of Revelation is both its frequency of occurrence and its almost consistent linkage to the adverb predicator ὡς (like) and the complex predicator ὡς + εἰμί (be + like) with the Usage of Comparison, PCmp [§6.9b]. Proximate predicator omission receives illustration in the following examples of noun predicators with the Usage of Benefaction with a Suppressed Patient and a Promoted Benefactive, B{P} [§6.1g]. The translations introduce the omitted predicators in bold print and the suppressed complement in braces, { }.

φωνὴν μεγάλην ὡς σάλπιγγος (1:10)
[A great sound (1/Pat)] like (ὡς) [**the sound** of a trumpet (2/Cmp)].

[φωνὴν] σάλπιγγος ([1:10b])
The sound (φωνή) [of a trumpet (1/Ben)] {sound (2/Pat)}.

οἱ ὀδόντες αὐτῶν ὡς λεόντων ἦσαν (9:8)
[Their teeth (1/Pat)] were like (ὡς + [εἰμί]) [**the teeth** of lions (2/Cmp)].

[ὀδόντες] λεόντων ([9:8b])
The teeth (ὀδούς) [of lions (1/Ben)] {teeth (2/Pat)}.

Valence Descriptions note such omitted predicators by placing their chapter and verse citations in brackets, [ ], and whenever the omitted predicators would be the second occurrence of the predicator in the verse, the citations end in "b." Since the omitted predicators are the DNC second complements of their licensing predicators, the Valence descriptions for the licensing predicators place the syntactic function of their second complement in brackets, [ ].

	ὡς (1:10)		φωνή [1:10b]	
	<Cmp. PCmp [§6.9b]>		<Ben. B{P} [§6.1g]>	
syn.	1	[2]	1	{{2}}
sem.	Pat	Cmp	Ben	Pat
lex.	N	DNC	N+gen	{N}

---

[25] BDF, 253 (§419.1).

	ὡς + [εἰμί] [9:8]		ὁδούς [9:8b]	
	<Cmp. PCmp [§6.9b]>		<Ben. B{P} [§6.1g]>	
syn.	1	[2]	1	{{2}}
sem.	Pat	Cmp	Ben	Pat
lex.	N	DNC	N+gen	{N}

6. Distant Predicator Retrieval

Distant predicator retrieval becomes necessary when parentheses intrude into a phrase licensed by a predicator. Since parentheses occur elsewhere in the NT, they are deemed grammatical in the text of Revelation.[26] Parentheses pose difficulty for interpretation because they introduce into the phrases licensed by predicators other predicators of equal or greater "rank." The ranking of predicators and their phrases from highest to lowest appears in the following table that places the highest-ranking phrases at the top left and indents lower ranking phrases, with phrases of equal rank separated by commas.

    verb phrase, complex predicator phrase, interjection phrase
        participle phrase, adjective phrase
            preposition phrase
                adverb phrase

What is distinctive about parentheses in the text of Revelation is the distance between the predicator that licenses complements and the complements that appear after the parentheses. The following examples illustrate a more straightforward parenthesis in the phrase licensed by οἶδά (know) with the Usage of Experience of a Content, EC [§5.5a] in 2:9, and a more distinctive parenthesis in the phrase licensed by the participle predicator ἔχων (having) with the Usage of Benefaction of a Patient, BP [§6.1c], in 13:1-3. Both translations set off the parentheses by dashes, —, and reintroduce the distant predicator in bold print.

οἶδά σου τὴν θλῖψιν καὶ τὴν πτωχείαν, ἀλλὰ πλούσιος εἶ, καὶ τὴν βλασφημίαν ἐκ τῶν λεγόντων Ἰουδαίους εἶναι ἑαυτούς (2:9)
[I (1/Exp)] know (οἶδά) [your oppression and poverty—but you are rich—and **know** the blasphemy of the ones saying that they are Jews and they are not (2/Con)].

θηρίον...ἔχον κέρατα δέκα καὶ κεφαλὰς ἑπτὰ καὶ ἐπὶ τῶν κεράτων αὐτοῦ δέκα διαδήματα καὶ ἐπὶ τὰς κεφαλὰς αὐτοῦ ὀνόμα[τα] βλασφημίας, καὶ τὸ θηρίον ὃ εἶδον ἦν ὅμοιον παρδάλει καὶ οἱ πόδες αὐτοῦ ὡς ἄρκου καὶ τὸ στόμα αὐτοῦ ὡς στόμα λέοντος. καὶ ἔδωκεν αὐτῷ ὁ δράκων τὴν δύναμιν αὐτοῦ καὶ τὸν θρόνον

---

[26] For a discussion of parenthesis, see BDF, 242 (§465).

αὐτοῦ καὶ ἐξουσίαν μεγάλην, καὶ μίαν ἐκ τῶν κεφαλῶν αὐτοῦ ὡς ἐσφαγμένην
εἰς θάνατον (13:1-3)
[A beast...(1/Ben)] having (ἔχων) [ten horns and seven heads and on its horns ten diadems and on its heads name[s] of blasphemy—and the beast which I saw was like a leopard and its feet [were] like [the feet] of a bear and its mouth was like [the] mouth of a lion and the dragon gave to it its power and its throne and great authority—and **having** one of its heads as if slain to [the point of] death (2/Pat)].

As an aid for interpretation, Valence Descriptions note such distant predicators by listing the chapter and verses of the complete phrase. Note that, since ἔχων in 13:1-3 licenses two Locative complements in which ἐπί requires completion by noun phrases with different lexical realizations, both are listed in the Valence Description.

	οἶδά (2:9) <*Exp.* EC [§5:5a]>		ἔχων (13:1-3) <*Ben.* BP [§6.1c]>			
syn.	1	2	1	2	C	C
sem.	Exp	Con	Ben	Pat	Loc	Loc
lex.	N	N+acc	N	N+acc	P/ἐπί [+gen]	P/ἐπί [+acc]

7. Contribution of the Study of the Distinctive Grammatical Characteristics

Both the distinctiveness and the grammaticality of these characteristics in the text of Revelation contribute to the Case Frame study. Identification of the motivations for the most exceptional novel usages and of parallels for the remaining usages and realizations removes these as possible examples of grammatical irregularities in the text and contributes significant observations concerning the licensing properties of NT predicators. The recognition of disharmonious coordination elsewhere in the NT also resolves as grammatical, albeit awkward, other proposed irregularities. Perhaps most significant is the recognition of the frequency of predicator omission and parentheses throughout the text. This recognition permits the reconsideration and ultimate resolution of numerous other proposed grammatical irregularities. The discussions of this chapter also establish the grammaticality of the licensing properties of *every* predicator in the text of Revelation. This grammaticality provides the stable basis for the coherent interpretation of the text which frequently is noted for its solecisms and difficult grammar.[27]

8. Conclusion to the Case Frame Study

The goal of this Case Frame study was to analyze and describe the licensing properties of all occurrences of predicators in the text of Revelation. To this end, the Case Frame study developed means of noting in Valence Descriptions the syntactic function, the

---

[27] For a detailed consideration of these solecisms, see Mot, *Irregularities*, 46–209.

7. Distinctive Grammatical Characteristics 181

semantic function, and lexical realization of all arguments and adjuncts of predicators in the text. These Valence Descriptions also incorporate notations concerning definite and indefinite null complements (Chapter 1). The study then augmented the Valence Descriptions to include notations on the events and non-events grammaticalized by predicators (Chapter 2) and usage features of the conceptualization of each event associated with each predicator usage (Chapter 3). The study then developed further notations for semantic features, occurrences of λέγω melding, and redundant complements, and a protocol for noting polysemous occurrences (Chapter 4). This permitted the exhaustive resolution of the licensing properties of all occurrences of all predicators in the text of Revelation into one or more usages or, in the case of polysemy, into two or three usages (Chapters 5 and 6). The study then demonstrated the grammaticality—in relation to other texts in the LXX or NT—of the distinctive grammatical characteristics of the text of Revelation (Chapter 7). As a consequence, the notations in Valence Descriptions provide comprehensive and exhaustive descriptions of the licensing properties of all occurrences of predicators in the text of Revelation. These Valence Descriptions now are ready for re-presentation according to strict protocols (Chapter 8) into lexicon entries (Chapter 9) that maintain all of the specific grammatical information about the licensing properties of each predicator in each of its occurrences.

Part III

LEXICON ENTRIES

8

FROM VALENCE DESCRIPTIONS TO LEXICON ENTRIES

All of the syntactic, semantic, lexical, and further information and notations concerning licensing properties in the Valence Descriptions of all occurrences of a predicator receives re-presentation in one or more Case Frame Lexicon entries for that predicator. Generation of entries requires a three-stage process. First, all occurrences of the predicator receive specification in Valence Descriptions. Second, the Valence Descriptions for all occurrences of the predicator with the same usage are re-presented according to protocols in a Generalized Valence Description that maintains all of the grammatical specificity and notations of the individual Valence Descriptions for the predicator with that usage. Third, all of the grammatical information and notations in each Generalized Valence Description of the predicator is re-presented according to protocols in a lexicon entry for the occurrences of the predicator with each usage. The following discussion illustrates the three-stage process of generating lexicon entries in relation to the verb predicator ποιέω (do, make). The discussion then clarifies the protocols for generating lexicon entries for predicator occurrences that admit to polysemous interpretation. The concluding discussions introduce further general and specific notations that may characterize particular lexicon entries.

1. Valence Descriptions for the Verb Predicator Ποιέω

This discussion distinguishes the occurrences of ποιέω according to its five observed usages in the text of Revelation, analyzes the occurrences of ποιέω with each usage in a subsection with the label for that usage, and generates the Valence Description for each occurrence. For ease of recognition, the presentation analyzes two occurrences with the same usage at a time and follows them with their associated Valence Descriptions before proceeding to the next pair of occurrences. Within this discussion, the Valence Descriptions for occurrences with coinstantiation of the first (Agent) complement follow the convention (§1.4) of listing the first complement of the infinitive with the syntactic function as "1" (no brackets) and the lexical realization as "N."

a. Valence Descriptions of Ποιέω with Usage AP [§6.3a]

Ποιέω occurs with the Usage of Effect on eight occasions.

τὰ πρῶτα ἔργα ποίησον (2:5)
[You (1/Agt)] do (ποιέω) [the first works (2/Pat)].

τὴν ἐξουσίαν τοῦ πρώτου θηρίου πᾶσαν ποιεῖ ἐνώπιον αὐτοῦ (13:12a)
[It (1/Agt)] wields (ποιέω) [all the authority of the first beast (2/Pat)] [before it (C/Loc)].

	ποιέω (2:5) <*Eff.* AP [§6.3a]>		ποιέω (13:12a) <*Eff.* AP [§6.3a]>		
syn.	1	2	1	2	C
sem.	Agt	Pat	Agt	Pat	Loc
lex.	N	N+acc	N	N+acc	P/ἐνώπιον

The translation of 13:14a introduces in double brackets, [[ ]], the contextual referents of the coinstantiated Agent (it/the other beast) and the DNC Patient (signs).

ποιεῖ σημεῖα μεγάλα, ἵνα καὶ πῦρ ποιῇ ἐκ τοῦ οὐρανοῦ καταβαίνειν εἰς τὴν γῆν ἐνώπιον τῶν ἀνθρώπων (13:13a)
[It (1/Agt)] does (ποιέω) [great signs (2/Pat)] [so that it even makes fire come down from heaven onto the earth before human beings (C/Res)].

ποιῆσαι ἐνώπιον τοῦ θηρίου (13:14a)
[[It/the other beast (1/Agt)]] to do (ποιέω) [[signs (2/Pat)]] [before the beast (C/Loc)].

	ποιέω (13:13a) <*Eff.* AP [§6.3a]>			ποιέω (13:14a) <*Eff.* AP [§6.3a]>		
syn.	1	2	C	1	[2]	C
sem.	Agt	Pat	Res	Agt	Pat	Loc
lex.	N	N+acc	V+ἵνα	N	DNC	P/ἐνώπιον

The translation of 17:17a introduces in double brackets, [[ ]], the contextual referent of the coinstantiated Agent (their hearts).

ἡ εἰκὼν τοῦ θηρίου...ποιήσῃ [ἵνα] ὅσοι ἐὰν μὴ προσκυνήσωσιν τῇ εἰκόνι τοῦ θηρίου ἀποκτανθῶσιν (13:15)
[The image of the beast (1/Agt)]...may make (ποιέω) [that as many as did not worship the image of the beast be killed (2/Pat)].

ποιῆσαι τὴν γνώμην αὐτοῦ (17:17a)
[[Their hearts (1/Agt)]] to do (ποιέω) [his intent (2/Pat)].

	ποιέω (13:15) <*Eff.* AP [§6.3a]>		ποιέω (17:17a) <*Eff.* AP [§6.3a]>	
syn.	1	2	1	2
sem.	Agt	Pat	Agt	Pat
lex.	N	V+ἵνα	N	N+acc

The translation of 17:17b introduces in double brackets, [[ ]], the contextual referent of the coinstantiated Agent (their hearts).

ποιῆσαι μίαν γνώμην (17:17b)
[[Their hearts (1/Agt)]] to do (ποιέω) [one intent (2/Pat)].

ὁ δίκαιος δικαιοσύνην ποιησάτω ἔτι (22:11)
Let [the just one (1/Agt)] [still (C/Tem)] do (ποιέω) [justice (2/Pat)].

	ποιέω (17:17b) <*Eff.* AP [§6.3a]>		ποιέω (22:11) <*Eff.* AP [§6.3a]>			
syn.	1	2	1	2	|	C
sem.	Agt	Pat	Agt	Pat	|	Tem
lex.	N	N+acc	N	N+acc	|	A/ἔτι

b. Valence Descriptions of Ποιέω with Usage APR [§6.6a]

Ποιέω occurs with the Usage of Agentive Modification on six occasions.

In 3:12, the first two words, ὁ νικῶν (the one conquering), are omitted because they are licensed not by the verb predicator but are introduced directly by Greek Grammar.[1]

ἐποίησεν ἡμᾶς βασιλείαν τῷ θεῷ καὶ πατρὶ αὐτοῦ (1:6)
[He (1/Agt)] made (ποιέω) [us (2/Pat)] [a kingdom, priests (3/Rst)] [for his God and Father (C/Ben)].

ποιήσω αὐτὸν στῦλον ἐν τῷ ναῷ τοῦ θεοῦ μου (3:12)
[I (1/Agt)] will make (ποιέω) [him (2/Pat)] [a pillar in the sanctuary of my God (3/Rst)].

	ποιέω (1:6) <*Mod.* APR [§6.6a]>					ποιέω (3:12) <*Mod.* APR [§6.6a]>		
syn.	1	2	3	|	C	1	2	3
sem.	Agt	Pat	Rst	|	Ben	Agt	Pat	Rst
lex.	N	N+acc	N+2	|	N+dat [+an]	N	N+acc	N+2

---

[1] BDF, 243–44 (§466.1), interprets ὁ νικῶν ποιήσω αὐτόν (the one conquering, I will make him) in 3:12 as an example of anacoluthon in which the N+acc pronoun αὐτόν (him) resumes the N+nom ὁ νικῶν (the one conquering), and Zerwick, *Analysis Philologica*, 573, interprets ὁ νικῶν as a Hebreism.

ἐποίησας αὐτοὺς τῷ θεῷ ἡμῶν βασιλείαν καὶ ἱερεῖς (5:10)
[You (1/Agt)] made (ποιέω) [them (2/Pat)] [a kingdom and priests (3/Rst)] [for our God (C/Ben)].

αὐτὴν ποταμοφόρητον ποιήσῃ (12:15)
[He (1/Agt)] might make (ποιέω) [her (2/Pat)] [swept away by a river (3/Rst)].

	ποιέω (5:10) <Mod. APR [§6.6a]>				ποιέω (12:15) <Mod. APR [§6.6a]>		
syn.	1	2	3	C	1	2	3
sem.	Agt	Pat	Rst	Ben	Agt	Pat	Rst
lex.	N	N+acc	N+2	N+dat [+an]	N	N+acc	Adj+2

ἠρημωμένην ποιήσουσιν αὐτήν (17:16)
[They (1/Agt)] will make (ποιέω) [her (2/Pat)] [desolated (3/Rst)].

καινὰ ποιῶ πάντα (21:5)
[I (1/Agt)] make (ποιέω) [all things (2/Pat)] [new (3/Rst)].

In 17:16, the participle ἠρημωμένη (desolated) functions as an adjective in relation to the licensing verb predicator and is listed as such in the Valence Description.

	ποιέω (17:16) <Mod. APR [§6.6a]>			ποιέω (21:5) <Mod. APR [§6.6a]>		
syn.	1	2	3	1	2	3
sem.	Agt	Pat	Rst	Agt	Pat	Rst
lex.	N	N+acc	Adj+2	N	N+acc	Adj+2

c. Valence Descriptions of Ποιέω with Usage APB [§6.1a]

Ποιέω occurs with the Usage of Agentive Benefaction on five occasions. As previously discussed (§6.1a n. 1), examples in which ποιέω licenses a second complement realized by the noun predicator πόλεμος (war, battle) attribute the P/μετά [+gen] (against) complement to the licensing properties of ποιέω.

The translation of 12:17 introduces in double brackets, [[ ]], the contextual referent of the coinstantiated Agent (the dragon).

ὅταν τελέσωσιν τὴν μαρτυρίαν αὐτῶν, τὸ θηρίον τὸ ἀναβαῖνον ἐκ τῆς ἀβύσσου ποιήσει μετ' αὐτῶν πόλεμον (11:7)
[When they complete their testimony (C/Tem)] [the beast coming up from the abyss (1/Agt)] will make (ποιέω) [war (2/Pat)] [against them (3/Ben)].

ποιῆσαι πόλεμον μετὰ τῶν λοιπῶν τοῦ σπέρματος αὐτῆς τῶν τηρούντων τὰς ἐντολὰς τοῦ θεοῦ καὶ ἐχόντων τὴν μαρτυρίαν Ἰησοῦ (12:17)

[[The dragon (1/Agt)]] to make (ποιέω) [war (2/Pat)] [against the rest of her offspring keeping the commandments of God and having the testimony of Jesus (3/Ben)].

	ποιέω (11:7) <Ben. APB [§6.1a]>				
syn.	1	2	3	|	C
sem.	Agt	Pat	Ben	|	Tem
lex.	N	N+acc	P/μετά [+gen]	|	V+ὅταν

	ποιέω (12:17) <Ben. APB [§6.1a]>		
syn.	1	2	3
sem.	Agt	Pat	Ben
lex.	N	N+acc	P/μετά [+gen]

The translations introduce in double brackets, [[ ]], the contextual referent of the coinstantiated Agent (the beast, cf. 13:4) in 13:7 and of the coinstantiated Agent (the ones dwelling on the earth, cf. 13:14a) in 13:14b.

ποιῆσαι πόλεμον μετὰ τῶν ἁγίων (13:7)
[[The beast (1/Agt)]] to make (ποιέω) [war (2/Pat)] [against the holy ones (3/Ben)].

ποιῆσαι εἰκόνα τῷ θηρίῳ (13:14b)
[[The ones dwelling on the earth (1/Agt)]] to make (ποιέω) [an image (2/Pat)] [for the beast (3/Ben)].

	ποιέω (13:7)			ποιέω (13:14b)		
	<Ben. APB [§6.1a]>			<Ben. APB [§6.1a]>		
syn.	1	2	3	1	2	3
sem.	Agt	Pat	Ben	Agt	Pat	Ben
lex.	N	N+acc	P/μετά [+gen]	N	N+acc	N+dat [+an]

The translation of 19:19 introduces in double brackets, [[ ]], the contextual referent of the coinstantiated Agent (the beast and the kings of the earth and their armies).

ποιῆσαι τὸν πόλεμον μετὰ τοῦ καθημένου ἐπὶ τοῦ ἵππου καὶ μετὰ τοῦ στρατεύματος αὐτοῦ (19:19)
[[The beast and the kings of the earth and their armies (1/Agt)]] to make (ποιέω) [war (2/Pat)] [against the one sitting on the horse and against his army (3/Ben)].

	ποιέω (19:19) <Ben. APB [§6.1a]>		
syn.	1	2	3
sem.	Agt	Pat	Ben
lex.	N	N+acc	P/μετά [+gen]

d. Valence Descriptions of Ποιέω with Usage APO [§5.7b]

Ποιέω occurs with the Usage of Compulsion on four occasions.

ποιήσω αὐτοὺς ἵνα ἥξουσιν καὶ προσκυνήσουσιν ἐνώπιον τῶν ποδῶν σου (3:9)
[I (1/Agt)] will make (ποιέω) [them (2/Pat)] [that they come and worship before your feet (2/Occ)].

ποιεῖ τὴν γῆν καὶ τοὺς ἐν αὐτῇ κατοικοῦντας ἵνα προσκυνήσουσιν τὸ θηρίον τὸ πρῶτον (13:12b)
[It (1/Agt)] makes (ποιέω) [the earth and the ones dwelling in it (2/Pat)] [that they worship the first beast (3/Occ)].

	ποιέω (3:9) <Cpl. APO [§5.7b]>			ποιέω (13:12b) <Cpl. APO [§5.7b]>		
syn.	1	2	3	1	2	3
sem.	Agt	Pat	Occ	Agt	Pat	Occ
lex.	N	N+acc	V+ἵνα	N	N+acc	V+ἵνα

καὶ πῦρ ποιῇ ἐκ τοῦ οὐρανοῦ καταβαίνειν εἰς τὴν γῆν ἐνώπιον τῶν ἀνθρώπων (13:13b)
[It (1/Agt)] [also (C/Mea)] may make (ποιέω) [fire (2/Pat)] [come down from heaven to the earth before human beings (3/Occ)].

ποιεῖ πάντας, τοὺς μικροὺς καὶ τοὺς μεγάλους, καὶ τοὺς πλουσίους καὶ τοὺς πτωχούς, καὶ τοὺς ἐλευθέρους καὶ τοὺς δούλους, ἵνα δῶσιν αὐτοῖς χάραγμα ἐπὶ τῆς χειρὸς αὐτῶν τῆς δεξιᾶς ἢ ἐπὶ τὸ μέτωπον αὐτῶν (13:16)
[It (1/Agt)] makes (ποιέω) [all the small and the great and the rich and the poor and the free and the slaves (2/Pat)] [that they give them a mark on their right hand or on their foreheads (3/Occ)].

	ποιέω (13:13b) <Cpl. APO [§5.7b]>					ποιέω (13:16) <Cpl. APO [§5.7b]>		
syn.	1	2	3	|	C	1	2	3
sem.	Agt	Pat	Occ	|	Mea	Agt	Pat	Occ
lex.	N	N+acc	V-i2	|	A/καί	N	N+acc	V+ἵνα

e. Valence Description of Ποιέω with Usage A{P} [§6.3b]

Ποιέω occurs with the Usage of Effect with a Suppressed Patient on one occasion. The following translation introduces in double brackets, [[ ]], the contextual referent of the coinstantiated Agent (it/the other beast).

ποιῆσαι μῆνας τεσσεράκοντα [καὶ] δύο (13:5)
[[It/the other beast (1/Agt)]] to act/work (ποιέω) {actions/works (2/Pat)} [for forty-two months (C/Tem)].

	ποιέω (13:5) <*Eff.* A{P} [§6.3b]>		
syn.	1	{{2)}}	C
sem.	Agt	Pat	Tem
lex.	N	{N}	N+acc

2. Generalized Valence Descriptions for the Verb Predicator Ποιέω

The Generalized Valence Description of a predicator groups together and re-presents in a single matrix all of the grammatical information and notations in all of the Valence Descriptions of occurrences of the predicator with the same usage. The following discussion develops the protocols for representing the predicator, citations, usage label with abbreviated and italicized event designation, configuration of entities with usage features, and bracketed sectional heading of the discussion of the usage in chevrons, < >, syntactic functions, semantic functions, lexical realizations, and notations within the Valence Descriptions for a predicator usage in the Generalized Valence Description for that usage. Although not applicable to ποιέω, which never is permissibly omitted by Greek grammar in the text of Revelation, Generalized Valence Descriptions also incorporate all of the information from the Valence Descriptions of predicators permissibly omitted in a given context and note the permissible omission of the predicator by placing its citation in brackets, [ ].

At the top of the Generalized Valence Description appear the predicator followed by a comma (,) and the usage label in chevrons, < >. The top of the Generalized Valence Description for each usage introduces after the predicator and comma an alphanumeric identifier for each usage of the predicator followed by a period (.). For predicators with only one usage, the alphanumeric identifier is "1." For predicators with usages of multiple events, the usages of each event receive consecutive numeric identifiers. For example, ποιέω has at least one usage associated with each of four different events. These usages receive four consecutive numerical identifiers: "1" for the usage of Effect (AP, A{P}), "2" for the usage of Agentive Modification (APR), "3" for the usage of Agentive Benefaction (APB), and "4" for the usage of Compulsion (APO). Although the ordering of usages is arbitrary, the listings in this study assign the identifier "1" to the usage of the most frequently grammaticalized event for that predicator in the NT, except when an alternate ordering better clarifies relationships among the usages. For predicators that grammaticalize two or three usages of the same event, the identifiers add a letter after the numeral to distinguish the usages of the same event. For example, ποιέω most frequently grammaticalizes the event of effect and does so with two different usages of effect, AP [§6:3a] and A{P} [§6.3b]. These receive the respective identifiers "1a" and "1b."

The row of syntactic functions of required complements continues to appear immediately below the predicator and other information. If a required complement consistently receives realization in all occurrences with that usage, its numerical syntactic function designation remains unmarked (no brackets or parentheses). If a required complement is realized or remains unrealized only as a definite null complement (DNC), its numerical syntactic function designation appears in brackets, [ ]. If a required complement remains unrealized as an indefinite null complement on at least one occasion, its numerical designation appears in parentheses, ( ). Thus the second argument for different usages may appear as 2, [2], or (2).

The semantic functions of required complements appear immediately under their associated syntactic functions. Since these semantic functions are the same for all occurrences of the predicator with a given usage, the semantic function row of the Generalized Valence Description of a usage is identical to the semantic function row of the individual Valence Descriptions of occurrences with that usage.

The lexical realizations of required complements appear under their associated semantic functions, with a separate row for each observed combination of lexical realizations of required complements. The combinations of lexical realizations are listed with the realizations of noun phrases (N) before verb phrases (V), before adjective phrases (Adj), before prepositional phrases (P), before adverb phrases (A), before definite null complements (DNC), before indefinite null complements (INC). To the right of each observed set of lexical realizations of required complements is the list of occurrences with that exact set of realizations. For predicators with more than eleven occurrences in a verse, the listings of occurrences avoid the use of alphanumeric citations ending in the letter "l" so that a citation ending in "k" is followed by a citation ending in "m." For ποιέω with the usage of Agentive Benefaction, there would be two rows of lexical realizations: the first with the set "N N+acc N+dat [+an]" followed by the citations of the occurrences with this set of realizations, and the second with the set "N N+acc P/μετά [+gen]" followed by the citations for the occurrences with this set of realizations. After the lexical realization and in brackets, [ ], appear the notations that directly qualify the lexical realizations of required complements. Such notations concern the +animate/–animate distinction [+an/–an] and the +response/–response distinction [+resp/–resp].

Generalized Valence Descriptions incorporate in parentheses, ( ), information concerning adjuncts immediately after the citation of the predicator occurrence. The parentheses replace the syntactic function "C" in the individual Valence Descriptions, and, since the use of parentheses in lists of occurrences is restricted to enclosing adjuncts, this change introduces no ambiguity. The descriptions of the adjuncts restate the information in the Valence Description by listing first the three-letter semantic function followed by a colon (:), followed by the lexical realization and any attending notations. For example, the Generalized Valence Description specifies the presence of the Locative adjunct of ποιέω with the usage of Effect in 13:12a by placing (Loc: P/ἐνώπιον) after the citation. Notations from the individual Valence Descriptions that do not directly specify the lexical realizations of complements appear in brackets, [ ], immediately after the citation and, if present, any adjuncts. Such notations specify occurrences with λέγω melding [LM], redundant complements [red.], indeclinable nouns with nominative case endings [ind. N+nom], and the ±animate distinction [±an] with adjuncts.

8. *From Valence Descriptions to Lexicon Entries* 193

These protocols for re-presenting the information in the Valence Descriptions for all occurrences of a predicator with the same usage ensure that the resulting Generalized Valence Description for the predicator with that usage maintains all of the grammatical specificity about the predicator's licensing properties. The protocols accommodate the following Generalized Valence Descriptions for the occurrences of ποιέω in the text of Revelation.

a. Generalized Valence Description for Ποιέω with Usage AP [§6.3a]

	ποιέω, 1a. <*Eff.* AP [§6.3a]>		
syn.	1	[2]	
sem.	Agt	Pat	
lex.	N	N+acc	Rev 2:5; 13:12a (Loc: P/ἐνώπιον), 13a (Res: V+ἵνα); 17:17a, 17b; 22:11 (Tem: A/ἔτι)
lex.	N	V+ἵνα	Rev 13:15
lex.	N	DNC	Rev 13:14a (Loc: P/ἐνώπιον)

b. Generalized Valence Description of Ποιέω with Usage APR [§6.6a]

	ποιέω, 2. <*Mod.* APR [§6.6a]>			
syn.	1	2	3	
sem.	Agt	Pat	Rst	
lex.	N	N+acc	N+2	Rev 1:6 (Ben: N+dat [+an]); 3:12; 5:10 (Ben: N+dat [+an])
lex.	N	N+acc	Adj+2	Rev 12:15; 17:16; 21:5

c. Generalized Valence Description of Ποιέω with Usage APB [§6.1a]

	ποιέω, 3. <*Ben.* APB [§6.1a]>			
syn.	1	2	3	
sem.	Agt	Pat	Ben	
lex.	N	N+acc	N+dat [+an]	Rev 13:14b
lex.	N	N+acc	P/μετά [+gen]	Rev 11:7 (Tem: V+ὅταν); 12:17; 13:7; 19:19

d. Generalized Valence Description of Ποιέω with Usage APO [§5.7b]

	ποιέω, 4. <*Cpl.* APO [§5.7b]>			
syn.	1	2	3	
sem.	Agt	Pat	Occ	
lex.	N	N+acc	V+ἵνα	Rev 3:9; 13:12b, 16
lex.	N	N+acc	V-i2	Rev 13:13b (Mea: A/καί)

e. Generalized Valence Description for Ποιέω with Usage A{P} [§6.3b]

	ποιέω, 1b. <*Eff.* A{P} [§6.3b]>		
syn.	1	{{2}}	
sem.	Agt	Pat	
lex.	N	{N}	Rev 13:5 (Tem: N+acc)

3. Lexicon Entries for the Verb Predicator Ποιέω

This discussion develops the protocols for generating the lexicon entries using the verb predicator ποιέω. The following lexicon entries for this predicator are complete except for two categories of inserted specifications developed in the discussion of the concluding sections of this chapter (§8.5 and §8.6).

The lexicon entry or entries for a predicator are narratives developed directly from the Generalized Valence Description or Generalized Valence Descriptions for that predicator. The lexicon entry for predicators with only one usage or the first entry for predicators with more than one usage begins with the information at the top of the Generalized Valence Description for the usage in the following format: predicator, comma (,), space, alphanumeric identifier ("1" for predicators with a single usage of an event or "1a" for predicators like ποιέω with more than one usage of the same event), period (.), space, usage label enclosed in chevrons, < >, and a restatement of the syntactic and semantic functions for each argument separated by a slash, /, and followed by a colon (:). Among these constituents, the predicator, alphanumeric identifier, and combined syntactic and semantic function descriptions appear in bold print. After the colon appears a list of the most frequent translations of the predicator with the usage. This protocol yields the following introduction to the first lexicon entry for ποιέω with the Usage of Effect.

ποιέω, 1a. <*Eff.* AP [§6.3a]> **1/Agt [2/Pat]**: make, do, wield, enact

Beneath this information appear in bold print the indented rows of lexical realizations, each of which is introduced by a dash (—) and followed by a colon (:). In plain print after the colon appears the list of occurrences with the set of lexical realizations as well as any adjuncts in parentheses, ( ), and any further notations in brackets, [ ]. Whenever the lexical realizations of required complements have a consistent translation, the translation appears before the lexical realization in plain print and in parentheses, ( ). For economy of presentation, the lists of occurrences wrap around under their associated set of lexical realizations. This protocol yields the following complete entry for the first usage of ποιέω.

ποιέω, 1a. <*Eff.* AP [§6.3a]> **1/Agt [2/Pat]**: make, do, wield
 —**N N+acc**: Rev 2:5; 13:12a (Loc: P/ἐνώπιον), 13a (Res: V+ἵνα); 17:17a, 17b; 22:11 (Tem: A/ἔτι)
 —**N** (that) **V+ἵνα**: Rev 13:15
 —**N DNC**: Rev 13:14a (Loc: P/ἐνώπιον)

This lexicon entry serves as a paradigm for verb predicators with only one usage. The development of lexicon entries for predicators with more than one usage follows the same protocols except that they omit the initial statement of the predicator and following comma (,), are slightly indented, and begin with the alphanumeric identifier in bold, with each usage appearing on a separate line. This protocol yields the following complete set of lexicon entries for ποιέω.

ποιέω, 1a. <*Eff.* AP [§6.3a]> **1/Agt [2/Pat]**: make, do, wield
—**N N+acc**: Rev 2:5; 13:12a (Loc: P/ἐνώπιον), 13a (Res: V+ἵνα); 17:17a, 17b; 22:11 (Tem: A/ἔτι)
—**N** (that) **V+ἵνα**: Rev 13:15
—**N DNC**: Rev 13:14a (Loc: P/ἐνώπιον)
1b. <*Eff.* A{P} [§6:3b]> **1/Agt {{2/Pat}}**: act, work
—**N {N}**: Rev 13:5 (Tem: N+acc)
2. <*Mod.* APR [§6.6a]> **1/Agt 2/Pat 3/Rst**: make
—**N N+acc N+2**: Rev 1:6 (Ben: N+dat [+an]); 3:12; 5:10 (Ben: N+dat [+an])
—**N N+acc Adj+2**: Rev 12:15; 17:16; 21:5
3. <*Ben.* APB [§6.1a]> **1/Agt 2/Pat 3/Ben**: make
—**N N+acc** (for) **N+dat [+an]**: Rev 13:14b
—**N** (war) **N+acc** (against) **P/μετά [+gen]**: Rev 11:7 (Tem: V+ὅταν); 12:17; 13:7; 19:19
4. <*Cpl.* APO [§5.7b]> **1/Agt 2/Pat 3/Occ**: make, compel, force
—**N N+acc** (that) **V+ἵνα**: Rev 3:9; 13:12b, 16
—**N N+acc** (to) **V-i2**: Rev 13:13b (Mea: A/καί)

Two clarifications are appropriate here. First, since the lists of citations appear immediately after the set of lexical realizations of required complements and following the colon (:), the list of citations for zero-place predicators (i.e., predicators without required complements) appears immediately after the dash (—) in the row of lexical realizations, as illustrated in the lexicon entry for ἄμμος (sand).

ἄμμος, 1. <*Spec.* — [§6.12]> **0/—**: sand
—Rev 12:18 (Ben: N+gen); 20:8 (Ben: N+gen)

Second, all occurrences of words that function as predicators in some contexts and non-predicators in other contexts appear in separate lexicon entries, for the predicator usage[s] and for the non-predicator occurrences. Unlike the lexicon entries for predicator usages, the entry for non-predicator occurrences are labeled as such in italics and the non-predicator occurrences do not have an introductory dash (—), as illustrated in the entries for ἔμπροσθεν (before).

ἔμπροσθεν, 1. <*Mot.* Θ[S]G [S=Θ] G→L [§5.2b]> **1/Thm 2/Loc**: before
—**N N+gen**: Rev 19:10; 22:8
2. <*non-predicator*>: in front
Rev 4:6

4. Lexicon Entries for Polysemous Predicator Occurrences

The previous discussions identified polysemous occurrences of verb and participle predicators that grammaticalize the event of transference with passive base forms (§3.4) and of noun predicators that grammaticalize the event of communication with the configuration BCE (§4.6). The discussions of usages then resolved usage sets of polysemous occurrences of verb predicators (§§5.1a, 5.1e, 5.2f and §§5.1j, 5.1k, 5.2g). The following discussion develops the protocols for generating lexicon entries for polysemous occurrences in relation to the noun predicator ἀποκάλυψις (revelation) that admits to a dual interpretation with usage BCE [§5.4f] and the two occurrences of ἵστημι (stand, station) that admit to three-fold interpretation with usages AΘ[S]G [S=A] G→L –imp. [§5.1j], A[Θ][S]G [Θ=A] [S=A] G→L pass. –imp. [§5.1k], and (A) Θ(S)G G=Θ G→L pass. [§5.2g]. The discussion translates and provides the Valence Descriptions for the polysemous occurrences, re-presents the content of the Valence Description for the occurrence of ἀποκάλυψις and the Valence Descriptions for the two occurrences of ἵστημι in Generalized Valence Descriptions, and generates the lexicon entries for the polysemous occurrence of ἀποκάλυψις and occurrences of ἵστημι.

a. Valence Descriptions for Ἀποκάλυψις in 1:1 and Ἵστημι in 8:3 and 12:18

As previously discussed (§4.6 and §5.1j), the occurrence of ἀποκάλυψις in 1:1 admits to dual interpretation and representation in a Valence Description and the occurrences of ἵστημι in 8:3 and 12:18 admit to three-fold interpretation and representation in Valence Descriptions. The translations of 1:1 introduce in double brackets, [[ ]], the contextual referents of the DNC Content (what will happen soon) with the first interpretation, of the DNC Agentive Benefactive (John) with the second interpretation, and of the DNC Experiencer (John's addressees) with both interpretations.

ἀποκάλυψις Ἰησοῦ Χριστοῦ (1:1)
[Jesus Christ's (1/Ben)] revelation (ἀποκάλυψις) [[of what will happen soon (2/Con)]] [[to John's addressees (3/Exp)]].
[[John's (1/Ben)]] revelation (ἀποκάλυψις) [of Jesus Christ (2/Con)] [[to John's addressees (3/Exp)]].

	ἀποκάλυψις (1:1) <Cmm. BCE || BCE [§5.4f]>						
syn.	1	[2]	[3]	||	[1]	2	[3]
sem.	Ben	Con	Exp	||	Ben	Con	Exp
lex.	N+gen	DNC	DNC	||	DNC	N+gen	DNC

The translations of 8:3 and 12:18 introduce in double brackets, [[ ]], the indefinite but circumscribed referent of the INC Agent (someone) with passivized Usage AΘ[S] G [S=A] G→L –imp. and the contextual referent of the never-realized co-referential Theme with Usage A[Θ][S]G [Θ=A] [S=A] G→L pass. –imp. (§5.1k).

ἄλλος ἄγγελος...ἐστάθη ἐπὶ τοῦ θυσιαστηρίου (8:3)
AΘ[S]G [S=A] G→L -imp. [§5.1j] [Another angel (2/Thm)]...was stationed (ἵστημι) [[by someone (1/Agt)]] [on the altar (3/Loc)].
A[Θ][S]G [Θ=A] [S=A] G→L pass. -imp. [§5.1k] [Another angel (1/Agt)]... stationed (ἵστημι) [[himself (2/Thm)]] [on the altar (3/Loc)].
(A)Θ(S)G G=Θ G→L pass. [§5.2g] [Another angel (1/Thm)]...stood (ἵστημι) [on the altar (2/Loc)].

	ἵστημι (8:3) <Tra. AΘ[S]G [S=A] G→L -imp. [§5.1j]>			‖ ‖
syn.	1	2	3	‖
sem.	Agt	Thm	Loc	‖
lex.	N	N+acc	P/ἐπί [+gen]	‖

	ἵστημι (8:3) <Tra. A[Θ][S]G [Θ=A] [S=A] G→L pass. -imp. [§5.1k]>			‖ ‖	ἵστημι (8:3) <(A)Θ(S)G G=Θ G→L pass. [§5.2g]>	
syn.	1	[[2]]	3	‖	1	2
sem.	Agt	Thm	Loc	‖	Thm	Loc
lex.	N	[N]	P/ἐπί [+gen]	‖	N	P/ἐπί [+gen]

ἐστάθη ἐπὶ τὴν ἄμμον τῆς θαλάσσης (12:18)
AΘ[S]G [S=A] G→L -imp. [§5.1j] [It (2/Thm)] was stationed (ἵστημι) [[by someone (1/Agt)]] [on the sand of the sea (3/Loc)].
A[Θ][S]G [Θ=A] [S=A] G→L pass. -imp. [§5.1k] [It (1/Agt)] stationed (ἵστημι) [[itself (2/Thm)]] [on the sand of the sea (3/Loc)].
(A)Θ(S)G G=Θ G→L pass. [§5.2g] [It (1/Thm)] stood (ἵστημι) [on the sand of the sea (2/Loc)].

	ἵστημι (12:18) <Tra. AΘ[S]G [S=A] G→L -imp. [§5.1j]>			‖ ‖
syn.	1	2	3	‖
sem.	Agt	Thm	Loc	‖
lex.	N	N+acc	P/ἐπί [+acc]	‖

	ἵστημι (12:18) <Tra. A[Θ][S]G [Θ=A] [S=A] G→L pass. -imp. [§5.1k]>			‖ ‖	ἵστημι (12:18) <Mot. (A)Θ(S)G G=Θ G→L pass. [§5.2g]>	
syn.	1	[[2]]	3	‖	1	2
sem.	Agt	Thm	Loc	‖	Thm	Loc
lex.	N	[N]	P/ἐπί [+acc]	‖	N	P/ἐπί [+acc]

b. The Generalized Valence Descriptions for These Polysemous Occurrences

The Generalized Valence Descriptions for these occurrences proceeds according to the same protocols as previously discussed (§8.2) except for the following modifications of the format.

The top of the Generalized Valence Descriptions continues to present the predicator, comma (,), alphanumeric identifiers ("1" for both predicators), period (.), and a single set of chevrons, < >, that incorporates the two usage labels for ἀποκάλυψις and the three usage labels for ἵστημι separated by double vertical lines, ||. Since the two labels for ἀποκάλυψις reference the same usage of the same event, the abbreviated event designation appears only once, at the beginning, and the bracketed sectional heading appears only once, at the end. The two or three sets of syntactic and semantic functions and lexical realizations continue to appear below this information, also separated by double vertical lines, ||. The citations then appear after the double and triple statements for the syntactic functions, the semantic functions, and the lexical realizations. Given the width of the resulting Generalized Valence Description for the occurrences of ἵστημι, the citations for its illustrative Generalized Valence Description appear on a separate line.

ἀποκάλυψις <Cmm. BCE || BCE [§5.4f]>

syn.	1	(2)	[3]	||	[1]	2	[3]	
sem.	Ben	Con	Exp	||	Ben	Con	Exp	
lex.	N+gen	INC	DNC	||	DNC	N+gen	DNC	Rev 1:1

ἵστημι, 1. <Tra. AΘ[S]G [S=A] G→L −imp. [§5.1j] || Tra. A[Θ][S]G [Θ=A] [S=A] G→L pass. −imp. [§5.1k] || Mot. (A)Θ(S)G G=Θ G→L pass. [§5.2g]>

syn.	1	2	3	||	1	[[2]]	3	||	1	2
sem.	Agt	Thm	Loc	||	Agt	Thm	Loc	||	Thm	Loc
lex.	N	N+acc	P/ἐπί [+acc]	||	N	[N]	P/ἐπί [+acc]	||	N	P/ἐπί [+acc]
		Rev 12:18								
lex.	N	N+acc	P/ἐπί [+gen]	||	N	[N]	P/ἐπί [+gen]	||	N	P/ἐπί [+gen]
		Rev 8:3								

c. The Lexicon Entries for These Polysemous Occurrences

Generation of the lexicon entries for these polysemous occurrences follows the previously established protocols (§5.3), including inserting translations after each of the statements of syntactic/semantic licensing properties and, where appropriate, translations in parentheses, ( ), before lexical realizations.

ἀποκάλυψις, 1. <Cmm. BCE || BCE [§5.4f]> 1/Ben [2/Con] [3/Exp]: revelation || [1/Ben] 2/Con [3/Exp]: revelation
—(of) N+gen DNC DNC || DNC (of) N+gen DNC: Rev 1:1

ἵστημι, 1. <Tra. AΘ[S]G [S=A] G→L −imp. [§5.1j] || Tra. A[Θ][S]G [Θ=A] [S=A] G→L pass. −imp. [§5.1k] || Mot. (A)Θ(S)G G=Θ G→L pass. [§5.2g]> 1/Agt 2/Thm 3/Loc: station, stand || 1/Agt [[2/Thm]] 3/Loc: station [[oneself]], stand [[oneself]] || 1/Thm 2/Loc: stand

—N N+acc (on) P/ἐπί [+acc] ‖ N (oneself) [N] (on) P/ἐπί [+acc] ‖ N (on) P/ ἐπί [+acc]: Rev 12:18
—N N+acc (on) P/ἐπί [+gen] ‖ N (oneself) [N] (on) P/ἐπί [+gen] ‖ N (on) P/ ἐπί [+gen]: Rev 8:3

5. Further Specifications of Lexicon Entries with General Application

Although generation of the lexicon entries in the manner previously described re-presents all of the information in the Valence Descriptions for each occurrence of every predicator in the text of Revelation, the entries in the Lexicon insert further descriptive information. The following discussion develops four categories of insertions that impact a number of lexicon entries. These insertions pertain to associated verb/participle and simple/complex predicators, permissibly omitted components of complex predicators, the interpretation of complements containing permissibly omitted forms of εἰμί (be), and tracking the occurrences of εἰμί.

a. Linking Associated Verb/Participle and Simple/Complex Predicators

The novelty of separating the lexicon entries for verbs and their associated participles and for simple predicators and their associated complex predicators may cause confusion. To address this, the lexicon entries for participle predicators and complex predicators insert after the predicator and in parentheses, ( ), a plain print notation that begins with a left chevron, <, followed immediately by the associated verb or simple predicator.

Most frequently, the verb and simple predicators associated with the participle and complex predicators also appear in the text of Revelation. When this occurs, the lexicon entries of the associated verb and simple predicator insert after the predicator and in parentheses, ( ), a plain print notation that begins with a right chevron, >, followed immediately by the participle predicator[s] and complex predicator with which they are associated. In such cases, the alphanumeric indicators of parallel usages are linked and set according to the indicators of the verb and simple predicator. For example, these protocols yield the following entries for the first usage of ποιέω and its associated participle predicators ποιήσας (making) and ποιῶν (doing, making) and for the sole usage of ἀληθινός (true) and its associated complex predicator ἀληθινός + [εἰμί] (be true).

ποιέω (>ποιήσας, ποιῶν), **1a.** <*Eff.* AP [§6.3a]> **1/Agt [2/Pat]**: make, do, wield
—N N+acc: Rev 2:5; 13:12a (Loc: P/ἐνώπιον), 13a (Res: V+ἵνα); 17:17a, 17b; 22:11 (Tem: A/ἔτι)
—N (that) V+ἵνα: Rev 13:15
—N DNC: Rev 13:14a (Loc: P/ἐνώπιον)

ποιήσας (<ποιέω), 1a. <Eff. AP [§6.3a]> 1/Agt 2/Pat: making, doing
—N N+acc: Rev 14:7; 19:20 (Loc: P/ἐνώπῖον)

ποιῶν (<ποιέω), 1a. <Eff. AP [§6.3a]> 1/Agt 2/Pat: making, doing
—N N+acc: Rev 16:14; 21:27; 22:2, 15

ἀληθινός (>ἀληθινός + [εἰμί]), 1. <Qual. P [§6.10a]> [1/Pat]: true
—N: Rev 6:10
—DNC: Rev 3:7, 14; 19:11

ἀληθινός + [εἰμί] (<ἀληθινός), 1. <Qual. P [§6.10a]> [1/Pat]: be true
—N: Rev [15:3b (Voc: N+nom)]; [16:7]; [19:2], 9b; 21:5; [22:6]

Less frequently, a participle or complex predicator occurs without its associated verb or simple predicator appearing elsewhere in the text of Revelation. In this situation, the Lexicon introduces a "dummy" entry for the lacking verb or simple predicator. The dummy entry includes only the information from the top of what would be the verb or simple predicator's Generalized Valence Description followed by a colon (:), translations, and a period (.) and with no lexical realizations beneath. (These are the only lexicon entries that end in a period.) Such dummy entries identify the lexical forms used by traditional grammars and lexicons and clarify the licensing properties of the verb predicators associated with passive participles. The following examples illustrate the lexicon entries for ἑλισσόμενος (being rolled up) and ἄμωμος + εἰμί (be without blemish) and dummy lexicon entries for ἑλίσσω (roll up) and ἄμωμος (without blemish).

ἑλισσόμενος (<ἑλίσσω), 1. <Eff. PA [§6.3c]> 1/Pat (2/Agt): being rolled up
—N DNC: Rev 6:14

ἑλίσσω (>ἑλισσόμενος), 1. <Eff. AP [§6.3a]> 1/Agt 2/Pat: roll up.

ἄμωμος + εἰμί (<ἄμωμος), 1. <Qual. P [§6.10a]> 1/Pat: be spotless, without blemish
—N: Rev 14:5

ἄμωμος (>ἄμωμος + εἰμί), 1. <Qual. P [§6.10a]> 1/Pat: spotless, without blemish.

Since the Lexicon (Chapter 9) includes only predicators, the lexicon entry for a complex predicator formed by joining a non-predicator and εἰμί (be) has no associated simple predicator entry and so no reference to an associated dummy entry.

b. Permissibly Omitted Components of Complex Predicators

As previously discussed (§7.4), the Valence Description of a complex predicator with a permissibly omitted component places both the omitted component of the complex predicator, most frequently the εἰμί (be) component, and its citation in brackets, [ ].

This presents a problem when re-presenting the content of the Valence Descriptions of occurrences in a Generalized Valence Description because one component of the complex predicator appears sometimes with and sometimes without enclosing brackets. When one component of the complex predicator always is realized, the Generalized Valence Description places brackets around the occasionally omitted component and uses the brackets around the citations to identify the occurrences with the omitted component. This protocol receives illustration in the following Generalized Valence Description and lexicon entry for ἐγγύς + [εἰμί] (be near).

	ἐγγύς + [εἰμί], 1. <Tem. PTem [§6.9d]>		
syn.	1	[2]	
sem.	Pat	Tem	
lex.	N	DNC	Rev [1:3b], [14b]; 22:10

ἐγγύς + [εἰμί], 1. <Tem. PTem [§6.9d]> 1/Pat [2/Tem]: be near
—N DNC: Rev [1:3b], [14b]; 22:10

c. Complements Containing Permissibly Omitted Forms of Εἰμί

As with the omission of the εἰμί (be) component of complex predicators, the omission of the simple verb predicator εἰμί as the licensing predicator of a verb phrase can cause difficulties for interpreting the function of the words in that verb phrase. The following examples illustrate two verb phrases licensed by an omitted form of the simple verb predicator with its two usages, εἰμί (1) (be, exist) and εἰμί (2) (be [for]). In both examples, δόξα (glory) realizes the first complement of εἰμί.

ἡ δόξα...τοῦ θεοῦ ἡμῶν ὅτι ἀληθιναὶ καὶ δίκαιαι αἱ κρίσεις αὐτοῦ (19:1-2)
[The glory of our God (1/Pat)]...is/exists ([εἰμί (1)]) [because your judgments are true and just (C/Cau)].

αὐτῷ ἡ δόξα καὶ τὸ κράτος εἰς τοὺς αἰῶνας [τῶν αἰώνων] (1:6)
[To him (2/Ben)] be ([εἰμί (2)]) [glory and might (1/Pat)] [into the ages of the ages (C/Tem)]!

	εἰμί (19:1-2) <Qual. P [§6.10a]>		εἰμί (1:6) <Ben. PB [§6.1f]>		
syn.	1	C	1	2	C
sem.	Pat	Cau	Pat	Ben	Tem
lex.	N	V+ὅτι	N	N+dat [+an]	P/εἰς

Although these translations and Valence Descriptions clarify that the non-required complements realize adjuncts of εἰμί, the absence of εἰμί in the contexts may mislead an interpreter to assess the non-required complements as adjuncts of δόξα (glory). To address this, the lexicon entry for δόξα introduces after the citations for 19:1-2 and 1:6 notations in brackets, [ ], that δόξα appears in verb phrases licensed by εἰμί (1) and εἰμί (2).

δόξα, 1. <*Ben.* B{P} [§6.1g]> [1/Ben] {{2/Pat}}: glory
—(of) N+gen {N}: Rev 15:8; 18:1; 19:1-2 [εἰμί 1]; 21:11, 23, 24, 26
—DNC {N}: Rev 1:6 [εἰμί 2]; 4:9, 11; 5:12, 13 [εἰμί 2]; 7:12 [εἰμί 2]; 11:13; 14:7; 16:9; 19:1 [εἰμί 1], 7

d. Tracking the Occurrences of Εἰμί

Lexicon entries track and note all occurrences of εἰμί (be) in a verse consecutively using alphanumeric citations (e.g., 1a, 1b, 1c…). The tracking applies to all occurrences, whether realized or permissibly omitted, of the εἰμί component of complex predicators and of the simple predicator εἰμί. As a consequence, the citations of complex predicators that appear only once in a verse may be listed by an alphanumeric citation, as illustrated in the following example in which the omitted εἰμί component of the complex predicator constitutes the eighth occasion of an omitted form of εἰμί in the verse.

ὁ δωδέκατος ἀμέθυστος (21:20)
[The twelfth (1/Pat)] is amethyst (ἀμέθυστος + [εἰμί]).

ἀμέθυστος + [εἰμί], 1. <*Qual.* P [§6.10a]> 1/Pat: be amethyst
—N: Rev [21:20h]

6. Further Specifications of Lexicon Entries with Particular Application

Each of the remaining seven specifications apply to one or a few lexicon entries and illustrate the types of clarifications introduced into lexicon entries. The first six are designed to assist in the interpretation of particular predicator occurrences and appear in brackets, [ ], immediately after the element of the lexicon entry which they concern, while the seventh applies to the format of one preposition predicator. The first specification references the sectional headings of previous discussions that offer clarifications concerning particular occurrences. The next four specifications introduce short narratives that disambiguate the licensing properties of predicators, identify the distant referents of DNC required complements, address novel instances of proximate omitted predicator retrieval or of the retrieval of proximate referents of DNC required complements, and clarify instances of predicator-imposed changes in the ±animate distinction for specific nouns. The sixth specification guides the interpretation of the lexical realization rows of some interjection predicators. The seventh applies only to the lexicon entry for the preposition predicator ἐπί. Given the limited application of these specifications, their discussion appears in summary fashion.

a. Previous Discussions of Occurrences

The label for each usage concludes with the section heading of the discussion of that usage, and the referenced section is assumed to provide all of the descriptive information for interpreting the occurrences of predicators with that usage. On occasion, however, the discussion of predicators with one usage may introduce information pertaining to the interpretation of specific occurrences of predicators with another usage. When this occurs, the lists of citations for a predicator with one usage incorporates in brackets, [ ], a reference to the section of the discussion of the other usage. For example, the first footnote (n. 1) in the discussion of the licensing properties of ποιέω with usage APB [§6.1a] makes an observation that clarifies the lexical realization (DNC) of the third complement of the noun predicator πόλεμος with usage B{P}B [§6.1h]. As a consequence, some occurrences in the list of citations for πόλεμος with a DNC third complement include a reference to the discussion in the footnote of §6.1a.

πόλεμος, 1. <*Ben.* B{P}B [§6.1h]> **[1/Ben] {{2/Pat}} (3/Ben)**: battle, war
—**DNC {N} DNC**: Rev 11:7 [§6.1a n. 1]; 12:7 [§6.1a n. 1], 17 [§6.1a n. 1]; 13:7 [§6.1a n. 1]; 16:14 [§6.1a n. 1]; 19:19 [§6.1a n. 1]; 20:8
—**DNC {N} INC**: Rev 9:7, 9

b. Disambiguating the Licensing Properties of Predicators

An example of disambiguating the licensing properties of predicators appears in 22:19b where the verb predicator ἀφαιρέω (take away) requires completion by an Agent, a Patient, and a Source argument and the lexical realization of the Source complement is listed as DNC even though the phrase contains P/ἀπό and P/ἐκ complements, both of which are standard realizations of Source complements. The short narrative after the citation of 22:19b explains that these two complements are licensed by the noun predicator μέρος (portion, part) and not by ἀφαιρέω, as illustrated in the following resolution of the licensing properties of ἀφαιρέω and μέρος in this context. The first translation introduces in double brackets, [[ ]], the definite contextual referent of the Source (that one/him) of ἀφαιρέω.

> ἐάν τις ἀφέλῃ ἀπὸ τῶν λόγων τοῦ βιβλίου τῆς προφητείας ταύτης, ἀφελεῖ ὁ θεὸς τὸ μέρος αὐτοῦ ἀπὸ τοῦ ξύλου τῆς ζωῆς καὶ ἐκ τῆς πόλεως τῆς ἁγίας τῶν γεγραμμένων ἐν τῷ βιβλίῳ τούτῳ (22:19)
> [If anyone takes away from the words of the book of this prophecy (C/Cnd)] [God (1/Agt)] will take away (ἀφαιρέω) [[from that one/him (3/Sou)]] [his portion of the tree of life and of the holy city written in this book (2/Thm)].

> τὸ μέρος αὐτοῦ ἀπὸ τοῦ ξύλου τῆς ζωῆς καὶ ἐκ τῆς πόλεως τῆς ἁγίας τῶν γεγραμμένων ἐν τῷ βιβλίῳ τούτῳ (22:19)
> [His (C/Ben)] portion (μέρος) {portion (2/Pat)} [of the tree of life and of the holy city written in this book (1/Par)].

The manner of incorporating such short narratives receives illustration in the lexicon entry for ἀφαιρέω.

ἀφαιρέω, 1. <Tra. AΘS[G] [G=A] +imp. [§5.1c]> 1/Agt (2/Thm) [3/Sou]: take away
—N INC (from) P/ἀπό: Rev 22:19a
—N N+acc DNC: Rev 22:19b (Cnd: V+ἐάν) [P/ἀπό and P/ἐκ are complements of μέρος]

c. Identifying the Distant Referents of DNC Required Complements

An example of identifying the distant referents of DNC required complements appears in 17:10 where the adjective predicator ὀλίγος (little, few) licenses but does not realize a Patient argument. Here the null Patient complement is deemed to have a definite referent based on its previous occurrence in 12:12, in which καιρός (time) is the referent of the Patient. The following translations place in double brackets, [[ ]], the definite referent of the DNC Patient (time) and the indefinite but circumscribed referent of the INC Instrument (some force), and the lexicon entry for ὀλίγος notes this information after the citation for 17:10.

ὅταν ἔλθῃ ὀλίγον αὐτὸν δεῖ μεῖναι (17:10)
[When he comes (C/Tem)] [that he remain only a little [[time]] (1/Occ)] is necessary (δεῖ) [[by some force (2/Ins)]].

ὀλίγον (17:10)
A little (ὀλίγος) [[time (1/Pat)]].

ὀλίγος, 1. <Qual. P [§6.10a]> [1/Pat]: [a] few, little
—N: Rev 3:4; 12:12
—DNC: Rev 2:14; 17:10 [DNC Patient referent from 12:12]

d. Specifying Novel Instances of Proximate Omitted Predicator Retrieval

This discussion considers three examples of specifying novel instances of proximate omitted predicator retrieval.

The first example appears in 3:4b where the predicator ἐν (by [means of]) is licensed by the participle predicator περιβεβλημένος (wrapped) which is permissibly omitted even though its first occurrence in the text of Revelation is in the following verse (3:5). The translation introduces in double brackets, [[ ]], the omitted participle predicator (wrapped) and the indefinite but circumscribed referents of the INC Instrument (clothing of some sort) and the INC Agent (someone). Although the retrieval of an omitted predicator from the immediately following context occurs elsewhere in the NT, it is rare, and the lexicon entry for ἐν (2) notes the omitted participle predicator in brackets, [ ], after the citation for 3:4b.

[[περιβεβλημένοι]] ἐν λευκοῖς (3:4b)
[They (1/Pat)] [[wrapped (περιβεβλημένος)]] [[by someone (2/Agt)]] [by/with white [[clothing of some sort]] (3/Ins)].

8. From Valence Descriptions to Lexicon Entries 205

ἐν, 2. <*Ins.* PI [§6.4e]> **1/Pat 2/Ins**: by [means of], through
—**N N+dat**: Rev 1:5, 16b; 2:16, 23, 27; 3:4b [περιβεβλημένος omitted], 5; 4:4; 5:2, 9; 6:8a, 8b, 8c; 7:9, 14; 8:7; 9:17, 19c, 20; 10:6a; 11:6, 12, 13b; 12:5; 13:10a, 10b; 14:2, 7, 9, 10b, 15; 15:1b; 16:8; 17:3, 16; 18:2, 8b, 16, 19a, 23c; 19:2, 11, 15a, 15b, 17b, 20a, 20b, 21; 21:10

The second and third examples appear in the maximal verb phrase in 1:15a. The interpretation of this verb phrase is difficult because (1) it contains a noun (χαλκολίβανον) whose meaning is uncertain, (2) its constituent predicators license two definite null complements, one of which derives its referent from χαλκολίβανον, and (3) the predicator of a constituent Temporal complement retrieves the referent of its DNC first complement in an atypical manner. The following discussion resolves the licensing properties of four of the verb phrase's constituent predicators and translates χαλκολίβανον by "bronze/shiny frankincense" based on the meanings of its constituent elements χαλκος (copper/bronze) and λίβανος (frankincense tree/frankincense) and on the contextual focus on white, bright, and shiny objects. The translations present increasing specificity of the licensed complements through the introduction of the referents of DNC and INC complements in bold print.

οἱ πόδες αὐτοῦ ὅμοιοι χαλκολιβάνῳ ὡς ἐν καμίνῳ πεπυρωμένης (1:15)
[His feet (1/Pat)] were like (ὅμοιος + [εἰμί]) [bronze/shiny frankincense like in a furnace when it is made to burn (2/Cmp)].

The translation of the constituent phrase licensed by ὡς (like) introduces in bold print the contextual referent of its DNC second complement (bronze/shiny frankincense).

χαλκολιβάνῳ ὡς ἐν καμίνῳ πεπυρωμένης (1:15a)
[Bronze/shiny frankincense (1/Pat)] like (ὡς) [**bronze/shiny frankincense in a furnace when it is made to burn (2/Cmp)**].

The translation of the constituent phrase licensed by ἐν (in) introduces in bold print the contextual referent of its DNC first complement (bronze/shiny frankincense).

ἐν καμίνῳ πεπυρωμένης (1:15)
[**Bronze/shiny frankincense** (1/Thm)] in (ἐν) [a furnace (2/Loc)] [when it is made to burn (C/Tem)].

The constituent Temporal complement receives interpretation as Part+gen (a genitive absolute) whose predicator is πεπυρωμένος (made to burn).[2] The translation

---

[2] For the interpretation of this occurrence as a genitive absolute, see Robert L. Thomas, *Revelation 1–7: An Exegetical Commentary* (Chicago, IL: Moody, 1992), 162; cf. Grant R. Osborne, *Revelation* (Baker Exegetical Commentary on the New Testament; Grand Rapids, MI: Baker, 2002), 162; Richard C. H. Lenski, *Interpretation of St. John's Revelation* (Minneapolis, MN: Augsburg, 1961); and Turner, *Syntax*, 314.

introduces in bold print the contextual referent of the predicator's DNC first complement (furnace), which is retrieved atypically from another complement of its licensing predicator ἐν (in), and the indefinite but circumscribed referent of its INC second complement (someone).

πεπυρωμένης (1:15)
[**The furnace** (1/Pat)] is made to burn (πεπυρωμένος) [**by someone** (2/Agt)].

The lexicon entries note after the citations in brackets, [ ], the referent of the DNC Patient complement of ὡς and of the DNC Patient of πεπυρωμένος. Only the affected rows of lexical realizations appear below.

ὡς, **1.** <*Cmp*. PCmp [§6.9b]> **(1/Pat) [2/Cmp]**: like, as [if]
— DNC N+2: Rev 1:15a [DNC = χαλκολίβανον from context]

πεπυρωμένος (<πυρόω), **1.** <*Eff*. PA [§6.3c]> **[1/Pat] (2/Agt)**: burned, made to burn
—DNC INC: Rev 1:15 [DNC = κάμινος from context]

e. Predicator-Imposed Changes in the ±Animate Distinction

An example of the novel occurrences of predicator-imposed changes in the ±animate distinction appears in 6:16 where the verb predicator λέγω (1) (say) occurs with usage ACE [§5.4a]. Although λέγω with this usage requires completion by an Agent, a Content, and an Experiencer whose noun phrase realization (N+dat) is restricted to +animate complements, the verb in this occurrence licenses and so imposes on the inherently –animate phrase "mountains and rocks" a +animate interpretation (required by the definition of the Experiencer complement to be +animate) that permits the use of the N+dat [+an] realization. The lexicon entry notes this information after the citation of 6:16. Given the length of the entry for λέγω (1), only the row of the entry containing the notation receives illustration.

λέγουσιν τοῖς ὄρεσιν καὶ ταῖς πέτραις· πέσετε ἐφ' ἡμᾶς... (6:16)
[**They** (1/Agt)] say (λέγω) [**to the mountains and rocks** (3/Exp)] ["**Fall on us...**" (2/Con)].

λέγω (>λέγων, λέγων + [εἰμί]), **1.** <*Cmm*. ACE [§5.4a]> **1/Agt [2/Con] [3/Exp]**: say, speak, describe
—N V+quo (to) N+dat [+an]: Rev 2:24a; 5:5; 6:16 [ὄρος & πέτρα +an]; 7:14a, 14b; 10:11; 14:18; 17:7a, 7b, 15; 19:9a, 9b, 10; 21:6; 22:6, 9, 10

f. Interpreting the Lexical Realization Rows of Some Interjection Predicators

Interjection predicators typically license their single Occurrence required complement by a following maximal verb phrase (V+). Some interjection predicators, however, appear on occasion without a following verb phrase complement. On such occasions, the unrealized Occurrence complement consistently has a definite referent (i.e., is

DNC) and retrieves this definite referent from the V+ complement of a preceding predicator. The lexicon entries for interjection predicators that license both V+ and DNC Occurrence complements introduce notations into the lexical realization rows in brackets, [ ], that the referent of the Occurrence can be found in the following V+ phrase or preceding V+ phrase, as illustrated in the following occurrences of the interjection predicator ἀμήν (amen). The translation introduces in double brackets, [[ ]], the contextual referent of the DNC Occurrence (blessing and glory and...be to our God into the ages of the ages) licensed by the second ἀμήν. The lexicon entry for ἀμήν clarifies the format of the bracketed information.

ἀμήν, ἡ εὐλογία καὶ ἡ δόξα καὶ...τῷ θεῷ ἡμῶν εἰς τοὺς αἰῶνας τῶν αἰώνων· ἀμήν (7:12)
Amen (ἀμήν) [blessing and glory and...be to our God into the ages of the ages (1/Occ)]: Amen (ἀμήν) [[blessing and glory and...be to our God into the ages of the ages]].

ἀμήν, 1. <*Qual.* O [§6.10b]> [**1/Occ**]: truth, amen
—[licensing following] **V+**: Rev 7:12a
—[referencing what precedes] **DNC**: Rev 1:6, 7; 3:14; 5:14; 7:12b; 19:4; 22:20

g. The Lexicon Entries for the Preposition Predicator Ἐπί

The protocols for generating lexicon entries produce unambiguous lexicon entries for all predicators in the text of Revelation except ἐπί with the Primary Usage of Location, ΘL [§5.3a] and the Primary Usage of Motion Terminating in a Locative, Θ[S]G [S=Θ] G→L [§5.2b]. With these two usages, the predicator licenses N+gen, N+dat, and N+acc complements with the same syntactic and semantic functions but widely divergent translations for each lexical realization of the second complement. As a consequence, the protocol that places the translations at the top of a lexicon entry would introduce a series of translations, not all of which would apply to each lexical realization of the second complement. To address this, the lexicon separates these two usages of ἐπί into three entries (1a, 1b, 1c) for Usage ΘL [§5.3a] and two entries (2a, 2b) for Usage Θ[S]G [S=Θ] G→L [§5.2b] according to the lexical realizations of their second complements and provides for each entry the applicable translations. Since the entries are long and receive clear illustration in the lexicon (Chapter 9), they are not repeated here.

7. Application of the Protocols for Generating Lexicon Entries

The development of the protocols for re-presenting all of the specific grammatical information and notations in the Valence Descriptions of all occurrences of a predicator into one or more lexicon entries for that predicator and the introduction of the final categories of notations within lexicon entries accommodate the generation of Case Frame lexicon entries for all predicators in the text of Revelation (Chapter 9).

9

THE CASE FRAME LEXICON FOR PREDICATORS IN THE TEXT OF REVELATION

ἀγαλλιάω, 1. <*Exp.* EC C→T [§5.5c]> 1/Exp [2/Top]: rejoice
—N DNC: Rev 19:7 (Cau: V+ὅτι)
ἀγαπάω (>ἀγαπῶν, ἠγαπημένος), 1. <*Exp.* EC [§5.5a]> 1/Exp 2/Con: love
—N N+acc: Rev 3:9; 12:11 (Tem: P/ἄχρι)
ἀγάπη, 1. <*Exp.* EC [§5.5a]> 1/Exp (2/Con): love
—(of) N+gen INC: Rev 2:4, 19
ἀγαπῶν (<ἀγαπάω), 1. <*Exp.* EC [§5.5a]> 1/Exp 2/Con: loving
—N N+acc: Rev 1:5
ἄγγελος (>ἄγγελος + εἰμί), 1. <*Ben.* B{P} [§6.1g]> [1/Ben] {{2/Pat}}: angel
—(of) N+gen {N}: Rev 1:1; 2:1, 8, 12, 18; 3:1, 5, 7, 14; 9:11; 12:7a, 7b, 9; 16:5; 22:6, 16
—DNC {N}: Rev 5:2, 11 (Loc: P/κύκλῳ [+gen]); 7:1, 2a, 2b, 11; 8:2, 3, 4, 5, 6, 8, 10, 12, 13; 9:1, 13, 14a, 14b, 15; 10:1, 5, 7, 8, 9, 10; 11:15; 14:6, 8, 9, 10, 15, 17, 18, 19; 15:1, 6, 7, 8; 16:1; 17:1, 7; 18:1, 21; 19:17; 20:1; 21:9, 12, 17; 22:8
ἄγγελος + εἰμί (<ἄγγελος), 1. <*Ben.* PB [§6.1f]> 1/Pat 2/Ben: be an angel
—N (of) N+gen: Rev 1:20a
ἁγιάζω, 1. <*Mod.* AP{R} [§6.6b]> 1/Agt 2/Pat {{3/Rst}}: make {holy}, sanctify
—N N+acc {Adj+2}: Rev 22:11 (Tem: A/ἔτι)
ἅγιος (>ἅγιος + [εἰμί]), 1. <*Qual.* P [§6.10a]> [1/Pat]: holy
—N: Rev 6:10; 11:2; 14:10; 20:6; 21:2, 10; 22:19
—DNC: Rev 3:7; 5:8; 8:3, 4; 11:18; 13:7, 10; 14:12; 16:6; 17:6; 18:20, 24; 19:8; 20:9; 22:11
ἅγιος + [εἰμί] (<ἅγιος), 1. <*Qual.* P [§6.10a]> 1/Pat: be holy
—N: Rev [4:8a], [8b], [8c]; [20:6a]
ἀγοράζω (>ἠγορασμένος), 1. <*Sep.* APS [§6.8a]> 1/Agt (2/Pat) (3/Sou): buy
—N N+acc (from) P/ἀπό: Rev 14:4 (Ben: N+dat [+an]; Cur: N+2)
—N N+acc (from) P/παρά [+gen, +an]: Rev 3:18a (Pur: V+ἵνα), [18b (Pur: V+ἵνα)], [13c (Pur: V-i1)]
—N N+acc DNC: Rev 18:11 (Tem: A/οὐκέτι)
—N (some of) P/ἐκ INC: Rev 5:9 (Ben: N+dat [+an]; Ins: P/ἐν)
—N INC INC: Rev 13:17

ἀδελφός, 1. <Ben. B{P} [§6.1g]> 1/Ben {{2/Pat}}: brother
—(of) N+gen {N}: Rev 1:9; 6:11; 12:10; 19:10; 22:9
ἀδικέω (>ἀδικῶν), 1. <Eff. AP [§6.3a]> 1/Agt (2/Pat): harm
—N N+acc: Rev 2:11 (Sou: P/ἐκ); 6:6; 7:2, 3 (Tem: V+ἄχρι); 9:4 (Mea: εἰ μή N+2), 10 (Tem: N+acc); 11:5a, 5b
—N DNC: Rev 9:19 (Ins: P/ἐν)
—N INC: Rev 22:11b (Tem: A/ἔτι)
ἀδίκημα, 1. <Ben. B{P}B [§6.1h]> 1/Ben {{2/Pat}} (3/Ben): misdeed
—(of) N+gen {N} INC: Rev 18:5
ἀδικῶν (<ἀδικέω), 1. <Eff. AP [§6.3a]> 1/Agt (2/Pat): harming
—N INC: Rev 22:11a
ᾄδω, 1. <Eff. AP [§6.3a]> 1/Agt (2/Pat): sing
—N N+acc: Rev 5:9; 15:3
—N INC: Rev 14:3 (Cmp: A/ὡς N+2; Loc: P/ἐνώπιον)
αἷμα, 1. <Ben. B{P} [§6.1g]> (1/Ben) {{2/Pat}}: blood
—(of) N+gen {N}: Rev 1:5; 5:9; 6:10; 7:14; 12:11; [16:3b], 6a; 17:6a, 6b; 18:24; 19:2
—DNC {N}: Rev 14:20
—INC {N}: Rev 6:12; 8:7, 8; 11:6; 16:3a, 4, 6b; 19:13
αἰνέω, 1. <Cmm. A{C}E [§5.4b]> 1/Agt {{2/Con}} 3/Exp: speak {praise} to, praise
—N {N} N+dat [+an]: Rev 19:5 (Voc: N+voc)
αἴρω, 1. <Eff. AP [§6.3a]> 1/Agt 2/Pat: take up, pick up [in travel], raise
—N N+acc: Rev 10:5 (Goa: P/εἰς [-an]); 18:21
αἰσχύνη, 1. <Exp. EC C->T [§5.5c]> [1/Exp] 2/Top: shame
—DNC (of/concerning) N+gen: Rev 3:18
αἰχμαλωσία, 1. <Ben. B{P}B [§6.1h]> (1/Ben) {{2/Pat}} [3/Ben]: captivity
—INC {N} DNC: Rev 13:10a, 10b
αἰών, 1. <Mat. M{P} [§6.5c]> (1/Mat) {{2/Pat}}: age
—(of) N+gen {N}: Rev 1:6a, 18a; 4:9a, 10a; 5:13a; 7:12a; 10:6a; 11:15a; 14:11a; 15:7a; 19:3a; 20:10a; 22:5a
—INC {N}: Rev 1:6b, 18b; 4:9b, 10b; 5:13b; 7:12b; 10:6b; 11:15b; 14:11b; 15:7b; 19:3b; 20:10b; 22:5b
αἰώνιος, 1. <Qual. P [§6.10a]> 1/Pat: everlasting
—N: Rev 14:6
τὸ ἀκάθαρτον (<ἀκάθαρτος), 1. <Spec. — [§6.12]> 0/—: unclean thing
—Rev 17:4 (Ben: N+gen)
ἀκάθαρτος, 1. <Qual. P [§6.10a]> (1/Pat): unclean
—N: Rev 16:13; 18:2a, 2b, 2c
—INC: Rev 17:4
ἀκμάζω, 1. <Qual. P [§6.10a]> 1/Pat: be ripe
—N: Rev 14:18
ἀκολουθέω (>ὁ ἀκολουθῶν + [εἰμί]), 1. <Mot. Θ[S]G [S=Θ] [§5.2a]> 1/Thm [2/Goa]: follow
—N N+dat [+an]: Rev 14:9; 19:14 (Loc: P/ἐπί [+dat])
—N DNC: Rev 6:8 (Loc: P/μετά [+gen]); 14:8, 13 (Loc: P/μετά [+gen])

ὁ ἀκολουθῶν + [εἰμί] (<ἀκολουθέω), 1. <Mot. Θ[S]G [S=Θ] [§5.2a]> 1/Thm 2/Goa: be the one following
—N N+dat [+an]: Rev [14:4 (Loc: V+ὅπου)]
ἀκούω (>ἀκούων, ὁ ἀκούων + [εἰμί]), 1. <Exp. EC [§5.5a]> 1/Exp (2/Con): hear, listen to
—N [-resp] N+acc [-an]: Rev 5:11, 13; 6:6; 7:4; 9:13, 16; 12:10; 14:2a, 2b; 18:4, 22a (Loc: P/ἐν; Tem: Α/ἔτι), 22b (Loc: P/ἐν; Tem: Α/ἔτι), 23 (Cau: V+ὅτι; Loc: P/ἐν; Tem: Α/ἔτι)
—N [+resp] N+acc [-an]: Rev 1:10; 4:1; 6:7 (Tem: V+ὅτε); 9:16; 10:4, 8
—N [+resp] N+gen [-an]: Rev 3:20; 11:12; 14:13; 21:3
—N [-resp] N+gen [+an]: Rev 6:3 (Tem: V+ὅτε); 8:13; 16:1, 5, 7
—N [+resp] N+gen [+an]: Rev 6:1 (Cmp: Α/ὡς N+2), 5 (Tem: V+ὅτε)
—N V+quo: Rev 13:9 (Cnd: V+εἰ)
—N (what) V+τί: Rev 2:7, 11, 17, 29; 3:6, 13, 22
—N DNC: Rev 3:3; 9:20; 22:8b
—N INC: Rev 6:6 (Cmp: Α/ὡς N+2); 19:1 (Cmp: Α/ὡς N+2; Loc: P/ἐν; Tem: P/μετά [+acc]), 6 (Cmp: Α/ὡς N+2)
ἀκούων (<ἀκούω), 1. <Exp. EC [§5.5a]> 1/Exp [2/Con]: hearing
—N [+resp] N+acc [-an]: Rev 1:3
—N DNC: Rev 22:17
ὁ ἀκούων + [εἰμί] (<ἀκούω), 1. <Exp. EC [§5.5a]> 1/Exp 2/Con: be the one hearing
—N [+resp] N+acc [-an]: Rev [22:8a]
ἀληθινός (>ἀληθινός + [εἰμί]), 1. <Qual. P [§6.10a]> [1/Pat]: true
—N: Rev 6:10
—DNC: Rev 3:7, 14; 19:11
ἀληθινός + [εἰμί] (<ἀληθινός), 1. <Qual. P [§6.10a]> 1/Pat: be true
—N: Rev [15:3b (Voc: N+nom)]; [16:7]; [19:2], 9b; 21:5; [22:6]
ἀλλά, 1a. <Coor. — — [§6.11a]> 1/— 2/—: but
—V+ V+: Rev 2:4, 6, 9a, 9b, 14, 20; 3:4, 9; 10:7, 9; 17:12; 20:6
1b. <Coor. --- --- [§6.11b]> 1/--- 2/---: but
—(that) V+ἵνα (that) V+ἵνα: Rev 9:5
ἀλληλουϊά, 1. <Qual. O [§6.10b]> [1/Occ]: alleluia
—[licensing following] V+: Rev 19:1 (Cau: V+ὅτι), 3
—[licensing following] V+ὅτι: Rev 19:6
—[referencing what precedes] DNC: Rev 19:4
ἄλλος, 1. <Qual. P [§6.10a]> [1/Pat]: another, other
—N: Rev 2:24; 6:4; 7:2; 8:3; 10:1; 12:3; 13:11; 14:6, 8, 9, 15, 17, 18; 15:1; 18:1, 4; 20:12
—DNC: Rev 17:10
ἅλυσις, 1. <Ben. B{P} [§6.1g]> (1/Ben) {{2/Pat}}: chain
—INC {N}: Rev 20:1
τὸ ἄλφα + [εἰμί], 1. <Qual. P [§6.10a]> 1/Pat: be the alpha
—N: Rev 1:8a; 21:6; [22:13]
ἁμαρτία, 1. <Ben. B{P}B [§6.1h]> 1/Ben {{2/Pat}} [3/Ben]: sin
—(of) N+gen {N} DNC: Rev 1:5; 18:4, 5

ἀμέθυστος + [εἰμί], 1. <Qual. P [§6.10a]> 1/Pat: be amethyst
—N: Rev [21:20h]
ἀμήν, 1. <Qual. O [§6.10b]> (1/Occ): truth, amen
—[licensing following] V+: Rev 7:12a
—[referencing what precedes] DNC: Rev 1:6, 7; 5:14; 7:12b; 19:4; 22:20
—INC: Rev 3:14
ἄμμος, 1. <Spec. — [§6.12]> 0/—: sand
—Rev 12:18 (Ben: N+gen); 20:8 (Ben: N+gen)
ἄμπελος, 1. <Ben. B{P} [§6.1g]> 1/Ben {{2/Pat}}: vineyard
—(of) N+gen {N}: Rev 14:18, 19
ἄμωμος (>ἄμωμος + εἰμί), 1. <Qual. P [§6.10a]> 1/Pat: spotless, without blemish.
ἄμωμος + εἰμί (<ἄμωμος), 1. <Qual. P [§6.10a]> 1/Pat: be spotless, be without blemish
—N: Rev 14:5
ἀνὰ μέσον, 1. <Loc. ΘL [§5.3a]> 1/Thm 2/Loc: in the middle of
—N N+gen: Rev 7:17
ἀναβαίνω (>ἀναβαίνων), 1a. <Mot. Θ[S]G [S=Θ] [§5.2a]> 1/Thm (2/Goa): come up, go up
—N (to) P/εἰς [-an]: Rev 11:12b (Ins: P/ἐν)
—N (before) P/ἐνώπιον: Rev 8:4 (Com: N+dat; Sou: P/ἐκ)
—N (onto) P/ἐπί [+acc]: Rev 20:9
—N (here) A/ὧδε: Rev 4:1; 11:12a
—N INC: Rev 14:11 (Cnd: V+εἰ; Tem: P/εἰς); 19:3 (Tem: P/εἰς)
1b. <Mot. ΘS(G) S=Θ [§5.2c]> 1/Thm [2/Sou]: come up, go up
—N (out of) P/ἐκ: Rev 9:2a (Cmp: V+ὡς); 17:8
—N DNC: Rev [9:2b]
ἀναβαίνων (<ἀναβαίνω), 1b. <Mot. ΘS(G) S=Θ [§5.2c]> 1/Thm 2/Sou: going up
—N (from) P/ἀπό: Rev 7:2
—N (out of) P/ἐκ: Rev 11:7; 13:1, 11
ἀναγινώσκω (>ἀναγινώσκων), 1. <Cmm. ACE [§5.4a]> 1/Agt 2/Con [3/Exp]: read.
ἀναγινώσκων (<ἀναγινώσκω), 1. <Cmm. ACE [§5.4a]> 1/Agt 2/Con [3/Exp]: reading
—N N+acc DNC: Rev 1:3
ἀνάπαυσις, 1. <Ben. B{P} [§6.1g]> [1/Ben] {{2/Pat}}: rest
—DNC {N}: Rev 4:8; 14:11 (Tem: N+gen)
ἀναπαύω, 1. <Qual. P [§6.10a]> 1/Pat: rest
—N: Rev 6:11 (Mea: A/ἔτι; Tem: N+acc; Tem: V+ἕως); 14:13 (Sou: P/ἐκ)
ἀνάστασις, 1. <Ben. B{P} [§6.1g]> [1/Ben] {{2/Pat}}: resurrection
—DNC {N}: Rev 20:5, 6
ἀνατολή, 1. <Ben. B{P} [§6.1g]> [1/Ben] {{2/Pat}}: rising
—(of) N+gen {N}: Rev 7:2; 16:12
—DNC {N}: Rev 21:13
ἄνεμος, 1. <Spec. — [§6.12]> 0/—: wind
—Rev 6:3; 7:1a (Ben: N+gen), 1b
ἀνήρ, 1. <Ben. B{P} [§6.1g]> 1/Ben {{2/Pat}}: husband
—(of) N+gen {N}: Rev 21:2

ἀνοίγω (>ἀνοίγων, ἠνεῳγμένος), 1. <Eff. AP [§6.3a]> 1/Agt [2/Pat]: open
—N N+acc: Rev 3:8, 20; 5:2, 3, 4, 5, 9; 6:1, 3, 5, 7, 9, 12; 8:1; 9:2; 11:19; 12:16; 13:6
    (Ben: P/εἰς [-an]; Pur: V-i1); 15:5 (Loc: P/ἐν); 19:11; 20:12a, 12b
—N DNC: Rev 3:7b
ἀνοίγων (<ἀνοίγω), 1. <Eff. AP [§6.3a]> 1/Agt [2/Pat]: opening
—N DNC: Rev 3:7a
ἄξιος (>ἄξιος + [εἰμί]), 1. <Cap. UO [§5.6b]> 1/Uns 2/Occ: worthy
—N (to) V-i1: Rev 5:4
ἄξιος + [εἰμί] (<ἄξιος), 1. <Cap. UO [§5.6b]> 1/Uns [2/Occ]: be worthy
—N (to) V-i1: Rev 4:11a (Cau: V+ὅτι; Voc: N+nom); [5:2], 9 (Cau: V+ὅτι), 12
—N DNC: Rev 3:4; 16:6
ἀπαρχή, 1. <Ben. B{P}B [§6.1h]> [1/Ben] {{2/Pat}} [3/Ben]: first fruits
—DNC {N} DNC: Rev 14:4
ἀπέρχομαι, 1a. <Mot. Θ[S]G [S=Θ] [§5.2a]> 1/Thm (2/Goa): go forth
—N (to) P/πρός [+acc, +an]: Rev 10:9
—N DNC: Rev 9:12; 11:14; 16:2
—N INC: Rev 12:17 (Pur: V-i1); 21:1, 4
  1b. <Mot. ΘS(G) S=Θ [§5.2c]> 1/Thm 2/Sou: go away
—N (from) P/ἀπό: Rev 18:14
ἀπεσταλμένος (<ἀποστέλλω), 1. <Tra. ΘA[S]G [S=A] -imp. [§5.1n]> 1/Thm [2/Agt] 3/
  Goa: sent
—N DNC (into) P/εἰς [-an]: Rev 5:6
ἄπιστος, 1. <Exp. EC C→T [§5.5c]> (1/Exp) [2/Top]: unfaithful
—INC DNC: Rev 21:8
ἀπό (>ἀπό + [εἰμί]), 1. <Mot. ΘS(G) S=Θ [§5.2c]> 1/Thm 2/Sou: [away] from
—N N+gen: Rev 1:4a [ind. N+nom], 4b, 5; 3:12; 6:16a, 16b; 7:2; 9:6; 14:3, 4, 20;
    16:12, 17; 18:10, 14a, 14b, 15b; 19:5; 20:11; 21:2, 10; 22:19a
  2. <Eff. PA [§6.3c]> 1/Pat 2/Agt: by, from
—N N+gen: Rev 12:6
  3. <Ins. PI [§6.4e]> 1/Pat 2/Ins: by, from
—N N+gen: Rev 9:18; 18:15a
  4. <Par. PPar [§6.7a]> 1/Pat 2/Par: of, from
—N N+gen: Rev 22:19b
  5. <Loc. ΘL [§5.3a]> 1/Thm 2/Loc: from
—N (far [from]) N+gen: Rev 12:14
—N ([from] afar) A/μακρόθεν: Rev 18:10, 15, 17
  6. <Tem. PTem [§6.9d]> 1/Pat 2/Tem: from, on
—N N+gen: Rev 13:8; 14:13; 16:18; 17:8
ἀπό + [εἰμί] (<ἀπό), 5. <Loc. LΘ [§5.3a]> 1/Thm 2/Loc: be of, be on
—N N+gen: Rev [21:13a], [13b], [13c], [13d]
ἀποδιδούς (<ἀποδίδωμι), 2. <Eff. AP [§6.3a]> 1/Agt 2/Pat: giving, producing
—N N+acc: Rev 22:2 (Mea: P/κατά [+acc])
ἀποδίδωμι (>ἀποδιδούς), 1. <Tra. AΘ[S]G [S=A] +imp. [§5.1a]> 1/Agt (2/Thm) [3/Goa]:
  give [back], pay [back]
—N DNC (to) N+dat [+an]: Rev 22:12 (Cmp: V+ὡς)

9. The Case Frame Lexicon

—N INC (to) **N+dat [+an]**: Rev 18:6 (Cmp: V+ὡς)
—N INC DNC: Rev 18:6b (Mea: A/καί)
2. <*Eff*. AP [§6.3a]> **1/Agt 2/Pat**: give, produce.
ἀποθνήσκω (>ἀποθνήσκων), 1. <*Qual*. P [§6.10a]> **1/Pat**: die
—N: Rev 3:2; 8:9, 11 (Cau: V+ὅτι; Ins: P/ἐκ); 9:6; 16:3
ἀποθνήσκων (<ἀποθνήκω), 1. <*Qual*. P [§6.10a]> **1/Pat**: dying
—N: Rev 14:13 (Man: P/ἐν; Tem: P/ἀπό)
ἀποκάλυψις, 1. <*Cmm*. BCE || BCE [§5.4f]> **1/Ben [2/Con] [3/Exp]**: revelation || [1/Ben] 2/Con [3/Exp]: revelation
—(of) **N+gen** DNC DNC || DNC (of) **N+gen** DNC: Rev 1:1
ἀποκρίνομαι, 1. <*Cmm*. ACE[B] [B=A] pass. [§5.4i]> **1/Agt [2/Con] [3/Exp]**: respond
—N DNC DNC: Rev 7:13 [LM]
ἀποκτανθῆναι...αὐτὸν + [εἰμί] (<ἀποκτείνω), 1. <*Eff*. PA [§6.3c]> **1/Pat (2/Agt)**: be...that one is killed
—N INC: Rev [13:10a] (Ins: P/ἐν)
ἀποκτείνω (>ἀποκτανθῆναι...αὐτὸν + [εἰμί]), 1. <*Eff*. AP [§6.3a]> **1/Agt [2/Pat]**: kill
—N **N+acc**: Rev 2:13 (Loc: P/παρά [+dat]), 23 (Ins: P/ἐν); 6:11a (Cmp: V+ὡς), [11b (Mea: A/καί)]; 9:5, 15, 18 (Ins: P/ἐκ), 20 (Ins: P/ἐν); 11:5, 7 (Tem: V+ὅταν), 13 (Ins: P/ἐν); 13:10b (Cnd: V+εἰ; Ins: P/ἐν), 15 (Cnd: V+ἐάν); 19:21 (Ins: P/ἐν)
—N DNC: Rev 6:8 (Ins: P/ἐν; Ins: P/ὑπό [+gen])
ἀπόλλυμι, 1. <*Eff*. AP [§6.3a]> **1/Agt 2/Pat**: destroy
—N **N+acc**: Rev 18:14 (Sou: P/ἀπό)
ἀποστείλας (<ἀποστέλλω), 1. <*Tra*. AΘ[S]G [S=A] –imp. [§5.1i]> **1/Agt [2/Thm] 3/Goa**: sending
—N DNC (to) **N+dat [+an]**: Rev 1:1 (Ins: P/διά [+gen])
ἀποστέλλω (>ἀπεσταλμένος, ἀποστείλας), 1. <*Tra*. AΘ[S]G [S=A] –imp. [§5.1i]> **1/Agt [2/Thm] 3/Goa**: send
2. <*Dis*. AΘO [§5.7a]> **1/Agt 2/Thm 3/Occ**: send [forth]
—N **N+acc** (to) **V-i2**: Rev 22:6
ἀπόστολος (>[ἀπόστολος] + εἰμί), 1. <*Ben*. B{P} [§6.1g]> **[1/Ben] {{2/Pat}}**: apostle
—(of) **N+gen {N}**: Rev 21:14
—DNC **{N}**: Rev 2:2a; 18:20
[ἀπόστολος] + εἰμί (<ἀπόστολος), 1. <*Ben*. PB [§6.1f]> **1/Pat [2/Ben]**: be an apostle
—N DNC: Rev [2:2b]
ἀποφέρω, 1. <*Tra*. AΘ[S]G [S=A] +imp. [§5.1a]> **1/Agt 2/Thm 3/Goa**: bring away, take away
—N **N+acc** (to) **P/εἰς [–an]**: Rev 17:3 (Man: P/ἐν)
—N **N+acc** (onto) **P/ἐπί [+acc]**: Rev 21:10 (Man: P/ἐν)
ἀποχωρίζω, 1. <*Sep*. APS [§6.8a]> **1/Agt 2/Pat [3/Sou]**: separate
—N **N+acc** DNC: Rev 6:14a (Cmp: V+ὡς), [14b]
ἀπώλεια, 1. <*Ben*. B{P}B [§6.1h]> **[1/Ben] {{2/Pat}} [3/Ben]**: destruction
—DNC **{N}** DNC: Rev 17:8, 11
ἀργυροῦς, 1. <*Qual*. P [§6.10a]> **1/Pat**: [made of] silver
—N: Rev 9:20

ἀριθμέω, 1. <Eff. AP [§6.3a]> 1/Agt 2/Pat: count
—N N+acc: Rev 7:9 [red.]
ἀριθμός, 1. <Ben. B{P} [§6.1g]> 1/Ben {{2/Pat}}: number
—(of) N+gen {N}: Rev 5:11; 7:4; 9:16; 13:17, 18a, 18b [εἰμί 1], 18c; 15:2; 20:8 [red.]
ἅρμα, 1. <Ben. B{P} [§6.1g]> 1/Ben {{2/Pat}}: chariot
—(of) N+gen {N}: Rev 9:9
ἀρνέομαι, 1. <Eff. AP [§6.3a]> 1/Agt 2/Pat: deny
—N N+acc: Rev 2:13 (Mea: A/καί; Tem: P/ἐν); 3:8
ἀρνίον, 1. <Spec. — [§6.12]> 0/—: lamb
—Rev 5:6 (Cmp: A/ὡς DNC), 8, 12, 13; 6:1, 16; 7:9, 10, 14, 17 (Loc: P/ἀνὰ μέσον); 12:11; 13:8, 11; 14:1, 4a, 4b, 10; 15:3; 17:14a, 14b; 19:7, 9; 21:9, 14, 22, 23, 27; 22:1, 3
ἁρπάζω, 1a. <Tra. AΘ[S]G [S=A] +imp. [§5.1a]> 1/Agt 2/Thm 3/Goa: carry off
—N N+acc (to) P/πρός [+acc, +an]: Rev 12:5
1b. <Tra. AΘ[S]G [S=A] G→L +imp. [§5.1b]> 1/Agt 2/Thm 3/Loc: carry off
—N N+acc (at) P/πρός [+acc, -an]: Rev 12:5b
ἄρσην, 1. <Qual. P [§6.10a]> [1/Pat]: male
—N: Rev 12:5
—DNC: Rev 12:13
ἀρχαῖος, 1. <Qual. P [§6.10a]> 1/Pat: ancient
—N: Rev 12:9; 20:2
ἀρχή (>ἀρχή + [εἰμί]), 1. <Ben. B{P} [§6.1g]> 1/Ben {{2/Pat}}: source, origin
—(of) N+gen {N}: Rev 3:14
ἀρχή + [εἰμί] (<ἀρχή), 1. <Ben. f[§6.1f]> 1/Pat [2/Ben]: be the source, be the origin
—N DNC: Rev 21:6; [22:13]
ἄρχων, 1. <Ben. B{P} [§6.1g]> 1/Ben {{2/Pat}}: ruler
—(of) N+gen {N}: Rev 1:5
ἀστήρ, 1. <Spec. — [§6.12]> 0/—: star
—Rev 1:16, 20a, 20b; 2:1, 28; 3:1; 6:13 (Ben: N+gen); 8:10, 11, 12; 9:1; 12:1, 4 (Ben: N+gen); 22:16
ἀσχημοσύνη, 1. <Exp. EC C→T [§5.5c]> 1/Exp [2/Top]: unseemliness
—(of) N+gen DNC: Rev 16:15
αὐλή, 1. <Ben. B{P} [§6.1g]> [1/Ben] {{2/Pat}}: courtyard
—DNC {N}: Rev 11:2 (Loc: P/ἔξωθεν)
ἀφαιρέω, 1. <Tra. AΘS[G] [G=A] +imp. [§5.1c]> 1/Agt (2/Thm) [3/Sou]: take away
—N INC (from) P/ἀπό: Rev 22:19a
—N N+acc DNC: Rev 22:19b (Cnd: V+ἐάν) [P/ἀπό and P/ἐκ are complements of μέρος]
ἀφίημι, 1. <Cap. AUO [§5.6a]> 1/Agt 2/Uns [3/Occ]: permit, tolerate
—N N+acc (to) V-i2: Rev 11:9
—N N+acc DNC: Rev 2:20
2. <Eff. AP [§6.3a]> 1/Agt 2/Pat: leave [behind]
—N N+acc: Rev 2:4

ἄχρι, 1. <Loc. ΘL [§5.3a]> 1/Thm 2/Loc: until, up to
—N N+gen: Rev 14:20; 18:5
2. <Tem. PTem [§6.9d]> 1/Pat 2/Tem: until
—N N+gen: Rev 2:10, 25, 26; 12:11; 20:3, 5
3. <non-predicator>: until
Rev 7:3; 15:8; 17:17
τὸ βαθύ (<βαθύς), 1. <Spec. — [§6.12]> 0/—: deep thing
—Rev 2:24 (Ben: N+gen)
βαθύς (>τὸ βαθύ), 1. <Qual. P [§6.10a]> 1/Pat: deep.
βάλλω, 1. <Tra. AΘ[S]G [S=A] -imp. [§5.1i]> 1/Agt (2/Thm) [3/Goa]: throw, put, cast
—N N+acc (into) P/εἰς [-an]: Rev 2:22; 8:7; 12:4, 9b, 13; 14:19a; 19:20 (Cur:
    Adj+2); 20:3, 10 (Loc: V+ὅπου), 14, 15 (Cnd: V+εἰ)
—N N+acc (before) P/ἐνώπιον: Rev 2:14; 4:9-10 (Tem: V+ὅταν)
—N N+acc (onto) P/ἐπί [+acc]: Rev 2:24; 14:16; 18:19
—N N+acc (behind) P/ὀπίσω: Rev 12:15 (Pur: V+ἵνα; Sou: P/ἐκ)
—N N+acc DNC: Rev 6:13 (Ins: P/ὑπό [+gen]); 12:9a, 9c (Com: P/μετά [+gen]),
    10, 16 (Sou: P/ἐκ); 18:21b (Man: A/οὕτως; Man: N+dat)
—N (some of) P/ἐκ (into) P/εἰς [-an]: Rev 2:10 (Pur: V+ἵνα)
—N DNC (into) P/εἰς [-an]: Rev 8:5; 14:19b; 18:21a
—N INC (into) P/εἰς [-an]: Rev 8:8 (Cmp: A/ὡς N+2)
βάπτω (>βεβαμμένος), 1. <Tra. AΘ[S]G [S=A] G→L +imp. [§5.1b]> 1/Agt 2/Thm 3/
    Loc: dip.
βασανιζόμενος (<βασανίζω), 1. <Eff. PA [§6.3c]> 1/Pat [2/Agt]: being tormented
—N DNC: Rev 12:2 (Pur: V-i1)
βασανίζω (>βασανιζόμενος), 1. <Eff. AP [§6.3a]> 1/Agt 2/Pat: torment
—N N+acc: Rev 9:5 (Tem: N+acc); 11:10; 14:10 (Ins: P/ἐν; Loc: P/ἐνώπιον); 20:10
    (Tem: N+gen; Tem: P/εἰς)
βασανισμός, 1. <Ben. B{P}B [§6.1h]> [1/Ben] {{2/Pat}} (3/Ben): torment
—(of) N+gen {N} INC: Rev 9:5a, 5b [εἰμί 1]
—DNC {N} (of) N+gen: Rev 14:11; 18:10, 15
—DNC {N} DNC: 18:7
βασιλεία, 1. <Ben. B{P} [§6.1g]> [1/Ben] {{2/Pat}}: kingdom, reign
—(of) N+gen {N}: Rev 11:15a; 12:10; 16:10; 17:17
—DNC {N}: Rev 1:6, 9; 5:10; 17:12, 18 (Loc: P/ἐπί [+gen])
βασιλεύς (>[βασιλεύς] + εἰμί), 1. <Ben. B{P} [§6.1g]> [1/Ben] {{2/Pat}}: king
—(of) N+gen {N}: Rev 1:5; 6:15; 15:3; 16:14; 17:2, 18; 18:3, 9; 19:16a, 19; 21:24
—DNC {N}: Rev 9:11; 10:11; 16:12 (Sou: P/ἀπό) 17:12b, 14b; 19:16b, 18
[βασιλεύς] + εἰμί (<βασιλεύς), 1. <Ben. PB [§6.1f]> 1/Pat [2/Ben]: be a king
—N (of) N+gen: Rev 17:14a
—N DNC: Rev 17:9c, [10 (Cur: N+1)], 12a
βασιλεύω, 1. <Ben. PB [§6.1f]> 1/Pat [2/Ben]: be king
—N DNC: Rev 5:10 (Loc: P/ἐπί [+gen]); 11:15 (Tem: P/εἰς), 17; 19:6; 20:4 (Com:
    P/μετά [+gen]; Tem: N+acc), 6 (Com: P/μετά [+gen]; Tem: N+acc); 22:5
    (Tem: P/εἰς)

βαστάζω (>βαστάζων), 1. <*Exp.* EC [§5.5a]> 1/Exp [2/Con]: bear, endure
 —N N+acc: Rev 2:2
 —N DNC: Rev 2:3 (Cau: P/διά [+acc])
 2. <*Eff.* AP [§6.3a])> 1/Agt 2/Pat: bear, carry.
βαστάζων (<βαστάζω), 2. <*Eff.* AP [§6.3a]> 1/Agt 2/Pat: bearing, carrying
 —N N+acc: Rev 17:7
βδέλυγμα, 1. <*Ben.* B{P} [§6.1g]> (1/Ben) {{2/Pat}}: abomination
 —(of) N+gen {N}: Rev 17:5
 —INC {N}: Rev 17:4; 21:27
βδελύσσομαι (>ἐβδελυγμένος), 1. <*Qual.* P [§6.10a]> 1/Pat: be polluted.
βεβαμμένος (<βάπτω), 1. <*Tra.* ΘA[S]G [S=A] G→L +imp. [§5.1g]> 1/Thm (2/Agt) 3/Loc: dipped
 —N INC ([terminating] in) N+dat [-an]: Rev 19:13
βήρυλλος + [εἰμί], 1. <*Qual.* P [§6.10a]> 1/Pat: be beryl
 —N: Rev [21:20d]
βιβλαρίδιον, 1. <*Ben.* B{P} [§6.1g]> [1/Ben] {{2/Pat}}: small scroll, small book
 —DNC {N}: Rev 10:2, 9, 10
βιβλίον, 1. <*Ben.* B{P} [§6.1g]> (1/Ben) {{2/Pat}}: scroll, book
 —(of) N+gen {N}: Rev 13:8 (Ben: N+gen); 21:27 (Ben: N+gen)
 —DNC {N}: Rev 1:11; 5:1, 2, 3, 4, 5, 8, 9; 10:8; 17:8 (Ben: N+gen); 20:12a, 12b, 12c, 12d; 22:7, 9, 10, 18, 19a, 19b
 —INC {N}: Rev 6:14
βίβλος, 1. <*Ben.* B{P} [§6.1g]> [1/Ben] {{2/Pat}}: scroll, book
 —DNC {N}: 3:5 (Ben: N+gen); 20:15 (Ben: N+gen)
βλασφημέω, 1. <*Ben.* A{P}B [§6.1b]> 1/Agt {{2/Pat}} 3/Ben: speak {blasphemy} against, blaspheme
 —N {N} N+acc: Rev 13:6; 16:9, 11 (Cau: P/ἐκ), 21 (Cau: P/ἐκ; Cau: V+ὅτι)
βλασφημία, 1. <*Ben.* B{P}B [§6.1h]> [1/Ben] {{2/Pat}} [3/Ben]: blasphemy
 —DNC {N} (against) P/πρός [+acc, +an]: Rev 13:6
 —DNC {N} DNC: Rev 2:9 (Sou: P/ἐκ); 13:1, 5; 17:3
βλέπω (>βλέπων, ὁ βλέπων + [εἰμί]), 1. <*Exp.* EC [§5.5a]> 1/Exp (2/Con): see, look at
 —N N+acc: Rev 1:11, 12; 5:3, 4; 11:9 (Par: P/ἐκ; Tem: N+acc); 16:15; 18:9
 —N DNC: Rev 22:8b
 —N INC: Rev 3:18; 9:20
βλέπων (<βλέπω), 1. <*Exp.* EC [§5.5a]> 1/Exp 2/Con: seeing
 —N N+acc: Rev 17:8; 18:18
ὁ βλέπων + [εἰμί] (<βλέπω), 1. <*Exp.* EC [§5.5a]> 1/Exp 2/Con: be the one seeing
 —N N+acc: Rev [22:8a]
βοηθέω, 1. <*Ben.* A{P}B [§6.1b]> 1/Agt {{2/Pat}} 3/Ben: provide {aid}
 —N {N} (to/for) N+dat [+an]: Rev 12:16
βότρυς, 1. <*Spec.* — [§6.12]> 0/—: bunch of grapes
 —Rev 14:18 (Ben: N+gen)
βρέχω, 1. <*Qual.* P [§6.10a]> 1/Pat: rain
 —N: Rev 11:6 (Tem: N+acc)

βύσσινος, 1. <Qual. P [§6.10a]> (1/Pat): [made of] fine linen
—DNC: Rev 19:8b
—INC: Rev 18:12, 16; 19:8a, 14
γάμος, 1. <Ben. B{P} [§6.1g]> 1/Ben {{2/Pat}}: marriage
—(of) N+gen {N}: Rev 19:7, 9
γάρ, 1. <Coor. — — [§6.11a]> 1/— 2/—: for
—V+ V+: Rev 1:3; 3:2; 9:19a, 19b; 13:18; 14:4, 13; 16:14; 17:17; 19:8, 10; 21:1,
  22, 23, 25; 22:10
γαστήρ, 1. <Ben. B{P} [§6.1g]> [1/Ben] {{2/Pat}}: womb
—DNC {N}: Rev 12:2
γεγραμμένος (<γράφω), 2. <Eff. PA [§6.3c]> 1/Pat [2/Agt]: written
—N DNC: Rev 1:3 (Loc: P/ἐν); 2:17 (Goa: P/ἐπί [+acc]); 5:1 (Loc: A/ἔσωθεν; Loc:
  A/ὄπισθεν); 14:1 (Loc: P/ἐπί [+gen]); 17:5 (Goa: P/ἐπί [+acc]); 19:12, 16;
  20:12 (Loc: P/ἐν), 15 (Loc: P/ἐν); 21:27 (Loc: P/ἐν); 22:18 (Loc: P/ἐν), 19
  (Loc: P/ἐν)
γεμίζω, 1. <Mat. APM [§6.5a]> 1/Agt 2/Pat 3/Mat: fill
—N N+acc (with) N+gen: Rev 15:8 (Sou: P/ἐκ)
—N N+acc (with) P/ἐκ: Rev 8:5
γέμω (>γέμων), 1. <Mat. PM [§6.5b]> 1/Pat 2/Mat: be full.
γέμων (<γέμω), 1. <Mat. PM [§6.5b]> 1/Pat 2/Mat: being full
—N (of) N+gen: Rev 4:6 (Loc: A/ἔμπροσθεν; Loc: A/ὄπισθεν), 8 (Sou: P/ἐκ); 5:8;
  15:7; 17:4; 21:9
—N (of) N+acc: Rev 17:3
γένος (>γένος + εἰμί), 1. <Ben. B{P} [§6.1g]> 1/Ben {{2/Pat}}: offspring.
γένος + εἰμί (<γένος), 1. <Ben. PB [§6.1f]> 1/Pat 2/Ben: be an offspring
—N (of) N+gen: 22:16
γίνομαι, 1. <Mod. PR [§6.6e]> 1/Pat 2/Rst: become
—N N+1: Rev 8:8; 16:3 (Cmp: DNC), 4; 18:2 (Cau: V+ὅτι)
—N Adj+1: Rev 1:18; 2:8, 10 (Tem: P/ἄχρι); 3:2; 6:12b (Cmp: V+ὡς); 11:13b;
  16:10
—N P/εἰς: Rev 8:11; 16:19
—N (in the Spirit) P/ἐν πνεύματι: Rev 1:10 (Tem: P/ἐν); 4:2 (Tem: A/εὐθέως)
—N (like) A/ὡς N+1: Rev 6:12c
2. <Eff. PA [§6.3c]> 1/Pat [2/Agt]: become, [come to] be done, [come to] be made
—N DNC: Rev 12:7 (Loc: P/ἐν); 16:17; 21:6
3. <Mot. Θ[S]G [S=Θ] G→L [§5.2b]> 1/Thm 2/Loc: come to be
—N (on) P/ἐν: Rev 1:9 (Cau: P/διά [+acc])
4. <Qual. P [§6.10a]> 1/Pat: come to be, happen
—N: Rev 1:1 (Man: P/ἐν), 19 (Tem: P/μετά [+acc]); 4:1 (Tem: P/μετά [+acc]);
  6:12a; 8:1 (Loc: P/ἐν, **Tem: V+ὅταν**; Tem: A/ὡς N+acc), 5, 7; 11:13a
  (Tem: P/ἐν), 15a (Loc: P/ἐν), 15b, 19; 12:10 (Cau: V+ὅτι; Tem: A/ἄρτι);
  16:2 (Loc: P/ἐπί [+acc]), 18a, 18b, 18c (Tem: V+ἀφ' οὗ), 18d (Loc: P/ἐπί
  [+gen]); 22:6 (Tem: P/ἐν)

γινώσκω, 1. <*Exp.* EC [§5.5a]> 1/Exp 2/Con: [come to] know
—N N+acc: Rev 2:24 (Cmp: V+ὡς)
—N (that) V+ὅτι: Rev 2:23; 3:9
—N (which) V+ποῖος: Rev 3:3
γλυκύς (>γλυκύς + εἰμί), 1. <*Exp.* CE [§5.5h]> 1/Con 2/Exp: sweet.
γλυκύς + εἰμί (<γλυκύς), 1. <*Exp.* CE [§5.5h]> 1/Con [2/Exp]: be sweet
—N DNC: Rev 10:9 (Cmp: V+ὡς; Loc: P/ἐν), 10 (Cmp: A/ὡς N+1; Loc: P/ἐν)
γλῶσσα (>γλῶσσα + εἰμί), 1. <*Ben.* B{P} [§6.1g]> (1/Ben) {{2/Pat}}: tongue, language
—(of) N+gen {N}: Rev 16:10
—INC {N}: Rev 5:9; 7:9; 10:11; 11:9; 13:7; 14:6
γλῶσσα + εἰμί (<γλῶσσα), 1. <*Ben.* PB [§6.1f]> 1/Pat (2/Ben): be a tongue, be a language
—N INC: Rev 17:15
γνώμη, 1. <*Exp.* EC C→T [§5.5c]> [1/Exp] [2/Top]: intent, opinion
—(of) N+gen DNC: Rev 17:17a
—DNC DNC: Rev 17:13, 17b
γόμος, 1. <*Mat.* B{P}M [§6.5d]> [1/Ben] {{2/Pat}} [3/Mat]: cargo
—(of) N+gen {N} DNC: Rev 18:11
—DNC {N} (of) N+gen {N}: Rev 18:12-13
γράφω (>γεγραμμένος), 1. <*Cmm.* ACE [§5.4a]> 1/Agt [2/Con] [3/Exp]: write
—N V+ (to) N+dat [+an]: Rev [1:4], 2:1, 8, 12, 18; 3:1, 7, 14
—N V+ DNC: Rev 14:13; 19:9
—N DNC DNC: Rev 21:5 (Cau: V+ὅτι)
2. <*Eff.* AP [§6.3a]> 1/Agt [2/Pat]: write, inscribe
—N N+acc: Rev 3:12 (Goa: P/ἐπί [+acc]); 10:4b; 13:8 (Loc: P/ἐν; Tem: P/ἀπό); 17:8 (Goa: P/ἐπί [+acc]; Tem: P/ἀπό)
—N (what) V+ὅ: Rev 1:11 (Goa: P/εἰς [–an]), 19 (Res: A/οὖν)
—N DNC: Rev 10:4a
γρηγορέω (>γρηγορῶν), 1. <*Qual.* P [§6.10a]> 1/Pat: be awake, stay awake
—N: Rev 3:3
γρηγορῶν (<γρηγορέω), 1. <*Qual.* P [§6.10a]> 1/Pat: being awake, being alert
—N: Rev 3:2; 16:15 (Pur: V+ἵνα)
γυμνός (>γυμνός + εἰμί), 1. <*Qual.* P [§6.10a]> 1/Pat: naked
—N: Rev 16:15; 17:16
γυμνός + εἰμί (<γυμνός), 1. <*Qual.* P [§6.10a]> 1/Pat: be naked
—N: Rev 3:17b
γυμνότης, 1. <*Ben.* B{P} [§6.1g]> 1/Ben {{2/Pat}}: nakedness
—(of) N+gen {N}: Rev 3:18
γυνή, 1. <*Ben.* B{P} [§6.1g]> 1/Ben {{2/Pat}}: wife
—(of) N+gen {N}: Rev 19:7; 21:9
2. <*Spec.* — [§6.12]> 0/—: woman
—Rev 2:20; 9:8; 12:1, 4, 6, 13, 14, 15, 16, 17; 14:4; 17:3, 4, 6, 7, 9, 18
γωνία, 1. <*Ben.* B{P} [§6.1g]> 1/Ben {{2/Pat}}: corner
—(of) N+gen {N}: Rev 7:1; 20:8
δάκρυον, 1. <*Ben.* B{P} [§6.1g]> [1/Ben] {{2/Pat}}: tear
—DNC {N}: Rev 7:17; 21:4

δέ, 1. <Coor. — — [§6.11a]> 1/— 2/—: and, but, however
—V+ V+: Rev 1:14; 2:5, 16, 24; 10:2; 19:12; 21:8
δεδεμένος (<δέω), 1. <Eff. PA [§6.3c]> 1/Pat (2/Agt): bound
—N INC: Rev 9:14 (Loc: P/ἐπί [+dat])
δεῖ, 1. <Nec. OI [§5.7d]> 1/Occ [2/Ins]: be necessary
—(to) V+i DNC: Rev 1:1; 4:1; 10:11; 11:5 (Cnd: V+εἰ; Man: Α/οὕτως); 17:10
(Tem: V+ὅταν); 20:3 (Tem: P/μετά [+acc]); 22:6
δείκνυμι, 1. <Cmm. ACE [§5.4a]> 1/Agt 2/Con 3/Exp: show
—N N+acc (to) N+dat [+an]: Rev 17:1; 21:9, 10; 22:1
—N (what) V+ὅ (to) N+dat [+an]: Rev 1:1; 4:1; 22:6
δεικνύω (>δεικνύων), 1. <Cmm. ACE [§5.4a]> 1/Agt 2/Con 3/Exp: show.
δεικνύων (<δεικνύω), 1. <Cmm. ACE [§5.4a]> 1/Agt 2/Con 3/Exp: showing
—N N+acc (to) N+dat [+an]: Rev 22:8
δειλός, 1. <Exp. CE [§5.5h]> (1/Con) [2/Exp]: cowardly
—INC DNC: Rev 21:8
δειπνέω, 1. <Eff. AP [§6.3a]> 1/Agt (2/Pat): eat
—N INC: Rev 3:20a (Loc: P/μετά [+gen]), [20b (Loc: P/μετά [+gen])]
δεῖπνον, 1. <Ben. B{P}B [§6.1h]> 1/Ben {{2/Pat}} [3/Ben]: dinner
—(of) N+gen {N} DNC: Rev 19:9, 17
δέκα, 1. <Qual. P [§6.10a]> 1/Pat: ten
—N: Rev 2:10; 12:3; 13:1a, 1b; 17:3, 7, 12a, 12b, 16
δέκατος, 1. <Par. PPar [§6.7a]> [1/Pat] [2/Par]: tenth
—DNC (of) N+gen: Rev 11:13
—DNC DNC: Rev 21:20
δεξιός, 1. <Qual. P [§6.10a]> [1/Pat]: right
—N: Rev 1:16; 10:2, 5; 13:16
—DNC: Rev 1:17, 20; 2:1; 5:1, 7
δεσπότης, 1. <Ben. B{P} [§6.1g]> [1/Ben] {{2/Pat}}: lord
—DNC {N}: Rev 6:10
δεῦρο, 1. <Qual. O [§6.10b]> 1/Occ: come!
—V+: Rev 17:1; 21:9
δεῦτε, 1. <Qual. O [§6.10b]> 1/Occ: come!
—V+: Rev 19:17
δεύτερος, 1. <Par. PPar [§6.7a]> [1/Pat] [2/Par]: second
—N DNC: Rev 2:11; 4:7; 6:3a, 3b; 8:8; 11:14; 14:8; 20:6, 14; 21:8
—DNC DNC: Rev 16:3; 19:3; 21:19
δέω, 1. <Eff. AP [§6.3a]> 1/Agt 2/Pat: bind
—N N+acc: Rev 20:2 (Tem: N+acc)
διά, 1. <Ins. PI [§6.4e]> 1/Pat 2/Ins: by [means of], through
—N N+gen: Rev 1:1; 21:24
2. <Cau. PCau [§6.9a]> 1/Pat 2/Cau: because of
—N N+acc: Rev 1:9; 2:3; 4:11; 6:9a, 9b; 7:15; 12:11a, 11b, 12; 13:14; 17:7; 18:8,
10, 15; 20:4a, 4b
Διάβολος + εἰμί, 1. <Qual. P [§6.10a]> 1/Pat: be the Devil
—N: Rev 20:2

διάδημα, 1. <Ben. B{P} [§6.1g]> [1/Ben] {{2/Pat}}: diadem
—DNC {N}: Rev 12:3; 13:1; 19:12
διαθήκη, 1. <Ben. B{P}B [§6.1h]> 1/Ben {{2/Pat}} [3/Ben]: covenant
—(of) N+gen {N} DNC: Rev 11:19
διακονία, 1. <Ben. B{P}B [§6.1h]> 1/Ben {{2/Pat}} (3/Ben): service
—(of) N+gen {N} INC: Rev 2:19
διακόσιοι, 1. <Qual. P [§6.10a]> 1/Pat: two hundred
—N: Rev 11:3; 12:6
διαυγής, 1. <Qual. P [§6.10a]> 1/Pat: transparent
—N: Rev 21:21
διαφθείρω (>διαφθείρων), 1. <Eff. AP [§6.3a]> 1/Agt 2/Pat: destroy
—N N+acc: Rev 8:9; 11:18a
διαφθείρων (<διαφθείρω), 1. <Eff. AP [§6.3a]> 1/Agt 2/Pat: destroying
—N N+acc: Rev 11:18b
διδάσκω, 1a. <Cmm. ACE [§5.4a]> 1/Agt 2/Con 3/Exp: teach
—N (to) V-i3 (to) N+dat [+an]: Rev 2:14
1b. <Cmm. AEC [§5.4d]> 1/Agt 2/Exp 3/Con: teach
—N N+acc (to) V-i2: Rev 2:20
διδαχή, 1. <Cmm. BCE [§5.4f]> [1/Ben] [2/Con] [3/Exp]: teaching
—(of) N+gen DNC DNC: Rev 2:14, 15
—DNC DNC DNC: Rev 2:24
δίδωμι, 1. <Tra. AΘ[S]G [S=A] +imp. [§5.1a]> 1/Agt (2/Thm) 3/Goa: give
—N N+acc (to) N+dat [+an]: Rev 1:1 (Pur: V-i3); 2:10, 17b, 21 (Pur: V+ἵνα), 26, 28 (Cmp: V+ὡς); 4:9; 6:2, 4b, 8 (Pur: V-i3), 11; 8:2, 3a (Pur: V+ἵνα); 9:1, 3 (Cmp: V+ὡς); 10:9; 11:1, 2, 13, 18; 12:14 (Pur: V+ἵνα); 13:2, 4, 5a, 5b, 7b, 15b (Pur: V+ἵνα), 16 (Loc: P/ἐπί [+gen]; Loc: P/ἐπί [+acc]); 14:7 (Cau: V+ὅτι); 15:7; 16:6 (Pur: V-i3,2), 9, 19; 17:13, 17b (Tem: V+ἄχρι); 18:7 (Cau: V+ὅτι; Mea: V+ὅσος); 19:7 (Cau: V+ὅτι); 20:4
—N N+acc (before) P/ἐνώπιον: Rev 3:8 (Cau: V+ὅτι) [red.]
—N (some of) N+gen (to) N+dat [+an]: Rev 2:17a [red.]
—N DNC (to) N+dat [+an]: Rev 21:6 (Man: A/δωρεάν; Sou: P/ἐκ)
—N DNC (onto) P/ἐπί [+acc]: Rev 8:3b (Com: N+dat)
—N INC (to) N+dat [+an]: Rev 2:23 (Cmp: P/κατά [+acc]; Goa: N+dat [+an])
2. <Eff. AP [§6.3a]> 1/Agt 2/Pat: give forth
—N N+acc: Rev 20:13a, 13b
3. <Del. AO[S]G [S=A] +imp. [§5.7c]> 1/Agt [2/Occ] 3/Goa: give, delegate
—N (that) V+ἵνα (to) N+dat [+an]: Rev 6:4a [red.]; 9:5; 19:8
—N (to) V-i3 (to) N+dat [+an]: Rev 2:7 [red.]; 3:21; 6:4a; 7:2 [red.]; 13:7a, 14, 15a (Res: V+ἵνα); 16:8
—N (to) V-i3 (to) P/εἰς [–an]: Rev 17:17a
—N DNC (to) N+dat [+an]: Rev 11:3
4. <Dis. AΘO [§5.7a]> 1/Agt 2/Thm 3/Occ: dispose
—N (some of) P/ἐκ (that) V+ἵνα: Rev 3:9
δίκαιος (>δίκαιος + [εἰμί]), 1. <Qual. P [§6.10a]> [1/Pat]: just
—DNC: Rev 22:11

9. *The Case Frame Lexicon* 221

δίκαιος + [εἰμί] (<δίκαιος), 1. <*Qual*. P [§6.10a]> **1/Pat**: be just
—N: Rev [15:3b (Voc: N+voc)]; 16:5 (Cau: V+ὅτι; Voc: N+Voc), [7b]; [19:2]
δικαιοσύνη, 1. <*Ben*. B{P} [§6.1g]> **[1/Ben]** {{2/Pat}}: justice, righteousness
—DNC {N}: Rev 19:11; 22:11
δικαίωμα (>δικαίωμα + εἰμί), 1. <*Ben*. B{P} [§6.1g]> **1/Ben** {{2/Pat}}: righteous deed
—(of) N+gen {N}: Rev 15:4
δικαίωμα + εἰμί (<δικαίωμα), 1. <*Ben*. PB [§6.1f]> **1/Pat 2/Ben**: be a righteous deed
—N (of) N+gen: Rev 19:8
διπλοῦς, 1. <*Qual*. P [§6.10a]> **[1/Pat]**: twofold
—DNC: Rev 18:6a, 6b
διπλόω, 1. <*Eff*. AP [§6.3a]> **1/Agt 2/Pat**: double
—N N+acc: Rev 18:6 (Cmp: P/κατά [+acc])
δισμυριάς (>δισμυριάς + [εἰμί]), 1. <*Mat*. M{P} [§6.5c]> **1/Mat** {{2/Pat}}: twenty-thousand-member group
δισμυριάς + [εἰμί] (<δισμυριάς), 1. <*Mat*. PM [§6.5b]> **1/Pat 2/Mat**: be a twenty-thousand-member group
—N (of) N+gen: Rev [9:16]
δίστομος, 1. <*Qual*. P [§6.10a]> **1/Pat**: two-edged
—N: Rev 1:16; 2:12
διψάω (>διψῶν), 1. <*Exp*. EC C→T [§5.5c]> **1/Exp (2/Top)**: be thirsty
—N INC: Rev 7:16 (Tem: A/ἔτι)
διψῶν (<διψάω), 1. <*Exp*. EC C→T [§5.5c]> **1/Exp (2/Top)**: being thirsty
—N DNC: Rev 22:17
—N INC: Rev 21:6
διώκω, 1. <*Mot*. Θ[S]G [S=Θ] [§5.2a]> **1/Thm 2/Goa**: pursue
—N N+acc: Rev 12:13 (Tem: V+ὅτε)
δόξα, 1. <*Ben*. B{P} [§6.1g]> **[1/Ben]** {{2/Pat}}: glory
—(of) N+gen {N}: Rev 15:8; 18:1; 19:1 [εἰμί 1]; 21:11, 23, 24, 26
—DNC {N}: Rev 1:6 [εἰμί 2]; 4:9, 11; 5:12, 13 [εἰμί 2]; 7:12 [εἰμί 2]; 11:13; 14:7; 16:9; 19:7
δοξάζω, 1. <*Eff*. AP [§6.3a]> **1/Agt 2/Pat**: glorify
—N N+acc: Rev 15:4 (Cau: V+ὅτι; Voc: N+voc); 18:7 (Cau: V+ὅτι; Ins: N+acc)
δοῦλος, 1. <*Ben*. B{P} [§6.1g]> **(1/Ben)** {{2/Pat}}: slave
—(of) N+gen {N}: Rev 1:1a, 1b; 7:3; 10:7; 11:18; 15:3; 19:2, 5; 22:3, 6
—DNC {N}: Rev 2:20
—INC {N}: Rev 6:15; 13:16; 19:18
δρέπανον, 1. <*Ben*. B{P} [§6.1g]> **[1/Ben]** {{2/Pat}}: sickle
—(of) N+gen {N}: Rev 14:15, 16, 18b, 19
—DNC {N}: Rev 14:14, 17, 18a
δύναμαι, 1. <*Cap*. UO [§5.6b]> **1/Uns 2/Occ**: be able
—N (to) V-i1: Rev 2:2; 3:8; 5:3 (Loc: P/ἐν; Loc: P/ἐπί [+gen]; Loc: P/ὑποκάτω); 6:17; 7:9; 9:20; 13:4, 17; 14:3 (Mea: A/εἰ μή N+1); 15:8
δύναμις, 1. <*Ben*. B{P} [§6.1g]> **[1/Ben]** {{2/Pat}}: power
—(of) N+gen {N}: Rev 1:16; 11:17; 13:2; 15:8; 17:13; 18:3; 19:1 [εἰμί 1]
—DNC {N}: Rev 3:8; 4:11; 5:12; 7:12 [εἰμί 2]; 12:10

δύο, 1. <Qual. P [§6.10a]> [1/Pat]: two
—N: Rev 9:12; 11:2, 3, 4a, 4b, 10; 12:14; 13:5, 11
—DNC: Rev 19:20
δώδεκα, 1. <Qual. P [§6.10a]> 1/Pat: twelve
—N: Rev 7:5a, 5b, 5c, 6a, 6b, 6c, 7a, 7b, 7c, 8a, 8b, 8c; 12:1; 21:12a, 12b, 12c, 14a, 14b, 14c, 16, 21a, 21b; 22:2
δωδέκατος, 1. <Par. PPar [§6.7a]> [1/Pat] [2/Par]: twelfth
—DNC DNC: Rev 21:20
δῶρον, 1. <Ben. B{P}B [§6.1h]> [1/Ben] {{2/Pat}} [3/Ben]: gift
—DNC {N} DNC: Rev 11:10
ἐβδελυγμένος (<βδελύσσομαι), 1. <Qual. P [§6.10a]> 1/Pat: befouled, polluted
—N: Rev 21:8
ἕβδομος, 1. <Par. PPar [§6.7a]> [1/Pat] [2/Par]: seventh
—N DNC: Rev 8:1l; 10:7; 11:15
—DNC DNC: Rev 16:17; 21:20
ἐγγύς + [εἰμί], 1. <Tem. PTem [§6.9d]> 1/Pat [2/Tem]: be near
—N DNC: Rev [1:3b]; 22:10
ἐγείρω, 1. <Mot. Θ[S](G) [S=Θ] [§5.2d]> 1/Thm [[2/Sou]]: get up
—N [N]: Rev 11:1
ἐγχρίω, 1. <Ins. API [§6.4a]> 1/Agt 2/Pat [3/Ins]: anoint
—N N+acc DNC: Rev 3:18 (Pur: V+ἵνα)
ἔθνος (>ἔθνος + εἰμί), 1. <Ben. B{P} [§6.1g]> (1/Ben) {{2/Pat}}: nation
—INC {N}: Rev 2:26; 5:9; 7:9; 10:11; 11:2, 9, 18; 12:5; 13:7; 14:6, 8; 15:3, 4; 16:19; 18:3, 23; 19:15; 20:3, 8 (Loc: P/ἐν); 21:24, 26; 22:2
ἔθνος + εἰμί (<ἔθνος), 1. <Ben. PB [§6.1f]> 1/Pat (2/Ben): be a nation
—N INC: Rev 17:15
εἰδωλόθυτος, 1. <Ben. PA{B} [§6.1i]> [1/Pat] (2/Agt) {3/Ben}: sacrificed {to idols}
—DNC INC {N}: Rev 2:14, 20
εἰδώς (<οἶδα), 1. <Exp. EC [§5.5a]> 1/Exp 2/Con: knowing
—N (that) V+ὅτι: Rev 12:12
εἴκοσι, 1. <Qual. P [§6.10a]> 1/Pat: twenty
—N: Rev 4:4a, 4b, 10; 5:8; 11:16; 19:4
εἰκών, 1. <Ben. B{P}B [§6.1h]> [1/Ben] {{2/Pat}} [3/Ben]: image
—DNC {N} (of) N+gen: Rev 13:15a, 15b, 15c; 14:9, 11; 15:2; 16:2; 19:20; 20:4
—DNC {N} DNC: Rev 13:14
εἰμί (>ὤν), 1. <Qual. P [§6.10a]> 1/Pat: be, exist
—N: Rev 1:4c, 8c, 19; 4:8e, 11b (Cau: P/διά [+acc]); [6:2a], [5a], [6a (Mea: N+gen)], [6b (Mea: N+gen)], [8a]; [7:9a]; [8:13a (Sou: P/ἐκ)], [13b (Sou: P/ἐκ)], [13c (Sou: P/ἐκ)]; 10:6 (Tem: A/οὐκέτι); 11:17b; [12:3a], [12 (Cau: V+ὅτι)]; 13:18b; 14:4a, [14a]; 16:5b, 5c; 17:8a, 8b, 8c, 8d, 10, 11a, 11b; [18:10a (Cau: V+ὅτι; Voc: N+voc)], [10b (Cau: V+ὅτι; Voc: N+voc)], [16a (Cau: V+ὅτι; Voc: N+voc)], [16b (Cau: V+ὅτι; Voc: N+voc)], [19a (Cau: V+ὅτι; Voc: N+voc)], [19b (Cau: V+ὅτι; Voc: N+voc)]; [19:1-2 (Cau: V+ὅτι)], [10a], [11a]; 21:1 (Tem: A/ἔτι), 4 (Cau: V+ὅτι; Tem: A/ἔτι), 25 (Loc: A/ἐκεῖ); [22:2], 3a (Tem: A/ἔτι), 5 (Tem: A/ἔτι), [9a], 12b, 14b

9. The Case Frame Lexicon 223

2. <*Ben.* PB [§6.1f]> **1/Pat 2/Ben**: be
   —**N** (of/for) **N+dat** [+**an**]: Rev [1:4a (Sou: P/ἀπό)], [6 (Tem: P/εἰς)]; [5:13b (Tem: P/εἰς)]; [7:10], [12b (Tem: P/εἰς)]

εἰς (>εἰς + [εἰμί]), **1.** <*Mot.* Θ[S]G [S=Θ] [§5.2a]> **1/Thm 2/Goa**: to, into, onto
   —**N N+acc** [-**an**]: Rev 1:11a, 11b, 11c, 11d, 11e, 11f, 11g, 11h; 2:10, 22a, 22b; 5:6; 6:13, 15a, 15b; 8:5, 7, 8; 9:1, 3, 9; 10:5; 11:9, 12; 12:4, 6, 9, 13, 14a, 14b; 13:3, 10b, 13; 14:19a, 19b; 15:8; 16:1, 2, 3, 4, 14, 16; 17:3, 8, 11, 17; 18:21; 19:9, 17, 20; 20:3, 8, 10a, 14, 15; 21:24, 26, 27; 22:14

2. <*Ben.* PB [§6.1f]> **1/Pat 2/Ben**: for
   —**N N+acc**: Rev 9:7, 15; 13:6, 10a; 22:2

3. <*Mod.* PR [§6.6e]> **1/Pat 2/Rst**: into
   —**N N+acc**: Rev 8:11; 11:6; 16:19

4. <*Tem.* PTem [§6.9d]> **1/Pat 2/Tem**: to, into
   —**N N+acc**: Rev 1:6, 18; 4:9, 10; 5:13; 7:12; 10:6; 11:15; 14:11; 15:7; 19:3; 20:10b; 22:5

εἰς + [εἰμί] (<εἰς), **2.** <*Ben.* PB [§6.1f]> **1/Pat 2/Ben**: be for
   —**N N+acc** [-**an**]: Rev [13:10a]; [22:2b]

εἷς, 1. <*Qual.* P [§6.10a]> [**1/Pat**]: one, a, an
   —**N**: Rev 8:13; 9:12; 17:12, 13, 17; 18:8, 10, 17, 19, 21; 19:17; 21:12b
   —**DNC**: Rev 17:10 [εἰμί 1]

2. <*Par.* PPar [§6.7a]> [**1/Pat**] [**2/Par**]: one
   —**DNC** (of) **N+gen**: Rev 4:8b; 21:21a
   —**DNC** (of) **P/ἐκ**: Rev 5:5; 6:1a, 1b; 7:13; 9:13; 13:3; 15:7; 17:1; 21:9
   —**DNC DNC**: Rev 4:8a; 17:10

εἰσέρχομαι, 1a. <*Mot.* Θ[S]G [S=Θ] [§5.2a]> **1/Thm 2/Goa**: enter, come
   —**N** (into) **P/εἰς** [-**an**]: Rev 15:8 (Tem: V+ἄχρι); 21:27 (Mea: εἰ μή N+1); 22:14 (Ins: N+dat)
   —**N** (to) **P/πρός** [+**acc**, +**an**]: Rev 3:20 (Cnd: V+ἐάν; Mea: A/καί)

1b. <*Mot.* Θ[S]G [S=Θ] G→L [§5.2b]> **1/Thm 2/Loc**: enter, come
   —**N** ([terminating] in) **P/ἐν**: Rev 11:11 (Tem: P/μετά [+acc])

ἐκ (>ἐκ + [εἰμί]), **1.** <*Mot.* ΘS(G) S=Θ [§5.2c]> **1/Thm 2/Sou**: [apart] from, out of
   —**N N+gen**: Rev 1:5, 16; 2:5, 7, 9; 3:5, 10, 12, 16; 4:5; 5:5b, 7; 6:4, 10, 14; 7:4, 5a, 5b, 5c, 6a, 6b, 6c, 7a, 7b, 7c, 8a, 8b, 8c, 9, 14, 17; 8:4, 10, 13; 9:1, 2a, 3, 17, 18b; 10:1, 4, 8, 10; 11:5, 7, 9, 11, 12; 12:15, 16; 13:1, 11, 13; 14:2, 10, 13a, 13b, 15, 17, 18, 20; 15:2a, 2b, 2c, 6, 8a, 8b; 16:1, 17, 21a; 17:8; 18:1a, 3a, 3b, 4a, 4b, 4c, 19; 19:2, 15, 21a, 21b; 20:1, 7, 9; 21:2, 3, 4, 6, 10; 22:1

2. <*Par.* PPar [§6.7a]> **1/Pat 2/Par**: some of
   —**N N+gen**: Rev 2:10; 3:9; 5:5a, 9; 6:1a, 1b; 7:13; 9:13; 11:9; 13:3; 15:7; 17:1, 11; 21:9; 22:19

3. <*Ins.* PI [§6.4e]> **1/Pat 2/Ins**: by [means of]
   —**N N+gen**: Rev 2:11; 3:18; 8:11; 9:2b, 18a; 17:2, 6a, 6b; 18:1b; 20:12

4. <*Mat.* PM [§6.5b]> **1/Pat 2/Mat**: [out] of
   —**N N+gen**: Rev 8:5; 14:8; 18:12

5. <*Exp.* EC [§5.5a]> **1/Exp 2/Con**: of, from
   —**N N+gen**: Rev 2:21, 22; 9:20, 21a, 21b, 21c, 21d; 16:11c; 18:20

6. <*Cau.* PCau [§6.9a]> 1/Pat 2/Cau: because of
—N N+gen: Rev 16:10, 11a, 11b, 21b
ἐκ + [εἰμί] (<ἐκ), 1. <*Mot.* ΘS(G) S=Θ [§5.2c]> 1/Thm 2/Sou: be from, be out of
—N N+gen: Rev [16:13a], [13b], [13c]; 17:11d
4. <*Mat.* PM [§6.5b]> 1/Pat 2/Mat: be [made] out of
—N N+gen: Rev 21:21b (Mea: A/ἀνά)
ἕκαστος, 1. <*Par.* PPar [§6.7a]> 1/Pat [2/Par]: each
—N (of) N+gen: Rev 21:21
—N DNC: Rev 2:23; 5:8; 6:11; 20:13; 22:2, 12
ἑκατόν, 1. <*Qual.* P [§6.10a]> 1/Pat: one hundred
—N: Rev 7:4; 14:1, 3; 21:17
ἐκβάλλω, 1. <*Tra.* AΘ[S]G [S=A] –imp. [§5.1i]> 1/Agt 2/Thm 3/Goa: cast [out]
—N N+acc (outside) A/ἔξωθεν: Rev 11:2
ἐκδικέω, 1. <*Sep.* APS [§6.8a]> 1/Agt 2/Pat 3/Sou: exact, avenge
—N N+acc (from) P/ἐκ: Rev 6:10; 19:2
ἐκεῖνος, 1. <*Qual.* P [§6.10a]> 1/Pat: that
—N: Rev 9:6; 11:13
ἐκκεντέω, 1. <*Eff.* AP [§6.3a]> 1/Agt 2/Pat: pierce
—N N+acc: Rev 1:7
ἐκκλησία, 1. <*Ben.* B{P} [§6.1g]> [1/Ben] {{2/Pat}}: church
—DNC {N}: Rev 1:4 (Loc: P/ἐν), 11, 20a, 29b; 2:1 (Loc: P/ἐν), 7, 8 (Loc: P/ἐν), 11, 12 (Loc: P/ἐν), 17, 18 (Loc: P/ἐν), 23, 29; 3:1 (Loc: P/ἐν), 6, 7 (Loc: P/ἐν), 13, 14 (Loc: P/ἐν), 22; 22:16
ἐκκλησία + εἰμί, 1. <*Ben.* PB [§6.1f]> 1/Pat [2/Ben]: be a church
—N DNC: Rev 1:20b
ἐκλεκτός (>ἐκλεκτός + [εἰμί]), 1. <*Eff.* PA [§6.3c]> 1/Pat 2/Agt: chosen.
ἐκλεκτός + [εἰμί] (<ἐκλεκτός), 1. <*Eff.* PA [§6.3c]> 1/Pat [2/Agt]: be chosen
—N DNC: Rev [17:14b]
ἐκπορεύομαι (>ἐκπορευόμενος), 1a. <*Mot.* Θ[S]G [S=Θ] [§5.2a]> 1/Thm 2/Goa: come [out]
—N (onto) P/ἐπί [+acc]: Rev 16:14 (Pur: V-i1)
1b. <*Mot.* ΘS(G) S=Θ [§5.2c]> 1/Thm 2/Sou: come [out]
—N (from) P/ἐκ: Rev 4:5; 9:17; 11:5 (Cnd: V+εἰ); 19:15 (Pur: V+ἵνα)
ἐκπορευόμενος (<ἐκπορεύομαι), 1b. <*Mot.* ΘS(G) S=Θ [§5.2c]> 1/Thm 2/Sou: coming out
—N (of/from) P/ἐκ: Rev 1:16; 9:18; 22:1
ἕκτος, 1. <*Par.* PPar [§6.7a]> [1/Pat] [2/Par]: sixth
—N DNC: Rev 6:12; 9:13, 14
—DNC DNC: Rev 16:12; 21:20
ἐκχέω, 1. <*Tra.* AΘ[S]G [S=A] +imp. [§5.1a]> 1/Agt 2/Thm 3/Goa: pour out
—N N+acc (to /onto/into) P/εἰς [–an]: Rev 16:1, 2, 3, 4
—N N+acc (onto) P/ἐπί [+acc]: Rev 16:8, 10, 12 (Pur: V+ἵνα), 17
2. <*Eff.* AP [§6.3a]> 1/Agt 2/Pat: [cause to] pour out
—N N+acc: Rev 16:6

ἐλαία + εἰμί, 1. <Qual. P [§6.10a]> 1/Pat: be an olive tree
—N: Rev 11:4
ἐλέγχω, 1. <Eff. AP [§6.3a]> 1/Agt 2/Pat: reprove
—N (however many) V+ὅσος ἐάν: Rev 3:19
ἐλεεινός (>ἐλεεινός + εἰμί), 1. <Exp. CE [§5.5h]> 1/Con [2/Exp]: pitiable.
ἐλεεινός + εἰμί (<ἐλεεινός), 1. <Exp. CE [§5.5h]> 1/Con [2/Exp]: be pitiable
—N DNC: Rev 3:17b
ἐλεύθερος, 1. <Qual. P [§6.10a]> (1/Pat): free
—INC: Rev 6:15; 13:16; 19:18
ἐλεφάντινος, 1. <Qual. P [§6.10a]> 1/Pat: [made of] ivory
—N: Rev 18:12
ἐλισσόμενος (<ἑλίσσω), 1. <Eff. PA [§6.3c]> 1/Pat [2/Agt]: being rolled up
—N DNC: Rev 6:14
ἑλίσσω (>ἐλισσόμενος), 1. <Eff. AP [§6.3a]> 1/Agt 2/Pat: roll up.
ἕλκος, 1. <Ben. B{P} [§6.1g]> [1/Ben] {{2/Pat}}: sore
—(of) N+gen {N}: Rev 16:11
—DNC {N}: Rev 16:2
Ἑλληνικός, 1. <Qual. P [§6.10a]> [1/Pat]: Greek
—DNC: Rev 9:11
ἐμέω, 1. <Tra. AΘS(G) S-A –imp. [§5.1m]> 1/Agt/Thm 3/Sou: vomit, spit
—N N+acc (out of/from) P/ἐκ: Rev 3:16
ἐμός, 1. <Qual. P [§6.10a]> 1/Pat: my
—N: Rev 2:20
ἔμπορος, 1. <Mat. M{P} [§6.5c]> (1/Mat) {{2/Pat}}: merchant
—(of) N+gen {N}: Rev 18:15
—INC {N}: Rev 18:3 (Ben: N+gen), 11 (Ben: N+gen), 23 (Ben: N+gen)
ἔμπροσθεν, 1. <Mot. Θ[S]G [S=Θ] G→L [§5.2b]> 1/Thm 2/Loc: before
—N N+gen: Rev 19:10; 22:8
2. <non-predicator>: in front
Rev 4:6
ἐν (>ἐν + [εἰμί]), 1. <Loc. ΘL [§5.3a]> [1/Thm] 2/Loc: in, on
—N N+dat: Rev 1:3, 4, 5, 9a, 9b, 9c, 16a; 2:1a, 1b, 8, 12, 18, 24; 3:1, 4a, 7, 12, 14; 4:1, 2b; 5:3, 6a, 6b, 13b; 6:5, 6; 7:15; 8:1, 9, 13; 9:11, 17; 10:2, 6b, 6c, 6d, 8, 9, 10; 11:1, 15, 19a, 19b; 12:1, 2, 3, 7, 8, 10, 12; 13:6, 8, 12; 14:5, 6, 10a, 13, 14, 17; 15:1a, 5; 16:3; 17:4; 18:7, 19b, 22a, 22b, 22c, 23a, 23b, 24; 19:1, 14, 17a, 17c; 20:6, 8, 12, 13a, 13b, 15; 21:22, 27; 22:2, 18, 19
—DNC N+dat: Rev 1:15 (Tem: Part+gen)
2. <Ins. PI [§6.4e]> 1/Pat 2/Ins: by [means of], through
—N N+dat: Rev 1:5, 16b; 2:16, 23, 27; 3:4b [περιβεβλημένος omitted], 5; 4:4; 5:2, 9; 6:8a, 8b, 8c; 7:9, 14; 8:7; 9:17, 19c, 20; 10:6a; 11:6, 12, 13b; 12:5; 13:10a, 10b; 14:2, 7, 9, 10b, 15; 15:1b; 16:8; 17:3, 16; 18:2, 8b, 16, 19a, 23c; 19:2, 11, 15a, 15b, 17b, 20a, 20b, 21; 21:10
3. <Mod. PR [§6.6e]> 1/Pat 2/Rst: in
—N (the Spirit) N+dat: Rev 1:10a; 4:2

4. <Tem. PTem [§6.9d]> 1/Pat 2/Tem: on, in
—N N+dat: Rev 1:1, 10b; 2:13; 9:6; 11:13a; 18:8a; 22:6
5. <Mot. Θ[S]G [S=Θ] G→L [§5.2b]> 1/Thm 2/Loc: [terminating] in, [terminating] on
—N N+dat: Rev 3:21a, 21b; 11:11; 18:6
ἐν + [εἰμί] (<ἐν), 1. <Loc. ΘL [§5.3a]> 1/Thm 2/Loc: be in
—N N+dat [–an]: Rev 2:7; [5:13a]; [7:9b]; [9:10], 19a, 19b, 19c; [21:8 (Ben: N+dat [+an])]; 22:3b
4. <Tem. PTem [§6.9d]> 1/Pat 2/Tem: be in
—N N+dat: Rev [10:7 (Tem: V+ὅταν)]
ἐν μέσῳ (>ἐν μέσῳ + [εἰμί]), 1. <Loc. ΘL [§5.3a]> 1/Thm 2/Loc: in the middle of
—N N+gen: Rev 1:13; 2:1; 5:6a, 6b; 6:6
ἐν μέσῳ + [εἰμί] (<ἐν μέσῳ), 1. <Loc. ΘL [§5.3a]> 1/Thm 2/Loc: be in the middle of
—N N+gen: Rev [4:6b]; [22:2 (Loc: A/ἐντεῦθεν; Loc: A/ἐκεῖθεν)]
ἔνατος, 1. <Par. PPar [§6.7a]> [1/Pat] [2/Par]: ninth
—DNC DNC: Rev 21:20
ἐνδεδυμένος (<ἐνδύω), 1. <Ins. PAI [§6.4d]> 1/Pat (2/Agt) 3/Ins: clothed
—N INC N+acc: Rev 1:13; 15:6; 19:14
ἐνδέκατος, 1. <Par. PPar [§6.7a]> [1/Pat] [2/Par]: eleventh
—DNC DNC: Rev 21:20
ἐνδύω (>ἐνδεδυμέμος), 1. <Ins. API [§6.4a]> 1/Agt 2/Pat 3/Ins: clothe.
ἐνδώμησις, 1. <Ben. B{P} [§6.1g]> 1/Ben {{2/Pat}}: building material
—(of) N+gen {N}: Rev 21:18
ἐντολή, 1. <Cmm. BCE [§5.4f]> 1/Ben (2/Con) [3/Exp]: commandment
—(of) N+gen INC DNC: Rev 12:17; 14:12
ἐνώπιον (>ἐνώπιον + [εἰμί]), 1. <Loc. ΘL [§5.3a]> 1/Thm 2/Loc: before, in front of
—N N+gen: Rev 3:2, 5a, 5b, 6, 8, 9; 4:5, 6, 10a; 5:8; 7:9a, 9b, 11; 8:2, 3; 9:13; 11:4, 16; 12:4, 10; 13:12, 14; 14:3a, 3b, 10a, 10b; 15:4; 16:19; 19:20; 20:12
2a. <Mot. Θ[S]G [S=Θ] [§5.2a]> 1/Thm 2/Goa: [to] before, in front of
—N N+gen: Rev 2:14; 4:10b; 8:4
2b. <Mot. Θ[S]G [S=Θ] G→L [§5.2b]> 1/Thm 2/Loc: [terminating] before, [terminating] in front of
—N N+gen: Rev 13:13
ἐνώπιον + [εἰμί] (<ἐνώπιον), 1. <Loc. ΘL [§5.3a]> 1/Thm 2/Loc: be before
—N N+gen: Rev [1:4d]; 7:15 (Cau: P/διά [+acc])
ἕξ (>ἑξακόσιοι ἑξήκοντα ἕξ + [εἰμί]), 1. <Qual. P [§6.10a]> 1/Pat: six.
ἑξακόσιοι (>ἑξακόσιοι ἑξήκοντα ἕξ + [εἰμί]), 1. <Qual. P [§6.10a]> 1/Pat: six hundred
—N: Rev 14:20
ἑξακόσιοι ἑξήκοντα ἕξ + [εἰμί] (<ἕξ, ἑξακόσιοι, ἑξήκοντα), 1. <Qual. P [§6.10a]> 1/Pat: be six hundred sixty-six
—N: Rev [13:18c]
ἐξαλείφω, 1. <Sep. APS [§6.8a]> 1/Agt 2/Pat 3/Sou: wipe out, wipe away
—N N+acc (from) P/ἐκ: Rev 3:5; 7:17; 21:4
ἐξελθών (<ἐξέρχομαι), 1b. <Mot. ΘS(G) S=Θ [§5.2c]> 1/Thm 2/Sou: coming out
—N (from) P/ἐκ: Rev 19:21

ἐξέρχομαι (>ἐξελθών), 1a. <*Mot.* Θ[S]G [S=Θ] [§5.2a]> 1/Thm (2/Goa): come forth
—N (into) P/εἰς [-an]: Rev 9:3 (Sou: P/ἐκ)
—N DNC: Rev 6:4
—N INC: Rev 6:2 (Cur: Adj+1; Pur: V+ἵνα)
1b. <*Mot.* ΘS(G) S=Θ [§5.2c]> 1/Thm [2/Sou]: come forth
—N (from) P/ἀπό: Rev 19:5
—N (from) P/ἐκ: Rev 14:15, 17, 18, 20 (Loc: P/ἄχρι; Sou: P/ἀπό); 15:6; 16:17 (Sou: P/ἀπό); 18:4-5 (Cau: V+ὅτι; Pur: V+ἵνα; Voc: N+voc)
—N (out/outside) A/ἔξω: Rev 3:12 (Tem: A/ἔτι)
—N DNC: Rev 20:8 (Pur: V-i1)
ἐξήκοντα (>ἑξακόσιοι ἑξήκοντα ἕξ + [εἰμί]), 1. <*Qual.* P [§6.10a]> 1/Pat: sixty
—N: Rev 11:3; 12:6
ἐξουσία, 1. <*Aut.* BOL [§5.7e]> [1/Ben] (2/Occ) (3/Loc): authority
—(of) N+gen (to) V-i1,3 DNC: Rev 9:10 (Ins: P/ἐν) [εἰμί 1]
—(of) N+gen DNC (over) P/ἐπί [+acc]: Rev 22:14
—(of) N+gen DNC DNC: Rev 9:19; 12:10; 13:12; 17:13
—DNC (to) V-i1 (over) P/ἐπί [+gen]: Rev 11:6b
—DNC (to) V-i1,3 (over) P/ἐπί [+acc]: Rev 6:8
—DNC (to) V-i1,3 DNC: Rev 11:6a (Pur: V+ἵνα); 13:5
—DNC INC (over) P/ἐπί [+gen]: Rev 2:26; 14:18; 20:6
—DNC INC (over) P/ἐπί [+acc]: Rev 13:7; 16:9
—DNC DNC DNC: Rev 9:3a, 3b; 13:2, 4; 17:12
—DNC INC INC: Rev 18:1
ἔξω + [εἰμί], 1. <*Loc.* Θ[L] [L=Θ] [§5.3b]> 1/Thm [[2/Loc]]: be outside
—N [N]: Rev [22:15]
ἔξωθεν, 1. <*Loc.* ΘL [§5.3a]> 1/Thm 2/Loc: [from] outside of
—N N+gen: Rev 11:2a; 14:20
2. <*non-predicator.*>: out
Rev 11:2b
ἐπάνω, 1. <*Loc.* ΘL [§5.3a]> 1/Thm 2/Loc: above
—N N+gen: Rev 6:8; 20:3
ἐπί (>ἐπί + [εἰμί]), 1a. <*Loc.* ΘL [§5.3a]> 1/Thm 2/Loc: on, over, before [+an]
—N N+gen: Rev 1:20; 2:26; 3:10b; 4:10; 5:1b, 3, 7, 10; 6:10, 16b; 7:3, 15a, 17; 8:13; 9:4, 11, 17; 10:1, 5a, 5b, 8a, 8b; 11:6, 10a, 10c; 13:1a, 8, 14a, 14b; 14:6b, 14b, 15, 16a, 18; 16:18; 17:1, 8a, 9, 18; 18:24; 19:18, 19, 21; 20:6
1b. <*Loc.* ΘL [§5.3a]> 1/Thm 2/Loc: on, at
—N N+dat: Rev 4:9; 5:13c; 7:10; 9:14; 19:4, 14; 21:5, 12
1c. <*Loc.* ΘL [§5.3a]> 1/Thm 2/Loc: on, over
—N N+acc: Rev 2:17; 3:20; 4:2, 4a, 4b, 9; 5:1a; 6:2, 4, 5, 8; 7:1a, 15b; 11:16a; 13:1b, 7; 14:1a, 14a, 16b; 15:2; 16:2, 9; 17:3; 19:11, 16a, 16b; 20:1, 11; 22:5, 14
2a. <*Mot.* Θ[S]G [S=Θ] G→L [§5.2b]> 1/Thm 2/Loc: [terminating] on, over, before [+an]
—N N+gen: Rev 3:10a; 7:1b, 1c, 17; 8:3a; 10:2a, 2b; 13:16a; 14:1b, 9a

2b. <*Mot.* Θ[S]G [S=Θ] G→L [§5.2b]> 1/Thm 2/Loc: [terminating] on, over
—N N+acc: Rev 2:17; 7:1d; 11:11a; 12:18; 13:16b; 14:9b, 16b; 18:17; 20:4a, 4b, 4c; 22:18a, 18b
2c. <*Mot.* Θ[S]G [S=Θ] [§5.2a]> 1/Thm 2/Goa: onto
—N N+acc: Rev 1:17; 2:24; 3:3, 12; 6:16a; 7:11, 16, 17; 8:3b, 10a, 10b; 11:11b, 16b; 14:16b; 16:8, 10, 12, 14, 17, 21; 17:5, 8b; 18:19; 20:9; 21:10
3a. <*Exp.* EC [§5.5a]> 1/Exp 2/Con: over
—N N+acc: Rev 1:7; 18:9, 11
3b. <*Exp.* EC C→T [§5.5c]> 1/Exp 2/Top: at, about, concerning
—N N+dat: Rev 10:11; 11:10b; 12:17; 18:20; 22:16
3c. <*Exp.* CE [§5.5h]> 1/Con 2/Exp: to
—N N+acc: Rev 14:6a, 6c
4. <*Mea.* PMea [§6.9c]> 1/Pat 2/Mea: at
—N N+gen: Rev 21:16
ἐπί + [εἰμί] (<ἐπί), 1a. <*Loc.* ΘL [§5.3a]> 1/Thm 2/Loc: be on
—N N+gen: Rev [4:4c]; [5:13a], [13b]; [10:1a]; [11:8]; [12:1b]; [21:14b]; [22:4]
1c. <*Loc.* ΘL [§5.3a]> (1/Thm) 2/Loc: be over, be on
—N N+acc: Rev [12:3b]; [19:12b]
—INC N+acc: Rev [9:7b (Cmp: A/ὡς N+1)]
ἐπιγεγραμμένος (<ἐπιγράφω), 2. <*Eff.* PA [§6.3c]> 1/Pat (2/Agt): written, inscribed
—N INC: Rev 21:12
ἐπιγράφω (>ἐπιγεγραμμένος), 1. <*Eff.* AP [§6.3a]> 1/Agt 2/Pat: write, inscribe.
ἐπιθυμέω, 1. <*Exp.* EC [§5.5a]> 1/Exp 2/Con: desire
—N (to) V-i1: Rev 9:6
ἐπιθυμία, 1. <*Exp.* EC [§5.5a]> 1/Exp [2/Con]: desire
—(of) N+gen DNC: Rev 18:14
ἐπιπίπτω, 1. <*Mot.* Θ[S]G [S=Θ] [§5.2a]> 1/Thm 2/Goa: fall
—N P/ἐπί [+acc]: Rev 11:11
ἐπιστρέφω (>ἐπιστρέψας), 1. <*Mot.* Θ[S]G [S=Θ] [§5.2a]> 1/Thm [2/Goa]: turn
—N DNC: Rev 1:12a (Pur: V-i1)
ἐπιστρέψας (<ἐπιστρέφω), 1. <*Mot.* Θ[S]G [S=Θ] [§5.2a]> 1/Thm [2/Goa]: turning
—N DNC: Rev 1:12b
ἐπιτίθημι, 1. <*Tra.* AΘ[S]G [S=A] G→L +imp. [§5.1b]> 1/Agt (2/Thm) 3/Loc: put, add
—N N+acc (on) P/ἐπί [+acc]: Rev 22:18b (Cnd: V+ἐάν)
—N INC (on) P/ἐπί [+acc]: Rev 22:18a
ἑπτά, 1. <*Qual.* P [§6.10a]> 1/Pat: seven
—N: Rev 1:4a, 4b, 11, 12, 16, 20a, 20b, 20c, 20d, 20e, 20f; 2:1a, 1b; 3:1a, 1b; 4:5a, 5b; 5:1, 5, 6a, 6b, 6c; 6:1; 8:2a, 8:2b, 6a, 6b; 10:3, 4a, 4b; 11:13; 12:3a, 3b; 13:1; 15:1a, 1b, 6a, 6b, 7a, 7b, 8a, 8b; 16:1a, 1b; 17:1a, 1b, 3, 7, 9a, 9b, 9c, 11; 21:9a, 9b, 9c
ἐραυνάω (>ὁ ἐραυνῶν + εἰμί), 1. <*Exp.* EC [§5.5a]> 1/Exp 2/Con: search.
ὁ ἐραυνῶν + εἰμί (<ἐραυνάω), 1. <*Exp.* EC [§5.5a]> 1/Exp 2/Con: be the one searching
—N N+acc: Rev 2:23
ἐργάζομαι, 1. <*Eff.* AP [§6.3a]> 1/Agt 2/Pat: work
—N N+acc: Rev 18:17

ἔργον, 1. <Ben. B{P} [§6.1g]> [1/Ben] {{2/Pat}}: work
—(of) N+gen {N}: Rev 2:2, 6, 19a, 19b, 22, 23, 26; 3:1, 2, 8, 15; 9:20; 14:13; 15:3; 16:11; 18:6; 20:12, 13; 22:12 [εἰμί 1]
—DNC {N}: Rev 2:5

ἔρημος, 1. <Qual. P [§6.10a]> (1/Pat): deserted
—INC: Rev 12:6 (Loc: V+ὅπου), 14; 17:3

ἐρημόω (>ἠρημωμένος), 1. <Mod. AP{R} [§6.6b]> 1/Agt 2/Pat {{3/Rst}}: make {desolated}
—N N+acc {Adj+2}: Rev 18:17 (Tem: N+dat), 19 (Tem: N+dat)

ἔρχομαι (>ἐρχόμενος, ὁ ἐρχόμενος + εἰμί), 1a. <Mot. Θ[S]G [S=Θ] [§5.2a]> 1/Thm [2/Goa]: come
—N (to) N+dat [+an]: Rev 2:5, 16 (Cnd: V+εἰ; Tem: A/ταχύ)
—N DNC: Rev 1:7 (Loc: P/μετά [+gen]); 3:11 (Tem: A/ταχύ); 5:7; 6:1, 3, 5, 7, 17; 7:13 (Sou: A/πόθεν); 8:3; 9:12 (Mea: A/ἔτι; Tem: P/μετά [+acc]); 11:14 (Tem: A/ταχύ), 18 (Pur: V+i); 14:7, 15 (Cau: V+ὅτι); 16:15 (Cmp: A/ ὡς V+), [15b]; 17:1, 10a (Tem: A/οὔπω), 10b; 18:10 (Tem: N+dat); 19:7; 21:9; 22:7 (Tem: A/ταχύ), 12 (Tem: A/ταχύ), 17a, 17b, 17c, 20a (Tem: A/ ταχύ), 20b (Voc: N+voc)

1b. <Mot. Θ[S]G [S=Θ] G→L [§5.2b]> 1/Thm 2/Loc: come
—N ([terminating] on) P/ἐπί [+gen]: Rev 3:10

ἐρχόμενος (<ἔρχομαι), 1a. <Mot. Θ[S]G [S=Θ] [§5.2a]> 1/Thm [2/Goa]: coming
—N DNC: Rev 1:4, 8; 4:8

ὁ ἐρχόμενος + εἰμί (<ἔρχομαι), 1a. <Mot. Θ[S]G [S=Θ] [§5.2a]> 1/Thm [2/Goa]: be the one coming
—N DNC: Rev 7:14 (Sou: P/ἐκ)

ἐσθίω, 1. <Eff. AP [§6.3a]> 1/Agt [2/Pat]: eat
—N N+acc: Rev 2:14, 20; 10:10; 17:16; 19:18
—N DNC: Rev 2:7 (Sou: P/ἐκ)

ἐσκοτωμένος (<σκοτόω), 1. <Mod. PA{R} [§6.6d]> 1/Pat [2/Agt] {{3/Rst}}: made {dark}, darkened
—N DNC {Adj+1}: Rev 16:10

ἑστηκώς (<ἵστημι), 4. <Loc. ΘL [§5.3a]> 1/Thm 2/Loc: standing
—N (from afar, at a distance) P/ἀπὸ μακρόθεν: Rev 18:10 (Cau: P/διά [+acc])
—N (in the middle of) P/ἐν μέσῳ: Rev 5:6

ἑστώς (<ἵστημι), 4. <Loc. ΘL [§5.3a]> 1/Thm 2/Loc: standing
—N (in/on) P/ἐν: 19:17
—N (before) P/ἐνώπιον: Rev 7:9; 11:4; 20:12
—N (on) P/ἐπί [+gen]: Rev 10:5, 8
—N (on) P/ἐπί [+acc]: Rev 7:1; 14:1; 15:2

ἑστώς + [εἰμί] (<ἵστημι), 4. <Loc. ΘL [§5.3a]> 1/Thm 2/Loc: standing
—N (on) P/ἐπί [+acc]: Rev [14:1a]
—N (with) P/μετά [+gen]: Rev [14:1b]

ἐσφαγμένος (<σφάζω), 1. <Eff. PA [§6.3c]> 1/Pat (2/Agt): slain
—N INC: Rev 5:6, 12; 6:9 (Cau: P/διά [+acc]); 13:3 (Goa: P/εἰς [-an]), 8; 18:24 (Loc: P/ἐπί [+gen])

ἐσφραγισμένος (<σφραγίζω), 1. <Eff. PA [§6.3c]> 1/Pat [2/Agt]: sealed
—N DNC: Rev 7:4a, 4b (Sou: P/ἐκ), 5a (Sou: P/ἐκ), [5b (Sou: P/ἐκ)], [5c (Sou: P/ἐκ)], [6a (Sou: P/ἐκ)], [6b (Sou: P/ἐκ)], [6c (Sou: P/ἐκ)], [7a (Sou: P/ἐκ)], [7b (Sou: P/ἐκ)], [7c (Sou: P/ἐκ)], [8a (Sou: P/ἐκ)], [8b (Sou: P/ἐκ)], 8c (Sou: P/ἐκ)

ἔσχατος (>ὁ ἔσχατος + [εἰμί]), 1. <Par. PPar [§6.7a]> [1/Pat] (2/Par): last
—N DNC: Rev 2:19; 15:1; 21:9
—DNC INC: Rev 2:8

ὁ ἔσχατος + [εἰμί], 1. <Par. PPar [§6.7a]> 1/Pat (2/Par): be the last
—N INC: Rev 1:17; [22:13]

ἑτοιμάζω (>ἡτοιμασμένος), 1. <Eff. AP [§6.3a]> 1/Agt 2/Pat: prepare
—N N+acc: Rev 8:6 (Pur: V+ἵνα); 16:12; 19:7

εὐαγγελίζω, 1a. <Cmm. ACE [§5.4a]> 1/Agt [2/Con] 3/Exp: proclaim
—N DNC (to) P/ἐπί [+acc]: Rev 14:6
1b. <Cmm. AE{C} [§5.4e]> 1/Agt 2/Exp {{3/Con}}: tell {good news}
—N N+acc {N}: Rev 10:7

εὐαγγέλιον, 1. <Cmm. BCE [§5.4f]> [1/Ben] (2/Con) [3/Exp]: gospel
—DNC INC DNC: Rev 14:6

εὐλογία, 1. <Ben. B{P}B [§6.1h]> [1/Ben] {{2/Pat}} [3/Ben]: blessing
—DNC {N} DNC: Rev 5:12, 13 [εἰμί 2]; 7:12 [εἰμί 2]

εὑρίσκω, 1. <Eff. AP [§6.3a]> 1/Agt 2/Pat: find
—N N+acc: Rev 9:6; 12:8 (Loc: P/ἐν; Tem: A/ἔτι); 14:5 (Loc: P/ἐν); 16:20; 18:14 (Tem: A/οὐκέτι), 21 (Tem: A/ἔτι), 22 (Loc: P/ἐν; Tem: A/ἔτι), 24 (Loc: P/ἐν); 20:11 (Ben: N+dat [+an]), 15
2. <Exp. ECCur [§5.5g]> 1/Exp 2/Con 3/Cur: find
—N N+acc Adj+2: Rev 2:2; 3:2; 5:4

εὐφραίνω, 1. <Exp. EC C→T [§5.5c]> 1/Exp [2/Top]: rejoice
—N (at/concerning) P/ἐπί [+dat]: Rev 18:20 (Cau: V+ὅτι; Voc: N+voc)
—N DNC: Rev 11:10 (Cau: V+ὅτι); 12:12 (Cau: P/διά [+acc]; Voc: N+voc)

εὐχαριστέω, 1. <Cmm. A{C}E [§5.4b]> 1/Agt {{2/Con}} 3/Exp: speak {thanks}
—N {N} (to) N+dat [+an]: Rev 11:17 (Cau: V+ὅτι; Voc: N+voc/nom)

εὐχαριστία, 1. <Cmm. B{C}E [§5.4g]> [1/Ben] {{2/Con}} [3/Exp]: thanksgiving
—DNC {N} DNC: Rev 4:9; 7:12 [εἰμί 2]

εὐώνυμος, 1. <Qual. P [§6.10a]> [1/Pat]: left
—DNC: Rev 10:2

ἐχθρός, 1. <Ben. B{P} [§6.1g]> 1/Ben {{2/Pat}}: enemy
—(of) N+gen {N}: Rev 11:5, 12

ἔχω (>ἔχων, ἔχων + [εἰμί]), 1a. <Ben. BP [§6.1c]> 1/Ben 2/Pat: have
—N N+acc: Rev 2:3, 10 (Tem: N+acc), 14b (Loc: A/ἐκεῖ), 15 (Cmp: A/ὁμοίως; Man: A/οὕτως; Mea: A/καί), 25, 29; 3:1b, 4 (Loc: P/ἐν), 8, 11, 17; 9:3, 4 (Loc: P/ἐπί [+gen]), 8, 9, 10, 11a (Cur: N+2; Loc: P/ἐπί [+gen]), 11b (Cur: N+2; Loc: P/ἐν); 11:6a (Pur: V+ἵνα), 6b; 12:6 (Loc: A/ὅπου; Loc: A/ἐκεῖ [red.]), 12b; [13:3 (Cmp: A/ὡς Adj+2)], 9, 11, 14; 14:11 (Cnd: V+εἰ; Tem: N+acc); 19:16 (Loc: P/ἐπί [+acc]); 20:6b; 21:23; 22:5 (Cau: V+ὅτι)

1b. <*Ben*. BP¹/P² [§6.1d]> **1/Ben 1/Pat¹/Pat²**: have
—**N N+acc/**(that) **V+ὅτι**: Rev 2:6
1c. <Ben. B[P]L [§6.1e]> **1/Ben [[2/Pat]] 3/Loc**: have [[a child]].
2a. <*Exp*. ECT [§5.5d]> **1/Exp 2/Con [3/Top]**: hold
—**N N+acc DNC**: Rev 2:24; 17:13
—**N** (that) **V+ὅτι** (against) **P/κατά [+gen]**: Rev 2:4, 20
—**N** (that) **V+ὅτι DNC**: Rev 12:12
2b. <*Exp*. EC¹/C²T [§5.5f]> **1/Exp 2/Con¹/Con² 3/Top**: hold
—**N N+acc/**(that) **V+ὅτι** (concerning/against) **P/κατά [+gen]**: Rev 2:14a
3. <*Eff*. AP [§6.3a]> **1/Agt 2/Pat**: hold, keep
—**N N+acc**: Rev 1:18; 6:9
ἔχων (<ἔχω), **1a.** <*Ben*. BP [§6.1c]> **1/Ben 2/Pat**: having
—**N N+acc**: Rev 2:7, 11, 12, 15, 17, 18; 3:1a, 6, 13, 22; 4:7, 8a; 5:6; 8:9; 9:17, 19a, [19b (Loc: P/ἐν)]; 12:3 (Loc: P/ἐπί [+acc]), 12a; 13:1-3, 17 (Cur: N+2), 18; 14:1, 6 (Pur: V-i1), [14 (Loc: P/ἐπί [+gen]; Loc: P/ἐν)], 17 (Cur: N+1; Mea: A/καί), 18a, 18b; 15:1, 6; 16:2, 9; 17:1, 3, 7, 9, 18 (Loc: P/ἐπί [+gen]); 18:1, 19 (Loc: P/ἐν); 19:12; 20:6a (Loc: P/ἐν); 21:11, 12a, 12b (Loc: P/ἐπί [+dat])
1c. <*Ben*. B[P] L [§6.1e]> **1/Ben [[2/Pat]] 3/Loc**: having [[a child]]
—**N [N]** (in) **P/ἐν**: Rev 12:2
3. <*Eff*. AP [§6.3a]> **1/Agt 2/Pat**: holding
—**N N+acc**: Rev 1:16 (Loc: P/ἐν); 3:7; 5:8; 6:2, 5 (Loc: P/ἐν); 7:2; 8:3, 6; 9:14; 10:2 (Loc: P/ἐν); 12:17; 15:2; 17:4 (Loc; P/ἐν; Loc: P/ἐπί [+acc]); 19:10; 20:1 (Loc: P/ἐπί [+acc]); 21:9, 15 (Pur: V+ἵνα)
ἔχων + [εἰμί] (<ἔχω), **1a.** <*Ben*. BP [§6.1c]> **1/Ben 2/Pat**: be having
—**N N+acc**: Rev [4:8b (Mea: P/κατά [+acc]; Mea: A/ἀνά)]; [21:14a]
3. <*Eff*. AP [§6.3a]> **1/Agt 2/Pat**: be holding
—**N N+acc**: Rev [6:2b], [5b (Loc: P/ἐν)]
ζάω (>ζῶν, ζῶν + εἰμί, ὁ ζῶν + εἰμί), **1.** <*Qual*. P [§6.10a]> **1/Pat**: be alive, live
—**N**: Rev 2:8; 3:1; 13:14; 20:4 (Tem: N+acc), 5 (Tem: V+ἄχρι)
ζεστός (>ζεστός + εἰμί), **1.** <*Qual*. P [§6.10a]> **1/Pat**: hot.
ζεστός + εἰμί (<ζεστός), **1.** <*Qual*. P [§6.10a]> **1/Pat**: be hot
—**N**: Rev 3:15a, 15b, 16
ζηλεύω, **1.** <*Exp*. EC [§5.5a]> **1/Exp [2/Con]**: be zealous
—**N DNC**: Rev 3:19 (Res: A/οὖν)
ζητέω, **1.** <*Mot*. Θ[S]G [S=Θ] [§5.2a]> **1/Thm 2/Goa**: seek
—**N N+acc**: Rev 9:6 (Tem: P/ἐν)
ζυγός, **1.** <*Ben*. B{P} [§6.1g]> **[1/Ben] {{2/Pat}}**: scale
—**DNC {N}**: Rev 6:5
ζωή, **1.** <*Ben*. B{P} [§6.1g]> **(1/Ben) {{2/Pat}}**: life
—**DNC {N}**: Rev 2:10; 3:5; 11:11 (Sou: P/ἐκ); 13:8; 17:8; 20:12, 15; 21:6, 27; 22:1, 2, 14, 17, 19
—**INC {N}**: Rev 2:7; 7:17; 16:3

ζῶν (<ζάω), 1. <Qual. P [§6.10a]> [1/Pat]: living
—N: Rev 7:2; 15:7 (Tem: P/εἰς)
—DNC: Rev 4:9 (Tem: P/εἰς), 10 (Tem: P/εἰς); 10:6 (Tem: P/εἰς); 19:20
ζῶν + εἰμί (<ζάω), 1. <Qual. P [§6.10a]> 1/Pat: be living
—N: Rev 1:17-18a
ὁ ζῶν + εἰμί (<ζάω), 1. <Qual. P [§6.10a]> 1/Pat: be the one living
—N: Rev 1:18b (Tem: P/εἰς)
ζώνη, 1. <Ben. B{P} [§6.1g]> [1/Ben] {{2/Pat}}: belt
—DNC {N}: Rev 1:13; 15:6
ἤ, 1a. <Coor. — — [§6.11a]> 1/— 2/—: or
—Complex Adj Complex Adj [cf. §2.7b]: Rev 3:15
 1b. <Coor. --- ---- [§6.11b]> 1/--- 2/----: or
—N N: Rev 13:17b
—(to) V-i1 (to) V-i1: Rev 13:17a
—(on) P/ἐπί [+gen] (on) P/ἐπί [+acc]: Rev 13:16; 14:9
ἠγαπημένος (<ἀγαπάω), 1. <Exp. CE [§5.5h]> 1/Con [2/Exp]: loved
—N DNC: Rev 20:9
ἠγορασμένος (<ἀγοράζω), 1. <Sep. PAS [§6.8b]> 1/Pat [2/Agt] 3/Sou: bought
—N DNC (from) P/ἀπό: Rev 14:3
ἥκω, 1. <Mot. Θ[S]G [S=Θ] [§5.2a]> 1/Thm [2/Goa]: have come
—N (onto) P/ἐπί [+acc]: Rev 3:3b
—N DNC: Rev 2:25; 3:3a (Cmp: V+ὡς; Cnd: V+ἐάν; Res: A/οὖν), 9; 15:4; 18:8
    (Cau: P/διά [+acc]; Tem: P/ἐν)
ἡμέρα, 1. <Spec. — [§6.12]> 0/—: day
—Rev 1:10; 2:10, 13 (Ben: N+gen [ind. N+nom]); 4:8; 6:17 (Ben: N+gen); 7:15;
    8:12; 9:6, 15; 10:7 (Ben: N+gen); 11:3, 6 (Ben: N+gen), 9, 11; 12:6, 10;
    14:11; 16:14 (Ben: N+gen); 18:8; 20:10; 21:25
ἥμισυς, 1. <Qual. P [§6.10a]> 1/Pat: half
—N: Rev 11:9, 11
 2. <Par. PPar [§6.7a]> [1/Pat] 2/Par: one half
—DNC (of) N+gen: Rev 12:14
ἠνεῳγμένος (<ἀνοίγω), 1. <Eff. PA [§6.3c]> 1/Pat [2/Agt]: opened
—N DNC: Rev 3:8; 4:1; 10:2, 8 (Loc: P/ἐν); 19:11
ἠνεῳγμένος + [εἰμί] (<ἀνοίγω), 1. <Eff. PA [§6.3c]> 1/Pat (2/Agt): be opened
—N INC: Rev [4:1a (Loc: P/ἐν)], [8]
ἠρημωμένος (<ἐρημόω), 1. <Mod. PA{R} [§6.6d]> 1/Pat [2/Agt] {{3/Rst}}: made
    {desolated}
—N DNC {Adj+1}: Rev 17:16
ἡτοιμασμένος (<ἑτοιμάζω), 1. <Eff. PA [§6.3c]> 1/Pat (2/Agt): prepared
—N (by) P/ἀπό: Rev 12:6 (Pur: V+ἵνα)
—N INC: Rev 9:7 (Pur: P/εἰς), 15 (Pur: P/εἰς); 21:2 (Cmp: A/ὡς N+1)
θάνατος (>θάνατος + εἰμί), 1. <Ben. B{P} [§6.1g]> (1/Ben) {{2/Pat}}: death
—(of) N+gen {N}: Rev 13:3b, 12
—DNC {N}: Rev 2:10, 23; 9:6a, 6b; 12:11; 13:3a; 18:8
—INC {N}: Rev 2:11; 6:8b; 20:6, 14b; 21:4 [εἰμί 1], 8

θάνατος + εἰμί (<θάνατος), 1. <Ben. PB [§6.1f]> 1/Pat (2/Ben): be death
—N INC: Rev 20:14; 21:18
θαῦμα, 1. <Exp. EC C→T [§5.5c]> [1/Exp] [2/Top]: wonder
—DNC DNC: Rev 17:6 [εἰμί 1]
θαυμάζω, 1. <Exp. EC C→T [§5.5c]> 1/Exp [2/Top]: be amazed
—N DNC: Rev 13:3 (Loc: P/ἐνώπιον); 17:6, 7 (Cau: P/διά [+acc]), 8 (Cau: V+ἵνα)
θαυμαστός (>θαυμαστός + [εἰμί]), 1. <Exp. CE [§5.5h]> 1/Con [2/Exp]: marvelous
—N DNC: Rev 15:1
θαυμαστός + [εἰμί] (<θαυμαστός), 1. <Exp. CE [§5.5h]> 1/Con [2/Exp]: be marvelous
—N DNC: Rev [15:3a (Voc: N+voc)]
θειώδης, 1. <Qual. P [§6.10a]> 1/Pat: yellow
—N: Rev 9:17
θέλω (>θέλων), 1. <Exp. EC [§5.5a]> 1/Exp [2/Con]: want
—N (to) V-i1: Rev 2:21; 11:5a, 5b
—N DNC: Rev 11:6
θέλων (<θέλω), 1. <Exp. EC [§5.5a]> 1/Exp [2/Con]: wanting
—N DNC: Rev 22:17
θεμέλιος, 1. <Ben. B{P}B [§6.1h]> (1/Ben) {{2/Pat}}) [3/Ben]: foundation
—INC {N} (of) N+gen: Rev 21:19a
—INC {N} DNC: Rev 21:14, 19b, [19c], [19d], [19e], [20a], [20b], [20c], [20d], [20e], [20f], [20g], [20h]
θεός (>θεός + εἰμί), 1. <Ben. B{P} [§6.1g]> [1/Ben] {{2/Pat}}: God
—(of) N+gen {N}: Rev 1:6; 3:2, 12a, 12b, 12c, 12d; 4:11; 5:10; 7:3, 10, 12; 11:13; 12:10a, 10b; 16:11; 19:1, 5, 6; 21:3c; 22:6
—DNC {N}: Rev 1:1, 2, 8, 9; 2:7, 18; 3:1, 14; 4:5, 8; 5:6, 9; 6:9; 7:2, 11, 15, 17; 8:2, 4; 9:4, 13; 10:7; 11:1, 11, 16a, 16b, 17, 19; 12:5, 6, 17; 13:6; 14:4, 7, 10, 12, 19; 15:1, 2, 3a, 3b, 7, 8; 16:1, 7, 9, 14, 19, 21; 17:17a, 17b; 18:5, 8, 20; 19:4, 9, 10, 13, 15, 17; 20:4, 6; 21:2, 3a, 3b, 10, 11, 22, 23; 22:1, 3, 5, 9, 18, 19
θεός + εἰμί (<θεός), 1. <Ben. PB [§6.1f]> 1/Pat 2/Ben: be God
—N (of/for) N+dat [+an]: Rev 21:7a
θεραπεία, 1. <Ben. B{P}B [§6.1h]> [1/Ben] {{2/Pat}} 3/Ben: healing
—DNC {N} (of) N+gen: Rev 22:2
θεραπεύω, 1. <Eff. AP [§6.3a]> 1/Agt 2/Pat: heal
—N N+acc: Rev 13:3, 12
θερίζω, 1. <Eff. AP [§6.3a]> 1/Agt [2/Pat]: gather
—N N+acc: Rev 14:16
—N DNC: Rev 14:15a (Cau: V+ὅτι), 15b
θερισμός, 1. <Ben. B{P}B [§6.1h]> [1/Ben] {{2/Pat}} 3/Ben: harvest
—DNC {N} (of) N+gen: Rev 14:15
θεωρέω (>θεωρῶν), 1. <Exp. EC [§5.5a]> 1/Exp 2/Con: see
—N N+acc: Rev 11:12
θεωρῶν (<θεωρέω), 1. <Exp. EC [§5.5a]> 1/Exp 2/Con: seeing
—N N+acc: Rev 11:11

θηρίον, 1. <Spec. — [§6.12]> 0/—: beast
—Rev 6:8 (Ben: N+gen); 11:7; 13:1, 2, 3, 4a, 4b, 4c, 11, 12a, 12b, 14a, 14b, 15a, 15b, 15c, 17, 18; 14:9, 11; 15:2; 16:2, 10, 13; 17:3, 7, 8a, 8b, 11, 12, 13, 16, 17; 18:2; 19:19, 20a, 20b; 20:4, 10

θλῖψις, 1. <Ben. B{P}B [§6.1h]> (1/Ben) {{2/Pat}} [3/Ben]: oppression
—DNC {N} DNC: Rev 2:10, 22
—INC {N} (of) N+gen: Rev 2:9
—INC {N} DNC: Rev 1:9; 7:14

θρίξ, 1. <Ben. B{P} [§6.1g]> [1/Ben] {{2/Pat}}: hair
—(of) N+gen {N}: Rev 1:14; 9:8b
—DNC {N}: Rev 9:8a (Cmp: A/ὡς N+2)

θρόνος, 1. <Ben. B{P} [§6.1g]> [1/Ben] {{2/Pat}}: throne
—(of) N+gen {N}: Rev 1:4; 2:13; 3:21a, 21b; 7:15a; 11:16; 12:5; 13:2; 16:10; 22:1, 3
—DNC {N}: Rev 4:2a, 2b, 3, 4a, 4b, 4c, 5a, 5b, 6a, 6b, 6c, 9, 10a, 10b; 5:1, 6, 7, 11, 13; 6:16; 7:9, 10, 11a, 11b, 15b, 17; 8:3; 14:3; 16:17; 19:4, 5; 20:4, 11, 12; 21:3, 5

θύϊνος, 1. <Qual. P [§6.10a]> 1/Pat: citron
—N: Rev 18:12

θυμός, 1. <Exp. EC [§5.5a]> [1/Exp] [2/Con]: passion
—(of) N+gen DNC: Rev 14:10, 19; 15:1, 7; 16:1, 19; 19:15
—DNC (for) N+gen: Rev 14:8; 18:3
—DNC DNC: Rev 12:12

θύρα, 1. <Ben. B{P} [§6.1g]> [1/Ben] {{2/Pat}}: door
—DNC {N}: Rev 3:8, 20a, 20b; 4:1

θυσιαστήριον, 1. <Ben. B{P}B [§6.1h]> [1/Ben] {{2/Pat}} [3/Ben]: altar
—DNC {N} DNC: Rev 6:9; 8:3a, 3b (Loc: P/ἐνώπιον), 5; 9:13 (Loc: P/ἐνώπιον); 11:1; 14:18; 16:7

θώραξ, 1. <Ben. B{P} [§6.1g]> (1/Ben) {{2/Pat}}: breastplate
—DNC {N}: Rev 9:9a (Cmp: A/ὡς N+2), 17
—INC {N}: Rev 9:9b

ἴασπις + [εἰμί], 1. <Qual. P [§6.10a]> 1/Pat: be jasper
—N: Rev [21:18a], [19b]

ἰδού, 1. <Qual. O [§6.10b]> 1/Occ: look!
—V+: Rev 1:7, 18; 2:10, 22; 3:8, 9a, 9b, 20; 4:1, 2; 5:5; 6:2 [εἰμί 1], 5 [εἰμί 1], 8 [εἰμί 1]; 7:9 [εἰμί 1]; 9:12; 11:14; 12:3 [εἰμί 1]; 14:1 [εἰμί 1], 14 [εἰμί 1]; 16:15; 19:11 [εἰμί 1]; 21:3, 5; 22:7, 12

ἰδών (<ὁράω), 1. <Exp. EC [§5.5a]> 1/Exp 2/Con: seeing
—N N+acc: Rev 17:6b

ἱερεύς (>ἱερεύς + εἰμί), 1. <Ben. B{P} [§6.1g]> [1/Ben] {{2/Pat}}: priest
—DNC {N}: Rev 1:6; 5:10

ἱερεύς + εἰμί (<ἱερεύς), 1. <Ben. PB [§6.1f]> 1/Pat 2/Ben: be a priest
—N (of) N+gen: Rev 20:6b

ἱμάτιον, 1. <Ben. B{P} [§6.1g]> [1/Ben] {{2/Pat}}: garment
—(of) N+gen {N}: Rev 3:4; 16:15
—DNC {N}: Rev 3:5, 18; 4:4; 19:13, 16

Ἰουδαῖος (>[Ἰουδαῖος] + εἰμί), 1. <Qual. P [§6.10a]> [1/Pat]: Jewish, Judean
—DNC: Rev 2:9b, [9c]; 3:9a, [9b]
[Ἰουδαῖος] + εἰμί (<Ἰουδαῖος), 1. <Qual. P [§6.10a]> 1/Pat: be Jewish, be Judean
—N: Rev 2:9b, [9c]; 3:9a, [9b]
ἶρις, 1. <Spec. — [§6.12]> 0/—: rainbow
—Rev 4:3 (Loc: P/κυκλόθεν); 10:1
ἴσος (>ἴσος + εἰμί), 1. <Cmp. PCmp [§6.9b]> 1/Pat 2/Cmp: equal.
ἴσος + εἰμί (<ἴσος), 1. <Cmp. PCmp [§6.9b]> 1/Pat [2/Cmp]: be equal
—N DNC: Rev 21:16b
ἵστημι (>ἑστηκώς, ἑστώς, ἑστώς + [εἰμί]), 1. <Tra. AΘ[S]G [S=A] G→L -imp. [§5.1j] ||
   Tra. A[Θ][S]G [Θ=A] [S=A] G→L pass. -imp. [§5.1k] || Mot. (A)Θ(S)G G=Θ G→L
   pass. [§5.2g]> 1/Agt 2/Thm 3/Loc: station, stand || 1/Agt [[2/Thm]] 3/Loc: station
   [[oneself]], stand [[oneself]] || 1/Thm 2/Loc: stand
   —N N+acc (on) P/ἐπί [+acc] || N (oneself) [N] (on) P/ἐπί [+acc] || N (on) P/
      ἐπί [+acc]: Rev 12:18
   —N N+acc (on) P/ἐπί [+gen] || N (oneself) [N] (on) P/ἐπί [+gen] || N (on) P/
      ἐπί [+gen]: Rev 8:3
2. <Mot. Θ[S]G [S=Θ] G→L [§5.2b]> 1/Thm 2/Loc: stand
   —N (on) P/ἐπί [+acc]: Rev 11:11
3. <Mot. (A)Θ(S)[G] [G=Θ] [G→L] pass. [§5.2h]> 1/Thm [[2/Loc]]: stand
   —N [N]: Rev 6:17
4. <Loc. ΘL [§5.3a]> 1/Thm 2/Loc: stand
   —N (at a distance) P/ἀπὸ μακρόθεν: Rev 18:15 (Cau: P/διά [+acc]), 17
   —N (on) P/ἐνώπιον: Rev 8:2; 12:4 (Pur: V+ἵνα)
   —N (on) P/ἐπί [+acc]: Rev 3:20
   —N (around/in the circle of) P/κύκλῳ: Rev 7:11
ἰσχυρός (>ἰσχυρός + [εἰμί]), 1. <Qual. P [§6.10a]> (1/Pat): strong
   —N: Rev 5:2; 10:1; 18:2, 10, 21; 19:6
   —INC: Rev 6:15; 19:18
ἰσχυρός + [εἰμί] (<ἰσχυρός), 1. <Qual. P [§6.10a]> 1/Pat: be strong
   —N: Rev [18:8]
ἰσχύς, 1. <Ben. B{P} [§6.1g]> [1/Ben] {{2/Pat}}: strength
   —DNC {N}: Rev 5:12; 7:12 [εἰμί 2]
ἰσχύω, 1. <Qual. P [§6.10a]> 1/Pat: be strong
   —N: Rev 12:8
καθαρός, 1. <Qual. P [§6.10a]> (1/Pat): pure, clean
   —N: Rev 15:6; 21:18a, 18b, 21
   —INC: Rev 19:8, 14
κάθημαι (>καθήμενος, καθήμενος + [εἰμί]), 1. <Loc. ΘL [§5.3a]> 1/Thm [2/Loc]: lie, sit
   —N (on/over) P/ἐπί [+gen]: Rev 17:9
   —N (where) A/οὗ: Rev 17:15
   —N DNC: Rev 18:7 (Cur: N+1)
καθήμενος (<κάθημαι), 1. <Loc. ΘL [§5.3a]> [1/Thm] [2/Loc]: lying, sitting
   —N (on) P/ἐπί [+gen]: Rev 17:1
   —N (on) P/ἐπί [+dat]: Rev 7:10; 19:4

—N (on) P/ἐπί [+acc]: Rev 11:16 (Loc: P/ἐνώπιον); 17:3
—N DNC: Rev 4:3, 4
—DNC (upon) P/ἐπάνω: Rev 6:8
—DNC (on) P/ἐπί [+gen]: Rev 4:10; 5:1, 7; 6:16; 7:15; 9:17; 14:6, 15, 16; 19:18, 19, 21
—DNC (on) P/ἐπί [+dat]: Rev 4:9; 5:13; 7:10; 21:5
—DNC (on) P/ἐπί [+acc]: Rev 4:2; 6:2, 4, 5; 14:14; 19:11; 20:11
καθήμενος + [εἰμί] (<κάθημαι), 1. <Loc. ΘL [§5.3a]> 1/Thm [2/Loc]: be sitting
—N (on) P/ἐπί [+acc]: Rev [4:2]
—N DNC: Rev [4:3 (Cmp: V+ὅμοιος)]; [14:14 (Cmp: V+ὅμοιος)]
καθίζω, 1. <Mot. Θ[S]G [S=Θ] G→L [§5.2b]> 1/Thm 2/Loc: sit down
—N (on) P/ἐπί [+acc]: Rev 20:4
—N (with/in the company of) P/μετά [+gen]: Rev 3:21a (Cmp: V+ὡς; Loc: P/ἐν), 21b (Loc: P/ἐν)
καί, 1a. <Coor. —— [§6.11a]> 1/— 2/—: and
—V+ V+: Rev 1:1, 4a, 6a, 7a, 7c, 8a, 10, 11a, 12a, 12b, 13a, 14b, 15a, 15b, 16a, 16c, 17a, 17b, 17c, 18a, 18b, 18d, 19a, 19b; 2:2d, 2e, 2f, 3a, 3b, 3c, 5a, 5b, 5c, 8a, 8c, 9c, 10a, 10b, 12, 13a, 13b, 14, 16, 17a, 18a, 18b, 19e, 20a, 20b, 21a, 21b, 23a, 23b, 23d, 26a, 27; 3:1a, 1c, 2, 3a, 3b, 3c, 3d, 4, 5a, 5b, 7a, 8a, 8b, 9a, 9b, 12a, 12b, 14a, 16, 17a, 17b, 17c, 18b, 19a, 19b, 20a, 20b, 20d, 20e, 21b; 4:1a, 1c, 2a, 3a, 3c, 4a, 4b, 4c, 5a, 5d, 6a, 6b, 7a, 7b, 7c, 7d, 8a, 8c, 9a, 10a, 10b, 11d, 11e; 5:1a, 2, 3, 4, 5a, 6a, 7a, 7b, 8a, 9a, 9c, 10a, 10c, 11a, 11b, 11e, 11f, 13a, 14a, 14b, 14c; 6:1a, 1b, 2a, 2b, 2c, 2d, 2e, 3, 4a, 4b, 4d, 5a, 5b, 5c, 5d, 6a, 6b, 6c, 7, 8a, 8b, 8c, 8d, 9a, 10a, 10c, 11a, 11b, 12a, 12b, 12c, 12d, 13, 14a, 14b, 15a, 16a, 16c, 17; 7:2a, 2b, 4, 9a, 9b, 9f, 10a, 11a, 11d, 13a, 13b, 14a, 14b, 14c, 14d, 15a, 15c, 17a, 17b; 8:1, 2a, 2b, 3a, 3b, 3c, 4, 5a, 5b, 5c, 5d, 6, 7a, 7b, 7d, 7e, 7f, 7g, 8a, 8b, 8c, 9a, 9b, 10a, 10b, 10c, 11a, 11b, 11c, 12a, 12b, 12e, 12f, 13a, 13b; 9:1a, 1b, 1c, 2a, 2b, 2c, 3a, 3b, 4, 5a, 5b, 6a, 6b, 6c, 6d, 7a, 7b, 7c, 8a, 8b, 9a, 9b, 10a, 10c, 11, 13a, 13b, 15a, 16, 17a, 17e, 17f, 20a, 21; 10:1a, 1b, 1c, 1d, 2a, 2b, 3a, 3b, 4a, 4b, 4c, 5a, 6a, 8a, 9a, 9b, 9c, 9d, 9e, 10a, 10b, 10c, 10d, 11a; 11:1a, 1b, 2a, 2b, 2c, 3a, 3b, 5a, 5b, 5c, 6a, 7a, 7b, 7c, 8a, 9a, 9f, 10a, 10b, 10c, 11a, 11c, 11d, 12a, 12b, 12c, 13a, 13b, 13c, 13d, 13e, 15a, 15b, 15d, 16a, 16b, 17b, 18a, 18b, 18c, 19a, 19b, 19c; 12:1a, 1b, 1c, 2a, 2b, 3a, 3b, 4a, 4b, 4c, 5a, 5b, 6, 7a, 7c, 8, 9a, 9c, 10a, 11a, 11c, 13, 14a, 15, 16a, 16b, 16c, 17a, 17b, 18; 13:1a, 2a, 2b, 2c, 2d, 3b, 3c, 4a, 4b, 4c, 5a, 5c, 6a, 7a, 7c, 8, 11a, 11b, 11c, 12a, 12b, 13a, 14a, 14b, 15a, 15c, 16a, 17; 14:1a, 1b, 2a, 3a, 3d, 5, 6a, 7a, 7b, 8, 9a, 9c, 10b, 11a, 11b, 13, 14a, 14b, 14c, 15a, 15b, 16a, 16b, 17a, 18a, 18b, 18c, 19a, 19b, 19c, 20a, 20b; 15:2a, 3a, 4a, 4b, 5a, 5b, 6a, 7, 8a, 8c; 16:1a, 1b, 2a, 2b, 2c, 3a, 3b, 3c, 4a, 4c, 5a, 6b, 7a, 8a, 8b, 9a, 9b, 9c, 10a, 10b, 10c, 11a, 11c, 12a, 12b, 13a, 15b, 16, 17a, 17b, 18a, 19a, 19b, 19c, 20a, 20b, 21a, 21b; 17:1a, 1b, 2a, 2b, 3a, 3b, 4a, 6a, 6c, 7a, 8a, 8b, 8c, 8d, 8e, 8f, 8g, 9, 10, 11a, 11b, 11c, 11d, 11e, 12, 13a, 14a, 14c, 15a, 15b, 15c, 15d, 16a, 16c, 16e, 16f, 18; 18:1, 2a, 2b, 3a, 3b, 4a, 5, 6b, 7a, 8c, 9a, 9b, 11a, 11b, 14a, 14b, 14d, 17a, 18, 19a, 19b, 21a, 21b, 21c, 22a, 22e,

22f, 23a, 23b, 24a; 19:2a, 2b, 3a, 3b, 4a, 4c, 5a, 6a, 7a, 7b, 7c, 8, 9a, 9b, 10a, 10b, 11a, 11b, 11e, 11f, 12, 13b, 14, 15a, 15b, 15c, 16a, 17a, 17b, 19a, 20a, 21a, 21b; 20:1a, 2a, 2c, 3a, 3b, 3c, 4a, 4b, 4c, 4g, 4i, 4j, 6c, 7, 8a, 9a, 9b, 9d, 9e, 10a, 10e, 11a, 11d, 12a, 12c, 12d, 12e, 13a, 13b, 13d, 14a, 15; 21:1a, 1c, 1d, 2, 3a, 3b, 3c, 3d, 4a, 4b, 5a, 6a, 7a, 7b, 9a, 9b, 10a, 10c, 14a, 15a, 16a, 16b, 16d, 17, 18a, 18b, 21a, 21b, 22a, 23a, 23b, 24a, 24b, 25, 26a, 27a; 22:1a, 2c, 3a, 3b, 3d, 4a, 4b, 5a, 5b, 5d, 6a, 6c, 7, 8a, 8c, 8d, 9a, 10, 11a, 11b, 11c, 11d, 12, 14, 17a, 17c, 17d, 19a

—**Complex Part Complex Part** [cf. §2.7b]: Rev 1:13b; 3:7b, 7c, 7d; 10:8b; 12:2c, 17c; 15:6b; 18:9c, 15, 16c, 19c; 19:13; 22:8b

—**Complex Adj Complex Part** [cf. §2.7b]: Rev 17:4c; 18:2f

—**Complex Adj Complex Adj** [cf. §2.7b]: Rev 3:14b, 17d, 17e, 17f, 17g; 6:10b; 9:17c, 17d, 20c, 20d, 20e, 20f; 11:2d, 9e, 11b; 12:5d; 15:1b, 3c, 3d; 16:2d, 7b; 17:4b, 14d, 14e, 16d; 19:18h; 20:6a; 21:5b, 10b, 12a; 22:6b

1b. (*Coor.* --- --- [§6.11b]) **1/--- 2/---**: and

—**N N**: Rev 1:2, 3a, 3b, 4b, 4c, 5b, 5c, 6b, 6c, 8b, 8c, 9a, 9b, 9c, 9d, 14a, 16b, 18e, 20; 2:2a, 2b, 8b, 9a, 9b, 17b, 19a, 19b, 19c, 19d, 20c, 22, 23c, 26b; 3:1b, 12c, 12d, 18a, 18c; 4:1b, 2b, 3b, 5b, 5c, 8d, 8e, 8f, 9b, 9c, 11a, 11b, 11c; 5:5b, 6b, 6d, 8b, 8c, 9d, 9e, 9f, 10b, 11c, 11d, 12a, 12b, 12c, 12d, 12e, 12f, 13e, 13f, 13g, 13h, 13i; 6:6d, 11d, 14c, 15b, 15c, 15d, 15e, 15f, 15g, 16b; 7:2c, 9b, 9c, 9d, 10b, 11b, 11c, 12a, 12b, 12c, 12d, 12e, 12f, 15b; 8:5e, 5f, 5g, 7c, 12c, 12d; 9:2d, 10b, 15b, 15c, 15d, 17b, 17g, 17h, 18a, 18b, 19b, 20b; 10:6b, 6c, 6d, 6e, 6f, 11b, 11c, 11d; 11:1c, 1d, 4, 8b, 9b, 9c, 9d, 15c, 17a, 18e, 18f, 18g, 18h, 19d, 19e, 19f, 19g; 12:3c, 3d, 3e, 7b, 7d, 9b, 10b, 10c, 10d, 10e, 12a, 12b, 14b, 14c; 13:1b, 1c, 1d, 2e, 2f, 3a, 5b, 6b, 7d, 7e, 7f, 10, 12c, 16b, 16c, 16d, 16e, 16f; 14:1c, 1d, 3c, 4, 6c, 6d, 6e, 7c, 7d, 7e, 9b, 10c, 11c, 11d, 12; 15:2b, 3b; 16:2e, 4b, 5b, 6a, 15a, 18b, 18c, 18d; 17:3c, 4d, 4e, 5a, 5b, 7b, 7c, 13b, 14b, 16b; 18:2c, 2d, 2e, 7b, 7c, 7d, 8a, 8b, 12a, 12b, 12c, 12d, 12e, 12f, 12g, 12h, 12i, 12j, 12k, 12m, 12n, 13a, 13b, 13c, 13d, 13e, 13f, 13g, 13h, 13i, 13j, 13k, 13m, 13n, 13o, 13p, 14c, 16a, 16b, 16d, 16e, 17b, 17c, 17d, 20a, 20b, 20c, 22b, 22c, 22d, 23c, 24b, 24c; 19:1a, 1b, 4b, 5b, 5c, 10c, 11c, 16c, 18a, 18b, 18c, 18d, 18e, 18g, 19b, 19c, 20b, 20c; 20:1b, 2b, 4d, 4f, 6b, 8b, 9c, 10b, 10d, 10f, 11b, 11c, 12b, 13c, 14b; 21:1b, 6b, 6c, 8a, 8b, 8c, 8d, 8e, 8f, 8g, 8h, 12b, 12c, 13a, 13b, 13c, 14b, 15b, 15c, 16e, 16f, 22b, 26b, 27b, 27c; 22:1b, 2a, 3c, 5c, 9b, 9c, 13a, 13b, 13c, 15a, 15b, 15c, 15d, 15e, 15f, 16, 16b, 17b

—**N** (if) **V+εἰ**: Rev 14:11e

—**N** (that) **V+ὅτι**: Rev 2:2c

—(that) **V+ἵνα** (that) **V+ἵνα**: Rev 13:1a

—(to) **V-i1** (that) **V+ἵνα**: Rev 6:4c

—(to) **V-i1** (to) **V-i1**: Rev 5:9b; 11:6b, 18d, 18h; 13:7b

—(to) **V-i3** (to) **V-i3**: Rev 17:17a, 17b; 19:11d

—**Adj+1** (so that) **V+ἵνα**: Rev 6:2f

—(from) **P/ἀπό** (from) **P/ἀπό**: Rev 1:4d, 5a; 6:16c

—(from/of) **P/ἀπό** (from/of) **P/ἐκ**: Rev 22:19b

—(because of) P/διά [+acc] (because of) P/διά [+acc]: Rev 6:9b; 12:11b; 20:4e
—(to) P/εἰς (to) P/εἰς: Rev 1:11b, 11c, 11d, 11e, 11f, 11g; 6:15h
—(from/of) P/ἐκ (from/of) P/ἐκ: Rev 15:2c, 2d, 8b; 16:11b, 13b, 13c; 17:6b; 18:4b
—(in/by) P/ἐν (in/by) P/ἐν: Rev 5:6b; 6:8e, 8f; 9:19a
—(in) P/ἐν (on) P/ἐπί [+gen]: Rev 5:13b
—(by) P/ἐν (by) P/ὑπό [+gen]: Rev 6:8g
—(in the middle of) P/ἐν μέσῳ (in the circle of) P/κύκλῳ: Rev 4:6c
—(before) P/ἐνώπιον (before) P/ἐνώπιον: Rev 3:5c; 7:9e; 14:3b, 10d
—(on) P/ἐπί [+gen] (in) P/ἐν: Rev 14:14d
—(on) P/ἐπί [+gen] (on) P/ἐπί [+gen]: Rev 10:5b, 8c
—(on) P/ἐπί [+gen] (on) P/ἐπί [+acc]: Rev 8:10d; 14:6b
—(on) P/ἐπί [+acc] (on) P/ἐπί [+acc]: Rev 19:16b; 20:4h
—(on) P/ἐπί [+gen] (under) P/ὑποκάτω: Rev 5:13c
—(with/against) P/μετά [+gen] (with/against) P/μετά [+gen]: Rev 19:19d
—(to) P/πρός [+acc] (at) P/πρός [+acc]: Rev 12:5c
—(under) P/ὑποκάτω (on) P/ἐπί [+gen]: Rev 5:13d
—(in front) A/ἔμπροσθεν (in back) A/ὄπισθεν: Rev 4:8d
—(from here) A/ἐντεῦθεν (from there) A/ἐκεῖθεν: Rev 22:2b
—(on the insider) A/ἔσωθεν (on the outside) A/ὄπισθεν: Rev 5:1b
—(around) A/κυκλόθεν (within) A/ἔσωθεν: Rev 4:8b
—(like) A/ὡς (like) A/ὡς: Rev 14:2b; 19:6b, 6c
2. <non-predicator>: also, even
Rev 1:7b; 2:6, 13c, 15, 28a, 28b; 3:10, 20c, 21a; 6:11c, 11e; 10:7; 11:8c; 13:13b, 15b; 14:10a, 17b; 18:6a; 20:10c; 21:16c

καινός, 1. <Qual. P [§6.10a]> [1/Pat]: new
—N: Rev 2:17; 3:12a, 12b; 5:9; 14:3; 21:1a, 1b, 2
—DNC: Rev 21:5

καίομαι (>καιόμενος, καιόμενος + [εἰμί]), 1. <Qual. P [§6.10a]> 1/Pat: burn
—N: Rev [8:10b]

καιόμενος (<καίομαι), 1. <Qual. P [§6.10a]> 1/Pat: burning
—N: Rev 4:5; 8:8 (Ins: N+dat), 10a (Cmp: V+ὡς); 19:20 (Ins: P/ἐν); 21:8 (Ins: N+dat)

καιόμενος + [εἰμί] (<καίομαι), 1. <Qual. P [§6.10a]> 1/Pat: be burning
—N: Rev [4:5a (Loc: P/ἐνώπιον)]

καιρός, 1. <Ben. B{P} [§6.1g]> [1/Ben] {{2/Pat}}: time
—(of) N+gen {N}: Rev 11:18 (Pur: V-i1)
—DNC {N}: Rev 1:3; 12:12, 14a, 14b, 14c; 22:10

κακός, 1. <Qual. P [§6.10a]> (1/Pat): evil, bad
—N: Rev 16:2
—INC: Rev 2:2

καλέω (>καλούμενος, κεκλημένος), 1. <Mod. APR [§6.6a]> 1/Agt 2/Pat 3/Rst: call
—N N+acc N+2: Rev 1:18 (Man: A/πνευματικῶς); 19:13
2. <Tra. ΘA(S)G G=A +imp. [§5.1h]> 1/Thm 2/Agt 3/Goa: call, summon.

9. The Case Frame Lexicon 239

καλούμενος (<καλέω), **1.** <*Mod.* PAR [§6.6c]> **1/Pat (2/Agt) 3/Rst**: being called, being summoned
—**N INC N+1**: Rev 1:9; 12:9; 16:16 (Man: A/Εβραϊστί); 19:11
καπνός, 1. <*Spec.* — [§6.12]> **0/—**: smoke
—Rev 8:4 (Ben: N+gen); 9:2a, 2b (Ben: N+gen), 2c (Ben: N+gen), 3, 17, 18; 14:11 (Ben: N+gen); 15:8 (Sou: P/ἐκ); 18:9 (Ben: N+gen), 18 (Ben: N+gen); 19:3 (Ben: N+gen)
καρδία, 1. <*Ben.* B{P} [§6.1g]> **(1/Ben) {{2/Pat}}**: heart
—(of) **N+gen {N}**: Rev 17:17; 18:7
—**INC {N}**: Rev 2:23
καρπός, 1. <*Ben.* B{P} [§6.1g]> **[1/Ben] {{2/Pat}}**: fruit
—(of) **N+gen {N}**: Rev 22:2b
—**DNC {N}**: Rev [2:7 (Sou: P/ἐκ)]; 22:2a
κατά, 1. <*Exp.* EC C→T [§5.5c]> **1/Exp 2/Top**: against
—**N N+gen**: Rev 2:4, 14, 20
2. <*Cmp.* PCmp [§6.9b]> **1/Pat 2/Cmp**: according to, in comparison to
—**N N+acc**: Rev 2:23; 18:6; 20:12, 13
3. <*Mea.* PMea [§6.9c]> **1/Pat 2/Mea**: by
—**N N+acc**: Rev 4:8; 22:2
καταβαίνω (>καταβαίνων), **1a.** <*Mot.* Θ[S]G [S=Θ] [§5.2a]> **1/Thm [2/Goal]**: come down
—**N** (onto/to) **P/εἰς [-an]**: Rev 13:13 (Loc: P/ἐνώπιον; Sou: P/ἐκ)
—**N** (onto) **P/ἐπί [+acc]**: Rev 16:21 (Cmp: Adj+1; Sou: P/ἐκ)
—**N** (to) **P/πρός [+acc, +an]**: Rev 12:12
—**N DNC**: Rev 20:9 (Sou: P/ἐκ)
1b. <*Mot.* ΘS(G) S=Θ [§5.2c]> **1/Thm 2/Sou**: come down
καταβαίνων (<καταβαίνω), **1b.** <*Mot.* ΘS(G) S=Θ [§5.2c]> **1/Thm 2/Sou**: coming down.
—**N** (out of) **P/ἐκ**: Rev 3:12 (Sou: P/ἀπό); 10:1; 18:1; 20:1; 21:2 (Sou: P/ἀπό), 10 (Sou: P/ἀπό)
καταβολή, 1. <*Ben.* B{P}B [§6.1h]> **[1/Ben] {{2/Pat}} 3/Ben**: foundation
—**DNC {N}** (of) **N+gen**: Rev 13:8; 17:8
κατακαίω, 1. <*Eff.* AP [§6.3a]> **1/Agt 2/Pat**: burn [up]
—**N N+acc**: Rev 8:7a, 7b, 7c; 17:16 (Ins: P/ἐν); 18:8 (Cau: V+ὅτι; Ins: P/ἐν)
καταπίνω, 1. <*Eff.* AP [§6.3a]> **1/Agt 2/Pat**: drink [up]
—**N N+acc**: Rev 12:16
κατασφραγίζω (>κατεσφραγισμένος), **1.** <*Eff.* AP [§6.3a]> **1/Agt 2/Pat**: seal.
κατεσθίω, 1. <*Eff.* AP [§6.3a]> **1/Agt 2/Pat**: devour
—**N N+acc**: Rev 10:9, 10; 11:5 (Cnd: V+εἰ); 12:4 (Tem: V+ὅταν); 20:9
κατεσφραγισμένος (<κατασφραγίζω), **1.** <*Eff.* PA [§6.3c]> **1/Pat (2/Agt)**: sealed
—**N INC**: Rev 5:1 (Ins: N+dat)
κατηγορέω (>κατηγορῶν), **1.** <*Ben.* A{P}B [§6.1b]> **1/Agt {{2/Pat}} 3/Ben**: make {an accusation against}.
κατηγορῶν (<κατηγορέω), **1.** <*Ben.* A{P}B [§6.1b]> **1/Agt {{2/Pat}} 3/Ben**: making {an accusation against}
—**N {N} N+acc**: Rev 12:10 (Loc: P/ἐνώπιον; Tem: N+acc)

κατήγωρ, 1. <Ben. B{P} [§6.1g]> 1/Ben {{2/Pat}}: accuser
—(of/against) N+gen {N}: Rev 12:10
κατοικέω (>κατοικῶν), 1. <Loc. ΘL [§5.3a]> 1/Thm 2/Loc: dwell
—N (where) A/ὅπου: Rev 2:13b
—N (where) A/ποῦ: Rev 2:13a (V+ὅπου)
κατοικητήριον, 1. <Ben. B{P} [§6.1g]> 1/Ben {{2/Pat}}: dwelling
—(of) N+gen {N}: Rev 18:2
κατοικῶν (<κατοικέω), 1. <Loc. ΘL [§5.3a]> 1/Thm 2/Loc: dwelling, inhabiting
—N N+acc: Rev 17:2
—N (in) P/ἐν: Rev 13:12
—N (on) P/ἐπί [+gen]: Rev 3:10; 6:10; 8:13; 11:10a, 10b; 13:8, 14a, 14b; 17:8
καυματίζω, 1. <Eff. AP [§6.3a]> 1/Agt 2/Pat: scorch
—N N+acc: Rev 16:8 (Ins: P/ἐν), 9 (Ins: N+acc)
κεῖμαι, 1. <Loc. ΘL [§5.3a]> 1/Thm (2/Loc): lie
—N (in) P/ἐν: Rev 4:2
—N INC: Rev 21:16 (Cur: Adj+1)
κεκερασμένος (<κεράννυμι), 1. <Eff. PA [§6.3c]> 1/Pat [2/Agt]: mixed
—N DNC: Rev 14:10 (Cur: Adj+1; Loc: P/ἐν)
κεκλημένος (<καλέω), 2. <Tra. ΘA(S)G G=A +imp. [§5.1h]> 1/Thm (2/Agt) 3/Goa: called, summoned
—N+acc INC (to) P/εἰς [-an]: Rev 19:9
κεκοσμημένος (<κοσμέω), 1. <Eff. PA [§6.3c]> 1/Pat (2/Agt): adorned
—N INC: Rev 21:2 (Ben: N+dat [+an]), 19
κεκοσμημένος + [εἰμί] (<κοσμέω), 1. <Eff. PA [§6.3c]> 1/Pat [2/Agt]: be adorned
—N DNC: Rev [21:19a (Ins: N+dat)]
κεκρυμμένος (<κρύπτω), 1. <Tra. ΘA[S]G [S=A] +imp. [§5.1f]> 1/Thm (2/Agt) (3/Goa): hidden
—N INC INC: Rev 2:17
κέντρον, 1. <Ben. B{P} [§6.1g]> [1/Ben] {{2/Pat}}: sting
—DNC {N}: Rev 9:10
κεραμικός, 1. <Qual. P [§6.10a]> 1/Pat: [made of] clay
—N: Rev 2:27
κεράννυμι (>κεκερασμένος), 1. <Eff. AP [§6.3a]> 1/Agt 2/Pat: mix
—N N+acc: Rev 18:6a [N+dat Patient from antecedent], 6b (Ben: N+dat [+an]; Loc: P/ἐν)
κέρας, 1. <Ben. B{P} [§6.1g]> [1/Ben] {{2/Pat}}: horn
—(of) N+gen {N}: Rev 9:13; 13:1b
—DNC {N}: Rev 5:6; 12:3; 13:1a, 11; 17:3, 7, 12, 16
κεφαλή, 1. <Ben. B{P} [§6.1g]> [1/Ben] {{2/Pat}}: head
—(of) N+gen {N}: Rev 1:14; 4:4; 9:7, 17a, 17b; 10:1; 12:1, 3b; 13:1b, 3; 14:14; 18:19; 19:12
—DNC {N}: Rev 9:19; 12:3a; 13:1a; 17:3, 7, 9
κεχρυσωμένος (<χρυσόω), 1. <Ins. PAI [§6.4d]> 1/Pat (2/Agt) 3/Ins: gilded, encrusted
—N INC (in/with) N+dat: Rev 17:4
—N INC (with) P/ἐν: Rev 18:16

κεχρυσωμένος + εἰμί, 1. <*Ins*. PAI [§6.4d]> **1/Pat (2/Agt) 3/Ins**: be gilded, be encrusted
—**N INC** (in/with) **N+dat**: Rev 17:4
κηρύσσω (>κηρύσσων), **1.** <*Cmm*. ACE [§5.4a]> **1/Agt 2/Con 3/Exp**: proclaim.
κηρύσσων (<κηρύσσω), **1.** <*Cmm*. ACE [§5.4a]> **1/Agt 2/Con (3/Exp)**: proclaiming
—**N V+quo INC**: Rev 5:2 (Ins: P/ἐν)
κιβωτός, 1. <*Ben*. B{P} [§6.1g]> **1/Ben {{2/Pat}}**: ark
—(of) **N+gen {N}**: Rev 11:19
κιθάρα, 1. <*Ben*. B{P} [§6.1g]> **[1/Ben] {{2/Pat}}**: harp
—(of) **N+gen {N}**: Rev 14:2; 15:2
—**DNC {N}**: Rev 5:8
κιθαρίζω (>κιθαρίζων), **1.** <*Eff*. A{P} [§6.3b]> **1/Agt {{2/Pat}}**: play {a harp}.
κιθαρίζων (<κιθαρίζω), **1.** <*Eff*. A{P} [§6.3b]> **1/Agt {{2/Pat}}**: playing {a harp}
—**N {N}**: Rev 14:2 (Ins: P/ἐν)
κινέω, 1. <*Tra*. AΘS(G) S=A +imp. [§5.1d]> **1/Agt 2/Thm 3/Sou**: move
—**N N+acc** (from) **P/ἐκ**: Rev 2:5 (Cnd: V+ἐάν); 6:14
κλαίω (>κλαίων), **1.** <*Qual*. P [§6.10a]> **1/Pat**: cry, weep
—**N**: Rev 5:4 (Cau: V+ὅτι; Mea: A/πολύ), 5; 18:9 (Tem: V+ὅταν), 11 (Cau: V+ὅτι)
κλαίων (<κλαίω), **1.** <*Qual*. P [§6.10a]> **1/Pat**: crying, weeping
—**N**: Rev 18:15, 19
κλείς, 1. <*Ben*. B{P}B [§6.1h]> **[1/Ben] {{2/Pat}} (3/Ben)**: key
—(of) **N+gen {N} INC**: Rev 3:7
—**DNC {N}** (of/to) **N+gen**: Rev 1:18; 9:1; 20:1
κλείω (>κλείων), **1.** <*Eff*. AP [§6.3a]> **1/Agt (2/Pat)**: close
—**N N+acc**: Rev 3:8; 11:6 (Pur: V+ἵνα); 21:25 (Tem: N+gen)
—**N DNC**: Rev 20:3 (Pur: V+ἵνα)
—**N INC**: Rev 3:7a
κλείων (<κλείω), **1.** <*Eff*. AP [§6.3a]> **1/Agt [2/Pat]**: closing
—**N DNC**: Rev 3:7b
κλέμμα, 1. <*Ben*. B{P}B [§6.1h]> **1/Ben {{2/Pat}} (3/Ben)**: theft
—(of) **N+gen {N} INC**: Rev 9:21
κληρονομέω, 1. <*Mot*. GΘS S=Θ [§5.2e]> **1/Goa 2/Thm [3/Sou]**: inherit
—**N N+acc DNC**: Rev 21:7
κλητός (>κλητός + [εἰμί]), **1.** <*Eff*. PA [§6.3c]> **1/Pat 2/Agt**: called.
κλητός + [εἰμί] (<κλητός), **1.** <*Eff*. PA [§6.3c]> **1/Pat [2/Agt]**: be called
—**N DNC**: Rev [17:14b]
κλίνη, 1. <*Ben*. B{P} [§6.1g]> **[1/Ben] {{2/Pat}}**: bed
—**DNC {N}**: Rev 2:22
κοιλία, 1. <*Ben*. B{P} [§6.1g]> **1/Ben {{2/Pat}}**: stomach
—(of) **N+gen {N}**: Rev 10:9, 10
κοινός, 1. <*Qual*. P [§6.10a]> **(1/Pat)**: common
—**INC**: Rev 21:27
κόκκινος, 1. <*Qual*. P [§6.10a]> **(1/Pat)**: scarlet
—**N**: Rev 17:3
—**INC**: Rev 17:4; 18:12, 16

κολλάω, 1. <*Eff.* AP [§6.3a]> 1/Agt 2/Pat: join
—N N+acc: Rev 18:5 (Loc: P/ἄχρι)
κολλούριον, 1. <*Ben.* B{P} [§6.1g]> [1/Ben] {{2/Pat}}: salve
—DNC {N}: Rev 3:18
κοπιάω, 1. <*Qual.* P [§6.10a]> 1/Pat: be weary
—N: Rev 2:3
κόπος, 1. <*Ben.* B{P} [§6.1g]> 1/Ben {{2/Pat}}: trouble, labor
—(of) N+gen {N}: Rev 2:2; 14:13
κόπτω, 1. <*Exp.* EC [§5.5a]> 1/Exp 2/Con: lament
—N (over) P/ἐπί [+acc]: Rev 1:7; 18:9 (Tem: V+ὅταν)
κοσμέω (>κεκοσμημένος, κεκοσμημένος + [εἰμί]), 1. <*Eff.* AP [§6.3a]> 1/Agt 2/Pat: adorn.
κράζω (>κράζων), 1. <*Cmm.* ACE [§5.4a]> 1/Agt [2/Con] [3/Exp]: call out
—N DNC (to) N+dat [+an]: Rev 7:2 (Ins: N+dat) [LM]
—N DNC DNC: Rev 6:10 (Ins: N+dat) [LM]; 7:10 (Ins: N+dat) [LM]; 18:2 (Ins: P/ἐν) [LM], 18 (Cur: Adj+1) [LM], 19 (Cur: Adj+1) [LM]; 19:17 (Ins: P/ἐν) [LM]
2. <*Eff.* A{P} [§6.3b]> 1/Agt {{2/Pat}}: make {a cry}, cry out
—N {N}: Rev 10:3a (Cmp: V+ὥσπερ; Ins: N+dat), 3b; 12:2 (Cur: Adj+1)
κράζων (<κράζω), 1. <*Cmm.* ACE [§5.4a]> 1/Agt 2/Con 3/Exp: calling out
—N V+quo (to) N+dat [+an]: Rev 14:15 (Ins: P/ἐν)
κρατέω (>κρατῶν), 1. <*Eff.* AP [§6.3a]> 1/Agt 2/Pat: hold [onto]
—N N+acc: Rev 2:13; 20:2
—N (what) V+ὅ: Rev 2:25 (Tem: V+ἄχρι οὗ); 3:11 (Pur: V+ἵνα)
κράτος, 1. <*Ben.* B{P} [§6.1g]> [1/Ben] {{2/Pat}}: strength, might
—DNC {N}: 1:6 [εἰμί 2]; 5:13 [εἰμί 2]
κρατῶν (<κρατέω), 1. <*Eff.* AP [§6.3a]> 1/Agt 2/Pat: holding [onto]
—N N+acc: Rev 2:1 (Loc: P/ἐν), 14, 15 (Man: A/ὁμοίως); 7:1 (Pur: V+ἵνα)
κραυγή, 1. <*Ben.* B{P} [§6.1g]> (1/Ben) {{2/Pat}}: shout
—INC {N}: Rev 21:4 [εἰμί 1]
κρίμα, 1. <*Exp.* ECT [§5.5d]> [1/Exp] [2/Con] [3/Top]: [rendered] judgment
—(of) N+gen (of) P/ἐκ DNC: Rev 18:20
—DNC (of) N+gen DNC: Rev 17:1
—DNC DNC DNC: Rev 20:4
κρίνας (<κρίνω), 1. <*Exp.* ECT [§5.5d]> 1/Exp 2/Con [3/Top]: judging
—N N+acc DNC: Rev 18:8
κρίνω (>κρίνας), 1. <*Exp.* ECT [§5.5d]> 1/Exp (2/Con) (3/Top): judge
—N N+acc DNC: Rev 11:18; 16:5 (Cau: V+ὅτι); 18:20; 19:2; 20:12 (Cmp: P/κατά [+acc]; Ins: P/ἐκ), 13 (Cmp: P/κατά [+acc])
—N DNC DNC: Rev 6:10 (Tem: P/ἕως; Voc: N+nom)
—N INC INC: Rev 19:11 (Ins: P/ἐν)
κρίσις, 1. <*Exp.* ECT [§5.5d]> [1/Exp] (2/Con) (3/Top): judgment
—(of) N+gen DNC INC: Rev 14:7
—(of) N+gen INC INC: Rev 16:7; 19:2
—DNC (of) N+gen INC: Rev 18:10

κρούω, 1. <*Eff*. AP [§6.3a]> 1/Agt [2/Pat]: knock
—N DNC: Rev 3:20
κρύπτω (>κεκρυμμένος), 1a. <*Tra*. AΘ[S]G [S=A] +imp. [§5.1a]> 1/Agt 2/Thm 3/Goa: hide
—N N+acc (into) P/εἰς [-an]: Rev 6:15
1b. <*Tra*. AΘS(G) S=A +imp. [§5.1d]> 1/Agt 2/Thm 3/Sou: hide
—N N+acc (from) P/ἀπό: Rev 6:16-17 (Cau: V+ὅτι)
κρυσταλλίζω (>κρυσταλλίζων), 1. <*Qual*. P [§6.10a]> 1/Pat: be clear as crystal.
κρυσταλλίζων (<κρυσταλλίζω), 1. <*Qual*. P [§6.10a]> 1/Pat: being clear as crystal
—N: Rev 21:11
κτίζω, 1. <*Eff*. AP [§6.3a]> 1/Agt 2/Pat: create
—N N+acc: Rev 4:11a, 11b; 10:6
κτίσις, 1. <*Ben*. B{P} [§6.1g]> 1/Ben {{2/Pat}}: creation
—(of) N+gen {N}: Rev 3:14
κτίσμα, 1. <*Spec*. — [§6.12]> 0/—: creature
—Rev 5:13; 8:9 (Loc: P/ἐν)
κυβερνήτης, 1. <*Ben*. B{P} [§6.1g]> [1/Ben] {{2/Pat}}: sailing-master
—DNC {N}: Rev 18:17
κυκλεύω, 1. <*Eff*. AP [§6.3a]> 1/Agt 2/Pat: encircle
—N N+acc: Rev 20:9
κυκλόθεν (>κυκλόθεν + [εἰμί]), 1. <*Loc*. ΘL [§5.3a]> 1/Thm 2/Loc: around
—N N+gen: Rev 4:3
2. <*non-predicator*>: all around
Rev 4:8
κυκλόθεν + [εἰμί] (<κυκλόθεν), 1. <*Loc*. ΘL [§5.3a]> 1/Thm 2/Loc: be around
—N N+gen: Rev [4:4]
κύκλῳ (>κύκλῳ + [εἰμί]), 1. <*Loc*. ΘL [§5.3a]> 1/Thm 2/Loc: around
—N N+gen: Rev 5:11; 7:11
κύκλῳ + [εἰμί] (<κύκλῳ), 1. <*Loc*. ΘL [§5.3a]> 1/Thm 2/Loc: be around
—N N+gen: Rev [4:6b]
κυριακός, 1. <*Qual*. P [§6.10a]> 1/Pat: dominical [Lord's]
—N: Rev 1:10
κύριος (>κύριος + εἰμί), 1. <*Ben*. B{P} [§6.1g]> [1/Ben] {{2/Pat}}: lord
—(of) N+gen {N}: Rev 4:11; 7:14; 11:4, 8, 15; 19:16a
—DNC {N}: Rev 1:8; 4:8; 11:17; 14:13; 15:3, 4; 16:7; 17:14b; 18:8; 19:6a, 16b; 21:22; 22:5, 6, 20, 21
κύριος + εἰμί (<κύριος), 1. <*Ben*. PB [§6.1f]> 1/Pat 2/Ben: be a lord
—N (of) N+gen: Rev 17:14a
λαβών (<λαμβάνω), 2. <*Mot*. (A)GΘS S=Θ [§5.2e]> [1/Goa] 2/Thm (3/Sou): receiving
—DNC N+acc INC: Rev 19:20
λαλέω (>λαλῶν), 1. <*Cmm*. ACE [§5.4a]> 1/Agt (2/Con) (3/Exp): speak, say
—N N+acc INC: Rev 10:3 (Tem: V+ὅτε), 4b
—N DNC (with) P/μετά [+gen]: Rev 1:12; 17:1 [LM]; 21:9 [LM]
—N DNC INC: Rev 10:4a
—N INC INC: Rev 13:11a (Cmp: V+ὡς), [11b], 15 (Mea: A/καί)

λαλῶν (<λαλέω), 1. <Cmm. ACE [§5.4a]> 1/Agt [2/Con] (3/Exp): speaking
—N N+acc INC: Rev 13:5
—N DNC (with) P/μετά [+gen]: Rev 4:1 [LM]; 10:8 (Mea: Α/πάλιν); 21:15
λαμβάνω (>λαβών, λαμβάνων), 1. <Tra. AΘS[G] [G=A] +imp. [§5.1c]> 1/Agt [2/Thm] [3/Sou]: take
—N N+acc (from) P/ἐκ: Rev 6:4; 10:10
—N N+acc DNC: Rev 3:11; 5:8, 9; 10:8
—N DNC (from) P/ἐκ: Rev 5:7
—N DNC DNC: Rev 10:9
2. <Mot. (A)GΘS S=Θ [§5.2e]> 1/Goa [2/Thm] (3/Sou): receive
—N N+acc DNC: Rev 4:11; 5:12; 17:12a (Tem: Α/οὔπω), 12b (Com: P/μετά [+gen]; Cmp: V+ώς; Tem: N+acc); 22:17 (Man: Α/δωρεάν)
—N N+acc INC: Rev 14:9 (Loc: P/ἐπί [+gen]; Loc: P/ἐπί [+acc]), 11; 20:4 (Loc: P/ἐπί [+acc])
—N DNC (from) P/παρά [+gen, +an]: Rev 2:28 (Mea: Α/καί)
—N DNC DNC: Rev 3:3 (Man: Α/πῶς); [17:12c]; 18:4
3. <Eff. AP [§6.3a]> 1/Agt 2/Pat: take [up]
—N N+acc: Rev 8:5; 11:17
λαμβάνων (<λαμβάνω), 2. <Mot. (A)GΘS G=Θ [§5.2e]> 1/Goa [2/Thm] [3/Sou]: receiving
—N DNC DNC: Rev 2:17
λαμπάς, 1. <Mat. M{P} [§6.5c]> (1/Mat) {{2/Pat}}: torch
—(of) N+gen {N}: Rev 4:5
—INC {N}: Rev 8:10
λαμπρός (>[λαμπρός] + [εἰμί]), 1. <Qual. P [§6.10a]> (1/Pat): bright
—N: Rev 15:6; 22:1, 16
—INC: Rev 18:14; 19:8
[λαμπρός] + [εἰμί] (<λαμπρός), 1. <Qual. P [§6.10a]> 1/Pat: be bright
—N: Rev [22:1]
λαός (>λαός + εἰμί), 1. <Ben. B{P} [§6.1g]> (1/Ben) {{2/Pat}}: people
—(of) N+gen {N}: Rev 18:4
—INC {N}: Rev 5:9; 7:9; 10:11; 11:9; 13:7; 14:6
λαός + εἰμί (<λαός), 1. <Ben. PB [§6.1f]> 1/Pat (2/Ben): be a people
—N (of) N+gen: Rev 21:3b
—N INC: Rev 17:15
λατρεύω, 1. <Ben. PB [§6.1f]> 1/Pat 2/Ben: serve, be a servant to
—N N+dat [+an]: Rev 7:15 (Loc: P/ἐν; Tem: N+gen); 22:3
λέγω (>λέγων, λέγων + [εἰμί]), 1. <Cmm. ACE [§5.4a]> 1/Agt [2/Con] [3/Exp]: say, speak
—N N+acc (to) N+dat [+an]: Rev 2:7, 11, 17, 29; 3:6, 13, 22; 17:7b
—N N+acc DNC: Rev 2:1, 8, 12, 18; 3:1, 7, 14
—N V+quo (to) N+dat [+an]: Rev 2:24a; 5:5; 6:16 [ὄρος & πέτρα +an]; 7:14a, 14b; 10:9b, 11; 14:18; 17:7a, 7b, 15; 19:9a, 9b, 10; 21:6; 22:6, 9, 10
—N V+quo DNC: Rev 1:8; 4:10; 5:14; 19:3 (Mea: Α/δεύτερον); 21:5a, 5b, 9; 22:17a, 17b, 20

—N (to) **V-i3** (to) **N+dat** [+an]: Rev 10:9a
—N (that) **V+ἵνα** (to) **N+dat** [+an]: Rev 6:11; 9:4; 14:3
—N **V+ὅτι** [+quo] (to) **DNC**: Rev 3:17; 18:7 (Loc: P/ἐν)
—N **DNC DNC**: Rev 2:24b
2. <*Mod.* APR [§6.6a]> **1/Agt 2/Pat 3/Rst**: call
—N **N+acc N+2**: Rev 8:11

λέγων (<λέγω), **1.** <*Cmm.* ACE [§5.4a]> **1/Agt 2/Con [3/Exp]**: saying
—N **V+quo** (to) **N+dat** [+an]: Rev 7:13; 9:14; 11:12; 16:1; 19:17
—N **V+quo DNC**: Rev 1:11, 17; 4:1, 8, 10; 5:9, 12 (Ins: N+dat), 13; 6:1a (Cmp: V+ὡς), [1b], 3, 5, 6 (Loc: P/ἐν), 7, 10; 7:3, 10, 12; 8:13 (Ins: N+dat); 10:4, 8; 11:1, 15, 17; 12:10; 13:4; 14:7 (Ins: P/ἐν), 8, 9 (Ins: P/ἐν), 13, 18; 15:3; 16:5, 7, 17; 17:1; 18:2 (Ins: P/ἐν), 4, 10, 16, 18, 19, 21; 19:1, 4, 5, 6; 21:3 (Sou: P/ἐκ), 9
—N (that) **V-i3** (to) **N+dat** [+an]: Rev 10:9a; 13:14
—N (that) **V+i DNC**: Rev 2:9; 3:9
2. <*Mod.* APR [§6.6a]> **1/Agt 2/Pat 3/Rst**: calling
—N **N+acc N+2**: Rev 2:2, 20

λέγων + [εἰμί], **1.** <*Cmm.* ACE [§5.4a]> **1/Agt 2/Con [3/Exp]**: be speaking
—N **V+quo DNC**: Rev [4:1b]

λευκαίνω, **1.** <*Mod.* AP{R} [§6.6b]> **1/Agt 2/Pat {{3/Rst}}**: make {white}
—N **N+acc {Adj+2}**: Rev 7:14 (Ins: P/ἐν)

λευκός (>λευκός + [εἰμί]), **1.** <*Qual.* P [§6.10a]> **(1/Pat)**: white
—N: Rev [1:14c (Cmp: A/ὡς DNC)]; 2:17; 3:5, 18; 4:4; 6:2, 11; 7:9, 13; 14:14; 19:11, 14a, 14b; 20:11
—INC: Rev 3:4

λευκός + [εἰμί] (<λευκός), **1.** <*Qual.* P [§6.10a]> **1/Pat**: be white
—N: Rev [1:14a (Cmp: V+/ὡς)], [14b (Cmp: A/ὡς N+1)]

λέων, **1.** <*Spec.* — [§6.12]> **0/—**: lion
—Rev 4:7; 5:5 (Sou: P/ἐκ); 9:8, 17; 10:3; 13:2

ληνός, **1.** <*Ben.* B{P} [§6.1g]> **[1/Ben] {{2/Pat}}**: winepress
—DNC {N}: Rev 14:19 (Mat: N+gen), 20a, 20b; 19:15 (Mat: N+gen)

λιβανωτός, **1.** <*Ben.* B{P} [§6.1g]> **[1/Ben] {{2/Pat}}**: censer
—DNC {N}: Rev 8:3, 5

λίθινος, **1.** <*Qual.* P [§6.10a]> **1/Pat**: [made of] stone
—N: Rev 9:20

λίθος, **1.** <*Spec.* — [§6.12]> **0/—**: stone
—Rev 4:3; 17:4; 18:12, 16, 21 (Cmp: A/ὡς DNC); 21:11a (Cmp: A/ὡς N+1), 11b, 19

λίμνη, **1.** <*Spec.* — [§6.12]> **0/—**: lake
—Rev 19:20 (Mat: N+gen); 20:10 (Mat: N+gen), 14 (Mat: N+gen), 15 (Mat: N+gen); 21:8

λιμός, **1.** <*Exp.* EC C→T [§5.5c]> **[1/Exp] (2/Top)**: hunger
—DNC INC: Rev 6:8; 18:8

λιπαρός, **1.** <*Qual.* P [§6.10a]> **(1/Pat)**: luxurious
—INC: Rev 18:14

λίνον, 1. <Ben. B{P} [§6.1g]> [1/Ben] {{2/Pat}}: linen
—DNC {N}: Rev 15:6
λόγος, 1. <Cmm. BCE [§5.4f]> [1/Ben] [2/Con] [3/Exp]: word, message
—(of) N+gen (of) N+gen DNC: Rev 3:10; 12:11; 22:7, 10, 18, 19
—(of) N+gen DNC DNC: Rev 1:2, 9; 3:8; 6:9 17:17; 19:9, 13; 20:4; 22:9
—DNC (of) N+gen DNC: Rev 1:3
—DNC DNC DNC: Rev 21:5; 22:6
λοιπός, 1. <Par. PPar [§6.7a]> [1/Pat] [2/Par]: rest
—N DNC: Rev 2:24 (Loc: P/ἐν); 8:13
—DNC (of) N+gen: Rev 9:20; 12:17; 20:5
—DNC DNC: Rev 3:2; 11:13; 19:21
λύσας (<λύω), 1. <Sep. APS [§6.8a]> 1/Agt 2/Pat 3/Sou: releasing
—N N+acc (from) P/ἐκ: Rev 1:5 (Ins: P/ἐν)
λυχνία (>λυχνία + εἰμί), 1. <Ben. B{P} [§6.1g]> (1/Ben) {{2/Pat}}: lampstand
—(of) N+gen {N}: Rev 2:5
—DNC {N}: Rev 1:20b; 2:1
—INC {N}: Rev 1:12, 13, 20a
λυχνία + εἰμί (<λυχνία), 1. <Ben. PB [§6.1f]> 1/Pat (2/Ben): be a lampstand
—N INC: Rev 11:4
λύχνος (>λύχνος + [εἰμί]), 1. <Ben. B{P} [§6.1g]> (1/Ben) {{2/Pat}}: lamp
—INC {N}: Rev 18:23; 22:5
λύχνος + [εἰμί] (<λύχνος), 1. <Ben. PB [§6.1f]> 1/Pat 2/Ben: be a lamp
—N (of) N+gen: Rev [21:23]
λύω (>λύσας), 1. <Sep. APS [§6.8a]> 1/Agt 2/Pat [3/Sou]: untie, release
—N N+acc (from) P/ἐκ: Rev 20:7 (Tem: V+ὅταν)
—N N+acc DNC: Rev 5:2; 9:14, 15 (Pur: V+ἵνα); 20:3 (Tem: N+acc)
μακάριος (>μακάριος + [εἰμί]), 1. <Qual. P [§6.10a]> 1/Pat: blessed.
μακάριος + [εἰμί] (<μακάριος), 1. <Qual. P [§6.10a]> 1/Pat: be blessed
—N: Rev [1:3a]; [14:13]; [16:15 (Pur: V+ἵνα)]; [19:9a]; [20:6a]; [22:7], [14a]
μανθάνω, 1. <Exp. EC [§5.5a]> 1/Exp 2/Con: learn
—N N+acc: Rev 14:3
μαργαρίτης + [εἰμί], 1. <Qual. P [§6.10a]> 1/Pat: be a pearl
—N: Rev [21:21a]
μαρτυρέω (>μαρτυρῶν), 1. <Cmm. ACE [§5.4a]> 1/Agt 2/Con [3/Exp]: testify
—N (to) N+acc (to) N+dat [+an]: Rev 22:16 (Top: P/ἐπί [+dat])
—N N+acc DNC: Rev 1:2a, [2b]
—N V+quo (to) N+dat [+an]: Rev 22:18
μαρτυρία, 1. <Cmm. BCE ‖ BCE [§5.4f]> [1/Ben] [2/Con] [3/Exp] ‖ [1/Ben] 2/Con [3/Exp]: testimony
—(of) N+gen DNC DNC) ‖ DNC (of) N+gen DNC: Rev 1:2, 9; 12:17; 19:10a, 10b; 20:4
—(of) N+gen DNC DNC ‖ [not applicable]: Rev 11:7; 12:11
—DNC DNC DNC ‖ [not applicable]: Rev 6:9
μαρτύριον, 1. <Cmm. BCE [§5.4f]> [1/Ben] [2/Con] [3/Exp]: testimony
—DNC DNC DNC: Rev 15:5

μαρτυρῶν (<μαρτυρέω), 1. <Cmm. ACE [§5.4a]> 1/Agt 2/Con [3/Exp]: testifying
—N N+acc DNC: Rev 22:20

μάρτυς, 1. <Cmm. BCE || BCE [§5.4f]> [1/Ben] (2/Con) [3/Exp] || (1/Ben) (2/Con) [3/Exp]: witness
—(of) N+gen INC DNC || INC (of) N+gen DNC: Rev 2:13; 11:13; 17:6
—DNC INC DNC || INC INC DNC: Rev 1:5; 3:14

μασάομαι, 1. <Eff. AP [§6.3a]> 1/Agt 2/Pat: gnaw
—N N+acc: Rev 16:10 (Cau: P/ἐκ)

μαστός, 1. <Ben. B{P} [§6.1g]> [1/Ben] {{2/Pat}}: breast
—DNC {N}: Rev 1:13

μάχαιρα, 1. <Ben. B{P} [§6.1g]> (1/Ben) {{21/Pat}}: sword
—DNC {N}: Rev 6:4
—INC {N}: Rev 13:10a, 10b, 14

μέγας (>μέγας + [εἰμί]), 1. <Qual. P [§6.10a]> (1/Pat): great
—N: Rev 1:10; 2:22; 5:2, 12; 6:4, 10, 12, 13, 17; 7:2, 10, 14; 8:8, 10, 13; 9:2, 14; 10:3; 11:8, 11, 12, 13, 15, 17, 19; 12:1, 3, 9, 10, 12, 14; 13:2, 13; 14:2, 7, 8, 9, 15, 18, 19; 15:1; 16:1, 9, 12, 14, 17, 18b, 19a, 19b, 21a (Cmp: A/ὡς Adj+1); 17:1, 5, 6, 18; 18:1, 2, 10, 16, 18, 19, 21b; 19:1, 2, 5, 17a, 17b; 20:1, 11; 21:3, 10, 12
—INC: Rev 11:18; 13:5, 16; 16:18a; 18:21a; 19:18; 20:12

μέγας + [εἰμί] (<μέγας), 1. <Qual. P [§6.10a]> 1/Pat: be great
—N: Rev [15:3a (Voc: N+voc)]; 16:21b (Mea: A/σφόδρα)

μεγιστάν (>μεγιστάν + εἰμί), 1. <Ben. B{P} [§6.1g]> [1/Ben] {{2/Pat}}: great one
—DNC {N}: Rev 6:15

μεγιστάν + εἰμί (<μεγιστάν), 1. <Ben. PB [§6.1f]> 1/Pat 2/Ben: be a great one
—N (of) N+gen: Rev 18:23

μεθύσκω, 1. <Eff. AP [§6.3a]> 1/Agt 2/Pat: make drunk
—N N+acc: Rev 17:2 (Ins: P/ἐκ)

μεθύω (>μεθύων), 1. <Qual. P [§6.10a]> 1/Pat: be drunk.

μεθύων (<μεθύω), 1. <Qual. P [§6.10a]> 1/Pat: being drunk
—N: Rev 17:6 (Ins: P/ἐκ)

μέλας (>[μέλας] + [εἰμί]), 1. <Qual. P [§6.10a]> 1/Pat: black
—N: Rev 6:5, 12 (Cmp: V+ὡς)

[μέλας] + [εἰμί] (<μέλας), 1. <Qual. P [§6.10a]> 1/Pat: be black
—N: Rev [6:12]

μέλλω (>μέλλων), 1. <Cap. UO [§5.6b]> 1/Uns 2/Occ: be about [to]
—N (to) V-i1: Rev 1:19; 2:10a, 10b; 3:2, 16 (Cau: V+ὅτι; Man: A/οὕτως); 10:4 (Tem: V+ὅτε), 7; 12:5; 17:8

μέλλων (<μέλλω), 1. <Cap. UO [§5.6b]> 1/Uns 2/Occ: being about [to]
—N (to) V-i1: Rev 3:10; 6:11; 8:13; 12:4

μεμιγμένος (<μίγνυμι), 1. <Ins. PAI [§6.4d]> 1/Pat (2/Agt) 3/Ins: mixed
—N INC (by means of/with) N+dat: Rev 15:2
—N INC (by means of/with) P/ἐν: Rev 8:7

μεμισημένος (<μισέω), 1. <Exp. CE [§5.5h]> 1/Con (2/Exp): hated
—N INC: Rev 18:2

μένω, 1. <Loc. ΘL [§5.3a]> 1/Thm [2/Loc]: remain
—N DNC: Rev 17:10 (Tem: A/ὀλίγον)
μέρος, 1. <Par. Par{P} [§6.7b]> [1/Par] {{2/Pat}}: portion, part
—(of) P/ἀπό {N}: Rev 22:19 (Ben: N+gen)
—(of) P/ἐκ {N}: Rev 22:19 (Ben: N+gen)
—DNC {N}: Rev 16:19; 20:6; 21:8 (Ben: N+gen)
μετά (>μετά + [εἰμί]), 1. <Loc. ΘL [§5.3a]> 1/Thm 2/Loc: with
—N N+gen: Rev 1:7; 3:20a, 20b, 21a, 21b; 6:8; 14:1, 13; 17:14b; 21:3b
2. <Ben. PB [§6.1f]> 1/Pat 2/Ben: against
—N N+gen: Rev 2:16; 11:7; 12:7, 17; 13:4, 7; 17:14a; 19:19a, 19b
3. <Exp. CE [§5.5h]> 1/Con 2/Exp: with
—N N+gen: Rev 1:12; 4:1b; 10:8; 17:1; 21:9, 15
4. <Ins. PI [§6.4e]> 1/Pat 2/Ins: with, by [means of]
—N N+gen: Rev 2:22; 14:4; 17:2; 18:3, 9
5. <Com. PCom [§6.2c]> 1/Pat 2/Com: [together] with
—N N+gen: Rev 3:4; 12:9; 17:12; 19:20; 20:4, 6
6. <Tem. PTem [§6.9d]> 1/Pat 2/Tem: after
—N N+acc: Rev 1:19; 4:1a, 1c; 7:1, 9; 9:12; 11:11; 15:5; 18:1; 19:1; 20:3
μετά + [εἰμί] (<μετά), 1. <Loc. ΘL [§5.3a]> 1/Thm 2/Loc: be with
—N N+gen: Rev [21:3a], 3c (Cur: N+1); [22:12a (Pur: V-i2,1)], [21]
μετανοέω, 1. <Exp. EC C→T [§5.5c]> 1/Exp [2/Top]: repent
—N (concerning/from) P/ἐκ: Rev 2:21b, 22; 9:20 (Res: V+ἵνα), 21; 16:11
—N DNC: Rev 2:5a, 5b, 16a (Res: A/οὖν), [16b], 21a; 3:3, 19; 16:9 (Pur: V-i1)
μετρέω, 1. <Eff. AP [§6.3a]> 1/Agt 2/Pat: measure
—N N+acc: Rev 11:1, 2 (Cau: V+ὅτι); 21:15, 16 (Ins: N+dat; Mea: P/ἐπί [+gen]),
17 (Ins: N+acc; Mea: N+gen)
μέτρον (>[μέτρον] + εἰμί), 1. <Ben. B{P} [§6.1g]> [1/Ben] {{2/Pat}}: measuring rod
—(of) N+gen {N}: Rev 21:17a
—DNC {N}: Rev 21:15 (Pur: V+ἵνα)
[μέτρον] + εἰμί (<μέτρον), 1. <Ben. PB [§6.1f]> 1/Pat 2/Ben: be a measuring rod
—N (of) N+gen: Rev [21:17b]
μέτωπον, 1. <Ben. B{P} [§6.1g]> [1/Ben] {{2/Pat}}: forehead
—(of) N+gen {N}: Rev 7:3; 13:16; 14:1, 9; 17:5; 22:4
—DNC {N}: Rev 9:4; 20:4
μηδείς, 1. <Qual. P [§6.10a]> (1/Pat): no, not any
—INC: Rev 2:10; 3:11
μῆκος, 1. <Ben. B{P} [§6.1g]> 1/Ben {{2/Pat}}: length
—(of) N+gen {N}: Rev 21:16a, 16b
μηρός, 1. <Ben. B{P} [§6.1g]> 1/Ben {{2/Pat}}: thigh
—(of) N+gen {N}: Rev 19:16
μήτε...μήτε, 1. <Coor. --- --- [§6.11b]> 1/--- 2/---: nor...nor
—N N: Rev 7:3
—P/ἐπί [+gen] P/ἐπί [+acc]: Rev 7:1
μήτηρ, 1. <Ben. B{P} [§6.1g]> 1/Ben {{2/Pat}}: mother
—(of) N+gen {N}: Rev 17:5

μίγνυμι (>μεμιγμένος), 1. <Ins. API [§6.4a]> 1/Agt 2/Pat 3/Ins: mix.
μικρός, 1. <Qual. P [§6.10a]> (1/Pat): small, little
—N: Rev 3:8; 6:11; 20:3, 12
—INC: Rev 11:18; 13:16; 19:5, 18
μιμνῄσκομαι, 1. <Exp. EC [§5.5a]> 1/Exp 2/Con: remember
—N N+acc: Rev 16:19 (Loc: P/ἐνώπιον; Pur: V-i1,2)
μισέω (>μεμισημένος), 1. <Exp. EC [§5.5a]> 1/Exp 2/Con: hate
—N N+acc: Rev 2:6a, 6b (Mea: A/καί); 17:16 (Cur: N+1)
μισθός, 1. <Ben. B{P}B [§6.1h]> [1/Ben] {{2/Pat}} [3/Ben]: wage
—(of) N+gen {N} DNC: Rev 22:12
—DNC {N} DNC: Rev 11:18
μνῆμα, 1. <Ben. B{P} [§6.1g]> (1/Ben) {{2/Pat}}: tomb
—INC {N}: Rev 11:9
μνημονεύω, 1. <Exp. EC [§5.5a]> 1/Exp 2/Con: remember
—N N+acc: Rev 18:5
—N (from where) V+πόθεν: Rev 2:5 (Res: A/οὖν)
—N (how) V+πῶς: Rev 3:3 (Res: A/οὖν)
μοιχεύω (>μοιχεύων), 1. <Ins. A{P}I [§6.4b]> 1/Agt {{2/Pat}} 3/Ins: commit {adultery}.
μοιχεύων (<μοιχεύω), 1. <Ins. A{P}I [§6.4b]> 1/Agt {{2/Pat}} 3/Ins: committing {adultery}
—N {N} (by/with) P/μετά [+gen]: Rev 2:22
μολύνω, 1. <Eff. AP [§6.3a]> 1/Agt 2/Pat: defile
—N N+acc: Rev 3:4; 14:4 (Ins: P/μετά [+gen])
μόνος, 1. <Qual. P [§6.10a]> 1/Pat: alone, only
—N: Rev 15:4
μουσικός, 1. <Qual. P [§6.10a]> (1/Pat): musical
—INC: Rev 18:22
μυκάομαι, 1. <Eff. A{P} [§6.3b]> 1/Agt {{2/Pat}}: make {a roar}, roar
—N {N}: Rev 10:3
μύλινος, 1. <Qual. P [§6.10a]> [1/Pat]: [made of] millstone
—DNC: Rev 18:21
μύλος, 1. <Ben. B{P} [§6.1g]> (1/Ben) {{2/Pat}}: mill, millstone
—INC {N}: Rev 18:22
μυριάς (>μυρίας + εἰμί), 1. <Mat. M{P} [§6.5c]> [1/Mat] {{2/Pat}}: ten-thousand-member group
—DNC {N}: Rev 5:11b; 9:16
μυρίας + εἰμί (<μυρίας), 1. <Mat. PM [§6.5b]> 1/Pat 2/Mat: be a ten-thousand-member group
—N (of) N+gen: Rev 5:11a
μυστήριον, 1. <Exp. EC [§5.5a]> [1/Exp] [2/Con]: secret, mystery
—(of) N+gen DNC: Rev 10:7
—DNC (of) N+gen: Rev 1:20; 17:7
—DNC DNC: Rev 17:5
ναί, 1. <Qual. O [§6.10b]> [1/Occ]: yes!
—[licensing following] V+: Rev 14:3; 16:7 (Voc: N+voc); 22:20

—[referencing what precedes] DNC: Rev 1:7
ναός (>ναός + εἰμί), 1. <Ben. B{P} [§6.1g]> [1/Ben] {{2/Pat}}: temple, sanctuary
—(of) N+gen {N}: Rev 3:12; 7:15; 11:1, 19a (Loc: P/ἐν), 19b; 15:5
—DNC {N}: Rev 11:1; 14:15, 17 (Loc: P/ἐν); 15:6, 8a, 8b; 16:1, 17; 21:22a
ναός + εἰμί (<ναός), 1. <Ben. PB [§6.1f]> 1/Pat 2/Ben: be a temple, be a sanctuary
—N (of) N+gen: Rev 21:22b
νεκρός (>νεκρός + εἰμί), 1. <Qual. P [§6.10a]> (1/Pat): dead
—DNC: Rev 1:17, 18; 2:8
—INC: Rev 1:5; 11:18; 14:13; 16:3; 20:5, 12a, 12b, 13a (Loc: P/ἐν), 13b (Loc: P/ἐν)
νεκρός + εἰμί (<νεκρός), 1. <Qual. P [§6.10a]> 1/Pat: be dead
—N: Rev 3:1
νεφρός, 1. <Ben. B{P} [§6.1g]> (1/Ben) {{2/Pat}}: kidney
—INC {N}: Rev 2:23
νικάω (>νικῶν), 1. <Eff. AP [§6.3a]> 1/Agt (2/Pat): conquer
—N N+acc: Rev 11:7; 12:11 (Cau: P/διά [+acc]); 13:7; 17:14 (Cau: V+ὅτι)
—N DNC: Rev 3:21b (Mea: A/καί); 5:5 (Res: V-i1)
—N INC: Rev 6:2b
νικῶν (<νικάω), 1. <Eff. AP [§6.3a]> [1/Agt] (2/Pat): conquering
—DNC DNC: Rev 2:7, 11, 17, 26; 3:5 (Man: A/οὕτως), 12, 21a; 15:2 (Sou: P/ ἐκ); 21:7
—DNC INC: Rev 6:2a
νοῦς, 1. <Ben. B{P} [§6.1g]> (1/Ben) {{2/Pat}}: mind
—DNC {N}: Rev 13:18
—INC {N}: Rev 17:9
νύμφη, 1. <Ben. B{P} [§6.1g]> (1/Ben) {{2/Pat}}: bride
—DNC {N}: Rev 21:9; 22:17
—INC {N}: Rev 18:23; 21:2
νυμφίος, 1. <Ben. B{P} [§6.1g]> (1/Ben) {{2/Pat}}: groom
—INC {N}: Rev 18:23
ξηραίνω, 1. <Eff. AP [§6.3a]> 1/Agt 2/Pat: dry [up]
—N N+acc: Rev 14:15; 16:12 (Pur: V+ἵνα)
ξύλινος, 1. <Qual. P [§6.10a]> 1/Pat: [made of] wood, wooden
—N: Rev 9:20
ξύλον, 1. <Spec. — [§6.12]> 0/—: tree
—Rev 2:7 (Ben: N+gen); 18:12a, 12b; 22:2a (Ben: N+gen) [εἰμί 1], 2b, 14 (Ben: N+gen), 19 (Ben: N+gen)
ὄγδοος (>ὄγδοος + εἰμί), 1. <Par. PPar [§6.7a]> [1/Pat] [2/Par]: eighth
—DNC DNC: Rev 21:20
ὄγδοος + εἰμί (<ὄγδοος), 1. <Par. PPar [§6.7a]> 1/Pat [2/Par]: be eighth
—N DNC: Rev 17:11c
ὁδηγέω, 1. <Tra. AΘ[S]G [S=A] +imp. [§5.1a]> 1/Agt 2/Thm 3/Goa: guide, lead
—N N+acc (to) P/ἐπί [+acc]: Rev 7:17
ὁδός, 1. <Ben. B{P}B [§6.1h]> [1/Ben] {{2/Pat}} [3/Ben]: way
—(of) N+gen {N} DNC: Rev 15:3
—DNC {N} (for) N+gen: Rev 16:12

ὀδούς, 1. <Ben. B{P} [§6.1g]> 1/Ben {{2/Pat}}: tooth
—(of) N+gen {N}: Rev 9:8a, [8b]
οἶδα (>εἰδώς), 1a. <Exp. EC [§5.5a]> 1/Exp [2/Con]: know
—N N+acc: Rev 2:2, 9, 17 (Mea: εἰ μή N+1), 19; 3:8; 19:12a (Mea: εἰ μή N+1)
—N (that) V+i: Rev 2:19
—N (that) V+ὅτι: Rev 2:2, 3:17
—N (where) V+ποῦ: Rev 2:13
—N DNC: Rev 7:14 (Voc: N+voc)
  1b. <Exp. EC¹/C² [§5.5e]> 1/Exp 2/Con¹/Con²: know
—N N+acc/(that) V+ὅτι: Rev 3:1, 15
οἶνος, 1. <Spec. — [§6.12]> 0/—: wine
—Rev 6:6; 14:8 (Mat: N+gen), 10 (Mat: N+gen); 16:19 (Mat: N+gen); 17:2 (Mat: N+gen); 18:3 (Mat: N+gen), 13; 19:15 (Mat: N+gen)
ὀλίγος, 1. <Qual. P [§6.10a]> [1/Pat]: [a] few, little
—N: Rev 3:4; 12:12
—DNC: Rev 2:14; 17:10 [DNC Patient referent from 12:12]
ὅλος, 1. <Qual. P [§6.10a]> 1/Pat: whole
—N: Rev 3:10; 6:12; 12:9; 13:3; 16:14
ὄλυνθος, 1. <Ben. B{P} [§6.1g]> 1/Ben {{2/Pat}}: late fig
—(of) N+gen {N}: Rev 6:13
ὀμνύω, 1. <Cmm. ACE [§5.4a]> 1/Agt 2/Con [3/Exp]: swear
—N V+ὅτι DNC: Rev 10:6 (Ins: P/ἐν)
ὅμοιος (>ὅμοιος + [εἰμί]), 1. <Cmp. PCmp [§6.9b]> 1/Pat 2/Cmp: like
—N N+dat: Rev 9:7b, 10; 11:1; 13:11; 21:18
  2. <Qual. P [§6.10a]> (1/Pat): [Son-of-Man]-like
—INC: Rev 1:13
ὅμοιος + [εἰμί] (<ὅμοιος), 1. <Cmp. PCmp [§6.9b]> 1/Pat 2/Cmp: be like
—N N+dat: Rev [1:15a]; [2:18]; [4:3a (Man: N+dat)], [3b (Man: N+dat)], [7a], [7b], [7c]; [9:7a], [19b]; 13:2a, [4]; [18:18]; [21:11])]
  2. <Qual. P [§6.10a]> 1/Pat: be [Son-of-Man]-like
—N: Rev [14:14]
ὁμοίωμα, 1. <Ben. B{P} [§6.1g]> 1/Ben {{2/Pat}}: likeness, appearance
—(of) N+gen {N}: Rev 9:7
ὁμολογέω, 1. <Cmm. ACE [§5.4a]> 1/Agt 2/Con [3/Exp]: declare
—N N+acc DNC: Rev 3:5 (Loc: P/ἐνώπιον)
ὄνομα (>ὄνομα + [εἰμί]), 1. <Ben. B{P} [§6.1g]> [1/Ben] {{2/Pat}}: name
—(of) N+gen {N}: Rev 2:3, 13; 3:5a, 5b, 8, 12a, 12b, 12c; 8:11; 11:13, 18; 13:1, 6, 8 [red.], 17a, 17b; 14:1a, 1b, 11; 15:2, 4; 16:9; 17:3, 8; 19:13; 21:14; 22:4
—DNC {N}: Rev 2:17; 3:4; 6:8 [εἰμί 2]; 9:11a [εἰμί 2], 11b; 17:5; 19:12, 16; 21:12a
  2. <Exp. EC [§5.5a]> [1/Exp] 2/Con: reputation
—DNC (that) V+ὅτι: Rev 3:1
ὄνομα + [εἰμί] (<ὄνομα), 1. <Ben. PB [§6.1f]> 1/Pat 2/Ben: be a name
—N (of) N+gen: Rev 21:12b
ὀξύς, 1. <Qual. P [§6.10a]> 1/Pat: sharp
—N: Rev 1:16; 2:12; 14:14, 17, 18a, 18b; 19:15

ὀπίσω, 1. <Loc. ΘL [§5.3a]> 1/Thm 2/Loc: behind
—N N+gen: Rev 1:10; 13:3
2. <Mot. Θ[S]G [S=Θ] [§5.2a]> 1/Thm 2/Goa: [to] behind
—N N+gen: Rev 12:15
ὅπου + [εἰμί], 1. <Loc. Θ[L] [L=Θ] [§5.3b]> 1/Thm [[2/Loc]]: be where
—N [N]: Rev [2:13]; [20:10 (Mea: A/καί)]
ὅρασις, 1. <Exp. EC [§5.5a]> [1/Exp] [2/Con]: vision, sight
—DNC DNC: Rev 4:3; 9:17
ὁράω (>ἰδών), 1. <Exp. EC [§5.5a]> 1/Exp (2/Con): see
—N N+acc: Rev 1:2, 7 (Mea: A/καί), 12, 17, 19, 20 (Loc: P/ἐπί [+gen]); [4:4]; 5:1 (Loc: P/ἐπί [+acc]), 2, 6 (Loc: P/ἐν μέσῳ; Loc: P/ἐν μέσῳ); 6:9 (Loc: P/ ὑποκάτω; Tem: V+ὅτε); 7:1 (Tem: P/μετά [+acc]), 2; 8:2; 9:1, 17 (Ins: P/ ἐν; Man: A/οὕτως); 10:1, 5; 11:19 (Loc: P/ἐν); 12:1 (Loc: P/ἐν), 3 (Loc: P/ ἐν); 13:1, 2, 11; 14:6; 15:1 (Loc: P/ἐν), 2; 16:13; 17:3, 6a, 6b, 8, 12, 15 (Loc: V+οὗ), 16, 18; 18:1 (Tem: P/μετά [+acc]), 7; 19:11, 17, 19; 20:1, 4a, [4b], 11, 12; 21:1, 2, 22 (Loc: P/ἐν); 22:4
—N (that) V+ὅτι: Rev 12:13
—N DNC: Rev 4:1 (Tem: P/μετά [+acc]); 6:2, 5, 8, 12 (Tem: V+ὅτε); 7:9 (Tem: P/ μετά [+acc]); 8:13; 14:1, 14; 15:5 (Tem: P/μετά [+acc])
—N INC: Rev 5:11; 6:1 (Tem: V+ὅτε); 15:2 (Cmp: A/ὡς N+2); 19:10; 22:9
ὀργή, 1. <Exp. EC C→T [§5.5c]> 1/Exp [2/Top]: anger
—(of) N+gen DNC: Rev 6:16, 17; 11:18; 14:10; 16:19; 19:15
ὀργίζω, 1. <Exp. EC C→T [§5.5c]> 1/Exp [2/Top]: be angry
—N (at) P/ἐπί [+dat]: Rev 12:17
—N DNC: Rev 11:18
ὄρος + εἰμί, 1. <Qual. P [§6.10a]> 1/Pat: be a mountain
—N: Rev 17:9b (Loc: V+ὅπου)
ὅσιος (>ὅσιος + [εἰμί]), 1. <Qual. P [§6.10a]> [1/Pat]: holy
—DNC: Rev 16:5
ὅσιος + [εἰμί] (<ὅσιος), 1. <Qual. P [§6.10a]> 1/Pat: be holy
—N: Rev [15:4]
ὅσος (>ὅσος + [εἰμί]), 1. <Cmp. PCmp [§6.9b]> 1/Pat 2/Cmp: as much as, as many as
—N N+1: Rev 21:16
2. <Qual. P [§6.10a]> [1/Pat]: however much, however many
—DNC: Rev 1:2; 2:24; 3:19; 13:15; 18:7, 17
ὅσος + [εἰμί] (<ὅσος), 1. <Cmp. PCmp [§6.9b]> 1/Pat 2/Cmp: be as much as, be as many as
—N N+1: Rev [21:16a (Mea: A/καί)]
οὐαί, 1. <Ben. B{P} [§6.1g]> [1/Ben] {{2/Pat}}: woe
—(for) N+acc {N}: Rev 8:13a [εἰμί 1], 13b [εἰμί 1], 13c [εἰμί 1]; 12:12 (Cau: V+ὅτι) [εἰμί 1]
—DNC {N}: Rev 9:12a, 12b; 11:14a, 14b; 18:10a [εἰμί 1], 10b [εἰμί 1], 16a [εἰμί 1], 16b [εἰμί 1], 19a [εἰμί 1], 19b [εἰμί 1]
οὐδέ, 1a. <Coor. — — [§6.11a]> 1/— 2/—: and not, nor
—V+ V+: Rev 9:20; 12:8

9. The Case Frame Lexicon 253

1b. <*Coor.* --- --- [§6.11b]> 1/--- 2/---: and not, nor
—**N N**: Rev 7:16b; 9:4a, 4b; 20:4; 21:23
—(in) **P/ἐν** (on) **P/ἐπί** [+gen]: Rev 5:3a
—(on) **P/ἐπί** [+gen] (under) **P/ὑποκάτω**: Rev 5:3b

οὐδέ...οὐδέ, 1a. <*Coor.* — — [§6.11a]> 1/— 2/—: nor...nor
—**V+ V+**: Rev 7:16a

οὐδείς, 1. <*Qual.* P [§6.10a]> (1/Pat): no, not any
—**INC**: Rev 2:17; 3:7a, 7b, 8, 17; 5:3, 4; 7:9; 14:3; 15:8; 18:11; 19:12

οὐρά, 1. <*Ben.* B{P} [§6.1g]> [1/Ben] {{2/Pat}}: tail
—(of) **N+gen {N}**: Rev 9:10b, 19a, 19b; 12:4
—**DNC {N}**: Rev 9:10a

οὖς, 1. <*Ben.* B{P} [§6.1g]> (1/Ben) {{2/Pat}}: ear
—**INC {N}**: Rev 2:7, 11, 17, 29; 3:6, 13, 22; 13:9

οὔτε, 1b. <*Coor.* --- --- [§6.11b]> 1/--- 2/---: nor
—(to) **V-iI** (to) **V-iI**: Rev 5:3, 4;

οὔτε...οὔτε, 1a. <*Coor.* — — [§6.11a]> 1/— 2/—: neither...nor
—**V+ V+**: Rev 3:15, 16

1b. <*Coor.* --- --- [§6.11b]> 1/--- 2/---: neither...nor
—**N N**: Rev 21:4a, 4b
—(to) **V-iI** (to) **V-iI**: Rev 9:20a, 20b
—(of) **P/ἐκ** (of) **P/ἐκ**: Rev 9:21a, 21b

οὗτος, 1. <*Qual.* P [§6.10a]> (1/Pat): this
—**N**: Rev 2:24; 9:18, 20; 11:10; 16:9; 19:9; 20:5; 21:5; 22:6, 7, 9, 10, 18a, 18b, 19a, 19b
—**DNC**: Rev 2:6; 4:1a; 7:1, 9, 13, 14, 15; 9:12; 11:4, 6; 12:12; 14:4a, 4b, 4c; 15:5; 16:5; 17:13, 14, 18; 18:1, 8, 15; 19:1; 20:3, 6, 14; 21:7; 22:8a, 8b, 16, 20
—**INC**: Rev 1:19; 4:1b, 15; 11:8

ὄφελον, 1. <*Qual.* O [§6.10b]> 1/Occ: would that, O that
—**V+**: Rev 3:15

ὀφθαλμός, 1. <*Ben.* B{P} [§6.1g]> [1/Ben] {{2/Pat}}: eye
—(of) **N+gen {N}**: Rev 1:14 (Cmp: A/ὡς N+2); 2:18 (Cmp: A/ὡς N+2); 3:18; 7:17; 19:12; 21:4
—**DNC {N}**: Rev 1:7; 4:6, 8; 5:6

ὄχλος (>ὄχλος + εἰμί), **1.** <*Spec.* — [§6.12]> 0/—: crowd
—Rev 7:9 (Sou: P/ἐκ) [εἰμί 1]; 19:1, 6

ὄχλος + εἰμί (<ὄχλος), **1.** <*Qual.* P [§6.10a]> 1/Pat: be a crowd
—**N**: Rev 17:15

ὄψις, 1. <*Ben.* B{P} [§6.1g]> 1/Ben {{2/Pat}}: face
—(of) **N+gen {N}**: Rev 1:16

παιδεύω, 1. <*Eff.* AP [§6.3a]> 1/Agt 2/Pat: discipline
—**N** (however many) **V+ὅσος ἐάν**: Rev 3:19

παίω, 1. <*Eff.* AP [§6.3a]> 1/Agt 2/Pat: strike
—**N+acc**: Rev 9:5

παρά, 1. <*Mot.* ΘS(G) S=Θ [§5.2c]> 1/Thm 2/Sou: from
—**N N+gen** [+an]: Rev 2:28; 3:18

2. <Loc. ΘL [§5.3a]> 1/Thm 2/Loc: with, among
—N N+dat: Rev 2:13
πάρειμι, 1. <Qual. P [§6.10a]> 1/Pat: be present
—N: Rev 17:8
παρεμβολή, 1. <Ben. B{P} [§6.1g]> 1/Ben {{2/Pat}}: encampment
—(of) N+gen {N}: Rev 20:9
παρθένος + εἰμί, 1. <Qual. P [§6.10a]> 1/Pat: be a virgin
—N: Rev 14:4
πᾶς, 1. <Qual. P [§6.10a]> [1/Pat]: every, all
—N: Rev 1:7a, 7b; 2:23; 5:6, 9, 13a; 6:14, 15; 7:1, 4, 9, 11, 16, 17; 8:7; 9:4a, 4b; 11:6; 12:5; 13:7, 12, 16; 14:6, 8; 15:4; 16:3, 20; 18:2a, 2b, 2c, 3, 12a, 12b, 12c, 14, 17a, 22a, 22b, 23; 19:5, 17, 21; 21:4, 19; 22:3
—DNC: Rev 4:11; 5:13b; 8:3; 13:8; 18:17b, 19, 24; 19:18; 21:5, 8, 27; 22:15, 18, 21
πάσχω, 1. <Exp. EC [§5.5a]> 1/Exp 2/Con: suffer
—N N+acc: Rev 2:10
πατάσσω, 1. <Eff. AP [§6.3a]> 1/Agt 2/Pat: strike
—N N+acc: Rev 11:6 (Ins: P/ἐν; Mea: V+ὁσάκις ἐάν); 19:15 (Ins: P/ἐν)
πατέω, 1. <Eff. AP [§6.3a]> 1/Agt 2/Pat: trample
—N N+acc: Rev 11:2 (Tem: N+acc); 14:20 (Loc: P/ἔξωθεν); 19:15
πατήρ, 1. <Ben. B{P} [§6.1g]> 1/Ben {{2/Pat}}: father
—(of) N+gen {N}: Rev 1:6; 2:28; 3:5, 21; 14:1
πεινάω, 1. <Exp. EC C→T [§5.5c]> 1/Exp (2/Top): be hungry
—N INC: Rev 7:16 (Tem: A/ἔτι)
πειράζω, 1. <Eff. AP [§6.3a]> 1/Agt 2/Pat: test
—N N+acc: Rev 2:2, 10; 3:10
πελεκίζω (>πεπελεκισμένος), 1. <Eff. AP [§6.3a]> 1/Agt 2/Pat: behead.
πέμπτος, 1. <Par. PPar [§6.7a]> [1/Pat] [2/Par]: fifth
—N DNC: Rev 6:9; 9:1
—DNC DNC: Rev 16:10; 21:20
πέμπω, 1. <Tra. AΘ[S]G [S=A] –imp. [§5.1i]> 1/Agt [2/Thm] [3/Goa]: send
—N N+acc (to) N+dat [+an]: Rev 11:10 (Cau: V+ὅτι)
—N N+acc DNC: Rev 14:15, 18
—N DNC (to) N+dat [+an]: Rev 1:11
—N DNC (to) P/εἰς [–an]: Rev 1:11b, 11c, 11d, 11e, 11f, 11g, 11h
2. <Dis. AΘO [§5.7a]> 1/Agt 2/Thm 3/Occ: send [forth]
—N N+acc (to) V-i2: Rev 22:16
πενθέω (>πενθῶν), 1. <Exp. EC C→T [§5.5c]> 1/Exp [2/Top]: mourn
—N DNC: Rev 18:11 (Ben: P/ἐπί [+acc]; Cau: V+ὅτι)
πένθος, 1. <Exp. EC C→T [§5.5c]> (1/Exp) (2/Top): mourning
—DNC INC: Rev 18:7a, 7b, 8
—INC INC: Rev 21:4 [εἰμί 1]
πενθῶν (<πενθέω), 1. <Exp. EC C→T [§5.5c]> 1/Exp [2/Top]: mourning
—N DNC: Rev 18:15, 19

9. The Case Frame Lexicon 255

πέντε, 1. <*Qual*. P [§6.10a]> [1/Pat]: five
—N: Rev 9:5, 10
—DNC: Rev 17:10
πεπελεκισμένος (<πελεκίζω), **1.** <*Eff*. PA [§6.3c]> 1/Pat (2/Agt): beheaded
—N INC: Rev 20:4 (Cau: P/διά [+acc])
πεπληρωμένος (<πληρόω), **1.** <*Eff*. PA [§6.3c]> 1/Pat [2/Agt]: fulfilled, completed
—N DNC: Rev 3:2 (Loc: P/ἐνώπιον)
πεπτωκώς (<πίπτω), **1b.** <*Mot*. Θ[S]G [S=Θ] [§5.2a]> 1/Thm 2/Goa: having fallen
—N (to) P/εἰς [-an]: Rev 9:1 (Sou: P/ἐκ)
πεπυρωμένος (<πυρόω), **1.** <*Eff*. PA [§6.3c]> [1/Pat] (2/Agt): burned, made to burn
—N INC: Rev 3:18 (Ins: P/ἐκ)
—DNC INC: Rev 1:15 [DNC = κάμινος from context]
περί, 1. <*Loc*. ΘL [§5.3a]> 1/Thm 2/Loc: around
—N N+acc: Rev 15:6
περιβάλλω (>περιβεβλημένος, περιβεβλημένος + [εἰμί]), **1.** <*Ins*. API [§6.4a]> 1/Agt [2/Pat] [3/Ins]: clothe, wrap
—N N+acc (by/with) N+acc: Rev 19:8
—N N+acc (by/with) P/ἐν: Rev 3:5 (Man: Α/οὕτως)
—N DNC DNC: Rev 3:18
περιβεβλημένος (<περιβάλλω), **1.** <*Ins*. PAI [§6.4d]> 1/Pat (2/Agt) 3/Ins: clothed, wrapped
—N INC (by/with) N+acc: Rev [3:4]; 7:9, 13; 10:1; 11:3; 12:1; 18:16
—N INC (by/with) P/ἐν: Rev 4:4
περιβεβλημένος + [εἰμί] (<περιβάλλω), **1.** <*Ins*. PAI [§6.4d]> 1/Pat (2/Agt) 3/Ins: be wrapped
—N INC (by/with) N+acc: Rev 17:4; [19:13]
περιεζωσμένος (<περιζώννυμι), **1.** <*Ins*. PAI [§6.4d]> 1/Pat (2/Agt) 3/Ins: wrapped
—N INC (with) N+acc: Rev 1:13 (Loc: P/πρός [+dat]); 15:6 (Loc: P/περί [+acc])
περιζώννυμι (>περιεζωσμένος), **1.** <*Ins*. API [§6.4a]> 1/Agt 2/Pat 3/Ins: wrap.
περιπατέω (>περιπατῶν), **1.** <*Mot*. Θ[S]G [S=Θ] [§5.2a]> 1/Thm (2/Goa): walk [around]
—N INC: Rev 3:4 (Cau: V+ὅτι; Com: P/μετά [+gen]; Man: P/ἐν); 9:20; 16:15 (Cur: Adj+1); 21:24 (Ins: P/διά [+gen])
περιπατῶν (<περιπατέω), **1.** <*Mot*. Θ[S]G [S=Θ] [§5.2a]> 1/Thm [2/Goa]: walking around
—N DNC: Rev 2:1 (Loc: P/ἐν μέσῳ)
πέτομαι (>πετόμενος), **1.** <*Mot*. Θ[S]G [S=Θ] [§5.2a]> 1/Thm 2/Goa: fly
—N (to) P/εἰς [-an]: Rev 12:14 (Goa: P/εἰς [-an]; Loc: V+ὅπου)
πετόμενος (<πέτομαι), **1.** <*Mot*. Θ[S]G [S=Θ] [§5.2a]> 1/Thm (2/Goa): flying
—N INC: Rev 4:7; 8:13 (Loc: P/ἐν); 14:6 (Loc: P/ἐν); 19:7 (Loc: P/ἐν)
πέτρα, 1. <*Spec*. — [§6.12]> 0/—: rock
—Rev 6:15 (Ben: N+gen), 16
πηγή, 1. <*Mat*. M{P} [§6.5c]> 1/Mat {{2/Pat}}: spring
—(of) N+gen {N}: Rev 7:17; 8:10; 14:7; 16:4; 21:6

πιάζω, 1. <*Eff.* AP [§6.3a]> 1/Agt 2/Pat: seize
—N N+acc: Rev 19:20 (Com: P/μετά [+gen])
πικραίνω, 1. <*Mod.* AP{R} [§6.6b]> 1/Agt 2/Pat {{3/Rst}}: make {bitter}
—N N+acc {Adj+2}: Rev 8:11; 10:9, 10
πίνω, 1. <*Eff.* AP [§6.3a]> 1/Agt [2/Pat]: drink
—N DNC: Rev 14:10 (Sou: P/ἐκ); 16:6; 18:3 (Sou: P/ἐκ)
πίπτω (>πεπτωκώς), 1a. <*Mot.* Θ[S]G [S=Θ] G→L [§5.2b]> 1/Thm [2/Loc]: fall [down]
—N (in front of) P/ἔμπροσθεν: Rev 19:10 (Pur: V-i1); 22:8 (Pur: V-i1; Tem: V+ὅτε)
—N (before) P/ἐνώπιον: Rev 4:10 (Tem: V+ὅταν); 5:8 (Tem: V+ὅτε); 7:11 (Goa: P/ἐπί [+acc])
—N (at) P/πρός [+acc, -an]: Rev 1:17 (Cmp: A/ὡς Adj+1; Tem: V+ὅτε)
—N DNC: Rev 5:14; 19:4
1b. <*Mot.* Θ[S]G [S=Θ] [§5.2a]> 1/Thm 2/Goa: fall
—N (to) P/εἰς [-an]: Rev 6:13 (Cmp: V+ὡς)
—N (onto) P/ἐπί [+acc]: Rev 6:16 (Cau: V+ὅτι); 7:16; 8:10b; 11:16
1c. <*Mot.* ΘS(G) S=Θ [§5.2c]> 1/Thm 2/Sou: fall
—N (from) P/ἐκ: Rev 8:10a
—N (from where) A/πόθεν: Rev 2:5
2. <*Qual.* P [§6.10a]> 1/Pat: fall, perish
—N: Rev 11:13; 14:8a, 8b; 16:19; 17:10; 18:2a, 2b
πίστις, 1. <*Exp.* EC C→T [§5.5c]> [1/Exp] [2/Top]: faith, belief
—(of) N+gen DNC: Rev 2:19; 13:10
—DNC (in/concerning) N+gen: Rev 2:13; 14:12
πιστός (>πιστός + [εἰμί]), 1. <*Exp.* EC C→T [§5.5c]> 1/Exp [2/Top]: faithful
—N (to/concerning) N+gen: Rev 2:13
—N DNC: Rev 1:5; 2:10, 13; 3:14; 19:11
πιστός + [εἰμί] (<πιστός), 1. <*Exp.* EC C→T [§5.5c]> 1/Exp [2/Top]: be faithful
—N DNC: Rev [17:14b]; 21:5; [22:6]
πλανάω (>πλανῶν), 1. <*Dis.* AΘO [§5.7a]> 1/Agt 2/Thm 3/Occ: mislead
—N N+acc (to) V-i2: Rev 2:20
2. <*Eff.* AP [§6.3a]> 1/Agt 2/Pat: mislead, lead astray
—N N+acc: Rev 13:14 (Cau: P/διά [+acc]); 18:23 (Ins: P/ἐν); 19:20 (Ins: P/ἐν); 20:3 (Tem: A/ἔτι; Tem: V+ἄχρι), 8 (Pur: V-i1)
πλανῶν (<πλανάω), 2. <*Eff.* AP [§6.3a]> 1/Agt 2/Pat: misleading
—N N+acc: Rev 12:9; 20:10
πλατεῖα, 1. <*Ben.* B{P} [§6.1g]> 1/Ben {{2/Pat}}: street
—(of) N+gen {N}: Rev 11:8; 21:21; 22:2
πλάτος, 1. <*Ben.* B{P} [§6.1g]> [1/Ben] {{2/Pat}}: width, wideness
—(of) N+gen {N}: Rev 20:9; 21:16b
—DNC {N}: Rev 21:16a
πλείων (>πλείων + [εἰμί]), 1. <*Cmp.* PCmp [§6.9b]> 1/Pat 2/Cmp: more, greater.
πλείων + [εἰμί] (<πλείων), 1. <*Cmp.* PCmp [§6.9b]> 1/Pat 2/Cmp: be more, be greater
—N (than) N+gen: Rev [2:19]

πλέω (>πλέων), 1. < *Eff.* A{P} [§6.3b]> 1/Agt {{2/Pat}}: sail {a boat}.
πλέων (<πλέω), 1. <*Eff.* A{P} [§6.3b]> 1/Agt {{2/Pat}}: sailing {a boat}
—N {N}: Rev 18:17 (Loc: P/ἐπί [+acc])
πληγή, 1. <*Ben.* B{P}B [§6.1h]> [1/Ben] {{2/Pat}} [3/Ben]: plague, wound
—(of) N+gen {N} (of) N+gen: Rev 13:3, 12
—(of) N+gen {N} DNC: Rev 13:14; 15:8; 16:21a, 21b
—DNC {N} of N+gen: Rev 18:4, 8
—DNC {N} DNC: Rev 9:18, 20; 11:6; 15:1, 6; 16:9; 21:9; 22:18
πληρόω (>πεπληρωμένος), 1. <*Eff.* AP [§6.3a]> 1/Agt 2/Pat: fill, complete
—N N+acc: Rev 6:11 (Mea: A/καί)
πλήσσω, 1. <*Eff.* AP [§6.3a]> 1/Agt 2/Pat: strike
—N N+acc: Rev 8:12 (Res: V+ἵνα)
πλοῖον, 1. <*Ben.* B{P} [§6.1g]> (1/Ben) {{2/Pat}}: boat
—DNC {N}: Rev 18:19
—INC {N}: Rev 8:9
πλούσιος (>πλούσιος + εἰμί), 1. <*Qual.* P [§6.10a]> [1/Pat]: rich
—DNC: Rev 6:15; 13:16
πλούσιος + εἰμί (<πλούσιος), 1. <*Qual.* P [§6.10a]> 1/Pat: be rich
—N: Rev 2:9; 3:17a
πλουτέω (>πλουτήσας), 1. <*Qual.* P [§6.10a]> 1/Pat: be rich
—N: Rev 3:17, 18; 18:3 (Ins: P/ἐκ), 19 (Ins: P/ἐν; Sou: P/ἐκ)
πλουτήσας (<πλουτέω), 1. <*Qual.* P [§6.10a]> 1/Pat: being rich
—N: Rev 18:15 (Sou: P/ἀπό)
πλοῦτος, 1. <*Ben.* B{P} [§6.1g]> [1/Ben] {{2/Pat}}: riches
—DNC {N}: Rev 5:12; 18:17
πλύνω (>πλύνων), 1. <*Eff.* AP [§6.3a]> 1/Agt 2/Pat: wash
—N N+acc: Rev 7:14
πλύνων (<πλύνω), 1. <*Eff.* AP [§6.3a]> 1/Agt 2/Pat: washing
—N N+acc: Rev 22:14 (Pur: V+ἵνα)
πνεῦμα (>πνεῦμα + εἰμί), 1. <*Ben.* B{P} [§6.1g] > (1/Ben) {{2/Pat}}: spirit
—(of) N+gen {N}: Rev 3:1; 11:11; 22:6
—DNC {N}: Rev 1:4, 10; 2:7, 11, 17, 29; 3:6, 13, 32; 4:2; 14:13; 17:3; 21:10; 22:17
—INC {N}: Rev 16:13 (Cmp: A/ὡς N+1)
  2. <*non-predicator*>: spirit, non-corporeal being
Rev 13:15; 18:2
πνεῦμα + εἰμί (<πνεῦμα), 1. <*Ben.* PB [§6.1f]> 1/Pat 2/Ben: be a spirit
—N (of) N+gen: Rev 4:5b; 5:6; 16:14; 19:10c
πνέω, 1. <*Mot.* Θ[S]G [S=Θ] G→L [§5.2b]> 1/Thm 2/Loc: blow
—N (on) P/ἐπί [+gen]: Rev 7:1
—N (on) P/ἐπί [+acc]: Rev 7:1
ποιέω (>ποιήσας, ποιῶν), 1a. <*Eff.* AP [§6.3a]> 1/Agt [2/Pat]: make, do, wield, enact
—N N+acc: Rev 2:5; 13:12a (Loc: P/ἐνώπιον), 13a (Res: V+ἵνα); 17:17a, 17b; 22:11 (Tem: A/ἔτι)
—N (that) V+ἵνα: Rev 13:15
—N DNC: Rev 13:14a (Loc: P/ἐνώπιον)

1b. <*Eff.* A{P} [§6.3b]> **1/Agt {{2/Pat}}**: act, work
—**N {N}**: Rev 13:5 (Tem: N+acc)
2. <*Mod.* APR [§6.6a]> **1/Agt 2/Pat 3/Rst**: make
—**N N+acc N+2**: Rev 1:6 (Ben: N+dat [+an]); 3:12; 5:10 (Ben: N+dat [+an])
—**N N+acc Adj+2**: Rev 12:15; 17:16; 21:5
3. <*Ben.* APB [§6.1a]> **1/Agt 2/Pat 3/Ben**: make
—**N N+acc** (for) **N+dat [+an]**: Rev 13:14b
—**N** (war) **N+acc** (against) **P/μετά [+gen]**: Rev 11:7 (Tem: V+ὅταν); 12:17; 13:7; 19:19
4. <*Cpl.* APO [§5.7b]> **1/Agt 2/Pat 3/Occ**: make, compel, force
—**N N+acc** (that) **V+ἵνα**: Rev 3:9; 13:12b, 16
—**N N+acc** (to) **V-i2**: Rev 13:13b (Mea: A/καί)
ποιήσας (<ποιέω), **1a.** <*Eff.* AP [§6.3a]> **1/Agt 2/Pat**: making, doing
—**N N+acc**: Rev 14:7; 19:20 (Loc: P/ἐνώπιον)
ποιμαίνω, 1. <*Eff.* AP [§6.3a]> **1/Agt 2/Pat**: shepherd
—**N N+acc**: Rev 2:27 (Cmp: V+ὡς; Ins: P/ἐν); 7:17; 12:5 (Ins: P/ἐν); 19:15 (Ins: P/ἐν)
ποιῶν (<ποιέω), **1a.** <*Eff.* AP [§6.3a]> **1/Agt 2/Pat**: making, doing
—**N N+acc**: Rev 16:14; 21:27; 22:2, 15
ποῖος, 1. <*Qual.* P [§6.10a]> **1/Pat**: what kind of
—**N**: Rev 3:3
πολεμέω, 1. <*Ben.* A{P}B [§6.1b]> **1/Agt {{2/Pat}} [3/Ben]**: wage {war}, battle
—**N {N}** (against) **P/μετά [+gen]**: Rev 2:16 (Ins: P/ἐν); 12:7a; 13:4; 17:14
—**N {N} DNC**: Rev 12:7b; 19:11 (Ins: P/ἐν)
πόλεμος, 1. <*Ben.* B{P}B [§6.1h]> **[1/Ben] {{2/Pat}} (3/Ben)**: battle, war
—**DNC {N} DNC**: Rev 11:7 [§6.1a n. 1]; 12:7 [§6.1a n. 1], 17 [§6.1a n. 1]; 13:7 [§6.1a n. 1]; 16:14 [§6.1a n. 1]; 19:19 [§6.1a n. 1]; 20:8
—**DNC {N} INC**: Rev 9:7, 9
πόλις (>πόλις + εἰμί), **1.** <*Ben.* B{P} [§6.1g]> **[1/Ben] {{2/Pat}}**: city
—(of) **N+gen {N}**: Rev 3:12; 16:19b
—**DNC {N}**: Rev 11:2, 8 (Loc: V+ὅπου), 13; 14:20; 16:19a; 18:10a, 10b, 16, 18, 19, 21; 20:9; 21:2 (Cmp: A/ὡς N+2), 10, 14, 15, 16a, 16b, 18, 19, 21, 23; 22:14, 19
πόλις + εἰμί (<πόλις), **1.** <*Ben.* PB [§6.1f]> **1/Pat [2/Ben]**: be a city
—**N DNC**: Rev 17:18
πολύς, 1. <*Qual.* P [§6.10a]> **1/Pat**: much, many
—**N**: Rev 1:15; 5:11; 7:9; 8:3; 9:9; 10:11; 14:2; 17:1; 19:1, 6a, 6b, 12
2. <*Par.* PPar [§6.7a]> **[1/Pat] 2/Par**: much, many
—**DNC** (of) **N+gen**: Rev 8:11
πονηρός, 1. <*Qual.* P [§6.10a]> **1/Pat**: evil
—**N**: Rev 16:2
πόνος, 1. <*Ben.* B{P} [§6.1g]> **(1/Ben) {{2/Pat}}**: pain, labor
—(of) **N+gen {N}**: Rev 16:11
—**DNC {N}**: Rev 16:10
—**INC {N}**: Rev 21:4 [εἰμί 1]

9. The Case Frame Lexicon 259

πορνεία, 1. <Ins. B{P}I [§6.4f]> 1/Ben {{2/Pat}} (3/Ins): sexual immorality
—(of) N+gen {N} DNC: Rev 2:21; 14:8; 17:2, 4; 18:3; 19:2
—(of) N+gen {N} INC: Rev 9:21

πορνεύσας (<πορνεύω), 1. <Ins. A{P}I [§6.4b]> 1/Agt {{2/Pat}} (3/Ins): engaging in {sexual immorality}
—N {N} INC: Rev 18:9

πορνεύω (>πορνεύσας), 1. <Ins. A{P}I [§6.4b]> 1/Agt {{2/Pat}} (3/Ins): engage in {sexual immorality}
—N {N} (with) P/μετά [+gen]: Rev 17:2; 18:3
—N {N} INC: Rev 2:14, 20

πορφυροῦς, 1. <Qual. P [§6.10a]> (1/Pat): purple
—INC: Rev 17:4; 18:16

ποταμός, 1. <Mat. M{P} [§6.5c]> [1/Mat] {{2/Pat}}: river
—(of) N+gen {N}: Rev 22:1
—DNC {N}: Rev 8:10; 9:14; 12:15, 16; 16:4, 12; 22:2

ποταμοφόρητος, 1. <Ins. P{I} [§6.4g]> [1/Pat] {{2/Ins}}: swept away {by a river}
—DNC {N}: Rev 12:15

ποτήριον, 1. <Ben. B{P} [§6.1g]> [1/Ben] {{2/Pat}}: cup
—DNC {N}: Rev 14:10 (Mat: N+gen); 16:19 (Mat: N+gen); 17:4; 18:6

ποτίζω, 1. <Ins. AP{I} [§6.4c]> 1/Agt 2/Pat {{3/Ins}}: provide {with a cup [of something able to be drunk]}
—N N+acc {N}: Rev 14:8

πούς, 1. <Ben. B{P} [§6.1g]> [1/Ben] {{2/Pat}}: foot
—(of) N+gen {N}: Rev 1:15, 17; 2:18; 3:9; 10:1, 2a; 11:11; 12:1; 13:2a, [2b]; 19:10; 22:8
—DNC {N}: Rev [10:2b]

πρός, 1a. <Mot. Θ[S]G [S=Θ] [§5.2a]> 1/Thm 2/Goa: to
—N N+acc [+an]: Rev 3:20; 10:9; 12:5a, 12

1b. <Mot. Θ[S]G [S=Θ] G→L [§5.2b]> 1/Thm 2/Loc: at
—N N+acc [-an]: Rev 1:17; 12:5b

2. <Loc. ΘL [§5.3a]> 1/Thm 2/Loc: at
—N N+dat [-an]: Rev 1:13

3. <Ben. PB [§6.1f] > 1/Pat 2/Ben: against
—N N+acc: Rev 13:6

προσευχή (>προσευχή + εἰμί), 1. <Cmm. BCE [§5.4f]> 1/Ben (2/Con) [3/Exp]: prayer
—(of) N+gen INC DNC: Rev 8:3, 4

προσευχή + εἰμί (<προσευχή), 1. <Cmm. CBE [§5.4h]> 1/Con 2/Ben [3/Exp]: be a prayer
—N (of) N+gen DNC: Rev 5:8

προσκυνέω (>προσκυνῶν), 1. <Exp. EC [§5.5a]> 1/Exp [2/Con]: worship
—N N+dat [+an]: Rev 4:10 (Tem: V+ὅταν); 7:11; 11:16; 13:4a (Cau: V+ὅτι), 4b, 15; 14:7; 19:4, 10a, 10c; 22:9b
—N N+acc: Rev 9:20; 13:8, 12; 14:9; 20:4
—N DNC: Rev 3:9 (Loc: P/ἐνώπιον); 5:14; 15:4 (Cau: V+ὅτι; Loc: P/ἐνώπιον); [19:10b]; 22:8 (Loc: P/ἔμπροσθεν), [9a]

προσκυνῶν (<προσκυνέω), 1. <Exp. EC [§5.5a]> 1/Exp [2/Con]: worshipping
—N N+dat: Rev 16:2; 19:20
—N N+acc: 14:11
—N DNC: Rev 11:1 (Loc: P/ἐν)
πρόσωπον, 1. <Ben. B{P} [§6.1g]> [1/Ben] {{2/Pat}}: face
—(of) N+gen {N}: Rev 6:16; 7:11; 9:7a, 7b; 10:1; 11:16; 12:14; 20:11; 22:4
—DNC {N}: Rev 4:7 (Cmp: A/ὡς N+2)
προφητεία, 1. <Cmm. BCE [§5.4f]> (1/Ben) [2/Con] (3/Exp): prophecy
—(of) N+gen DNC DNC: Rev 11:6
—DNC (of) N+gen DNC: Rev 22:7, 10, 18
—DNC DNC DNC: Rev 1:3; 22:19
—INC DNC INC: Rev 19:10
προφητεύω, 1a. <Cmm. A{C}E [§5.4b]> 1/Agt {{2/Con}} (3/Exp): speak {prophecy}, prophesy
—N {N} INC: Rev 11:3 (Tem: N+acc)
1b. <Cmm. ACE C→T [§5.4c]> 1/Agt 2/Top [3/Exp]: prophesy
—N (about) P/ἐπί [+dat] DNC: Rev 10:11 (Mea: A/πάλιν)
προφήτης, 1. <Ben. B{P} [§6.1g]> [1/Ben] {{2/Pat}}: prophet
—DNC {N}: Rev 10:7; 11:10, 18; 16:6; 18:20, 24; 22:6, 8
προφῆτις, 1. <Ben. B{P} [§6.1g]> [1/Ben] {{2/Pat}}: prophetess
—DNC {N}: Rev 2:20
πρωϊνός, 1. <Qual. P [§6.10a]> 1/Pat: [of the] morning
—N: Rev 2:28, 22:16
πρῶτος (>πρῶτος + [εἰμί], ὁ πρῶτος + [εἰμί]), 1. <Par. PPar [§6.7a]> [1/Pat] (2/Par): first, former
—N DNC: Rev 2:4, 5; 4:1, 7; 13:12a, 12b; 20:6; 21:1a, 1b, 19
—N INC: Rev 1:17
—DNC DNC: Rev 2:19; 8:7; 16:2; 21:4
—DNC INC: Rev 2:8
πρῶτος + [εἰμί] (<πρῶτος), 1. <Par. PPar [§6.7a]> 1/Pat [2/Par]: be first
—N DNC: Rev [20:5]
ὁ πρῶτος + [εἰμί] (<πρῶτος), 1. <Par. PPar [§6.7a]> 1/Pat [2/Par]: be the first
—N DNC: Rev 1:17; [22:13]
πρωτότοκος, 1. <Par. PPar [§6.7a]> 1/Pat 2/Par: firstborn
—N (of) N+gen: Rev 1:5
πτέρυξ, 1. <Ben. B{P} [§6.1g]> [1/Ben] {{2/Pat}}: wing
—(of) N+gen {N}: Rev 9:9; 12:14
—DNC {N}: Rev 4:8
πτῶμα, 1. <Ben. B{P} [§6.1g]> 1/Ben {{2/Pat}}: corpse
—(of) N+gen {N}: Rev 11:8, 9a, 9b
πτωχεία, 1. <Ben. B{P} [§6.1g]> 1/Ben {{2/Pat}}: poverty
—(of) N+gen {N}: Rev 2:9
πτωχός (>πτωχός + εἰμί), 1. <Qual. P [§6.10a]> [1/Pat]: poor
—DNC: Rev 13:16

πτωχός + εἰμί (<πτωχός), 1. <Qual. P [§6.10a]> 1/Pat: be poor
—N: Rev 3:17b
πυλών, 1. <Ben. B{P} [§6.1g]> [1/Ben] {{2/Pat}}: gate
—(of) N+gen {N}: Rev 21:15, 25
—DNC {N}: Rev 21:12a, 12b, 13a, 13b, 13c, 13d, 21a, 21b; 22:14
πῦρ, 1. <Spec. — [§6.12]> 0/—: fire
—Rev 1:14; 2:18; 3:18; 4:5; 8:5 (Ben: N+gen), 7, 8; 9:17, 18; 10:1; 11:5; 13:13; 14:10, 18; 15:2; 16:8; 17:16; 18:8; 19:12, 20; 20:9, 10, 14a, 14b, 15; 21:8
πύρινος, 1. <Qual. P [§6.10a]> 1/Pat: red
—N: Rev 9:17
πυρόω (>πεπυρωμένος), 1. <Eff. AP [§6.3a]> 1/Agt 2/Pat: burn, make to burn.
πυρρός, 1. <Qual. P [§6.10a]> 1/Pat: red
—N: Rev 6:4; 12:3
πύρωσις, 1. <Ben. B{P}B [§6.1h]> (1/Ben) {{2/Pat}} 3/Ben: burning
—INC {N} (of) N+gen: Rev 18:9, 18
ῥάβδος, 1. <Ben. B{P} [§6.1g]> (1/Ben) {{2/Pat}}: staff
—DNC {N}: 2:27; 12:5; 19:15
—INC {N}: Rev 11:1
ῥίζα (>ῥίζα + εἰμί), 1. <Ben. B{P} [§6.1g]> 1/Ben {{2/Pat}}: root
—(of) N+gen {N}: Rev 5:5
ῥίζα + εἰμί (<ῥίζα), 1. <Ben. PB [§6.1f]> 1/Pat 2/Ben: be a root
—N (of) N+gen: Rev 22:16
ῥομφαία, 1. <Ben. B{P} [§6.1g]> [1/Ben] {{2/Pat}}: sword
—(of) N+gen {N}: Rev 2:16; 19:21
—DNC {N}: Rev 1:16; 2:12; 6:8; 19:15
ῥυπαίνω, 1. <Qual. P [§6.10a]> 1/Pat: be filthy
—N: Rev 22:11 (Tem: A/ἔτι)
ῥυπαρός, 1. <Qual. P [§6.10a]> (1/Pat): filthy
—INC: Rev 22:11
σάκκος, 1. <Ben. B{P} [§6.1g]> (1/Ben) {{2/Pat}}: sackcloth
—DNC {N}: Rev 11:3
—INC {N}: Rev 6:12
σάλπιγξ, 1. <Ben. B{P} [§6.1g]> (1/Ben) {{2/Pat}}: trumpet
—(of) N+gen {N}: Rev 8:13
—DNC {N}: Rev 8:2, 6; 9:14
—INC {N}: Rev 1:10; 4:1
σαλπίζω, 1. <Eff. A{P} [§6.3b]> 1/Agt {{2/Pat}}: blow {a trumpet}
—N {N}: Rev 8:6, 7, 8, 10, 12, 13; 9:1, 13; 10:7; 11:15
σάπφιρος + [εἰμί], 1. <Qual. P [§6.10a]> 1/Pat: be sapphire
—N: Rev [21:19c]
σάρδιον + [εἰμί], 1. <Qual. P [§6.10a]> 1/Pat: be sardius
—N: Rev [21:20b]
σαρδόνυξ + [εἰμί], 1. <Qual. P [§6.10a]> 1/Pat: be sardonyx
—N: Rev [21:20a]

σάρξ, 1. <*Ben.* B{P} [§6.1g]> 1/Ben {{2/Pat}}: flesh
—(of) N+gen {N}: Rev 17:16; 19:18a, 18b, 18c, 18d, 18e, 21
Σατανᾶς + εἰμί, 1. <*Qual.* P [§6.10a]> 1/Pat: be Satan
—N: Rev 20:2
σειόμενος (<σείω), 1. <*Eff.* PA [§6.3c]> 1/Pat 2/Agt: being shaken
—N (by) P/ὑπό [+gen]: Rev 6:13
σείω (>σειόμενος), 1. <*Eff.* AP [§6.3a]> 1/Agt 2/Pat: shake.
σημαίνω, 1. <*Cmm.* ACE [§5.4a]> 1/Agt 2/Con [3/Exp]: indicate, make known
—N N+acc DNC: Rev 1:1
σημεῖον, 1. <*Cmm.* BCE [§5.4f]> (1/Ben) (2/Con) (3/Exp): sign
—DNC DNC DNC: Rev 13:14; 19:20
—DNC DNC INC: Rev 13:13
—DNC INC DNC: Rev 16:14
—INC DNC DNC: Rev 12:1, 3; 15:1
σιδηροῦς, 1. <*Qual.* P [§6.10a]> 1/Pat: [made of] iron
—N: Rev 2:27; 9:9; 12:5; 19:15
σιρικός, 1. <*Qual.* P [§6.10a]> (1/Pat): [made of] silk
—INC: Rev 18:12
σκεῦος, 1. <*Mat.* B{P}M [§6.5d]> (1/Ben) {{2/Pat}} [3/Mat]: vessel
—DNC {N} (of) P/ἐκ: Rev 18:12b
—DNC {N} DNC: Rev 18:12a
—INC {N} DNC: Rev 2:27
σκηνή, 1. <*Ben.* B{P} [§6.1g]> [1/Ben] {{2/Pat}}: tent
—(of) N+gen {N}: Rev 13:6; 21:3
—DNC {N}: Rev 15:5 (Ben: N+gen)
σκηνόω (>σκηνῶν), 1. <*Loc.* ΘL [§5.3a]> 1/Thm 2/Loc: dwell in a tent
—N (over) P/ἐπί [+acc]: Rev 7:15
—N (with) P/μετά [+gen]: Rev 21:3
σκηνῶν (<σκηνόω), 1. <*Loc.* ΘL [§5.3a]> 1/Thm 2/Loc: dwelling in a tent
—N (in) P/ἐν: 12:12; 13:6
σκορπίος, 1. <*Spec.* — [§6.12]> 0/—: scorpion
—Rev 9:3 (Ben: N+gen), 5, 10
σκοτίζω, 1. <*Mod.* AP{R} [§6.6b]> 1/Agt 2/Pat {{3/Rst}}: make {dark}, darken
—N N+acc {Adj+2}: Rev 8:12
σκοτόω (>ἐσκοτωμένος), 1. <*Mod.* AP{R} [§6.6b]> 1/Agt 2/Pat {{3/Rst}}: make {dark}, darken
—N N+acc {Adj+2}: Rev 9:2 (Ins: P/ἐκ)
σμάραγδος + [εἰμί], 1. <*Qual.* P [§6.10a]> 1/Pat: be emerald
—N: Rev [21:19e]
σοφία, 1. <*Exp.* EC C→T [§5.5c]> [1/Exp] (2/Top): wisdom
—DNC INC: Rev 5:12; 7:12 [εἰμί 2]; 13:18; 17:9
σπέρμα, 1. <*Ben.* B{P} [§6.1g]> 1/Ben {{2/Pat}}: offspring
—(of) N+gen {N}: Rev 12:17
σταυρόω, 1. <*Eff.* AP [§6.3a]> 1/Agt 2/Pat: crucify
—N N+acc: Rev 11:8 (Loc: A/ὅπου; Mea: A/καί)

σταφυλή, 1. <Spec. — [§6.12]> 0/—: bunch of grapes
  —Rev 14:18 (Ben: N+gen)
στέφανος, 1. <Ben. B{P} [§6.1g]> [1/Ben] {{2/Pat}}: crown
  —(of) N+gen {N}: Rev 3:11; 4:10
  —DNC {N}: Rev 2:10 (Ben: N+gen); 4:4; 6:2; 9:7; 12:1 (Mat: N+gen); 14:14
στῆθος, 1. <Ben. B{P} [§6.1g]> [1/Ben] {{2/Pat}}: chest, breast
  —DNC {N}: Rev 15:6
στηρίζω, 1. <Eff. AP [§6.3a]> 1/Agt 2/Pat: strengthen
  —N N+acc: Rev 3:2
στολή, 1. <Ben. B{P} [§6.1g]> [1/Ben] {{2/Pat}}: robe
  —(of) N+gen {N}: Rev 7:14; 22:14
  —DNC {N}: Rev 6:11; 7:9, 13
στόμα, 1. <Ben. B{P} [§6.1g]> [1/Ben] {{2/Pat}}: mouth
  —(of) N+gen {N}: Rev 1:16; 2:16; 3:16; 9:17, 18, 19; 10:9, 10; 11:5; 12:15, 16, 16b;
       13:2a, 2b, 6; 14:5; 16:13a, 13b, 13c; 19:15, 21
  —DNC {N}: Rev 13:5
στράτευμα, 1. <Ben. B{P} [§6.1g]> [1/Ben] {{2/Pat}}: army
  —(of) N+gen {N}: Rev 19:19a, 19b
  —DNC {N}: Rev 9:16 (Mat: N+gen); 19:14 (Loc: P/ἐν)
στρέφω, 1. <Mod. APR [§6.6a]> 1/Agt 2/Pat 3/Rst: turn
  —N N+acc (into) P/εἰς: Rev 11:6
στρηνιάσας (<στρηνιάω), 1. <Qual. P [§6.10a]> 1/Pat: living in luxury
  —N: Rev 18:9
στρηνιάω (>στρηνιάσας), 1. <Qual. P [§6.10a]> 1/Pat: live in luxury
  —N: Rev 18:7
στρῆνος, 1. <Ben. B{P} [§6.1g]> 1/Ben {{2/Pat}}: extreme strength
  —(of) N+gen {N}: Rev 18:3
στῦλος, 1. <Mat. M{P} [§6.5c]> [1/Mat] {{2/Pat}}: pillar
  —(of) N+gen {N}: Rev 10:1
  —DNC {N}: Rev 3:12 (Loc: P/ἐν)
συγκοινωνέω, 1. <Com. PComL [§6.2a]> 1/Pat [2/Com] 3/Loc: be a partner
  —N DNC (in) N+dat [-an]: Rev 18:4
συγκοινωνός, 1. <Com. Com{P}L [§6.2b]> 1/Com {{2/Pat}} 3/Loc: partner
  —(of/with) N+gen {N} (in) P/ἐν: Rev 1:9 (Loc: P/ἐν)
συμβουλεύω, 1. <Cmm. ACE [§5.4a]> 1/Agt 2/Con 3/Exp: recommend, speak as advice
  —N (to) V-i3 (to) N+dat [+an]: Rev 3:18
συνάγω (>συνηγμένος), 1. <Tra. AΘ[S]G [S=A] +imp. [§5.1a]> 1/Agt 2/Thm 3/Goa:
  bring together, assemble
  —N N+acc (to) P/εἰς [-an]: Rev 16:14 (Tem: N+gen), 16; 20:8
  2. <Tra.AΘ[S]G [S=A] +imp. [§5.1a] || Tra. A[Θ][S]G [Θ=A] [S=A] pass. +imp.
  [§5.1e] || Mot. (A)Θ(S)G G=Θ pass. [§5.2f]> 1/Agt 2/Thm 3/Goa: bring together
  || 1/Agt [[2/Thm]] 3/Goa: bring [oneself] together || 1/Thm 2/Goa: come together
  —N N+acc (to) P/εἰς [-an] || N [N] (to) P/εἰς [-an] || N (to) P/εἰς [-an]: Rev
      19:17-18 (Pur: V+ἵνα)

3. <Mot. (A)Θ(S)[G] [G=Θ] [G→L] pass. [§5.2h]> 1/Thm [[2/Loc]]: be gathered, be together.
συναγωγή (>συναγωγή + [εἰμί]), 1. <Ben. B{P} [§6.1g]> 1/Ben {{2/Pat}}: synagogue
—(of) N+gen {N}: Rev 3:9
συναγωγή + [εἰμί] (<συναγωγή), 1. <Ben. BP [§6.1f]> 1/Pat 2/Ben: be a synagogue
—N (of) N+gen: Rev [2:9d]
σύνδουλος (>σύνδουλος + εἰμί), 1. <Ben. B{P} [§6.1g]> 1/Ben {{2/Pat}}: fellow slave
—(of) N+gen {N}: Rev 6:11
σύνδουλος + εἰμί (<σύνδουλος), 1. <Ben. PB [§6.1f]> 1/Pat 2/Ben: be a fellow slave
—N (of) N+gen: Rev 19:10b; 22:9b
συνηγμένος (<συνάγω), 3. <Mot. (A)Θ(S)[G] [G=Θ] [G→L] pass. [§5.2h]> 1/Thm [[2/Loc]]: gathered
—N [N]: Rev 19:19 (Pur: V-i1)
συντρίβω, 1. <Eff. AP [§6.3a]> 1/Agt 2/Pat: crush
—N N+acc: Rev 2:27
σύρω, 1. <Eff. AP [§6.3a]> 1/Agt 2/Pat: drag away
—N N+acc: Rev 12:4
σφάζω (>ἐσφαγμένος), 1. <Eff. AP [§6.3a]> 1/Agt 2/Pat: slay
—N N+acc: Rev 5:9; 6:4
σφραγίζω (>ἐσφραγισμένος, ἐσφραγισμένος + [εἰμί]), 1. <Eff. AP [§6.3a]> 1/Agt [2/Pat]: seal
—N N+acc: Rev 7:3 (Loc: P/ἐπί [+gen]); 22:10
—N (what) V+ὅ: Rev 10:4
—N DNC: Rev 20:3 (Loc: P/ἐπάνω; Pur: V+ἵνα)
σφραγίς, 1. <Ben. B{P} [§6.1g]> [1/Ben] {{2/Pat}}: seal
—(of) N+gen {N}: Rev 5:2, 5, 9; 7:2; 9:4
—DNC {N}: Rev 5:1; 6:1, 3, 5, 7, 9, 12; 8:1
σωτηρία, 1. <Ben. B{P}B [§6.1h]> [1/Ben] {{2/Pat}} [3/Ben]: salvation
—(of) N+gen {N} DNC: Rev 19:1 [εἰμί 1]
—DNC {N} DNC: Rev 7:10 [εἰμί 2]; 12:10
ταλαίπωρος (>ταλαίπωρος + εἰμί), 1. <Exp. EC C→T [§5.5c]> 1/Exp 2/Top: wretched.
ταλαίπωρος + εἰμί (<ταλαίπωρος), 1. <Exp. EC C→T [§5.5c]> 1/Exp (2/Top): be wretched
—N INC: Rev 3:17b
ταλαντιαῖος, 1. <Qual. P [§6.10a]> [1/Pat]: weighing a talent
—DNC: Rev 16:21
τε καί, 1. <Coor. --- --- [§6.11b]> 1/--- 2/---: and
—N N: Rev 19:18
τεῖχος, 1. <Ben. B{P} [§6.1g]> [1/Ben] {{2/Pat}}: wall
—(of) N+gen {N}: Rev 21:14, 15, 17, 18, 19
—DNC {N}: Rev 21:12
τέκνον, 1. <Ben. B{P} [§6.1g]> 1/Ben {{2/Pat}}: child
—(of) N+gen {N}: Rev 2:23; 12:4, 5
τελέω, 1. <Eff. AP [§6.3a]> 1/Agt 2/Pat: finish, complete, accomplish
—N N+acc: Rev 10:7 (Cmp: V+ὡς), 11:7; 15:1 (Ins: P/ἐν), 8; 17:17; 20:3, 5, 7

9. The Case Frame Lexicon 265

τέλος (>τέλος + [εἰμί]), 1. <Ben. B{P} [§6.1g]> [1/Ben] {{2/Pat}}: end, goal
—DNC {N}: Rev 2:26
τέλος + [εἰμί] (<τέλος), 1. <Ben. PB [§6.1f]> 1/Pat [2/Ben]: be the end
—N DNC: Rev 21:6; [22:13]
τεσσεράκοντα, 1. <Qual. P [§6.10a]> 1/Pat: forty
—N: Rev 7:4; 11:2; 13:5; 14:1, 3; 21:17
τέσσαρες, 1. <Qual. P [§6.10a]> 1/Pat: four
—N: Rev 4:4a, 4b, 6, 8, 10; 5:6, 8a, 8b, 14; 6:1, 6; 7:1a, 1b, 1c, 2, 4, 11; 9:13, 14, 15; 11:16; 14:1, 3a, 3b; 15:7; 19:4a, 4b; 20:8; 21:17
τέταρτος, 1. <Par. PPar [§6.7a]> [1/Pat] [2/Par]: fourth
—N DNC: Rev 4:7; 6:7a, 7b; 8:12
—DNC (of) N+gen: Rev 6:8
—DNC DNC: Rev 16:8; 21:19
τετράγωνος, 1. <Qual. P [§6.10a]> 1/Pat: four-cornered, rectangular
—N: Rev 21:16
τέχνη, 1. <Ben. B{P} [§6.1g]> [1/Ben] {{2/Pat}}: craft
—DNC {N}: Rev 18:22
τεχνίτης, 1. <Ben. B{P} [§6.1g]> 1/Ben {{2/Pat}}: craftsman
—(of) N+gen {N}: Rev 18:22
τηλικοῦτος (>τηλικοῦτος + [εἰμί]), 1. <Qual. P [§6.10a]> 1/Pat: so great.
τηλικοῦτος + [εἰμί] (<τηλικοῦτος), 1. <Qual. P [§6.10a]> 1/Pat: be so great
—N: Rev [16:18 (Man: A/οὕτω)]
τηρέω (>τηρῶν), 1. <Eff. AP [§6.3a]> 1/Agt [2/Pat]: keep, hold
—N N+acc: Rev 2:26 (Tem: P/ἄχρι); 3:8, 10a
—N DNC: Rev 3:3
2. <Sep. APS [§6.8a]> 1/Agt 2/Pat 3/Sou: keep
—N N+acc (from) P/ἐκ: Rev 3:10b (Cau: V+ὅτι; Mea: A/καί)
τηρῶν (<τηρέω), 1. <Eff. AP [§6.3a]> 1/Agt [2/Pat]: keeping
—N N+acc: Rev 1:3; 12:17; 14:12; 16:15 (Pur: V+ἵνα); 22:7, 9
—N DNC: Rev 2:26 (Tem: P/ἄχρι)
τίθημι, 1a. <Tra. AΘ[S]G [S=A] +imp. [§5.1a]> 1/Agt 2/Thm 3/Goa: place, put, set
—N N+acc (to) P/εἰς [–an]: Rev 11:9
—N N+acc (to) P/ἐπί [+acc]: Rev 1:17
1b. <Tra. AΘ[S]G [S=A] G→L +imp. [§5.1b]> 1/Agt 2/Thm 3/Loc: place, put
—N N+acc (on) P/ἐπί [+gen]: Rev 10:2
τίκτω, 1. <Eff. AP [§6.3a]> 1/Agt [2/Pat]: bear, give birth to
—N N+acc: Rev 12:4b, 5, 13
—N DNC: Rev 12:2, 4a
τιμή, 1. <Ben. B{P} [§6.1g]> [1/Ben] {{2/Pat}}: honor
—(of) N+gen {N}: Rev 21:26
—DNC {N}: Rev 4:9, 11; 5:12, 13 [εἰμί 2]; 7:12 [εἰμί 2]
τίμιος, 1. <Qual. P [§6.10a]> 1/Pat: precious
—N: Rev 17:4; 18:12, 16; 21:19
τιμιότης, 1. <Ben. B{P} [§6.1g]> 1/Ben {{2/Pat}}: wealth
—(of) N+gen {N}: Rev 18:19

τιμιώτατος, 1. <Cmp. PCmp [§6.9b]> 1/Pat [2/Cmp]: most precious
—N DNC: Rev 18:12; 21:11
τίς + εἰμί, 1. <Qual. P [§6.10a]> 1/Pat: be who?
—N: Rev 7:13
τόξον, 1. <Ben. B{P} [§6.1g]> [1/Ben] {{2/Pat}}: bow
—DNC {N}: Rev 6:2
τοπάζιον + [εἰμί], 1. <Qual. P [§6.10a]> 1/Pat: be topaz
—N: Rev [21:20e]
τόπος, 1. <Ben. B{P} [§6.1g]> [1/Ben] {{2/Pat}}: place
—(of) N+gen {N}: Rev 2:5; 6:14; 12:8, 14 (Loc: A/ὅπου)
—DNC {N}: Rev 12:6; 16:16; 18:17; 20:11
τοσοῦτος, 1. <Qual. P [§6.10a]> 1/Pat: so much, such
—N: Rev 18:7, 17
τρεῖς, 1. <Qual. P [§6.10a]> 1/Pat: three
—N: Rev 6:6; 8:13; 9:18; 11:9, 11; 16:13, 19; 21:13a, 13b, 13c, 13d
τρέφω, 1. <Eff. AP [§6.3a]> 1/Agt 2/Pat: feed
—N N+acc: Rev 12:6 (Loc: A/ἐκεῖ; Tem: N+acc), 14 (Loc: A/ἐκεῖ; Loc: P/ἀπό; Tem: N+acc)
τρέχω (>τρέχων), 1. <Mot. Θ[S]G [S=Θ] [§5.2a]> 1/Thm 2/Goa: run.
τρέχων (<τρέχω), 1. <Mot. Θ[S]G [S=Θ] [§5.2a]> 1/Thm 2/Goa: running
—N (to) P/εἰς [–an]: Rev 9:9
τρίτος, 1. <Par. PPar [§6.7a]> [1/Pat] [2/Par]: third
—N DNC: Rev 4:7; 6:5a, 5b; 8:10a; 11:14; 14:9
—DNC (of) N+gen: Rev 8:7a, 7b, 8, 9a, 9b, 10b, 11, 12a, 12b, 12c, 12d, 12e; 9:15, 18; 12:4
—DNC DNC: Rev 16:4; 21:19
τρίχινος, 1. <Qual. P [§6.10a]> 1/Pat: [made of] hair
—N: Rev 6:12
τρυγάω, 1. <Tra. AΘS[G] [G=A] +imp. [§5.1c]> 1/Agt 2/Thm [3/Sou]: gather
—N N+acc DNC: Rev 14:18 (Cau: V+ὅτι), 19
τυφλός (>τυφλός + εἰμί), 1. <Qual. P [§6.10a]> 1/Pat: blind.
τυφλός + εἰμί (<τυφλός), 1. <Qual. P [§6.10a]> 1/Pat: be blind
—N: Rev 3:17b
ὑακίνθινος, 1. <Qual. P [§6.10a]> 1/Pat: blue
—N: Rev 9:17
ὑάκινθος + [εἰμί], 1. <Qual. P [§6.10a]> 1/Pat: be hyacinth
—N: Rev [21:20g]
ὑάλινος, 1. <Qual. P [§6.10a]> 1/Pat: [made of] glass
—N: Rev 4:6; 15:2a, 2b
ὕδωρ, 1. <Spec. — [§6.12]> 0/—: water
—Rev 1:15; 7:17 (Ben: N+gen); 8:10, 11a, 11b; 11:6; 12:15 (Cmp: A/ὡς N+2); 14:2, 7; 16:4, 5, 12 (Ben: N+gen); 17:1, 15; 19:6; 21:6 (Ben: N+gen); 22:1 (Ben: N+gen), 17 (Ben: N+gen)
υἱός (>υἱός + εἰμί), 1. <Ben. B{P} [§6.1g]> [1/Ben] {{2/Pat}}: son
—(of) N+gen {N}: Rev 1:13; 2:14, 18; 7:4; 14:14; 21:12

—DNC {N}: Rev 12:5
υἱός + εἰμί (<υἱός), 1. <Ben. PB [§6.1f]> 1/Pat 2/Ben: be a son
—N (of/for) N+dat [+an]: Rev 21:7b
ὑπάγω, 1a. <Mot. Θ[S]G [S=Θ] [§5.2a]> 1/Thm [2/Goa]: go
—N (to) P/εἰς [-an]: Rev 13:10 (Cnd: V+εἰ); 17:8, 11
—N DNC: Rev 14:4
1b. <Mot. Θ[S](G) [S=Θ] [§5.2d]> 1/Thm [[2/Sou]]: go
—N [N]: Rev 10:8; 16:1
ὑπό, 1. <Eff. PA [§6.3c]> 1/Pat 2/Agt: by
—N N+gen: Rev 6:8, 13
ὑποκάτω (>ὑποκάτω + [εἰμί]), 1. <Loc. ΘL [§5.3a]> 1/Thm 2/Loc: under
—N N+gen: Rev 5:3; 6:9
ὑποκάτω + [εἰμί] (<ὑποκάτω), 1. <Loc. ΘL [§5.3a]> 1/Thm 2/Loc: be under
—N N+gen: Rev [5:13]; [12:1b]
ὑπομονή, 1. <Exp. ECT [§5.5d]> [1/Exp] [2/Con] [3/Top]: endurance
—(of) N+gen DNC DNC: Rev 2:2, 19; 13:10; 14:12
—DNC DNC DNC: Rev 1:9 (Loc: P/ἐν); 2:3; 3:10
ὑψηλός, 1. <Qual. P [§6.10a]> 1/Pat: high
—N: Rev 21:10, 12
ὕψος, 1. <Ben. B{P} [§6.1g]> 1/Ben {{2/Pat}}: height
—(of) N+gen {N}: Rev 21:16
φαίνω, 1. <Qual. P [§6.10a]> 1/Pat: be bright, shine
—N: Rev 1:16 (Cmp: V+ὡς; Ins: P/ἐν); 8:12a (Tem: N+acc), [12b (Man: A/ὁμοίως)]; 18:23 (Cau: V+ὅτι; Loc: P/ἐν; Tem: A/ἔτι); 21:23 (Loc: N+dat [-an])
φανερόω, 1. <Cmm. ACE [§5.4a]> 1/Agt 2/Con (3/Exp): make known, reveal
—N N+acc DNC: Rev 15:4
—N N+acc INC: Rev 3:18
φαρμακεία, 1. <Ben. B{P} [§6.1g]> 1/Ben {{2/Pat}}: magic
—(of) N+gen {N}: Rev 18:23
φάρμακον, 1. <Ben. B{P} [§6.1g]> 1/Ben {{2/Pat}}: magic potion
—(of) N+gen {N}: Rev 9:21
φέρω, 1. <Tra. AΘ[S]G [S=A] +imp. [§5.1a]> 1/Agt 2/Thm 3/Goa: carry, bring, drive [by wind]
—N N+acc (to/into) P/εἰς [-an]: Rev 21:24, 26
φεύγω, 1a. <Mot. Θ[S]G [S=Θ] [§5.2a]> 1/Thm (2/Goa): flee
—N (into) P/εἰς [-an]: Rev 12:6 (Pur: V+ἵνα)
—N INC: Rev 16:20
1b. <Mot. ΘS(G) S=Θ [§5.2c]> 1/Thm 2/Sou: flee
—N (from) P/ἀπό: Rev 9:6; 20:11
φθείρω, 1. <Eff. AP [§6.3a]> 1/Agt 2/Pat: corrupt, ruin
—N N+acc: Rev 19:2 (Ins: P/ἐν)
φιάλη, 1. <Ben. B{P} [§6.1g]> [1/Ben] {{2/Pat}}: bowl
—(of) N+gen {N}: Rev 16:2, 3, 4, 8, 10, 12, 17
—DNC {N}: Rev 5:8; 15:7; 16:1 (Mat: N+gen); 17:1; 21:9

φιλέω (>φιλῶν), 1. <Exp. EC [§5.5a]> 1/Exp 2/Con: love, like
—N N+acc: Rev 3:19
φιλῶν (<φιλέω), 1. <Exp. EC [§5.5a]> 1/Exp 2/Con: liking
—N N+acc: Rev 22:15
φλόξ, 1. <Mat. M{P} [§6.5c]> 1/Mat {{2/Pat}}: flame
—(of) N+gen {N}: Rev 1:14; 2:18; 19:12
φοβέομαι (>φοβούμενος), 1. <Exp. EC [§5.5a]> 1/Exp [2/Con]: fear, be afraid of
—N N+acc: Rev 2:10; 14:7 (Cau: V+ὅτι); 15:4 (Cau: V+ὅτι; Voc: N+voc)
—N DNC: Rev 1:17
φόβος, 1. <Exp. EC [§5.5a]> [1/Exp] [2/Con]: fear
—DNC (of) N+gen: Rev 18:10, 15
—DNC DNC: Rev 11:11
φοβούμενος (<φοβέομαι), 1. <Exp. EC [§5.5a]> 1/Exp 2/Con: fearing
—N N+acc: Rev 11:18; 19:5
φονεύς, 1. <Ben. B{P} [§6.1g]> (1/Ben) {{2/Pat}}: murderer
—INC {N}: Rev 21:8; 22:15
φόνος, 1. <Ben. B{P}B [§6.1h]> 1/Ben {{2/Pat}} (3/Ben): murder
—(of) N+gen {N} INC: Rev 9:21
φρέαρ, 1. <Ben. B{P} [§6.1g]> [1/Ben] {{2/Pat}}: pit
—(of) N+gen {N}: Rev 9:1, 2a
—DNC {N}: Rev 9:2b, 2c
φυλακή, 1. <Ben. B{P}B [§6.1h]> (1/Ben) {{2/Pat}} [3/Ben]: prison
—DNC {N} (of/for) N+gen: Rev 18:2a, 2b, 2c; 20:7
—INC {N} DNC: Rev 2:10
φυλή, 1. <Ben. B{P} [§6.1g]> (1/Ben) {{2/Pat}}: tribe
—(of) N+gen {N}: Rev 1:7; 5:5; 7:4, 5a, 5b, 5c, 6a, 6b, 6c, 7a, 7b, 7c, 8a, 8b, 8c; 9:9; 21:12
—INC {N}: Rev 5:9; 7:9; 11:9; 13:7; 14:6
φύλλον, 1. <Ben. B{P} [§6.1g]> 1/Ben {{2/Pat}}: leaf
—(of) N+gen {N}: Rev 22:2
φωνέω, 1. <Cmm. ACE [§5.4a]> 1/Agt [2/Con] 3/Exp: speak loudly, shout
—N DNC (to) N+dat [+an]: Rev 14:18 (Ins: N+dat) [LM]
φωνή, 1. <Ben. B{P} [§6.1g]> (1/Ben) {{2/Pat}}: voice, sound
—(of) N+gen {N}: Rev [1:10b], 15a, 15b; 3:20; [4:1b]; 5:11; 6:1, 7; 8:13b; 9:9a, 9b; 10:3b, 7; 14:2b, 2c, [2e]; 18:22a, 22b, 23; 19:1 (Loc: P/ἐν), 6a, 6b, 6c
—DNC {N}: Rev 1:10a (Cmp: A/ὡς DNC; Loc: P/ὀπίσω), 12; 4:1a (Cmp: A/ὡς DNC); 5:2, 12; 6:10; 7:2, 10; 8:13a; 9:13; 10:3a, 8 (Sou: P/ἐκ); 14:2d, 7, 9, 15, 18; 18:2; 19:17
—INC {N}: Rev 4:5; 6:6 (Loc: P/ἐν); 8:5; 10:4 (Sou: P/ἐκ), 8; 11:12 (Sou: P/ἐκ), 15, 19; 12:10 (Loc: P/ἐν); 14:2a (Cmp: A/ὡς N+2; Sou: P/ἐκ), 13 (Sou: P/ἐκ); 16:1 (Sou: P/ἐκ), 17, 18; 18:4 (Sou: P/ἐκ); 19:5; 21:3 (Sou: P/ἐκ)
φῶς, 1. <Ben. B{P} [§6.1g]> 1/Ben {{2/Pat}}: light
—(of) N+gen {N}: Rev 18:23; 21:24; 22:5a, 5b
φωστήρ, 1. <Ben. B{P} [§6.1g]> 1/Ben {{2/Pat}}: light
—(of) N+gen {N}: Rev 21:11

9. The Case Frame Lexicon

φωτίζω, 1. <*Eff.* AP [§6.3a]> 1/Agt [2/Pat]: illuminate
—N N+acc: Rev 18:1 (Ins: P/ἐκ); 21:23
—N DNC: Rev 22:5 (Loc: P/ἐπί [+acc])

χαίρω, 1. <*Exp.* EC C→T [§5.5c]> 1/Exp [2/Top]: rejoice
—N (at/concerning) P/ἐπί [+dat]: Rev 11:10 (Cau: V+ὅτι)
—N DNC: Rev 19:7 (Cau: V+ὅτι)

χαλκηδών + [εἰμί], 1. <*Qual.* P [§6.10a]> 1/Pat: be chalcedony
—N: Rev [21:19d]

χαλινός, 1. <*Ben.* B{P} [§6.1h]> (1/Ben) {{2/Pat}} 3/Ben: bridle
—INC {N} (of) N+gen: Rev 14:20

χαλκοῦς, 1. <*Qual.* P [§6.10a]> 1/Pat: [made of] bronze
—N: Rev 9:20

χάραγμα, 1. <*Ben.* B{P}B [§6.1h]> [1/Ben] {{2/Pat}} [3/Ben]: mark, stamp
—(of) N+gen {N} DNC: Rev 14:11; 16:2; 19:20
—DNC {N} DNC: Rev 13:16, 17; 14:9; 20:4

χάρις, 1. <*Ben.* B{P}B [§6.1h]> [1/Ben] {{2/Pat}} [3/Ben]: grace, gift
—(of) N+gen {N} DNC: Rev 22:21
—DNC {N} (to/for) N+dat: Rev 1:4

χείρ, 1. <*Ben.* B{P} [§6.1g]> 1/Ben {{2/Pat}}: hand
—(of) N+gen {N}: Rev 1:16, [17], [20]; [2:1]; [5:1], [7]; 6:5; 7:9; 8:4; 9:20; 10:2, 5, 8, 10; 13:16; 14:9, 14; 17:4; 19:2; 20:1, 4

χήρα (>χήρα + εἰμί), 1. <*Ben.* B{P} [§6.1g]> 1/Ben {{2/Pat}}: widow.

χήρα + εἰμί (<χήρα), 1. <*Ben.* PB [§6.1f]> 1/Pat (2/Ben): be a widow
—N INC: Rev 18:7

χιλίαρχος, 1. <*Ben.* {B}{P} [§6.1j]> {{1/Ben}} {{2/Pat}}: {commander} {of a thousand}
—{N} {N}: Rev 6:15; 19:18

χιλιάς (>χιλιάς + εἰμί), 1. <*Mat.* M{P} [§6.5c]> [1/Mat] {{2/Pat}}: {thousand-member group}
—(of) N+gen {N}: Rev 21:16
—DNC {N}: Rev 5:11b; 7:4, 5a, 5b, 5c, 6a, 6b, 6c, 7a, 7b, 7c, 8a, 8b, 8c; 11:13; 14:1, 3

χιλιάς + εἰμί (<χιλιάς), 1. <*Mat.* PM [§6.5b]> 1/Pat 2/Mat: be a thousand-member group
—N (of) N+gen: Rev 5:11

χίλιοι, 1. <*Qual.* P [§6.10a]> 1/Pat: one thousand
—N: Rev 11:3; 12:6; 14:20; 20:2, 3, 4, 5, 6, 7

χλιαρός (>χλιαρός + εἰμί), 1. <*Qual.* P [§6.10a]> 1/Pat: tepid, lukewarm.

χλιαρός + εἰμί (<χλιαρός), 1. <*Qual.* P [§6.10a]> 1/Pat: be tepid, be lukewarm
—N: Rev 3:16

χλωρός, 1. <*Qual.* P [§6.10a]> (1/Pat): yellow-green
—N: Rev 6:8; 8:7
—INC: Rev 9:4

χοῖνιξ, 1. <*Mat.* M{P} [§6.5c]> 1/Mat {{2/Pat}}: quart
—(of) N+gen {N}: Rev 6:6a [εἰμί 1], 6b [εἰμί 1]

χορτάζω, 1. <*Eff.* AP [§6.3a]> 1/Agt 2/Pat: feed [to satisfaction]
—N N+acc: Rev 19:21 (Sou: P/ἐκ)

χόρτος, 1. <Spec. — [§6.12]> 0/—: grass
—Rev 8:7; 9:4 (Ben: N+gen)
χρεία, 1. <Exp. EC [§5.5a]> [1/Exp] (2/Con): need
—DNC (of) N+gen: Rev 21:23 (Pur: V+ἵνα); 22:5
—DNC INC: Rev 3:17
Χριστός, 1. <Ben. B{P} [§6.1g]> [1/Ben] {{2/Pat}}: Christ
—(of) N+gen {N}: Rev 11:15; 12:10
—DNC {N}: Rev 1:1, 2, 5; 20:4, 6
χρυσίον + [εἰμί], 1. <Qual. P [§6.10a]> 1/Pat: be gold
—N: Rev [21:18b], [21c (Cmp: A/ὡς N+1)]
χρυσόλιθος + [εἰμί], 1. <Qual. P [§6.10a]> 1/Pat: be chrysolite
—N: Rev [21:20c]
χρυσόπρασος + [εἰμί], 1. <Qual. P [§6.10a]> 1/Pat: be chrysoprase
—N: Rev [21:20f]
χρυσοῦς, 1. <Qual. P [§6.10a]> 1/Pat: [made of] gold, golden
—N: Rev 1:12, 13, 20; 2:1; 4:4; 5:8; 8:3a, 3b; 9:13, 20; 14:14; 15:6, 7; 17:4; 21:15
χρυσόω (>κεχρυσωμένος, κεχρυσωμένος + εἰμί), 1. <Ins. API [§6.4a]> 1/Agt 2/Pat 3/Ins: gild.
ψεύδομαι, 1. <Cmm. A{C}E [§5.4b]> 1/Agt {{2/Con}} (3/Exp): speak {a lie}, lie
—N {N} INC: Rev 3:9
ψευδοπροφήτης, 1. <Ben. B{P} [§6.1g]> [1/Ben] {{2/Pat}}: false prophet
—DNC {N}: Rev 16:13; 19:20; 20:10
ψεῦδος, 1. <Cmm. BCE [§5.4f]> [1/Ben] (2/Con) (3/Exp): lie
—DNC INC INC: Rev 14:5; 21:27; 22:15
ψηφίζω, 1. <Eff. AP [§6.3a]> 1/Agt 2/Pat: count, calculate
—N N+acc: Rev 13:18
ψυχή, 1. <Ben. B{P} [§6.1g]> [1/Ben] {{2/Pat}}: life, self
—(of) N+gen {N}: Rev 6:9; 12:11; 16:3 (Loc: P/ἐν); 18:13, 14; 20:4
—DNC {N}: Rev 8:9
ψυχρός (>ψυχρός + εἰμί), 1. <Qual. P [§6.10a]> 1/Pat: cold.
ψυχρός + εἰμί (<ψυχρός), 1. <Qual. P [§6.10a]> 1/Pat: be cold
—N: Rev 3:15a, 15b, 16
τὸ ὦ + [εἰμί], 1. <Qual. P [§6.10a]> 1/Pat: be the omega
—N: Rev 1:8a; 21:6; [22:13]
ὧδε + [εἰμί], 1. <Loc. Θ[L] [L=Θ] [§5.3b]> 1/Thm [[2/Loc]]: be here
—N [N]: Rev 13:10b, 18a; 14:12; [17:9a]
ᾠδή, 1. <Ben. B{P} [§6.1g]> [1/Ben] {{2/Pat}}: song
—(of) N+gen {N}: Rev 15:3a, 3b
—DNC {N}: Rev 5:9; 14:3a, 3b
ὠδίνω (>ὠδίνων), 1. <Exp. E{C} [§5.5b]> 1/Exp {{2/Con}}: suffer {birth pains}.
ὠδίνων (<ὠδίνω), 1. <Exp. E{C} [§5.5b]> 1/Exp {{2/Con}}: suffering {birth-pains}
—N {N}: Rev 12:2
ὤν (<εἰμί), 1. <Qual. > P [§6.10a] 1/Pat: being
—N: Rev 1:4b, 8b; 4:8f; 11:17a; 16:5b

ὥρα, 1. <*Spec.* — [§6.12]> **0/—**: hour
—Rev 3:3, 10 (Ben: N+gen); 9:15; 11:13; 14:7 (Ben: N+gen), 15 (Pur: V+i); 17:12; 18:10, 17, 19

ὡς (>ὡς + [εἰμί]), 1. <*Cmp.* PCmp [§6.9b]> **(1/Pat) [2/Cmp]**: like, as [if]
—**N N+1**: Rev 1:14c; 16:13; 21:11, 21
—**N N+2**: Rev 2:18; 6:1, 12b; 9:8a, 9a; 12:15; 14:2a, 2b; 21:2; 22:1
—**N V+**: Rev 1:14a, 14b; 2:24, 27, 28; 3:3, 21; 6:11, 12a, 13, 14; 9:2, 3; 10:7, 9; 13:11; 16:15; 17:12; 18:6; 22:12
—**Adj V+**: Rev 8:10
—**Adj+1 Adj+1**: Rev 16:21
—**N DNC**: Rev 1:10, 17; [4:1], 7; 5:6; 16:3; 18:21
—**DNC N+2**: Rev 1:15a [DNC = χαλκολίβανον from context]
—(something) **INC N+2**: Rev 6:6; 8:8; 14:3; 15:2; 19:1, 6a, 6b, 6c
2. <*Tem.* PTem [§6.9d]> **1/Pat 2/Tem**: about
—**N N+acc**: Rev 8:1

ὡς + [εἰμί] (<ὡς), 1. <*Cmp.* PCmp [§6.9b]> **(1/Pat) [2/Cmp]**: be [something] like, be as if
—**N N+1**: Rev [1:15b], [16]; [9:5 (Tem: V+ὅταν)], [7c], [9b], [17]; [10:1b], [1c], [10]; [13:2b]; [19:12a]; [20:8]
—**N Adj+1**: Rev 13:3
—**N DNC**: Rev 9:8b; [13:2a]; [14:2a]
—(something) **INC N+1**: Rev [4:6a (Loc: P/ἐνώπιον)]; [9:7b]

APPENDIX

A. Thematic Role Definitions
(Abbreviations in Valence Descriptions—
Event Configurations/Usage Labels)

Agent (Agt–A): The animate entity that actively instigates an action and/or is the ultimate cause of a change in another entity.

Benefactive (Ben–B): The ultimate entity for which an action is performed or for which, literally or figuratively, something happens or exists.

Cause (Cau–Cau): The circumstantial motivation for an action or event.

Comitative (Com–Com): The entity or event associated with another entity or event.

Comparative (Cmp–Cmp): The entity or event compared to another entity or event.

Condition (Cnd): The entity or event required for another event to occur.

Content (Con–C): What is experienced in a sensory, cognitive, or emotional event or activity.

Current (Cur–Cur): The present state of an entity.

Experiencer (Exp–E): The animate entity that undergoes a sensory, cognitive, or emotional event or activity.

Goal (Goa–G): The literal or figurative entity towards which something moves.

Instrument (Ins–I): The means by which an action is performed or something happens.

Locative (Loc–L): The literal or figurative place in which an entity is situated or an event occurs.

Manner (Man–Man): The circumstantial qualification of an action or event.

Material (Mat–M): The sensible or metaphorical substance of an entity.

Measure (Mea–Mea): The quantification of an action or event or price of an entity.

Occurrence (Occ–O): The complete circumstantial scene of an action or event.

Partitive (Par–Par): The entity specified as part of a whole or as part of a series.

Patient (Pat–P): The entity undergoing an action or the object of predication.

Purpose (Pur–Pur): The goal of a complete action or event.

Result (Res–Res): The consequence of a complete event.

Resultative (Rst–R): The final state of an entity.

Source (Sou–S): The literal or figurative entity from which something moves.

Temporal (Tem–Tem): The time, either durative or punctual, of an action or event.

Theme (Thm–Θ): The entity moving from one place to another or located in a place.

Topic (Top–T): That which a sensory, cognitive, or emotional event or activity concerns.
Unspecified (Uns–U): The entity awaiting specification of its semantic function.
Vocative (Voc–Voc): The directly addressed entity.

B. Event and Non-Event Designations, Abbreviations, and Configurations

event	base	inco.	rein.	bifu.
authority (*Aut.*)	BOL			
benefaction (*Ben.*)	PB	APB, BPL	BPB	BP^1/P^2
capacity (*Cap.*)	UO	AUO		
causation (*Cau.*)	PCau			
communication (*Cmm.*)	ACE	ACEB	BCE	
communion (*Com.*)	PCom	PComL		
comparison (*Cmp.*)	PCmp			
compulsion (*Cpl.*)	APO			
delegation (*Del.*)	AOSG			
disposition (*Dis.*)	AΘO			
effect (*Eff.*)	AP			
experience (*Exp.*)	EC	ECT, ECCur		EC^1/C^2, EC^1/C^{2}T
instrumentality (*Ins.*)	PI	API	BPI	
location (*Loc.*)	ΘL			
materiality (*Mat.*)	PM	APM	BPM	
measurement (*Mea.*)	PMea			
modification (*Mod.*)	PR	APR		
motion (*Mot.*)	ΘSG			
necessity (*Nec.*)	OI			
partition (*Par.*)	PPar			
separation (*Sep.*)	APS			
temporality (*Tem.*)	PTem			
transference (*Tra.*)	AΘSG			

non-event	*base*
qualification (*Qual.*)	P, O
coordination (*Coor.*)	— —, --- ---
specification (*Spec.*)	—

C. Usage Labels by Event or Non-Event (92 Usages)

1. Usages of Transference (13)

[§5.1a] AΘ[S]G [S=A] +Imp.
[§5.1b] AΘ[S]G [S=A] G→L +Imp.
[§5.1c] AΘS[G] [G=A] +Imp.
[§5.1d] AΘS(G) S=A +Imp.

[§5.1e] A[Θ][S]G [Θ=A] [S=A] Pass. +Imp.
[§5.1f] ΘA[S]G [S=A] +Imp.
[§5.1g] ΘA[S]G [S=A] G→L +Imp.
[§5.1h] ΘA(S)G G=A +Imp.
[§5.1i] AΘ[S]G [S=A] −Imp.
[§5.1j] AΘ[S]G [S=A] G→L −Imp.
[§5.1k] A[Θ][S]G [Θ=A] [S=A] G→L Pass. −Imp.
[§5.1m] AΘS(G) S=A −Imp.
[§5.1n] ΘA[S]G [S=A] −Imp.

2. Usages of Motion (8)

[§5.2a] Θ[S]G [S=Θ]
[§5.2b] Θ[S]G [S=Θ] G→L
[§5.2c] ΘS(G) S=Θ
[§5.2d] Θ[S](G) [S=Θ]
[§5.2e] GΘS S=Θ/(A)GΘS S=Θ
[§5.2f] (A)Θ(S)G G=Θ Pass.
[§5.2g] (A)Θ(S)G G=Θ G→L Pass.
[§5.2h] (A)Θ(S)[G] [G=Θ] [G→L] Pass.

3. Usages of Location (2)

[§5.3a] ΘL
[§5.3b] Θ[L] [L=Θ]

4. Usages of Communication (9)

[§5.4a] ACE
[§5.4b] A{C}E
[§5.4c] ACE C→T
[§5.4d] AEC
[§5.4e] AE{C}
[§5.4f] BCE
[§5.4g] B{C}E
[§5.4h] CBE
[§5.4i] ACE[B] [B=A] Pass.

5. Usages of Experience (8)

[§5.5a] EC
[§5.5b] E{C}
[§5.5c] EC C→T
[§5.5d] ECT
[§5.5e] EC^1/C^2
[§5.5f] EC/C^2 T
[§5.5g] ECCur
[§5.5h] CE

6. Usages of Capacity (2)

[§5.6a] AUO
[§5.6b] UO

7. Usage of Disposition (1)

[§5.7a] AΘO

8. Usage of Compulsion (1)

[§5.7b] APO

9. Usage of Delegation (1)

[§5.7c] AO[S]G [S=A] +imp.

10. Usage of Necessity (1)

[§5.7d] OI

11. Usage of Authority (1)

[§5.7e] BOL

12. Usages of Benefaction (10)

[§6.1a] APB
[§6.1b] A{P}B
[§6.1c] BP
[§6.1d] BP/¹P²
[§6.1e] B[P]L
[§6.1f] PB
[§6.1g] B{P}
[§6.1h] B{P}B
[§6.1i] PA{B}
[§6.1j] {B}{P}

13. Usages of Communion (3)

[§6.2a] PComL
[§6.2b] Com{P}L
[§6.2c] PCom

14. Usages of Effect (3)

[§6.3a] AP
[§6.3b] A{P}
[§6.3c] PA

15. Usages of Instrumentality (7)

[§6.4a] API
[§6.4b] A{P}I
[§6.4c] AP{I}
[§6.4d] PAI
[§6.4e] PI
[§6.4f] B{P}I
[§6.4g] P{I}

16. Usages of Materiality (4)

[§6.5a] APM
[§6.5b] PM
[§6.5c] M{P}
[§6.5d] B{P}M

17. Usages of Modification (5)

[§6.6a] APR
[§6.6b] AP{R}
[§6.6c] PAR
[§6.6d] PA{R}
[§6.6e] PR

18. Usages of Partition (2)

[§6.7a] PPar
[§6.7b] Par{P}

19. Usages of Separation (2)

[§6.8a] APS
[§6.8b] PAS

20. Usage of Causation (1)

[§6.9a] PCau

21. Usage of Comparison (1)
[§6.9b] PCmp

22. Usage of Measurement (1)
[§6.9c] PMea

23. Usage of Temporality (1)
[§6.9d] PTem

24. Usages of the Non-Event Qualification (2)
[§6.10a] P   [§6.10b] O

25. Usages of the Non-Event Coordination (2)
[§6.11a] — —   [§6.11b] --- ---

26. Usage of the Non-Event Specification (1)
[§6.12] —

BIBLIOGRAPHY

Ackerman, Farrell, and John Moore. "Valence and the Semantics of Causativization." *BLS* 20 (1994): 1-13.
Aland, Barbara, Kurt Aland, Johannes Karavidopoulos, Carlo M. Martini, and Bruce M. Metzger (eds). *The Greek New Testament*. 4th rev. edn. Stuttgart: Biblia-Druck, 1993.
Allan, Rutger J. *The Middle Voice in Ancient Greek: A Study in Polysemy*. ASCP 11; Amsterdam: Giessen, 2003.
Allerton, D.J. *Valency and the English Verb*. New York: Academic Press, 1982.
Bakker, Egbert. "Voice, Aspect, and Aktionsart: Middle and Passive in Ancient Greek." In *Voice: Form and Function*, edited by Barbara Fox and Paul J. Hopper, 23-47. Typological Studies in Language; Amsterdam/Philadelphia: Benjamins, 1994.
Brighton, Louis A. *Revelation*. Concordia Commentary; St. Louis, MO: Concordia, 1999.
Brinton, Laurel J. *The Structure of Modern English: A Linguistic Introduction*. Amsterdam/Philadelphia: Benjamins, 2000.
Cornish, Francis. "Implicit Internal Arguments, Event Structures, Predication and Anaphoric Reference." In *The Grammar-Pragmatics Interface: Essays in Honor of Jeanette K. Gindel*, edited by Nancy Hedberg and Ron Zacharski, 189-216. Amsterdam/Philadelphia: Benjamins, 2007.
Cruse, D.A. "Some Thoughts on Agentivity." *JLing* 9 (1973): 11-23.
Danove, Paul L. "The Action of Forgiving in the New Testament." In *Forgiveness: Selected Papers from the 2008 Annual Conference of the Villanova University Theology Institute*, edited by Darlene Fozard Weaver and Jeffrey S. Mayer, 41-66. Villanova, PA: Villanova University Press, 2008.
Danove, Paul L. "A Comparison of the Usage of ἀκούω and ἀκούω-Compounds in the Septuagint and New Testament." *FN* 14 (2001): 65-85.
Danove, Paul L. "A Comparison of the Usages of δίδωμι and δίδωμι Compounds in the Septuagint and New Testament." In *The Language of the New Testament: Context, History, and Development*, edited by Stanley E. Porter and Andrew W. Pitts, 365-400. LBS 6; Leiden: Brill, 2013.
Danove, Paul L. "Distinguishing Goal and Locative Complements of New Testament Verbs of Transference." *FN* 39-40 (2007): 51-68.
Danove, Paul L. *Grammatical and Exegetical Study of New Testament Verbs of Transference: A Case Frame Guide to Interpretation and Translation*. SNTG 13; LNTS 329; London: T&T Clark, 2009.
Danove, Paul L. "The Grammatical Uses of ἀκούω in the Septuagint & the New Testament." *Forum: A Journal of the Foundations and Facets of Western Culture* (New Series) 2, no. 2 (1999): 239-61.
Danove, Paul L. "Λέγω Melding in the Septuagint and New Testament." *FN* 16 (2003): 19-31.

Danove, Paul L. *Linguistics and Exegesis in the Gospel of Mark: Applications of a Case Frame Analysis and Lexicon.* JSNTSup 218; SNTG 10; Sheffield: Sheffield Academic Press, 2001.

Danove, Paul L. *New Testament Verbs of Communication: A Case Frame and Exegetical Study.* LNTS 520; London: Bloomsbury, 2015.

Danove, Paul L. "New Testament Verbs of Communication with Active and Middle Forms: The Distinction." In *In Mari Via Tua: Studies in Honor of Antonio Piñero*, edited by Jesús Peláez and Israel Muñoz Gallarte, 133–56. Estudios de Filología Neotestamentaria 11; Córdoba: El Almendro, 2016.

Danove, Paul L. "A Reconsideration of Λέγω Melding in the New Testament." *FN* 27-28 (2015-16): 92–108.

Danove, Paul L. *Theology of the Gospel of Mark: A Semantic, Narrative, and Rhetorical Study of the Characterization of God.* London/New York: T&T Clark, 2019.

Danove, Paul L. "The Theory of Construction Grammar and its Application to New Testament Greek." In *Biblical Greek Language and Linguistics: Open Questions in Current Research*, edited by Stanley E. Porter and Don Carson, 119–51. JSNTSup 80; Sheffield: Sheffield Academic Press, 1993.

Dowty, David R. "Thematic Proto-Roles and Argument Selection." *Language* 67, no. 3 (1991): 547–619.

Fillmore, Charles J. "The Case for Case." In *Universals in Linguistic Theory*, edited by Emmon Bach and Robert T. Harms, 1–88. New York: Holt, Reinhart & Winston, 1968.

Fillmore, Charles J. "Pragmatically Controlled Zero Anaphora." *BLS* 12 (1986): 95–107.

Fillmore, Charles J. "Topics in Lexical Semantics." In *Current Issues in Linguistic Theory*, edited by Roger W. Cole, 76–138. Bloomington, IN: Indiana University Press, 1977.

Fillmore, Charles J., and Paul Kay. *Construction Grammar.* Stanford: CSLI, 1999.

Fraser, Bruce, and John Robert Ross. "Idioms and Unspecified N[oun] P[hrase] Deletion." *LInq* 1 (1970): 264–65.

Fried, Mirjam, and Jan-Ola Östman. "Construction Grammar: A Thumbnail Sketch." In *Construction Grammar in a Cross-Language Perspective*, edited by Mirjam Fried and Jan-Ola Östman, 11–86. Amsterdam/Philadelphia: Benjamins, 2004.

Goddard, Cliff. *Semantic Analysis: A Practical Introduction.* Oxford: Oxford University Press, 1998.

Goldberg, Adele. "The Inherent Semantics of Argument Structure: The Case of the English Ditransitive Construction." *CogLing* 3-1 (1992): 37–64.

Grundmann, Walter. "δεῖ, δέον ἐστί." *TDNT* 2: 22–25.

Harris, Randy Allen. *The Linguistics Wars.* New York: Oxford University Press, 1993.

Heil, John Paul. *The Book of Revelation: Worship for Life in the Spirit of Prophecy.* Cascade Books; Eugene, OR: Wipf & Stock, 2014.

Hovav, Malka Rappaport, and Beth Levin. "The English Dative Alternation: The Case for Verb Sensitivity." *JLing* 44 (2008): 129–67.

Jackendoff, Ray S. "The Proper Treatment of Measuring Out, Telicity, and Perhaps Even Quantification in English." *Natural Language and Linguistic Theory* 11 (1996): 317–18.

Janneris, Antonius Nicholas. *An Historical Greek Grammar.* London: MacMillan, 1897.

Kay, Paul, and Charles J. Fillmore. "Grammatical Constructions and Linguistic Generalizations: The 'What's X doing Y?' Construction." *Language* 75, no. 1 (1999): 1–33.

Kühner, R., and B. Gerth. *Ausführliche Grammatik der Griechische Sprache. Teil II.* Munich: Max Hueber, 1963.

Lambrecht, Knud, and K. Lemoine. "Definite Null Objects in (Spoken) French: A Construction Grammar Account." In *Grammatical Constructions: Back to the Roots*, edited by Mirjam Fried and Hans C. Boas, 13-55. CAL 4; Amsterdam/Philadelphia: Benjamins, 2005.

Lehrer, Adrienne. "Checklist for Verbs of Speaking." *Acta Linguistica Hungarica* 38, nos. 1-4 (1988): 143-61.

Lenski, Richard C. H. *Interpretation of St. John's Revelation*. Minneapolis, MN: Augsburg, 1961.

Levin, Beth. *English Verb Classes and Alternations: A Preliminary Investigation*. Chicago: University of Chicago Press, 1993.

Lyons, J. *Introduction to Theoretical Linguistics*. London: Cambridge University Press, 1969.

Matthews, Peter Hugoe. *Syntax*. Cambridge: Cambridge University Press, 1981.

McCawley, James D. *Grammar and Meaning: Papers on Syntactic and Semantic Topics*. New York: Academic Press, 1976.

Messies, G. *The Morphology of Koine Greek, as Used in the Apocalypse of St. John: A Study in Bilingualism*. Supplements to Novum Testament 27; Leiden: Brill, 1971.

Mittwoch, Anita. "Idioms and Unspecified N[oun] P[hrase] Deletion." *LInq* 2, no. 2 (1971): 255-59.

Mot, Laurentiu Florentin. *Morphological and Syntactic Irregularities in the Book of Revelation: A Greek Hypothesis*. LBS 11; Leiden: Brill, 2013.

Newmeyer, Frederick J. *Linguistic Theory in America: The First Quarter-Century of Transformational Generative Grammar*. New York: Academic Press, 1980.

Osborne, Grant R. *Revelation*. Baker Exegetical Commentary on the New Testament; Grand Rapids, MI: Baker, 2002.

Pesetsky, David. *Zero Syntax: Experiencers and Cascades*. Cambridge, MA: MIT Press, 1995.

Pinker, Steven. *Learnability and Cognition: The Acquisition of Argument Structure*. Cambridge, MA: MIT Press, 1987.

Porter, Stanley E. *Idioms of the Greek New Testament*. Sheffield: Sheffield Academic Press, 1992.

Rijksbaron, Albert. *The Syntax and Semantics of the Verb in Classical Greek: An Introduction*. 3rd edn. Linguistic Contributions to the Study of Greek Literature; Amsterdam: Giessen, 2002.

Robertson, A.T. *A Short Grammar of the New Testament* (New York: Hodder & Stoughton, 1908.

Saeed, John I. *Semantics*. Oxford: Blackwell, 1997.

Sag, Ivan A., and Jorge Hankamer. "Toward a Theory of Anaphoric Processing." *L&P* 7, no. 3 (1984): 325-45.

Smalley, Stephen S. *The Revelation of John: A Commentary on the Text of the Apocalypse*. Downers Grove, Ill: Intervarsity, 2005.

Smyth, Herbert Weir. *Greek Grammar*. Cambridge, MA: Harvard University Press, 1959.

Smyth, Herbert Weir. *Greek Series for Colleges and Schools*. New York: American Book Company, 1906.

Somers, H. L. *Valency and Case in Computational Linguistics*. Edinburgh: Edinburgh University Press, 1987.

Speas, Margaret. *Phrase Structure in Natural Language*. Nordrecht: Kluwer, 1990.

Talmy, Leonard. "Lexicalization Patterns: Semantic Structure in Lexical Forms." In *Language Typology and Syntactic Distinction*. Vol. 3, *Grammatical Categories and the Lexicon*, edited by T. Shopen, 57-149. Cambridge: Cambridge University Press, 1985.

Tesnière, Lucien. Éléments de Syntaxe Structurale. Paris: C. Klincksieck, 1959.
Thayer, Joseph H. *Thayer's Greek-English Lexicon of the New Testament: Coded with Strong's Concordance Numbers*. Edinburgh: T. & T. Clark, 1908.
Thomas, Robert L. *Revelation 1–7: An Exegetical Commentary*. Chicago, IL: Moody, 1992.
Turner, Nigel. *A Greek Grammar of the New Testament*. Vol. 3, *Syntax*. Edinburgh: T. & T. Clark, 1963.
Valesco, D. García, and C. Portrero Muñiz. "Understood Objects in Functional Grammar." *WPiFG* 76 (2002): 1–22.
Wallace, Daniel B. *Greek Grammar Beyond the Basics: With Scripture, Subject, and Greek Word Indexes*. Grand Rapids: Zondervan, 1996.
Zerwick, Maximilian. *Analysis Philologica Novi Testamenti Graeci*. 3rd edn. SPIB 107. Rome: Sumptibus Pontificii Instituti Biblici, 1966.
Zerwick, Maximilian. *Biblical Greek: Illustrated by Examples*, translated by Joseph Smith. 2nd edn. SPIB 114. Rome: Scripti Pontificium Institutum Biblicum, 1985.

INDEX OF AUTHORS

Ackerman, F. 12
Aland, B. 4
Allan, R. 37, 50, 64
Allerton, D. J. 26

Bakker, E. 164
Brighton, L. A. 89
Brinton, L. J. 127

Cornish, F. 26
Cruse, D. A. 13

Danove, P. L. 3, 8, 12, 27, 39, 47, 58, 67, 70, 80, 83, 84, 86, 108, 135, 162, 164
Dowty, D. R. 12

Fillmore, C. J. 3, 5, 12, 24, 26, 28, 83
Fraser, B. 28
Fried, M. 5, 24, 26

Gerth, B. 85
Goddard, C. 30, 63, 109
Goldberg, A. 67
Grundmann, W. 127

Hankamer, J. 28
Harris, R. A. 4
Heil, J. P. 89
Hovav, M. R. 67

Jackendoff, R. S. 58
Janneris, A. N. 79

Kay, P. 3, 5, 24, 28
Kühner, R. 85

Lambrecht, K. 26
Lehrer, A. 67
Lemoine, K. 26
Lenski, R. C. H. 205

Levin, B. 5, 67
Lyons, J. 50

Matthews, P. H. 26
McCawley, J. D. 4
Messies, G. 154, 176
Mittwoch, A. 26
Mot, L. F. 163, 176, 180

Newmeyer, F. J. 4

Osborne, G. R. 205

Pesetsky, D. 67
Pinker, S. 67
Porter, S. E. 39, 84, 85
Portrero Muñiz, C. 26

Rijksbaron, A. 164
Robertson, A. T. 85
Ross, J. R. 28

Saeed, J. I. 12, 50
Sag, I. A. 28
Smalley, S. S. 161
Smyth, H. W. 79, 84, 85, 134
Somers, H. L. 12
Speas, M. 67

Talmy, L. 63, 109
Tesnière, L. 5
Thayer, J. H. 37
Thomas, R. L. 205
Turner, N. 85, 205

Valesco, D. G. 26

Wallace, D. B. 79

Zerwick, M. 85, 169, 187

Made in United States
North Haven, CT
10 July 2024